Richard H. Kern

Richard Hovendon Kern.
Daguerreotype.
Courtesy, Huntington Library, San Marino, California.

Richard H. Kern

EXPEDITIONARY ARTIST IN THE FAR SOUTHWEST, 1848–1853

by
David J. Weber

Published for the
AMON CARTER MUSEUM
by the
UNIVERSITY OF NEW MEXICO PRESS
Albuquerque

Some material presented in this book has been introduced in two recent articles by David J. Weber:

"Raising the Blindfold: The Earliest Published Graphic Images of the Desert Southwest," *Southwest Art* (August 1984).

"The Artist, the Lithographer, and the Desert Southwest," *Gateway Heritage,* 5 (Fall 1984).

Library of Congress
Cataloging in Publication Data

Weber, David J.
   Richard H. Kern: expeditionary artist in the far Southwest, 1848–1853.

   Bibliography: p.
   Includes index.
   1. Kern, Richard H., 1821–1853.
2. Southwest, New Mexico, in art.
3. Artists—United States—Biography.
4. Explorers—United States—Biography.
I. Kern, Richard H., 1821–1853.
II. Amon Carter Museum of Western Art.
III. Title.
NC139.K47W4   1985   741′.092′4 [B]
                                     84-19497
ISBN 0-8263-0770-1

The Amon Carter Museum was established in 1961 under the will of the late Amon G. Carter for the study and documentation of westering North America. The program of the museum, expressed in permanent collections, exhibitions, publications, and special events, reflects many aspects of American culture, both historic and contemporary.

This book was prepared in conjunction with the exhibit "Richard Kern's Watercolors" produced by the Amon Carter Museum, Fort Worth, and on view at the Amon Carter Museum from March 8, 1985 to April 28, 1985; at the Museum of Fine Arts, Santa Fe, New Mexico, from May 12, 1985 to June 30, 1985; and at the Colorado Historical Society, Denver, Colorado, from July 8, 1985 to September 1, 1985.

As of all good things, one can have too much of history—particularly where art is concerned. We labor still under the nineteenth-century delusion that the history of a thing provides a sufficient account of that thing. It doesn't. The history of art is not art, any more than the history of religion is religion. The essence of art consists in the individual experience of artist and onlooker. History has nothing to do with our most intimate esthetic satisfactions. All that the study of history can do for us, in so far as we are artists or lovers of art, is to make us familiar with alien conventions and in this way prepare our habit-ridden minds to receive a communication from the far-off artists who worked with those conventions.

Aldous Huxley,
"American Sources of Modern Art"
The New Republic, May 30, 1933

Contents

List of Maps

Acknowledgments

IMPETUS FOR THIS BOOK came from Ron Tyler, Assistant Director for Collections and Programs at the Amon Carter Museum, who asked me to prepare a study of Richard Kern to be published in conjunction with an exhibit of the exciting collection of original Kern watercolors and pencil drawings that the Amon Carter Museum had acquired in the mid-1970s. Although Richard Kern's career in the Far Southwest lasted but five years, seven years have passed since Ron Tyler first asked me to write about it. I am grateful to Ron Tyler for his patience and his confidence. He and Carol Clark, then Curator of Painting at the Amon Carter and now Maurice and Charles Prendergast Executive Fellow at Williams College Museum of Art, Massachusetts, guided me through the literature of art history, rescued me when I needed help, and read the entire manuscript.

In the initial stages of research for this book, Robert Hine's biography of Edward Kern, first published in 1962, pointed me toward essential sources. When I had questions that his book did not answer, Professor Hine responded generously and cheerfully by digging into his research notes of twenty years ago and finding the answers!

In following Richard Kern's trails across the Far Southwest, as well as to Panama, Washington, and Philadelphia, I have received generous aid from many people whose assistance is gratefully acknowledged in the notes. Extraordinary advice came from Pat Richmond of Crestone, Colorado, who deserves special mention. Mrs. Richmond has spent years tracing the route of Frémont's fourth expedition through the San Juan Mountains in all kinds of weather. Her research, done on horseback, skiis, and in hiking boots, has corrected misconceptions that previous writers have had about the route and has enabled me to pinpoint the locations of several of Richard Kern's watercolors from the expedition.

Similarly, Andrew Wallace of Northern Arizona University facilitated my efforts to follow Sitgreaves across central Arizona. By happy coincidence, Professor Wallace was preparing a book on the exploration of the Colorado plateau and had retraced much of the difficult route by jeep and on foot. We have enjoyed a fruitful collaboration, in which I have been the greater beneficiary.

The chapters on the Frémont and Gunnison expeditions have been read by historian Mary Lee Spence of the University of Illinois, who has been editing Frémont's papers, and biologist Richard G. Beidleman of Colorado College, who has been editing a diary that Frederick Creutzfeldt kept on the Gunnison expedition. As with Pat Richmond and Andrew Wallace, I am grateful to professors Spence and Beidleman for their generosity, and for advice so sound that I invariably took it.

Most of the manuscripts pertaining to Richard Kern are in the Huntington Library, San Marino, California. There, Associate Curator Vivian Rust helped with her usual efficiency to make material available to me both in person and by mail. For giving me access to previously unused manuscripts in their private collection, I am grateful to Fred and Helen Cron of Milford, Pennsylvania. In Philadelphia, Carol Spawn, Librarian at the Academy of Natural Sciences and Gladys Breuer, Associate Curator at the Franklin Institute, provided invaluable assistance. Thanks to Ms. Breuer, I was able to locate previously unknown documents at the Franklin Institute. At the Amon Carter Museum, librarian Milan Hughston and research assistant Ben Huseman brought their special knowledge to bear on difficult questions. At my own institution, I am grateful to the remarkable staff of the DeGolyer Library, especially to Jim Phillips and Clif Jones, and to Marilyn Duncan of the Fondren Library who tenaciously pursued items through interlibrary loan.

Dedman College of Southern Methodist University, where it is a joy to teach and write, made it possible for me to fulfill my promise to Ron Tyler. An SMU Research Leave gave me time to complete the research and writing; meanwhile, my generous and wise colleague, don Luis Martín, assumed my duties as department chair and left me alone. Joan Rosendahl did the initial typing of the manuscript, and Kathleen Triplett expeditiously made the many revisions that a book invariably requires before going to press.

I must acknowledge but can never fully thank the specialists who read the *entire* manuscript and offered corrections of fact and challenges to some of my interpretations. In addition to Carol Clark and Ron Tyler, they are: Ronald L. Davis, Director of the DeGolyer Institute of American Studies and accomplished historian of American society and culture in my own department at SMU; William H. Goetzmann, Stiles

Professor of American Studies at the University of Texas, Austin, whose monumental work on exploration and art of the nineteenth-century American West has influenced me greatly; David H. Miller of Cameron University, Lawton, Oklahoma, who has written on the Gunnison expedition and on Balduin Möllhausen and who knows the mid-nineteenth century American West intimately; Harry Nissen of Dallas, an accomplished draftsman, watercolorist, and aficionado of history; and my brother, Dan Weber of Cerrillos, New Mexico, himself an artist and explorer in the tradition of Richard Kern.

Somehow, my best friend and talented wife, Carol Bryant Weber, made time in her own busy schedule to read the manuscript and bring it up to her high standards. Directly and indirectly, she has contributed to this book with criticism, advice, encouragement, and love.

DAVID J. WEBER
Southern Methodist University
Autumn 1983

Richard H. Kern

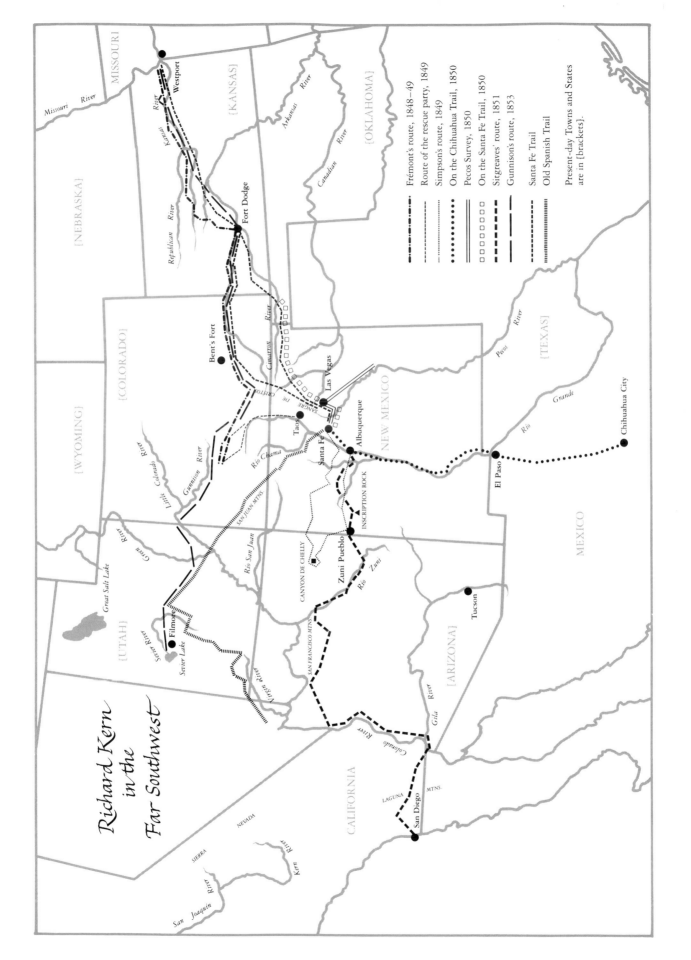

Richard Kern in the Far Southwest

- I -

Introduction

IF IT CAN BE SAID that a region has a heart, the heart of the Southwest is surely Inscription Rock. Towering above pine groves and red sandstone bluffs in western New Mexico, not far from the Arizona border and the Continental Divide, this great promontory is visible for miles.[1] On the vertical walls of the gigantic *peñol,* known to Spaniards and Mexicans as El Morro, Indians had made their marks long before Columbus's discovery of America, and Europeans since the time of Juan de Oñate had scratched or carved their names as reminders to posterity that they had passed by this place. Among the thousands of names and inscriptions still visible in the soft, buffcolored sandstone, none stands out more clearly than that of "R. H. Kern/ Artist." Midway through the last century, before the press of humanity caused us to redefine petroglyphs as graffiti, Richard Kern made his mark indelibly on the symbolic heart of the Southwest. As an artist whose views of Southwestern peoples and places were widely reprinted in his day and since, Kern also helped to make a lasting impression on the way Americans have perceived the Far Southwest.

The brief Southwestern career of Richard Hovendon Kern began with a disaster that took many lives; it ended in violence that took his life. Philadelphia born and bred, Kern first entered the Far Southwest in 1848 as an artist with John C. Frémont's fourth expedition. Kern was one of the lucky ones. When the Great Pathfinder led his men into the starvation and bitter cold of a Rocky Mountain winter in southern Colorado, Kern survived. Five years later, in October 1853, while employed as an artist on John W. Gunnison's survey of the 38th parallel, Kern's luck ran out. With Gunnison, Richard Kern met his death at the hands of Indians in Utah. Between his first trip

3

west in 1848 and his murder five years later, Kern visited the Navajo country with James H. Simpson and crossed central Arizona with Lorenzo Sitgreaves, sketching deserts, basins, ranges, ruins, villages, and peoples that no other artist had ever recorded. These activities put him in the vanguard of a small group of artists who gave Americans the first graphic images of the Far Southwest, a region newly acquired from Mexico.

By the time of the War with Mexico, artists had recorded scenes throughout much of the western half of the continent, scouring the Great Plains, penetrating the central Rockies, and visiting the Pacific and Gulf coasts. From as early as 1820, when Titian Peale and Samuel Seymour were assigned to accompany Stephen H. Long's expedition to the Rockies, official American exploring parties had included artists. Between 1832 and 1834, George Catlin and Karl Bodmer had accompanied fur traders up the Missouri and helped to make the Plains Indian the prototype of the American Indian in the minds of white Americans. A few years later, in 1837, Alfred Jacob Miller became the first American artist to enter the Rockies, where he did soft-toned, romantic watercolors of mountain men setting traps and trading with Indians at the annual rendezvous. By 1846, images of Indians, buffalo, treeless expanses of prairies, and improbably high and rugged peaks had been brought to public view through lithographs, engravings, and special exhibits of oils

and watercolors in America's major cities.[2] Meanwhile, on the Pacific, artists from many lands had sketched scenes along the coast of Spanish and Mexican California. Their work began to find its way into print as early as 1798, when George Vancouver's three-volume account of his voyages appeared with engravings of sketches by J. Sykes.[3] Along the Gulf Coast, Texas was slower to inspire artistic endeavor. Views of Texas were not available to the American public until the time of the successful Texas revolt from Mexico in 1836.[4]

While artists reconnoitered much of the West in the first half of the nineteenth century, they ignored the Far Southwest. The vast stretch from the coastal ranges of California to the Rio Grande, where Richard Kern would find his milieu, remained a terra incognita in American graphics until the United States acquired the region by force of arms in 1846–47.

Dating back to the mid-sixteenth century explorations of Francisco Vázquez de Coronado, Spaniards had crisscrossed the present states of Arizona and New Mexico. Beginning in 1598, they had planted permanent settlements in the region, and Spanish mapmakers and engineers had measured and plotted much of the West by 1800. During nearly three centuries of Spanish sovereignty, however, no graphic image of the region based on firsthand observation appears to have been printed.[5]

During the last years of Spanish control, and increasingly after Mexico won independence from Spain in 1821,

Fig. 1. *Burial of Mr. Pattie.* Engraving from *The Personal Narrative of James O. Pattie of Kentucky,* Timothy Flint, ed. (Cincinnati, 1831).

American trappers and merchants found their way into Arizona, New Mexico, Nevada, Utah, and southern Colorado. Some of these foreigners, together with a handful of Mexicans, wrote accounts of the region that began to find their way into print. Amateur artists were among them, such as Alexander Barclay, but their work did not come into public view. While nearly all of the books, pamphlets, and articles concerning the Far Southwest published prior to the outbreak of war in 1846 appeared without illustrations, there were three notable exceptions.[6]

The earliest published work purporting to show graphic images of either Arizona or New Mexico was *The Personal Narrative of James O. Pattie,* published in Cincinnati in 1831 and

Fig. 2. *Mexican Girls. Costumes of the Poblanas.* Engraving "adapted" from Carl Nebel. George Wilkins Kendall, *Narrative of the Texan Santa Fe Expedition,* 2 vols. (New York, 1844).

containing five engravings illustrating highlights of Pattie's adventures as a trapper in northern Mexico. These illustrations, which show trappers wearing stovepipe hats, are a worthy companion to Pattie's often fanciful prose. A depiction of *Mr. Pattie Wounded by an Indian Arrow* while trapping on the Puerco River, for example, shows Pattie in a lush forest more appropriate to the imagination of a Cincinnati engraver than to the realities of that arid New Mexico tableland. Similarly inventive was an engraving allegedly showing the burial of Pattie's father in San Diego, which calls attention to a freshly dug grave near the high walls of a palatial structure, suggesting the Escorial of Spain's Philip II rather than the crumbling, one-story walls of the San Diego presidio (fig. 1). These engravings clearly are not copies of an artist's firsthand observations. All five of the illustrations that accompanied Pattie's *Narrative* have fallen into deserved obscurity.[7]

Another illustrated firsthand account of travel in the desert Southwest was George Wilkins Kendall's *Narrative of the Texan Santa Fe Expedition,* published in London and New York in 1844.[8] This popular account of the sufferings of a group of hapless Texans sent to "liberate" New Mexico in 1841 contained five engravings—all copied from earlier works. Two included incidents on the Great Plains, by then familiar to Americans; two others were views of places in central Mexico, copied from a book published in London in 1828.[9]

One scene, an engraving of two women framed in a doorway smoking *cigarillos,* appears to have been based on a drawing done in Santa Fe or in El Paso, and has been reproduced frequently to illustrate books about the Southwest (fig. 2). But it is actually an adaptation from a lithograph of a scene in the central Mexican city of Puebla, drawn by the German artist Carl Nebel between 1829 and 1834.[10]

Along with Kendall's *Narrative,* Josiah Gregg's classic firsthand account of the Santa Fe trade, *Commerce of the Prairies,* appeared in 1844. It contained six full-page and six half-page engravings. Most of these engravings illustrated scenes of life and adventure on the prairies, to which Americans had access in other sources, but the two-volume work also included views of life in New Mexico: *A Kitchen Scene, Gold Washing, The Mexican Horseman, A Mining Scene,* and a finely done full-page engraving of a Santa Fe caravan approaching Santa Fe, with the city in the distance (fig. 3). None of these were drawn from actual observation, but art historian Robert Taft has surmised that the often reproduced *Arrival of the Caravan at Santa Fé* may have been drawn from a daguerreotype made by Gregg.[11] If so, it would represent the first authentic published image of Santa Fe. It seems unlikely, however, that Taft's contention is correct. Gregg probably did not have a camera at that time. Moreover, if Gregg had a daguerreotype view of Santa Fe, the publisher need not have gone through the un-

necessary step of having an artist, E. Didier, draw the scene, then have the engraver, A. L. Dick, work from the drawing.[12] Engravers were certainly capable of drawing from daguerreotypes.

When war broke out in 1846 between Mexico and the United States, no authentic printed images were available of the heart of the region that American forces were about to conquer. "Manifest Destiny," as Bernard DeVoto has written, "was blindfolded."[13] The war itself, though, produced considerable demand for graphic images. Americans wanted to see the theaters of combat and to glory vicariously in scenes of American victory. Photography was still in its infancy, but through engravings and the increasingly popular art of lithography, publishers began to meet public demand by producing individual prints and illustrations for books and magazines. Scenes along Gen. Zachary Taylor's route into northeastern Mexico and along Gen. Winfield Scott's arduous climb from Veracruz to Mexico City quickly became available.[14] In 1847, the first authentic graphic images of the Far Southwest, from the Rio Grande to the coastal ranges of California, also began to appear.

The earliest genuine views of the region to find their way into print were probably the illustrations that appeared in John T. Hughes's colorful chronicle of the "triumphant" three-thousand-mile march through northern Mexico of an undisciplined, profane group of Missouri volunteers under Col. Alexander Doniphan. Published in Cincinnati in

Fig. 3. *Arrival of the Caravan at Santa Fé.* Engraving of a drawing by E. Didier. Josiah Gregg, *Commerce of the Prairies: or the Journal of a Santa Fe trader*, 2 vols. (New York, 1844).

1847, and reprinted frequently thereafter, *Doniphan's Expedition* contained a number of crude but charming wood engravings based on sketches drawn by Lachlan Allan Maclean, a Scottish-born schoolteacher from Missouri. Corporal Maclean, who served in John Reid's Company D and who helped design Fort Marcy in Santa Fe, did a number of his sketches in the Southwest, probably in-

cluding those entitled *Bent's Fort*, *Mexican Group*, *Mexican Cart*, and *Mexican Woodsman* (fig. 4).[15]

Other men talented with a brush or pencil, such as Samuel Chamberlain and Alfred Waugh, found themselves in New Mexico and Arizona during the War with Mexico, but they did not have the fortune of seeing their work appear in print. As a result, their works had no

Fig. 4. *Fort Bent.* Woodcut based on a drawing by Lachlan Allan Maclean. John T. Hughes, *Doniphan's Expedition* (Cincinnati, 1847).

significant impact on their contemporaries.[16] Two exceptions were John Mix Stanley and James W. Abert. Lithographs of their work in the Southwest appeared in 1848 and, in quality and quantity, far exceeded the modest prints of Maclean's casual sketches.

Lithographs of the work of John Mix Stanley graced the pages of a government report that appeared in three printings in 1848: *Notes of a Military Reconnoissance* [sic] *from Fort Leavenworth, in Missouri, to San Diego, in California.*[17] The *Notes* were mainly the written report of Lt. William H. Emory, a West Point graduate and member of the U.S. Army Corps of Topographical Engineers, who had been assigned to accompany invading United States forces under Lt. Col. Stephen Watts Kearny.

Fig. 5. *San Felippe {sic}, New Mexico*. Lithograph based on an oil painting by John Mix Stanley. Lt. Col. W. H. Emory, *Notes of a Military Reconnoissance {sic}* (Washington, D.C., 1848).

At the head of the Army of the West, Kearny was to march over the Santa Fe Trail into New Mexico, seize the province, then continue to California and take possession of that territory, too. Emory's task was to study and map the area through which Kearny passed, and he did this admirably.

That Emory's report contained any illustrations at all was the result of a happy accident. Emory had encountered John Mix Stanley in Santa Fe and had persuaded him to make the journey to California. An itinerant draftsman with an eye for description rather than interpretation, Stanley already had substantial experience in the West, painting in and around Detroit, Chicago, Ft. Snelling, Minnesota, and in the Indian Territory that would become

Oklahoma. For Emory, Stanley did a number of drawings that appeared in the published report: fourteen botanical sketches, and twenty-six lithographs of people and places along the southern trail to California—the so-called Gila River route (fig. 5). In the 1850s Stanley would earn an enduring reputation for his work on the Pacific Railroad surveys, including the redrawing of a dozen sketches by Richard Kern.[18]

In the same year that Emory's report appeared with Stanley's illustrations, the Senate and the House issued separate printings of Lt. James W. Abert's *Examination of New Mexico in the Years 1846–'47*, which contained two dozen lithographs. All the illustrations apparently were derived from sketches or watercolors done by Abert himself. A West Point graduate and topographical engineer, James Abert enjoyed the patronage of his father, Col. John James Abert, head of the Topographical Bureau of the United States Army. Young Abert had originally started for New Mexico with Kearny and Emory, but had fallen ill on the Plains and remained behind to recover at Bent's Fort on the Arkansas before continuing to Santa Fe. While Emory, with John Mix Stanley in his retinue, proceeded on to California, James Abert remained in New Mexico. There he filled his sketchbook with drawings of Indian Pueblos, antiquities, remarkable scenes, and Mexican towns, including what would become the first authentic view of Santa Fe (fig. 6). Thus, Abert's New Mexico

scenes complemented the work of Stanley, whose published views of the region consisted largely of views along the Gila River in today's Arizona.[19]

With the publication of lithographs of the work of Stanley and Abert in 1848, the artists' reconnaissance of the Far Southwest had begun.[20] Richard H. Kern was not far behind. That year, as government reports found their way into the hands of readers eager to learn about the lands just acquired through the Treaty of Guadalupe Hidalgo, Richard Kern made his way west over the Santa Fe Trail. Time and chance would divert him to New Mexico, where he would make signal contributions to the artists' discovery of the American Southwest and participate in what one writer has called "a revolutionary phenomenon: the artist as explorer."[21]

Richard Kern has not been forgotten, but his achievements have been obscured. Lithographs of his work have been reprinted frequently, yet often without attribution. Although the broad outline of his life has been known, his career was so intertwined with that of his younger brother, Edward, that their very different achievements have blurred in historical memory. Edward, who began his career in the West three years before Richard, and who continued to work for another seven years after Richard's death in 1853, has been the subject of two biographies. Easily the best is Robert V. Hine's gracefully written and meticulously researched book *In the Shadow of Frémont: Edward Kern and the*

Fig. 6. *La Ciudad de Santa Fé.* Lithograph based on a drawing by Lt. James W. Abert. *Report of Lieut. J. W. Abert of His Examination of New Mexico* (Washington, D.C., 1848).

Art of American Exploration, 1845–1860, first published in 1962 and reissued in 1982.[22] If Edward's achievements were obscured by the "Shadow of Frémont," as Hine suggests, so too have Richard's achievements lain hidden in the longer shadow of his brother, Edward.

This study of Richard Kern's westering, which owes much to Hine's biography of Edward Kern, helps to disentangle the lives of the two brothers. Although Edward Kern had gone west ahead of Richard, working as an artist on Frémont's third expedition, no official report of that expedition was published and Edward's work did not appear in print. The preponderance of the art of Western exploration done by the two brothers came from Richard.[23] Both brothers accompanied John C.

Frémont on his tragic fourth expedition of 1848–49, but most of the extant images of that expedition came from Richard's brush and pen. The two brothers also worked for Lt. James H. Simpson, who in 1849 made the first official American reconnaissance of the Navajo country, but the majority of the surviving graphic art from that expedition is Richard's. Both brothers worked at odd jobs in New Mexico for a year and a half after their contract with Simpson had expired. Many of Richard's watercolors and sketches from these months survive; only a few of Edward's are known. In the summer of 1851, the brothers' careers diverged. Edward returned east and would find new adventures in the Orient. Richard continued west to California with an exploring party headed by Lorenzo Sitgreaves, and gave the American public its first graphic images of central Arizona and some of its indigenous peoples. Returning east early in 1852, Richard became a recognized authority on the ethnology and topography of the Southwest, which he had helped to map. He was called upon to testify before the Senate regarding the best route for a transcontinental railroad. Soon his reputation and expertise won him an appointment on the 38th parallel survey led by John W. Gunnison. With Gunnison, Richard made another entrada into the Southwest, but this time he did not survive to put the finishing touches on the sketches he did along the way. Another artist, John Mix Stanley, would do that work for him.

Like many documentary artists who portrayed the West before the days of the camera, Richard Kern was known best to his contemporaries through lithographs of his work. His original sketches and watercolors of Southwestern subjects apparently never appeared on public exhibition. Some originals, however, have been preserved. Nearly all of them are located in three collections, two of which have only recently come to light. Each collection has its own character.[24]

Prior to 1959, the only known collection of Richard Kern's original work, beyond some crude sketches in his diaries at the Huntington Library, was housed at the Philadelphia Academy of Natural Sciences. This collection, presented in 1898 as a gift to the Academy by Frances J. Duffy, contains seventy-two wash drawings, watercolors, and pen-and-ink sketches by the Kern brothers, the majority by Richard. All represent views done on Simpson's 1849 reconnaissance of the Navajo country and appeared as lithographs in the government report of the expedition. The original drawings, however, have been little known and seldom reproduced. Many are printed in this volume, some for the first time, with permission of the Director of the Philadelphia Academy.

The largest collection of Richard Kern's work, containing some two hundred sketches and drawings, was discovered in 1958. This Kern "archive," which also includes correspondence, diaries, and drawings by Edward

Kern, had been in the possession of William E. Kern, an artist and nephew of Richard and Edward. In the mid-1890s or so, William Kern moved his uncles' drawings and papers from Philadelphia, up the Delaware to Dingman's Ferry, Pennsylvania. William Kern had married Eugenia Mercer, who owned the Belleview Hotel in Dingman's Ferry. The Kern papers, stored in two wooden crates, were stashed away in a crawl space off the basement and forgotten. There they remained until 1958 when Fred and Ann Cron, who had bought the hotel in 1941, removed them to make room for plumbing repairs. The Crons started to burn the papers, but saved most of them when they recognized their value. The next year, the Crons permitted *Life* magazine to publish a portion of Edward's journal of Frémont's third expedition, together with some of the sketches.[25] In the 1960s and 1970s, however, the Crons would not permit scholars such as Robert Hine or Frank McNitt to see the collection or quote from the papers. Mr. Cron believed that this would depreciate the value of the collection, and he resented unscrupulous dealers who had tried to take advantage of him.[26]

The present owners of the collection, Fred and Helen Cron, have permitted scholars to see portions of the collection on just two previous occasions. As a result, a few of the sketches from the Cron's collection were subsequently reproduced in the *Southwest* volume of *Handbook of North American Indians* (1979) and in *The Rocky Mountains: A Vision for the Nineteenth Century* (1983) by Patricia Trenton and Peter Hassrick.[27] It has been my singular fortune to see the entire collection, and to be permitted to take notes and photographs. I am grateful to Fred and Helen Cron for their hospitality and generosity.

Most of the drawings by Richard Kern in the Cron collection are pencil sketches, done in six small sketchbooks (7″ × 4½″), and on single sheets of various sizes pasted into a scrapbook. Of the approximately two hundred drawings in this collection that can be attributed to Richard Kern, only a few are finished work or watercolors. The remainder have limited aesthetic appeal, but are of considerable historical and ethnographic interest. Reproductions of a number of drawings from this collection appear in this volume, most published for the first time, with the gracious permission of Fred and Helen Cron.

In the early 1960s, still another group of drawings by Richard Kern came to light. These consisted of an album of twenty-one finished watercolors and four pencil sketches. The collection seems to have been found about 1960 in a trunk in a garage in Pennsylvania and offered for sale to Harold McCracken, a noted authority on Western art and then director of the Buffalo Bill Historical Center in Cody, Wyoming. McCracken bought the album for his personal collection. In 1975 the Amon Carter Museum of Western Art acquired the collection from Kennedy Galleries in New York. The Amon Carter Museum displayed the entire album for the first time in March 1985, an exhibit that coincided with the publication of this biography of Richard Kern.[28]

Most of Richard Kern's drawings in the Amon Carter Museum are scenes from his adventures in the Southwest. None had appeared as lithographs, and none were previously known to students of Western art. These long-forgotten drawings differ in one important respect from the originals in the private collection and in the Philadelphia Academy of Natural Sciences. The works in the latter collections show us Kern the scientist and draftsman, producing careful, informative drawings to be used as illustrations for scientific reports. The collection at the Amon Carter Museum contains exquisite drawings of considerable aesthetic appeal. Most, if not all, were redrawn from field sketches, but Kern probably had not intended to put them on exhibit. First, the drawings fitted into an album of $6\frac{1}{2}'' \times 8\frac{3}{4}''$ and were too small to have been regarded as suitable for an exhibition in the mid-nineteenth century. Second, the album is labeled "Memorabilia," perhaps by Kern himself. Kern's addition of separate titles to many of the drawings, done perhaps in Washington D.C. in 1852–53, suggests that he may have gathered these pieces together to show to family and friends.[29] Twenty-four of the twenty-five drawings from the Amon Carter Museum collection are reproduced in this volume, nearly all for the first time, with the permission of the museum's director.

Beautifully colored and executed, Kern's drawings from the Amon Carter collection give us a new appreciation of Kern the artist, rather than Kern the draftsman. Indeed, the appearance of three of Kern's watercolors from this collection in a recently published book, *Visions of America* by Ron Tyler, led two British reviewers to praise Kern excessively. Of the 130 images in the book, critic Geoffrey Grigson wrote, only two by American artists belonged there "by right of art and not of record."[30] This effusive accolade went only to Winslow Homer and Richard Kern.

Since I am aware that "biography must always be a flawed achievement and the biographer, a man who fails before he begins," it may be best to deny at the outset that this is a biography in the usual sense of telling the story of a life.[31] Although I have had the good fortune to locate fresh information about Kern's early training and teaching in Philadelphia, too little is known of his life before he went West in 1848. Of his years in the West, we have only the record of his journeys through physical space. Kern kept diaries of his travels, but he left us few clues about his inner world or what he might have learned about himself while he was discovering the Southwest. In this respect, Kern was typical of his contemporaries. As historian Robert Hine has succinctly put it: "The white man in the West has been little concerned with inner revelations. (He was either introspectively impotent or too busy.)"[32]

If this book cannot examine the relationship between Kern's inner and outer lives, it can and does provide a view of the relationships between the artist and his subjects and the artist and his society. Particularly striking is the dependence of artists of the early West on the federal government. It is one of the paradoxes of American history that Westerners, who profess rugged individualism and rail against the intervention of federal government in their affairs, have also turned to Washington and depended upon it for massive aid.[33] In the Southwest, even our earliest and most enduring visual images of the region owe a large debt to federal patronage of those artists who examined the region in the late 1840s and early 1850s, just ahead of the camera.

Posterity's largest debt, however, belongs to the artists themselves, who left us priceless images of a world that has vanished. Yet the quantity or quality of those images cannot be the only measures of the achievements of these artist-explorers. An appreciation of their work must also take into account the extraordinary hardships and risks that they endured to get to the scene of their subjects. Many, like Richard Kern, left the comfort and safety of eastern studios to enter lands beyond the frontier. Their adventures and their art are inextricably interwoven; the artists themselves are often as interesting as the subjects they sought to portray. As one art historian has so eloquently explained:

> In Europe, the tour de force generally received its scale from the artists' Ambition, set resplendently within a major tradition. In America, it consisted in simply "getting there." The artist became the hero of his own journey—which replaced the heroic themes of mythology—by vanquishing physical obstacles enroute to a destination. For the ambition of the artistic enterprise was substituted the ambition of the artist's Quest—itself a major nineteenth-century theme. In this displacement of the heroic from the work of art to the persona of the artist lay, perhaps, part of the attraction of unexplored territory for the American artist at mid-century.[34]

-2-

The Disaster in the Mountains:
West with Frémont, 1848-1849

WHAT RESTLESSNESS Edward's letters must have aroused in his brother. Letters from Edward, two years his junior, arrived from time to time at Richard Kern's studio at 62 Filbert Street in Philadelphia. The correspondence reported extraordinary adventures in the western wilderness, and contrasted sharply with Richard's routine as a city-based artist ateacher of drawing.

Edward Kern had once taught drawing and shared the studio on Filbert Street until opportunity beckoned and swept him away to work in the shadow of one of the best-known and most glamorous figures of his day, John C. Frémont. On two widely publicized government-sponsored expeditions between 1842 and 1844, the handsome and energetic Frémont, a lieutenant in the U.S. Army Corp of Topographical Engineers, had reconnoitered the Rockies, the Great Basin, and explored as far west as California and Oregon.

His explorations won him fame in part because of the writing skills of his ambitious young wife, Jessie Benton, daughter of the influential senator from Missouri, Thomas Hart Benton. By 1845 Frémont had become a national hero. Young men, thirsty for adventure, jostled for a post on his next expedition, destined for the Mexican province of Alta California. For the single position of artist, forty-two men applied. In May 1845 the honor of drawing for Frémont had gone to Edward Kern (fig. 1).[1]

While Richard Kern had remained behind in Philadelphia, planning to fulfill an artist's dream of journeying to France and Switzerland, Edward had headed west in the summer of 1845. "Ned," as his family knew him, had traveled down the Ohio and Mississippi to St. Louis, then boarded a steamer with Frémont and headed up the Missouri to Westport, the launching place

Fig. 7. Edward Kern.
Daguerreotype.
Courtesy, Huntington Library.

for Frémont's earlier expeditions. At Westport Ned entered an exotic world that he described in a letter to his home-bound brother as "a dirty place filled with Indians, Spaniards, Jews & all sorts & sizes of folks." Dressed in fringed moccasins and skin pants with fringe, and looking "quite aboriginal," Ned began to draw. He did sketches of the prairies and of the Indians in camp, and sent those rough drawings back to Phil-adelphia for his older brother to finish. Along with the sketches, Ned sent in-structions to "Dick," as Richard was known to family and friends: "put some horses in the fore ground & carry dis-tant green up to the lead mark." He told Dick about Indian dress and colors for drawing Indians. The Indian women, Ned said, "are up & down like a plained board no grace no poetry." Ned had been surprised at the ordinariness of Indian women. His only familiarity with them had been through the works of other artists, such as John Gadsby Chapman, whose *Baptism of Pochahontas* hung in the rotunda of the United States Capital Building. It took a "good deal of imagination" to paint Indian women as Chapman did, Ned told his brother.[2] Although Ned probably did not know it, Chapman had never painted an Indian from life. Nor had Richard Kern, and he must have wished he was seeing the remarkable sights of the West with his brother.

In sending sketches and instructions back to Dick, Ned apparently hoped to get his brother on a government contract, too. Dick could prepare the lithographs for the expedition's published report. Ned urged his brother to learn to draw on a lithographer's stone. He advised Dick to "get a peep" at Frémont's earlier reports and to examine the style of engraving in which the flowers were done. That style, done on stone, had pleased Frémont, Ned wrote, "so if you have time get to work at it as you may as well have the work as anybody."[3]

While Richard Kern stayed home, painting and teaching, Edward Kern's journey west with Frémont took him across the Rockies, through the Great Basin, and over the Sierras into California. Traveling below the 42nd parallel, Frémont was in Mexican territory most of the way. The Pathfinder's party arrived in Alta California at a moment

when relations between Mexico and the United States were disintegrating and the two nations lurched uncertainly toward war. Even before American naval forces seized Monterey, California's capital, in July of 1846, the ambitious Frémont had joined a group of dissident American emigrants in the Sacramento Valley and helped launch a local revolt, known as the Bear Flag Rebellion. Inevitably, these events enveloped Edward Kern. Although he had no military experience, Ned soon found himself in command of John Sutter's fort on the Sacramento River. Reliable and diplomatic, Ned managed the position effectively and without antagonizing Sutter, a congenial Swiss expatriate who years later would remember Ned fondly.[4]

Back at home, Richard first heard about his brother's appointment as commander of Fort Sutter in the newspapers. "We presumed you did not write because you were too proud of your 'blushing honors.'" Dick told Ned.[5] But it was not Ned's modesty that kept him from informing his family of his position, just the slowness of the mail from the Pacific. Ned had sent Dick a lengthy account of his adventures, including stories of Indian attacks, perfidious Mexicans, and how Frémont had put him in charge of Fort Sutter and given him responsibility for guarding a group of prisoners of war. "Little did I think when sitting at home in our office in F[ilbert] St.," Ned told Dick, "that I would ever raise to be a Mil[itary] character, a rale Commandante of a Fort, with power to do as I pleased and shoot people if they do not obey me, and all that sort of thing."[6]

While Edward had become a military commander in California, Richard Kern, twenty-four years old when his younger brother went west in 1845, had quietly consolidated his position as a successful art teacher and artist in Philadelphia.[7] In that burgeoning port and mill city, an artist could make a comfortable living. By the 1840s New York and Boston had eclipsed Philadelphia as the nation's cultural capital, but Philadelphia still boasted the Pennsylvania Academy of Fine Arts, as well as excellent galleries where a young artist could study the work of more accomplished hands, or perhaps sell a painting or drawing.[8] Indeed, painting in Kern's day may have been "more popular in America than at any other time in our history," as one writer has concluded. Artists had begun to acquire respectability, and "to be a painter was not then in the United States financially hazardous."[9] The egalitarian ethos of the young American republic suggested to many Americans that anyone could be an artist and a number of inexpensive drawing manuals encouraged this delusion. These books enthusiastically explained to would-be artists how anyone who could write could also draw. Effort and perseverance were more important than talent, according to the self-help books then in fashion.[10]

Many of the artists who went west in the mid-nineteenth century were self-taught, but Richard and Edward Kern had received professional training. The brothers had grown up in a large, prosperous family that encouraged education. The brothers' home at 37 Crown Street near Franklin Square (fig. 8) stood a short walk from Philadelphia's commercial and cultural centers and its finest schools.[11] Just five blocks from the Kerns' home the Delaware flowed on its way to the sea. On the river front, the Kerns' father, John Kern III, a first-generation American of German descent, worked as deputy collector of customs of the Port of Philadelphia. Father and sons enjoyed good conversation in a home with many books. A friend of the boys, Matthias Weaver, who often visited the family, joined the Kerns for Sunday dinner in January 1842 when Richard was not yet twenty-one. Weaver was impressed that

> The Father and sons treat each other in a very familiar way—they address each other as persons of the same age . . . there is all due respect shown to the Father in its proper place—Dick made me laugh intolerably with his queer remarks—he told their old cat to behave with decency for there were strangers there![12]

Seven blocks or so from the Kerns' front door was the Franklin Institute. There the brothers studied drawing and perhaps other subjects as well. Certainly both Dick and Ned possessed a good education in literature, science, and the arts. They knew poetry, spelled flawlessly, and quickly learned the use of scientific instruments and trigonometry.

Fig. 8. The three-story Kern family home at 37 Crown St. Photograph of a drawing by Richard H. Kern. Courtesy, Huntington Library.

The Franklin Institute had been founded in 1824 to disseminate knowledge of the applied sciences. By Kern's day, it was the premier technological organization in America, devoted to the extension as well as the dissemination of scientific knowledge. In its own building on Seventh Street between Chestnut and Market (today the Atwater-Kent Museum), the Institute operated a high school and a museum, published an important journal, and sponsored evening classes and lectures. The Drawing School, where the Kerns studied, was the most popular unit of the Institute; its principal teacher, William Mason, enjoyed considerable respect. An engraver and painter of landscapes and still life, Mason had practiced his craft since his apprenticeship in 1804 in his native Connecticut. In 1810 he had moved to Philadelphia, where he had opened his own engraving firm. In 1834 he had taken charge of the Drawing School of the Institute. Consistent with the Institute's mission, Mason taught practical drawing—architectural, landscape, ornamental drawing, mechanical drafting, and lettering. For the Kern brothers, this would prove ideal training for the precise recording expected of an artist-explorer in the West.[13]

Richard and Edward Kern must have been among William Mason's star pupils. By his late teens, in 1840 and 1841, Dick had become sufficiently accomplished to have two of his oils exhibited at the Artists' Fund Society in Philadelphia.[14] When Mason died, late in the winter of 1843–44, the Kern brothers applied as a team for his position as Principal of the Drawing School. The brothers intended to continue using Mason's teaching methods, and had purchased his "models, Drawing patterns, and Materials." The brothers named eight prominent citizens as references, and some testified to the high opinion Mason had of his former students.[15] One who wrote a letter on their behalf was Dr. Henry S. Patterson, who had hired the Kerns to continue a series of drawings that Mason had begun. Patterson was pleased with the brothers' work and reported that he had often heard Mason speak warmly of their abilities: "Their long course of instruction under Mr. Mason renders them particularly fitted to teach his peculiar

system, which I believe to be the best and most philosophical ever offered to the public."[16] William H. Strickland, an architect, engineer, and officer of the Institute since 1824, also wrote a letter of support for the Kerns. Strickland referred to himself as "a member of the late Wm. Mason's family," and told the Kerns that he had often heard Mason "express admiration of your talents." Mason had intended, Strickland said, "to have made arrangements with you to take charge of the classes during his last illness," but death came too quickly.[17]

It is not clear if the Kerns got the position of Principal of the Drawing School, but they did take Mason's place as a teacher. They apparently held the position jointly.[18] The brothers also operated their "office" on Filbert Street as a partnership. Their simple announcement, "R. H. and E. M. Kern, teachers of drawing, 62 Filbert St.," first appeared in the Philadelphia *Directory* in 1845 and continued to appear year after year, even while Ned was in the West.[19] After Ned left Philadelphia with Frémont, another brother, John, joined Dick in the studio. Fourteen years Dick's senior, John was the oldest of six Kern brothers and Dick and Ned affectionately called him "old man." John had also studied with William Mason, and beginning in 1847, if not before, taught drawing at 62 Filbert. John was never listed as a partner of "R. H. and E. M. Kern." With John's help, however, Dick could assure his absent brother that "business is good, and the income certain: there is sufficient for old man and self."[20]

To make the income certain, Richard Kern worked at a variety of tasks in his studio. In addition to teaching, painting in oils, and drawing with washes, pen, and pencil, he prepared technical illustrations for members of Philadelphia's prominent scientific community. Home of the American Philosophical Society, the Academy of Natural Sciences, the Peale Museum of Natural History and Art, and the Franklin Institute, Philadelphia was the nation's scientific capital, offering Kern unique opportunities. He did botanical drawings for Dr. Joseph Carson's two-volume *Illustrations of Medical Botany* (1847), and illustrations in microscopic anatomy for *A System of Human Anatomy,* edited by Dr. Paul B. Goddard (1848).[21] Both jobs came to Kern through Dr. Joseph Leidy, a young curator of the Academy of Natural Sciences of Philadelphia who would become one of the nation's leading paleontologists. Leidy himself hired Kern to illustrate papers published in the Academy's annual reports.[22] Scientific illustration was painstakingly hard work, with little pay Some artists found themselves annoyed at having to draw dull subjects such as skulls and "shells for crabbed Conchologists." "Oh it is a waste of time— a squandering of talents entrusted to me by Heaven—a wearing out of body— and a crushing of mind," Kern's friend Matthias Weaver lamented in his diary.[23] But the work, which may have suited Kern's temperament better than

it did Weaver's, enabled him to indulge his interests in science.

By 1848, Dick had acquired the skills of the lithographer, as Ned had urged him to do. A drawing that Dick did of a fossil for Leidy was made, he said, "from Nature on stone" (fig. 9).[24] Prior to the introduction of lithography, prints had been made from carved blocks of wood or from metal plates, but drawing with crayon on reusable stone proved faster, less expensive, and lent itself to the mass production of illustrations. Philadelphia, where lithography had first been introduced to America from Europe in 1819, remained one of the nation's centers of the trade and Dick probably had no difficulty locating a teacher.[25]

In addition to this varied work in his studio, Richard Kern continued to teach classes at the Franklin Institute. Teaching not only assured him of a reasonably steady income—teachers' salaries at the Institute came directly from student tuition—but also gave him the opportunity to meet people from a wide variety of professions and trades. Among Dick's students at the Institute was John Wilkes, son of the controversial Lt. Charles Wilkes who had led a worldwide naval exploring expedition between 1838 and 1842. The Kerns' friend Joseph Drayton, a prominent Philadelphia draftsman who had accompanied Wilkes' expedition and who used his connections in 1845 to help Edward Kern land his job with Frémont, had brought young Wilkes to Richard Kern's class at the Institute. Also attending

Fig. 9. *Merycoidodon Culbertsonii. Leidy.*
Drawn "from nature on stone" by Richard H.
Kern. *Proceedings of the Academy of Natural
Sciences of Philadelphia* (Philadelphia, 1850).

Kern's class was a brother of the flamboyant and popular Egyptologist, George Robins Gliddon. The Kerns had known the senior Gliddon for some time. Richard had attended his "lectures on Ancient Egypt" and had done some drawing for him. Ned also worked for Gliddon and had promised to bring him a bearskin from the West. One of Dr. Samuel George Morton's sons also studied under Kern. A physician and professor of anatomy with wide-ranging interests, including significant work in geology and craniology, the senior Morton was one of the leading American scientists of his day. Morton admired the Kerns' "eminent talent," and sent students and business to the brothers. He had depended upon them for "drawing and colouring where extreme accuracy were requisite." Dick, in turn, cultivated Morton for his patronage and considered himself a close acquaintance of the doctor and his family.[26]

By the time of Edward's return from California, probably in 1848, Richard Kern had made a place for himself within Philadelphia's scientific community. Not only did he do illustrations for scientists and teach their friends and relatives, he was also one of them. As with the scientists of his day, Kern had eclectic interests and the kind of drawing he did required knowledge of botany and anatomy. Kern received regular invitations to Sunday evening "soirées" at the home of Dr. Morton, where resident scientists and visitors exchanged ideas.[27] In May of 1847, the prestigious and selective Philadelphia Academy of

Natural Sciences had honored Kern by electing him to membership. In September of 1847 the Academy had also taken into its ranks his brother Benjamin, a medical doctor who had been nominated by Joseph Leidy, Samuel Morton, and Richard Kern. In October, at the recommendation of Joseph Leidy and George Gliddon, the Academy invited Edward Kern's membership, although he was still in the Far West.[28]

When Ned returned from his remarkable adventures and began to talk about another trip west, the Kerns' connections with the Philadelphia scientific establishment paid off handsomely. Three Kern brothers—Ned, Dick, and Ben—would be chosen to accompany the Pathfinder, but the circumstances of what would become known as Frémont's fourth expedition were much less glamorous than those that had surrounded Ned's departure on Frémont's third expedition in 1845.

Frémont had returned from California in disgrace. During the military occupation of California, Frémont had become involved in a power struggle with a senior officer, Gen. Stephen Watts Kearny. Frémont lost. Kearny ordered Frémont back to Washington, where he was placed under arrest and court-martialed in the fall of 1847. In late January 1848, perhaps about the time that Ned returned to Philadelphia, Frémont was found guilty of mutinous acts and disobedience and sentenced to be dismissed from the service. The issues were complicated and neither side emerged blameless. Although James K. Polk, a sympathetic president, commuted Frémont's sentence, the proud explorer resigned his army commission.[29]

Summer of 1848 found John C. Frémont eager to find a way to restore luster to his tarnished reputation. His immediate ambition coincided with a long-held dream of his father-in-law, Thomas Hart Benton. For years, the senior Senator from Missouri had hoped to see railroad tracks stretch westward from St. Louis to the Pacific. A transcontinental railroad, Benton argued, would tap the rich trade of Asia—"the brightest jewel in the diadem of commerce." Whatever nation dominated that trade, Benton predicted, would acquire "the first rank in the arts, the sciences, in national power and individual wealth."[30]

The argument must have had strong appeal for three St. Louis businessmen, who agreed to underwrite the costs of a survey to be led by Benton's son-in-law. Cut off from the support of the Army Corps of Topographical Engineers that had financed his earlier explorations, Frémont probably found Benton's scheme a godsend. He began to assemble a team, asking veterans of his previous expeditions to join him. Among the veterans who stepped forward was Edward Kern, who also volunteered the services of two of his brothers, Benjamin and Richard. Benjamin was the oldest of the three and a trained physician. "Doc" had traveled as far as St. Louis with Ned in 1845, apparently for his health, and he may have met Frémont then.[31] For Dick, this would be the first trip west.

Whether Ned had to talk long and hard to convince Dick to leave the comfort of his studio and the security of Philadelphia, we do not know. He certainly understood that this would not be a pleasure excursion, resembling a sketching tour along the Hudson. "Our route will be a hard and dangerous one," Dick told Dr. Morton.[32] The journey across the continent also involved considerable financial risk. Although Dick later explained to a friend that he had left because he feared that the studio on Filbert Street would not support all three brothers, and "John could have all the business of the office," joining Frémont offered no financial security.[33] Frémont could not afford to pay all of his men, but he apparently convinced them that Congress would soon pass a railroad survey bill and then, as one of the veterans put it, "when the work was finished Govt. would pay us."[34]

Whatever the risks, a trip west with Frémont must have seemed irresistible to someone with Richard Kern's restless, curious, and energetic nature. To a friend, Dick cavalierly explained the trip across the continent as "an opportunity to improve myself [in] landscape painting."[35] He had few ties with family to break. Dick had not married, so there would be no tearful parting with a spouse. His father had died in 1842 and his mother the following year. Dick's closest kin were five brothers and two sisters, and two of the brothers would be traveling with him. Finally, Dick

seems to have possessed some of the Romantic restlessness that characterized many men of his generation. Life "in the field," he later noted, was "much more congenial to my semi savage habits than living in a civilized community."[36] Before leaving home he wrote in the album of his older sister, Mary, a poem he entitled: "Separation from the German":

When to the land where the citron flowers
    blooming,
The swan speeds his southwardly flight;
When the red of the evening in the far west
    is sinking
And through the deep woods steal the
    shadows of night,
Then doth my heart with deep grief
    complain
That never, ah never shall I see thee again.
Parting, ah parting, parting gives pain.[37]

In Kern's day, cities such as Philadelphia were reeling from the effects of rapid industrialization and urban growth. These cities became the breeding grounds of Romantic artists who sought to escape from the troubled man-made urban environment into pure "Nature." As Kern's best friend and fellow artist, Matthias Weaver, noted in his diary: "The farther we live from Nature the further from happiness."[38]

Only in wilderness, Romantics believed, could one see the works of the creator undefiled by man. Nature seemed the ideal milieu for the artist who sought to express emotion, be it rapture or melancholy, and to interpret the message of the creator for his fellow human beings. Thomas Cole, who died the year

Fig. 10. *Lansdown,* June 16, 1847. Watercolor by Richard H. Kern. Courtesy, Fred W. Cron.

that Kern went west, had helped bring new respectability to painting the American landscape. Cole and his disciples, who came to be called the Hudson River School, had rebelled against the painting of historical events, biblical scenes, allegories, and portraiture, and had turned to the picturesque American countryside for inspiration. Richard Kern, who considered himself a man "of Feeling and Thought," had followed their lead. He had made a sojourn up the Hudson to Lake George and into the White Mountains of New Hampshire—popular places among contemporary artists who did plein air sketching. Dick's watercolor of *Lansdown,* June 16, 1847, across the Schuylkill River (fig. 10); an unfinished watercolor, *View on Lake George from Ft.*

Fig. 11. *Après nature par Richd H. Kern 1846.* Courtesy, Fred W. Cron.

George, August 8, 1846, done for "Joe Leidy"; and a pencil sketch of a cow, *Aprés nature par Richard H. Kern 1846* (fig. 11), are among the few remaining works that Dick did "from nature" in the East. Now, beyond the Hudson and the Catskills, the Mississippi and the Rockies lay before him. Like Thomas Cole on the Hudson, Richard Kern the Romantic packed his flute for the trip.[39]

Romanticism, as one writer has explained, "resists definition, but in general it implies an enthusiasm for the strange, remote, solitary, and mysterious."[40] The Far West, more than any other area of the country, had all of these ingredients, but it was not a terra incognita for Richard Kern. He had received a firsthand report on the region from his brother. It also seems likely that Dick had seen images and artifacts of life in the Pacific Northwest and on the Plains. Collections assembled from the expeditions of Lewis and Clark, Stephen H. Long, and other sources were on permanent exhibit in the Peale Museum in Philadelphia, along with drawings done by the two Philadelphia artists who accompanied Long—Titian Peale and Samuel Seymour.[41] Kern also had opportunities to see portraits and genre scenes of Plains Indians. Ned might have disabused Dick of glorifying Indians as James Fenimore Cooper had done, but Indians held special fascination for the Romantic artist. George Catlin, who had worked and exhibited in Philadelphia put it forcibly:

> Black and blue cloth and civilization are destined . . . to obliterate the grace and beauty of Nature. Man, in the simplicity and loftiness of his nature, unrestrained and unfettered by the disguises of art, is surely the most beautiful model for the painter; and the country from which he hails is unquestionably the best school of the arts in the world.[42]

In his late teens, Richard Kern might have seen Catlin's Indian gallery when it was exhibited in Philadelphia, or he might have leafed through the hundreds of illustrations in Catlin's *Letters and Notes on the Manners, Customs, and Conditions of North American Indians,* published in 1841, or Catlin's beautiful *North American Indian Portfolio,* published in 1844.[43] Closer to home, it seems likely that the Kern brothers admired the colored lithographs in Thomas McKenney's and James Hall's three-volume portfolio, *History of the Indian Tribes of North America,* published in Philadelphia between 1836 and 1844.[44] When Richard Kern headed west, then, he probably took with him certain preconceived images about the Plains and Plains tribes. Nothing, however, could have prepared him for the vivid colors, extraordinary topography, and unique Indians he would see in the desert Southwest.

In addition to whatever preconceptions Kern might have had about the West, he also carried with him the sensibilities and conventions of an artist and the curiosity and drafting skills of a scientist. Indeed, Kern personified "the union of science and art" that was quintessentially Philadelphian and a matter of self-conscious pride to her leading citizens.[45] "In that city's important naturalist circle," one historian has explained, "the artist and the scientist performed interchangeable functions." Detailed drawings were essential for scientific description and classification, and so "the artist was the scientist and vice versa."[46] Philadelphia artist-scientists such as William Bartram, George Ord, Alexander Wilson, John James Audubon, and Charles Willson Peale and his numerous progeny had shown the way. Thus, along with his flute and brushes, Kern also packed up a small library and equipment for assembling an ornithological collection.

In 1848, as Thoreau preached but did not practice, Richard Kern headed "westward into the future, with a spirit of enterprise and adventure."[47] He also took along a sense of humor, which probably helped him through the tedium and privation that lay ahead. Kern appreciated a drink of "Mountain Dew," enjoyed puns and ribald jokes with friends, and the fellowship of fraternal organizations that had begun to spring up in cities like Philadelphia, where neighborhood life was deteriorating under the influence of rapid industrialization.[48] With fellow artists and friends, he enjoyed, as he put it, "the library . . . the festive board, the music room, the rambling study, [the] love of nature, and the gallery, where communion was held with brothers through their works hanging around."[49] In the evenings, he played chess, practiced his flute, attended lectures and the theater, and spent time "reading, talking, and smoking" with friends. He may well have participated in late-night street serenades with Matthias Weaver and other young bachelors as well. When he was nearly twenty-one, Matthias Weaver described him as "something of a marked character not settled yet."[50] Although an oil portrait of Dick, painted by Ned, suggests a somber demeanor (fig. 12), two photographic images reveal the impish smile and dancing eyes of a gregarious man who appears to have enjoyed life (frontispiece and fig. 13). "Gloire trois fois, gloire a Bacchus," Kern wrote in French in a poem celebrating Bacchus, the Roman god of wine and revelry, and Venus, the goddess of beauty and love.[51] The Frémont expedition, however, would be no bacchanal.

Fig. 12. *Richard Kern.*
Oil portrait by Edward M. Kern.
Courtesy, Smithsonian Institution.

If Frémont was to prove that a route west from St. Louis along the 38th parallel was practical for a railroad, he had to cross the Rockies in winter. Thus he made no effort to get the expedition off in summer or to postpone departure until the next spring. Instead, Frémont and his entourage began to rendezvous in St. Louis in late September, with winter coming on.

Fig. 13. Richard H. Kern.
Photograph.
Courtesy, Smithsonian Institution.

Fig. 14. Benjamin Jordon Kern.
Daguerreotype.
Courtesy, Huntington Library.

Four Kern brothers arrived in St. Louis ahead of Frémont. Ned and Dick understood from Frémont that they would serve as the artists on the survey; Ben would be the expedition's doctor and naturalist (fig. 14). John Kern, the "old man," had come only as far as St. Louis, perhaps to see his brothers off; he returned to Philadelphia, where he would continue to operate the studio.

With the hearty endorsement of Dick and Ned, John applied for their position at the Franklin Institute. His brothers had resigned in June, recommending him for their position. John also hoped to pick up some of Dick's business as an illustrator for scientific reports.[52]

At St. Louis, the Kern brothers found themselves part of a group of over thirty men who planned to join Frémont. Half of them, including Dick and Ben, were greenhorns, but the rest were experienced mountain explorers. Sixteen of the men had accompanied Frémont on earlier expeditions. These veterans included Alexander Godey, an ebullient and skillful hunter who had been on Frémont's second and third expeditions; Charles Preuss, the stoic topographer and mapmaker on Frémont's first and second expeditions; and, of course, Edward Kern.[53]

The party left St. Louis on October 3, heading up the Missouri on the steamer *Martha*. On Sunday October 8, they landed at the mouth of the Kansas and made camp near Westport. There Ned had written a tantalizing letter to Dick three years before. Today a suburb of Kansas City, Westport was then a popular place to assemble men and supplies before moving west. All three of Frémont's earlier expeditions had used it as a launching point. For nearly two weeks, the Kerns and their companions prepared for departure. Then, on the "clear and pleasant afternoon" of October 20, Dick noted in the small diary that he kept on the journey, the party moved about six miles on a trial run. "Everything went off well with the exception of some packs on wild mules and they went off too."[54] If Dick felt great excitement and anticipation, he never confided such emotions to his diary.

Traveling twenty-five to thirty miles on good days, Frémont's caravan of pack mules followed the Kansas River west-ward through rain and prairie fires, past sites where Topeka and Salina would spring up in the next decades. Along the way, Dick and Ned made sketches when time permitted. Sometimes, Ned noted, they worked "by the fire light till I was nearly blinded by the smoke and ashes."[55] Some of these drawings are lost (such as a sketch of Frémont's camp made on October 22), or in private collections.[56] Others have been preserved in the pages of Richard's diary, where he apparently made hasty sketches in order to record a moment or to serve as the basis for a more polished drawing.

By the end of October, a week of travel had put them on the Smoky Hill Fork of the Kansas, where Richard got his first sight and taste of buffalo (fig. 15). South of present Hays, Kansas, they left the timbered bottom lands of the Smoky Hill and struck southward over the rolling prairie toward the Arkansas, with "not a stick of timber in sight." Snow began to fall on November 4 and the early morning temperatures dropped to well below freezing, but the group proceeded with no incident more serious than what Richard described as "the pleasure" of being thrown over his mule's head, landing "in safety on the ground."

The group reached the Arkansas River on November 7, then proceeded west over the Santa Fe Trail, a road that Benjamin Kern described as "a good one and much traveled."[57] On November 9, just past Chouteau's Island and still in Kansas, they got their first

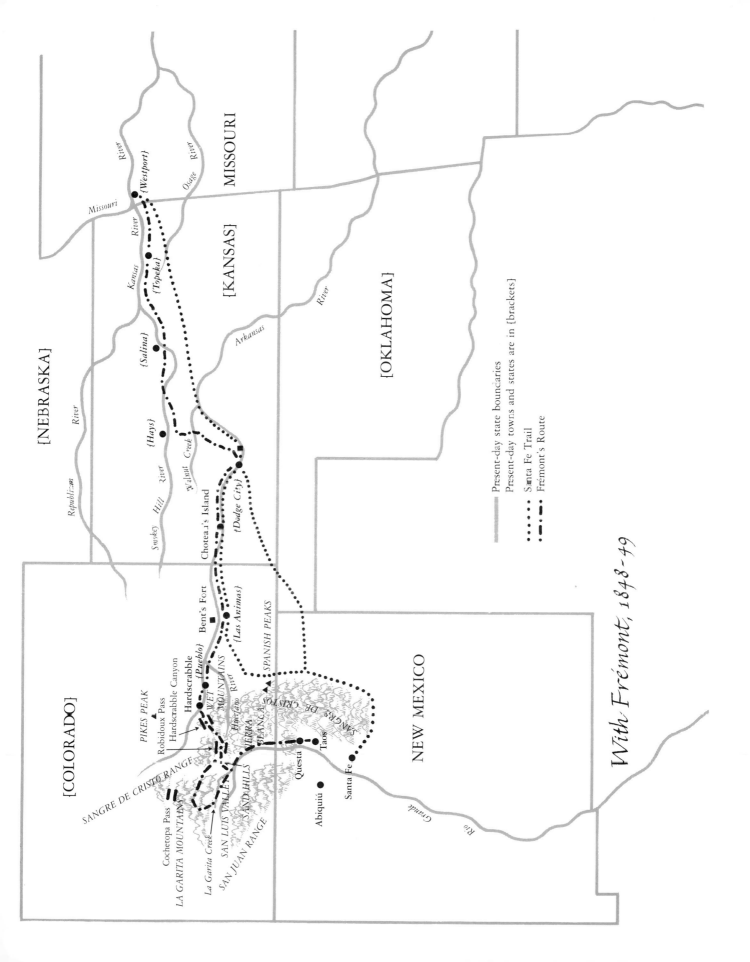

With Frémont, 1848–49

Fig. 15. *Sunday Oct. 29, 1848 . . . before crossing Smoky Hill Fork—Smoky Hills in the Distance.* Watercolor by Richard or Edward Kern. Courtesy, Fred W. Cron.

glimpse of the Rockies, over 150 miles beyond, snow already on the peaks. That same day, Dick reported, they "came across a large village of Kiowas, with some Comanches." No romantic about Indians, Dick pronounced them "a set of wild looking rascals"—"red devils" who annoyed the party. The next day, November 10, the Kiowas traveled along with Frémont's group and Dick noted

that "it was a queer compound, civilization and barbarism traveling in company." That night, the Kiowas camped nearby: "Ned and I were as busy as we could be sketching them." These sketches are lost or in private collections except for a drawing of a tepee that Dick made in his diary that romantic evening (fig. 16): "The night was a queer one—Indians singing, our

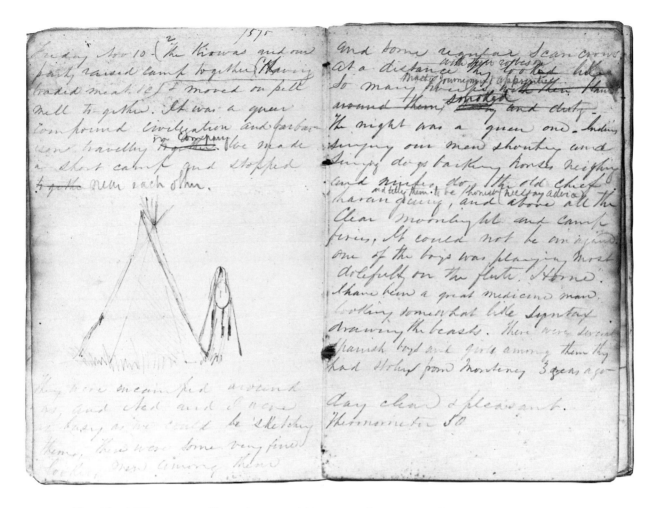

Fig. 16. A Kiowa tepee, November 10, 1848. Rough sketch in the diary of Richard H. Kern. Courtesy, Huntington Library.

men shouting and singing, dogs barking, horses neighing. . . . One of the boys was playing most dolefully on the flute, 'home.'" (fig. 17).

By mid-November the small party had reached Bent's Fort, a splendid adobe stronghold and trading emporium built in the early 1830s on the north side of the Arkansas. The party camped in snow on the south side of the river for a couple of days, and Richard Kern busied himself making sketches. Some 100 miles farther west he could see the Front Range of the Rockies, including Pikes Peak and the Spanish Peaks, which Indians called the Breasts of the World,

Fig. 17. *Saturday Evening Camp, Nov. 11, 1848.* Watercolor by Richard or Edward Kern. Courtesy, Fred W. Cron.

demurely covered with snow (fig. 18). Several years later, Dick did a watercolor of *Pike's Peak* in winter, as it might have looked in 1848 (plate 16).[58]

At Bent's Fort, Frémont stocked up on supplies and probably tried to engage a guide. None of Frémont's men knew the route, but it was his custom to hire a guide along the way. The news they picked up at Bent's Fort was gloomy. "Both Indians and whites here," Frémont wrote to his father-in-law, "report the snow to be deeper in the mountains than has for a long time been

Fig. 18. *Spanish Peaks from Our Camp, Nov. 17, 1848.* Watercolor by Richard or Edward Kern. Courtesy, Fred W. Cron.

known so early in the season, and they predict a severe winter. . . . Still I am not discouraged."[39]

On November 19 they broke camp and forged ahead, passing sand hills that Kern sketched in his diary. Two days later they reached Pueblo, where a few former trappers inhabited what Dick described as "a fort built of Adobes—a miserable looking place, the inside resembling a menagerie—a compound of Spaniards, Horses mules dogs chickens and bad stench." Here old-timers also warned Frémont against plunging into record snows and cold,

while Frémont tried to persuade "Old Bill" Williams to hire on as a guide. An eccentric but experienced mountain man who would turn sixty-two with the new year, Old Bill had worked briefly in 1845 as a guide for Frémont's third expedition. Williams happened to be passing the winter at Pueblo, mending an arm that an Indian bullet had shattered the previous July. Frémont must have known that Williams, despite his reputation for monumental binges and his penchant for solitude, knew the southern Rockies as well as any man. Williams finally agreed to lead the party, "but it was not without some hesitation," one contemporary remembered. Williams thought "we could manage to get through, though not without considerable suffering."[60] If Williams made such a remark, it would prove to be a colossal understatement.

Their guide finally secured, Frémont's men headed into a mountain winter. Frémont's plan, notable for its directness if not for its attention to detail, was to ascend the Rio Grande to its headwaters, then descend into the Colorado basin, proceed westward across the Great Basin and over the Sierras to Monterey.[61] To get to the Rio Grande, they left the Arkansas a day beyond Pueblo and headed southwest toward Hardscrabble, an adobe village where a small group of former trappers and their families ranched and farmed. This would be the last outpost of white civilization along their route, and Dick described it as "a miserable place containing about a dozen houses Corn Cribs and Corrals." But even that dreary place looked good to a trail-weary artist. Dick pronounced the adobe houses "very comfortable—they seemed like palaces to us, as we enjoyed the luxuries of a table & stools." At Hardscrabble, local women prepared a feast of chicken and baked pumpkin for the explorers. Frémont purchased 130 bushels of corn to sustain the pack animals in the snow-covered mountains, where they would find it difficult to forage.[62]

On foot because their horses were loaded with corn, Frémont's men trudged out of the village on Saturday afternoon, November 25, and headed southwest along the north branch of Hardscrabble Creek, through the Wet Mountains. Dick sketched the mountains as they entered them and recorded colors in his diary, such as rocks of "copper green blue and brownish black."

On November 27 they passed through Hardscrabble Canyon, where Dick did a dramatic painting that he later mislabeled *Robidoux' Pass* (plate 1). Dick laconically described Hardscrabble Canyon in his diary as "sandstone— white and salmon color probably 1200 to 1500 feet Rocks high rugged & bald plenty of snow." Earlier visitors knew the Hardscrabble as the Río de Piedras Amarillas, or the Río de Peñasco Amarillo—the river of yellow rocks—and Dick's watercolor appropriately suggests yellow hues on the cliff sides. He exaggerated the height and narrowness of the canyon in his painting, but he clearly captured the impact that it made on a newcomer from the East. As his brother Benjamin noted, some places in the canyon "seemed scarcely ever to get much sun so high are the mountains and so narrow the pass."[63]

With snow falling every day and the wind howling, they picked their way up the Huerfano River on December 2. The next day they painfully forced their animals across the Sangre de Cristos, through deep snow, over Robidoux Pass (today's Mosca Pass), at 9,713 feet. Once across, they descended into the San Luis Valley, toward the great hills of drifting sands that centuries of prevailing winds had piled up on the west

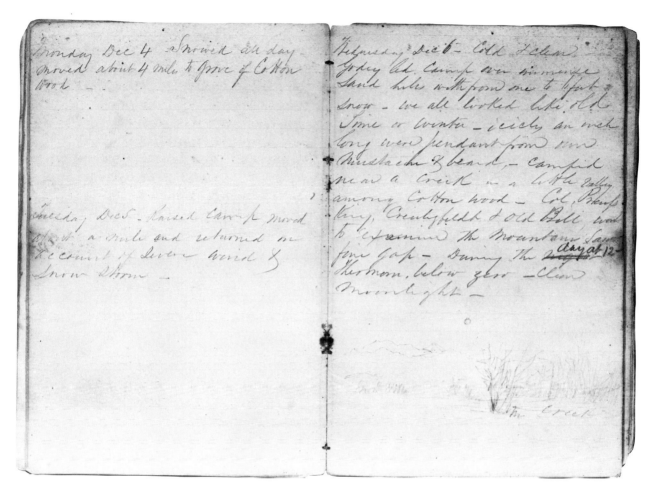

Fig. 19. Scene apparently drawn from the sand hills near Medano Creek, San Luis Valley, December 6, 1848. Rough sketch in the diary of Richard H. Kern. Courtesy, Huntington Library.

side of the mountains. Skirting "the immense sand hills" in subzero temperatures, Dick noted on December 6: "we all looked like old Time or Winter—icicles an inch long were pendant from our moustache & beard." Dick's fingers must have been nearly frozen as he sketched the "creek in a little valley among cotton wood" on a cold, clear, moonlit night (fig. 19), probably Médano Creek near the same spot where today's summer visitors to the Great Sand Dunes National Monument wade in cool water.

Two more snowy, bitter days of hard travel, without firewood, took them to the northern edge of the sandhills. Frémont was apparently headed toward the Saguache Valley and intended to cross the formidable San Juan Range to the Gunnison by way of Cochetopa or Carnero pass.[64] Toward that end, Frémont followed a short cut along the Carnero River, recommended by Old Bill Williams. Along the way, Old Bill seems to have made a mistake that would prove tragic.[65] After skirting "Hell's Gate" of the Carnero by taking to the piñón-covered hills to the south side, he missed finding his way back to the main stream. Instead, the party followed Coolbroth Canyon and Cave Creek into the La Garita Mountains, a part of the San Juan Range. Up the valley to the west, twin-peaked Boot Mountain rose before them.

On December 14, after four days of beating their way through narrow canyons in deep snow and blizzards, they reached a high ridge. They had hoped this would be the Continental Divide, but instead they found themselves near the top of Boot Mountain, which reaches to 12,422 feet with still higher elevations beyond. Some of the men must have been discouraged at the sight, but Kern found it "one of the finest mountain views in the world." He made a sketch that has since been lost.

For the next two days they continued moving west, descending Boot Mountain and then climbing a ridge toward the top of its taller neighbor, Mesa Mountain (12,944 feet). On the sixteenth, Dick said, they "reached the summit of the hill but the wind and the snow were so dreadful we had to return. Had the animals gone over the hill or had we remained there a half an hour longer the whole party might have been lost." As it was, the animals had already suffered horribly. Corn had run out and the deep snow prevented them from foraging. Mules ate saddles, straps, bedrolls, and one another's manes and tails, then began to die. Dick described the "desolate and cheerless sight" of "dead mules and pack and riding saddles lying on the trail."

Still they pushed forward. On the December 17 they made their way over Mesa Mountain by using handmade mauls to beat a trail through the deep snow for their dying mules. At day's end they settled into a pine grove on Wanamaker Creek that they would call Camp Dismal. When morning came on December 18, Benjamin Kern recalled, "I waked up and found 8 inches snow on my bed, peeped out and told Dick the expedition was destroyed and if we all got to some settlement with our lives we would be doing well."[66] A blizzard raged all that day and Frémont's men had the first of many meals of mule meat, sometimes sprinkled with corn meal.

While a scouting party went ahead, the Kerns and others remained at Camp Dismal for several more days; according to Benjamin, these were "days of horror desolation [and] despair." The snow was so deep that the men topped trees for firewood, leaving behind tall tree stumps—still visible today at heights ranging from four to thirty feet. Mules

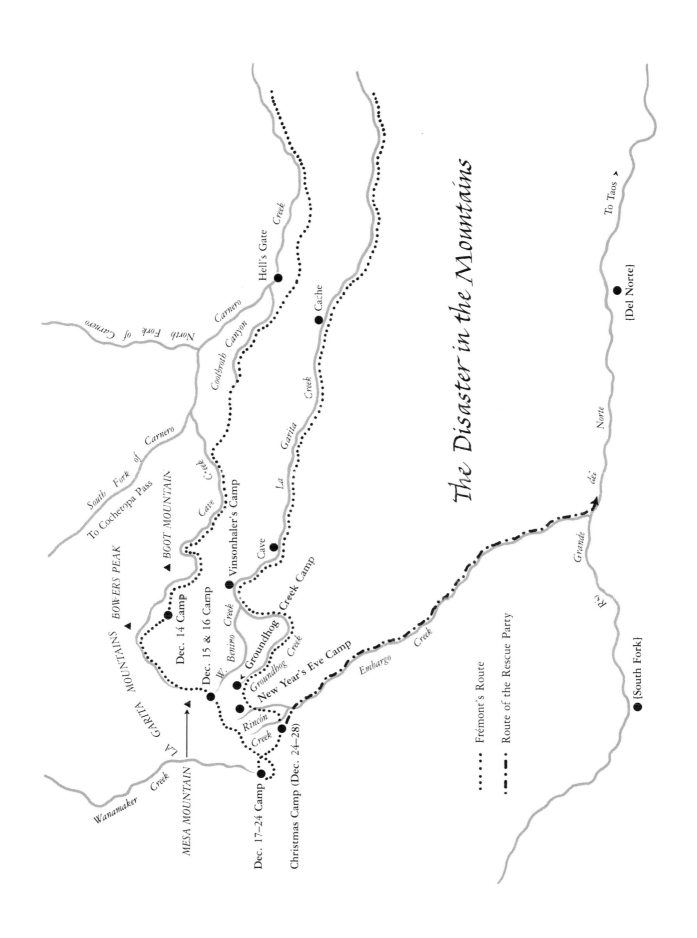

The Disaster in the Mountains

continued to die. At this site, the "bleached, honeycombed, lichen-covered bones" of the mules' skeletons could still be found in abundance nearly one hundred years later.[67]

All efforts to move forward failed. On the twenty-third they began a retreat, moving slowly through a trench in the deep snow, hoping to reach the Rio Grande and the settlements of New Mexico. Christmas Day brought a reprieve. With Alexander Godey as chief cook, the men prepared "Elk stew & pies, rice dough nuts coffee biscuits & hot stuff [alcohol]."[68] Supplies, however, were running low and finding game in the deep snow proved nearly impossible. Thus, the day after Christmas, Frémont sent four men—Williams, Henry King, Thomas Breckinridge, and Frederick Creutzfeldt—to descend the Rio Grande to Abiquiú, the first sizable town in New Mexico, to get help. He expected the rescue party to return in no more than sixteen days.

Meanwhile, Frémont's men split into several groups and continued to move down the mountain, attempting to follow the rescue party. The weather was pleasant for a week after Christmas, but moving baggage without mules was a laborious task and the men made only a few miles a day. The three Kern brothers, along with a British adventurer, Capt. Andrew Cathcart, and two Indian boys, were the slowest. Within a week they had fallen a few miles behind the other two groups.

Historians have criticized Frémont's decision to use precious time and resources moving gear instead of heading for help, but the Kerns never complained. Their luggage probably contained "clothes, surgical instruments, medicines, drawing equipment, sketches, [and] bird and plant collections," as one historian has surmised.[69] The baggage contained the means for the Kerns' livelihood, and time spent attempting to save it probably seemed a wise investment.

The last day of the year, Dick, Ned, and Benjamin apparently consolidated some of their equipment and "made a bale of about 200 pds to drag to next camp." The work was exhausting, but Dick noted that the day was "pleasant with occasional summery clouds" and that the new camp was "on a fine plateau with a grove of pines." He took out his sketchbook and watercolors that New Year's Eve to record the scene near the head of Embargo Creek (plate 2). He entitled the painting *In The Chowatch Mts., New Mexico, Dec. 31, 1848.* Dick mistakenly believed the party to be in the "Chowatch," or Saguache, Mountains of New Mexico, a range to the north that early travelers sometimes confused with the La Garita Mountains.[70] Although their camp was well into what is today Colorado, Kern was correct in saying that they were in New Mexico. Since 1819, New Mexico's border had officially extended north to the Arkansas River. Not until the Compromise of 1850 was New Mexico's boundary pushed southward to the 38th parallel (it was moved farther south, to its present line at the 37th parallel, with the creation of Colorado Territory in 1861).

That lonely New Year's Eve in the mountains, Ben wrote, "[we] made ourselves merry & sang several songs in our crude way—after supper Dick read Tom Hood [an English poet] & Ned minced boiled mule meat for pies for tomorrow's New Years treat."[71] It may be that on evenings such as this, "Dick blowed the flute a little to cheer us up," as Ben would write on another occasion.[72]

On New Year's Day, in addition to savoring minced mule-meat pie, the Kerns' party followed in the wake of the two other groups and moved a few miles over another ridge to a new camp on Groundhog Creek, which flows into La Garita Creek. Here they constructed a shelter and waited for the next ten days for the return of the rescue party. As a mountain storm came and went, the Kerns retrieved baggage that they had left strewn along the trail above them. But as their luggage grew heavier, the Kerns began to burn some of their books and sift out the items they most wanted to keep.[73] While they waited at the Groundhog Camp, Frémont's group went down the La Garita to the Rio Grande to watch for the rescue party.

Apparently confident that help would arrive on time, the Kerns finally moved out of camp and continued downstream on January 11, the day the relief party was scheduled to arrive. But help did not come. When it was clear that the rescue party would not show up that

day—if at all—Frémont took Alexander Godey, Charles Preuss, and two others, and set out down the Rio Grande for help. He left the remainder of the men under the command of Lorenzo Vinsonhaler, an Ohioan and veteran of Frémont's third expedition, with instructions to move all the baggage to the Rio Grande, then to follow until they should meet a rescue party.

While Frémont went for help, most of the remaining men struggled for several days to move the baggage, as ordered. But it soon became clear that their progress in the bitter cold was too slow; food nearly gone. In order to move more quickly, the Kerns and others cached most of their equipment, hoping to return for it. Among the items the Kerns left behind were specimens of birds that the brothers had collected along the way.[74] In his diary on January 11, Edward sketched the place where they had made the cache, showing a cave in the cliffs. Some of the men, including Dick, had slept there. The men called this place "the point of Rock," and Ned named the stream that is today La Garita Creek "Proulx Creek," in honor of a French veteran of three previous Frémont expeditions, Rafael Proue, who had frozen to death two days before. Proue was "the first of our party who perished," Ned later recalled.[75]

A watercolor, *Point of Rocks, Proulx Creek* (fig. 20), done by either Richard or Edward Kern, also shows the scene of the cache. With its distinctive formations in the cliffs on the north side of the creek, and with the twin peaks of the

Fig. 20. *Point of Rocks, Proulx Creek.* Watercolor by Richard or Edward Kern. Courtesy, Fred W. Cron.

heavily forested Blue Mountain in the background, the site of the watercolor is identifiable today. The spot is a mile or so from the prominent landmark from which La Garita Creek takes its name— the great cliffs of La Garita (the sentry box) that Frémont's men called "Point of Rocks." The site was probably chosen because this landmark, visible from the Rio Grande, would make it easy to lo-

cate the cache. Then, too, the cliffs pictured in the watercolor are on the north side of La Garita Creek. Sunshine on warm rock on the cliff's southern exposure would have melted the deep snow near the base of the cliffs, facilitating the men's work.

A second watercolor, signed by Richard Kern and entitled *On Proulx' Creek, Chowatch Mts., N.M., 1849,* apparently shows this same scene (plate 3). But this watercolor contains one notable inaccuracy. In the place of the heavily forested Blue Mountain, which appears dark in the previous watercolor, Kern has painted a twin-peaked, snow-covered bald mountain. This mountain appears to be craggier than Blue Mountain and the artist has reversed the height of the peaks. Curiously, the mountain resembles Boot Mountain as seen from Cave Creek, which the party had ascended a few weeks before. Two explanations suggest themselves. Kern almost certainly completed this watercolor after the Frémont party emerged from the mountains, and perhaps several years later. Formations in the cliffs on La Garita Creek and Cave Creek are similar, and Kern might have confused them—especially if his sketches, or those of one of his brothers, had become jumbled in the chaos surrounding the expedition's demise. It is also possible that Kern's *On Proulx' Creek* was painted with aesthetic concerns, rather than accuracy, foremost in the artist's mind. He may have deliberately idealized the mountains in the background and reversed the peaks to improve the composition of the scene.[76]

Unencumbered after making their cache, the enfeebled, starving, and frostbitten men still managed to travel only a few miles a day down La Garita Creek. They saw no game animals, and men began to die. As their plight became increasingly desperate, they began to quarrel among themselves. At this juncture, Vinsonhaler committed

what Richard Kern termed "a piece of rascality without parallel." The Kerns wanted the entire group to stay together for mutual support, but Vinsonhaler adopted what Dick condemned as an "each man for himself" attitude. Vinsonhaler moved ahead on January 22 with the "strong" men, leaving the "weak," Dick wrote, "to get along as we could or perish." The latter group included the three Kerns and half a dozen others: Andrew Cathcart and Micajah McGehee, who had come along for adventure; Elijah T. Andrews, Henry Rohrer, and John S. Stepperfeldt, on their first trip into the Far West; and Charles Taplin, a veteran of previous Frémont expeditions.[77]

The Kerns and their companions managed only a few more miles before Elijah Andrews could go no farther. Determined to stick together and not abandon the weak, they made camp and waited for fate to take its course. They "looked for muscles & snails & earth worms," Dick wrote, but "found none." Within a few days, Andrews and Rohrer had died. The men talked of eating human flesh, but apparently decided against it.[78] Rescue became their only hope. These, Dick wrote, "were days of misery & death would soon have ended them." Edward described what must have been the resigned attitude of most of the men:

> I had long passed the cravings of hunger, and was gradually sinking into a sleep . . . I felt happy and contented sitting nearly all day by the fire in a kind of stupor listless and careless of when my

time would come—for I was expecting it.[79]

Instead of death, Alexander Godey appeared before the snowblinded men. Benjamin Kern describes the moment best:

> On the 28th of January about 12 in the morning During a snow storm as we all sat silently around our little willow fire Taplin suddenly exclaimed by God there is a halloo. Tis but a wolf again we said—rising to his feet he said Christ there's a man on horseback over the river, we gave a shout you may be sure, almost in an instant Godey was with us. . . . Oh he has bread we cried and some of us trembled with joy at the sight of it.[80]

His spirits revived, Dick did a watercolor sketch the following day of the men huddled around a campfire at the Relief Camp, with the Sierra Blanca (that Kern mistakenly called "White and Wet" Mountains) in the background (plate 4). They were on the Rio Grande, probably a mile or so south of today's Alamosa.[81]

Under Godey's supervision, rescuers took the debilitated survivors down the Rio Grande. They arrived at Questa, the first of the New Mexico settlements, on February 9, and "slept in a house," as Dick gratefully noted in his diary. By February 12, all three Kern brothers had reached Taos where Dick, and perhaps Ned and Benjamin too, stayed at the home of the prominent French-Canadian trader and long-time resident of Taos, Carlos Beaubien.[82] "We are slowly recovering from the effects

of our starvation," Benjamin Kern wrote to a friend a week later, "but feel very tottering in the knees. We escaped from the mountains with little else than that which was on our backs."[83]

They were lucky to have escaped at all. From Godey, they had learned of the fate of some of the less fortunate. Henry King, who had gone with the first rescue party, had lost the will to live and sat down to freeze to death. There is good evidence that his starving companions survived on his flesh. Two of those who had gone with Vinsonhaler and the so-called strong men also died. All together, ten of thirty-three men had been lost to the ravages of winter. On his initial journey to the Far West, then, Richard Kern, along with his two brothers, had survived what historian William Goetzmann has called "one of the greatest disasters in the history of American exploration," and what another historian has more vehemently described as "one of the most hare-brained exploring expeditions ever undertaken in this country."[84]

Only a few days after the Kerns reached Taos, the ambitious and driven Frémont left for California by way of the more southerly Gila route. He had seen enough snow for one winter. Most of the survivors went with Frémont, but the three Kerns, Old Bill Williams, and two members of the allegedly weak group, Andrew Cathcart and John Stepperfeldt, had had their fill of Frémont's leadership and chose to stay behind. A few days after Frémont's departure, Edward explained part of the reason. Frémont, Edward wrote, "has broken faith with all of us. Dick and I were to have accompanied him as his Artists and Doc as Medico and Naturalist." Once on the trail, however, they discovered that instead they were to be "muleteers each with his number of packs. . . . This you must believe was somewhat cutting to our dignity—not that any of us were unwilling to assist in any work *if necessity* required it—but this was not the case." Edward explained Frémont's antipathy toward them by observing that the Kerns, "particularly" Dick and Ben, were not disposed toward flattery, and that Frémont "loves to be told of his greatness." Frémont, Ned charged, was "jealous of anyone who may know as much or more of any subject than himself." Indeed, there is some evidence to substantiate the Kerns' judgment. One historian has recently suggested that Frémont's vanity may have made it impossible for him "to allow those around him to function as 'successfully' as he did."[85]

The Kerns, then, had decided that it was better to part company with Frémont, rather than to have an angry confrontation en route to California. Frémont, Ned wrote, "has left us without even his good wishes or a thought of our future—and owing *me money*."[86]

Several years later, Alexander Godey offered a less flattering explanation for the Kerns' antipathy. Frémont had done no wrong, Godey argued, but the failure of the expedition represented a pro-

found loss of opportunity for the Kern brothers. The Kerns "had been the most strenuous advocates for the organization of the expedition in Washington," Godey wrote. Like other members of the expedition, the Kerns had gone along without pay, but "being scientific men," they had hoped to be recompensed by future appropriations from Congress after the expedition succeeded. Instead, they had lost everything, and became embittered toward Frémont.[87]

Just what Frémont thought of the Kerns is not clear, but something may be surmised from private comments that he made to his wife about the lack of courage and nerve of members of his party. Indeed, Frémont may have been pleased to see the Kerns stay in New Mexico; but Ned thought otherwise. Frémont feared leaving them behind, Ned wrote, for "the greatest dread that he has at present is that a *true* and *correct* account of the proceedings above [in the mountains] and here [in New Mexico] may be made public."[88]

It may have been with that in mind that on March 19 Richard Kern revised a portion of his diary, sending it east with John Stepperfeldt, who had it published in his hometown newspaper in Illinois. Papers in New York, Philadelphia, and perhaps elsewhere, reprinted the story. The revisions that Dick made in his diary charged Frémont with ignoring the signs of deep snow and imminent disaster: "with the wilfully blind eyes of rashness and self-conceit and confidence he pushed on."

Dick's judgment has been echoed by a recent psychological study of Frémont that characterizes him as impetuous, obsessive, narcissistic, and erratic.[89] More specifically, Dick accused Frémont of failing to have the dead mules butchered and packed to sustain the men; causing Proue's death through "harsh treatment"; delegating authority to the incompetent Vinsonhaler; taking army rations at Taos and moving on to California without sharing those provisions with the rest of his command; and exhibiting heartlessness. Richard Kern's assertions were reprinted years later, in an effort to discredit Frémont during his 1856 presidential campaign. Point by point, Alexander Godey denied Kern's charges and placed the blame on Old Bill Williams and on himself, for urging Frémont to follow Williams's advice.[90]

Whatever the truth, there can be no doubt that Richard Kern held Frémont responsible for the disaster. In the autumn of 1849, when Kern learned that Frémont had attempted to absolve himself of responsibility and shift the blame to Old Bill Williams, Dick's anger boiled over. From Capt. Andrew Cathcart, the British adventurer who had been among the Kerns' disgruntled "weak" messmates, Dick sought evidence against Frémont. "You have seen some of Frémont's letters," Dick wrote to Cathcart in London, "and I want from you a short extract of your journal, from Dec. 12 until Jany 28th with also what it cost you for provisions."[91] There is no evidence that Cathcart's journal reached

Kern, nor did Kern publish anything else to discredit Frémont, but the bitterness remained. Well over a year after the event, Dick told an acquaintance in Philadelphia:

> I do not think I shall ever allude again in public to our disaster in the San Juan Mountains. I cannot in justice speak of events *without* tracing them to their causes, and as I would handle the subject ungloved, it would ultimately lead to personal consequences and they you know should never be resorted to except as the ultimatum. Beside the subject is a very painful one to me, and I speak of it as little as possible. I am willing to leave it with the past.[92]

By then, a personal tragedy had visited itself upon the Kerns and had made the subject of Frémont's expedition even more painful.

The high hopes that Dick had in going west with Frémont must have intensified his disappointment. The Kern brothers had little to show for their work and sufferings; they received no pay, and most of their sketches from the expedition seem to have been lost. The only known original drawings by the Kerns from Frémont's fourth expedition are a group of nine drawings in a private collection and four of Richard Kern's watercolors in the Amon Carter Museum (plates 1, 2, 3, and 4).[93] Other drawings may exist. Months after the expedition ended, Dick was doing some sketches for Andrew Cathcart and promised to send them to him in London.[94] Sketches attributed to either Dick or Ned seem to be the basis for

Fig. 21. *In a Canyon of the San Juan Mountains*. Engraving apparently based on a drawing by either Richard or Edward Kern. Publisher's prospectus for John C. Frémont, *Memoirs of My life* (1887). Courtesy, Huntington Library.

four highly romanticized engravings done for Frémont's *Memoirs,* published in 1887 (fig. 21).[95] But Frémont never published an account of the fourth expedition, so whatever work by the Kerns might have survived the disaster, or whatever sketches they might have done from memory upon their safe return, never appeared in print during the artists' lifetimes. Neither fame nor fortune followed Richard Kern westward with Frémont.

Plate 1. *Robidoux' Pass, White Mts., N.M., 1848*. Watercolor by Richard H. Kern. Courtesy, Amon Carter Museum, Fort Worth, Texas.

Plate 2. *In the Chowatch Mts., New Mexico, Dec. 31, 1848.* Watercolor by Richard H. Kern. Courtesy, Amon Carter Museum, Fort Worth, Texas.

Plate 3. *On Proulx' Creek, Chowatch Mts., N.M., 1849*. Watercolor by Richard H. Kern. Courtesy, Amon Carter Museum, Fort Worth, Texas.

Plate 4. *Relief Camp on the Rio Grande del Norte, N.M., Jan. 29, 1849 {White and Wet Mts. in Distance}*. Watercolor by Richard H. Kern. Courtesy, Amon Carter Museum, Fort Worth, Texas.

Plate 5. *Valley of Taos, Looking South. N.M., 1849.* Watercolor by Richard H. Kern. Courtesy, Amon Carter Museum, Fort Worth, Texas.

Plate 6. *Pareda, N.M., 1850.* Watercolor by Richard H. Kern. Courtesy, Amon Carter Museum, Fort Worth, Texas.

Plate 7. *Interior of the Jesuit College, Chihuahua, 1850.* Watercolor by Richard H. Kern. Courtesy, Amon Carter Museum, Fort Worth, Texas.

Plate 8. *La Parroquia, Santa Fe, New Mexico, 1849.* Watercolor by Richard H. Kern. Courtesy, Amon Carter Museum, Fort Worth, Texas.

Plate 9. *From Near the Summit of "Kern's Peak," Rocky Mts Near Santa Fe, N.M., Sept. 1850 {Looking North}.* Watercolor by Richard H. Kern. Courtesy, Amon Carter Museum, Fort Worth, Texas.

Plate 10. *New Mexican Aqueduct. Santa Fe Creek, New Mexico, 1851.* Watercolor by Richard H. Kern. Courtesy, Amon Carter Museum, Fort Worth, Texas.

Plate 11. *Rock and Pueblo of Acoma, N.M., 1851.* Watercolor by Richard H. Kern. Courtesy, Amon Carter Museum, Fort Worth, Texas.

Plate 12. *Acoma.* Watercolor by Richard H. Kern. Courtesy, Amon Carter Museum, Fort Worth, Texas.

Plate 13. *Acoma.* Watercolor by Richard H. Kern. Courtesy, Amon Carter Museum, Fort Worth, Texas.

Plate 14. *Interior of the Church of San Miguel, Pueblo of Zuni, N.M., 1851.* Watercolor by Richard H. Kern. Courtesy, Amon Carter Museum, Fort Worth, Texas.

Plate 15. *Smithsonian Institute {From Capitol Grounds, Sept. 1852}*. Watercolor by Richard H. Kern. Courtesy, Amon Carter Museum, Fort Worth, Texas.

Plate 16. *Pike's Peak, 1848. "Mon Songe" {1853}.* Watercolor by Richard H. Kern. Courtesy, Amon Carter Museum, Fort Worth, Texas.

-3-
To the Navajo Country with Simpson, 1849

FOR THE MOMENT, the ordeal in the mountains had apparently satisfied Richard Kern's thirst for adventure. "Dick and Doc," Edward wrote to their older sister, Mary, planned to "return to the States by the earliest opportunity." They would travel with a caravan heading over the Santa Fe Trail to St. Louis, then home to Philadelphia—to "Zion."[1] Mary could expect to see them that summer. But some unfinished business remained.

Sometime in late February, Benjamin Kern teamed up with Old Bill Williams and enlisted the aid of eight New Mexican guides to go back up the Rio Grande and retrieve their equipment and collections, along with the baggage of the rest of Frémont's party.[2] "All the sketches Ned's instruments &c are up the hill," Benjamin had explained to a friend," and "our means of support here are very slender."[3]

During Doc's absence, Dick and Ned settled in at Taos. "We are quartered in a suite of rooms that you would say would make capital stabling," Ned wrote to Mary, "but 'tis among the best in town, and sociable too for we sometimes receive visits from the Donkeys, dogs &c." Ned did the cooking while Dick "does up what ever small chores may be to do." They had made friends and the contrast with their horrible suffering a month earlier must have made their situation seem very comfortable. "We are anxiously waiting [Ben's] return; to move eastward," Ned told Mary.[4] In late March, however, they learned that Ben would never return.

Ben and Old Bill had managed to reach the cache, and had loaded it on their mules. Then tragedy struck On or about March 21, the two were murdered, apparently by a band of Utes eager for revenge for a savage attack by United States forces out of Taos a week before.

News of the murders of Doc and Old Bill reached Taos on March 25 and must have been devastating. Three years his senior, Benjamin had been one of Dick's favorite brothers. A mutual friend, who knew them when they were younger, commented that "Dick Kern listens to the sayings of the Doctor as though he were a second Solomon sent to instruct the 19th Century—there is no use for one brother to so worship another." Now Ben was gone. Dick gave up his plans to return to Philadelphia that spring. As he told his brother John, months later, "I would have returned long ago, but Doc's death has kept me here in the hopes of finding out who were the actual murderers." Fatalistically, Dick added that he had made arrangements "in the case of my death to refund you $50."[5]

Ned and Dick remained at Taos until early summer, hoping perhaps to recover Ben's body and their equipment, as well as to learn the identity of the murderers. Soon after they heard of Ben's death, a rumor reached the brothers that some of the items from the chache had turned up in a Mexican village near Abiquiú. On April 6, Dick wrote to the commander of a militia company at Abiquiú, Capt. John Chapman, asking his help in retrieving the property. Chapman acted promptly. As he explained in a letter to Dick, "I . . . proceeded to the Village where the villains live, and arrested three of them, and searched their Houses . . . I found the villains dressed in Cloathing of the deceased."[6] Chapman sent some goods to Dick, and arrested the "villains," but they were never convicted. They appear to have been innocent of the murders and had come into possession of the Kerns' stolen goods through trade with the Utes. Richard Kern himself became convinced that Utes had done the deed.[7]

The Kerns never recovered all of their belongings or Ben's body. For several years they tried to retrieve their property, but the odds were against them. As one Ute explained, "most of it has been consumed, and that residue has changed hands so frequently that no human power can gather it into one parcel again."[8]

Somehow Dick and Ned eked out a living that sad spring, and Dick explored the mountains near Taos to do some sketches and watercolors. Although the circumstances that led to their lengthy stay were unhappy, the Kern brothers enjoy the distinction of being "the first real artists" to visit Taos, a community that has come to be famed for its colony of artists in the twentieth century.[9]

One of Richard Kern's watercolors from that spring shows the *Valley of Taos, Looking South,* with snow lingering on the mountain tops and the valley floor turned green (plate 5). Also remaining from that spring are several pencil drawings, including *"La Cruz del Muerto," Foot of Taos Mountain* (fig. 22), and *Salto del Rito de los Venados near Taos* (fig. 23). The sites of these drawings cannot be identified with precision. Whatever stream Kern termed the Rito de los Venados, for example, is no longer

Fig. 22. *"La Cruz del Muerto," Foot of Taos Mountains, N.M., 1849.* Pencil drawing by Richard H. Kern. Courtesy, Amon Carter Museum.

known by that name. The idealized waterfall that he drew, however, was probably inspired by the Salto de Agua near the town of Arroyo Seco, at the north end of Taos Valley. In this drawing, and in his view of Taos Valley, Kern did not record precisely what he saw, but captured instead the essence of these scenes. In redrawing his *Salto del Rito,* for example, from a field sketch done on May 18, 1848, Kern modified the scene considerably—adding more water, changing the number and position of trees, and the sizes of boulders—in order to improve composition (fig. 24). *"La Cruz del Muerto"* (the cross of the

Fig. 23. *Salto del Rito de Los Venados Near Taos, New Mexico, 1849.* Pencil drawing by Richard H. Kern. Courtesy, Amon Carter Museum.

Fig. 24. Untitled field sketch of a waterfall, dated May 18,
1848. Richard H. Kern. Courtesy, Fred W. Cron. Compare
with figure 23.

Fig. 25. James Hervey Simpson, August 1857. Photograph. Courtesy, Minnesota Historical Society.

In early summer, the Kern brothers said goodbye to friends in Taos and made the sixty-mile journey south to Santa Fe. New Mexico's capital for nearly two and a half centuries, Santa Fe bustled with the activities of American troops who had invaded the territory two summers before. The Kerns probably relocated in Santa Fe in order to be on hand should their equipment and collections be recovered, but also to live in a place that afforded better opportunities for employment than did Taos. They did not have to wait long.

Sometime in early July, employment appeared fortuitously in the form of James Hervey Simpson, a thirty-six-year-old lieutenant and engineer in the United States Army Corps of Topographical Engineers (fig. 25). The Kerns and Simpson probably found one another kindred spirits. A prodigy, Simpson had entered West Point at age fifteen. Although he would find no beauty in the stark vegetation of the Southwest, and the local cuisine made him nauseous, he had a driving, informed curiosity that the Kerns must have admired. In mid-March 1849, just a few months before his arrival in Santa Fe, Simpson had been overseeing the construction of a lighthouse in Michigan when orders arrived that changed his life. He was to report to Fort Smith, Arkansas, and from there to accompany Captain Randolph B. Marcy and a train of emigrants bound for the newly discovered gold fields of California. Simpson was to explore and survey a wagon road from Fort Smith to Santa Fe, a route that

dead man) might have been drawn at any number of places at the foot of Taos Mountain. As one contemporary noted, rustic crosses, held in place by piles of stone, were "thickly scattered over the country, from one end of it to the other," marking those places where New Mexicans had been killed by Indians or bandits. The road from Taos to Santa Fe offered the traveler frequent reminders of the deaths of other wayfarers, and the cross became a motif for Kern.[10]

would follow the Canadian River much of the way and serve as a southern alternative to the Santa Fe Trail.[11]

Some 820 miles out of Fort Smith, laboriously measured by chain, had brought Simpson to Santa Fe on June 28. His original instructions had called for him to proceed to California, but new orders, which reached him in Santa Fe on July 2, attached him to the command of the military and civil governor of New Mexico, Lt. Col. John M. Washington. In Santa Fe, Simpson was to prepare, "without delay," a report and map of the expedition from Fort Smith. The change of orders caught Simpson without "drawing paper and other appliances." The orders also pressured him to perform in a month "the labor which, with more time . . . I would prefer to have extended through several months." Simpson solved these problems by using "such means as were at hand," and by hiring the two Kern brothers to help prepare the maps.[12] Richard also did the two drawings that appeared as the sole illustrations in Simpson's published *Report*. One consisted of several views of what Simpson termed a "fish with legs," found in a pond of "disgustingly yellowish" water, twenty-one miles east of Galisteo, New Mexico (fig. 26). Kern and Simpson became overly excited about the anthropomorphic characteristics of this amphibian, declaring that its "hind feet resemble the human hand." Although Kern exaggerated the human quality of the feet, his experience at scientific drawing in Philadelphia enabled him

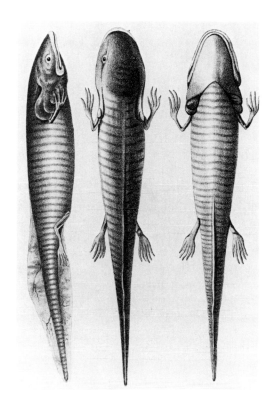

Fig. 26. The "fish with legs." Lithograph based on a drawing by Richard H. Kern. James H. Simpson, *Report of Exploration . . . Fort Smith, Arkansas, to Santa Fe* (Washington, D.C., 1850).

to draw with reasonable accuracy what is clearly a salamander in the larval stage. The "fish with legs" intrigued the head of the Topographical Bureau, J. J. Abert, who asked Simpson to send a specimen to Washington. Simpson promised to obtain a specimen for Abert, but whether he ever discovered that his fish was a salamander is not clear.[13]

The other illustration in Simpson's report was Kern's *View of Santa Fe and Vicinity from the East* (fig. 27), one of

Fig. 27. *View of Santa Fe and Vicinity from the East.* Lithograph based on a drawing by Richard H. Kern. James H. Simpson, *Report of Exploration . . . Fort Smith, Arkansas, to Santa Fe* (Washington, D.C., 1850).

his best known illustrations and one of the two earliest published views of Santa Fe. In this sketch, Kern deliberately distorted some of the topography, but accurately portrayed the scattered, haphazard arrangement of adobe dwellings surrounding the square Santa Fe plaza. Another rustic cross stands in a pile of stones in the foreground. Either Kern or the lithographer, Peter Duval of Philadelphia, patriotically exaggerated the size of the American flag over the adobe plaza.[14]

In August, the Kerns' work on the maps of the Ft. Smith to Santa Fe route had scarcely been completed before Simpson hired the brothers again, this time for a far more dangerous but potentially exciting position. Governor Washington had decided to lead a military expedition to punish the Navajos for repeated raids on the New Mexico settlements and to secure a treaty with them. Lieutenant Simpson was to "accompany the expedition, making such a survey of the country as the movement of the troops will permit."[15] The Kerns went as Simpson's assistants on this 41-day, 590-mile journey. Edward Kern, as topographer and "first assistant" would render the first reliable map of the Navajo country. Richard as "second assistant" and artist, would do "portraits of distinguished chiefs, costume, scenery, singular geological formations, petrifactions, ruins, and *fac similes* of ancient inscriptions."[16]

American trappers, Mexican traders, and Mexican military forces had entered the Navajo country on previous occasions. Indeed, Colonel Washington's troops would follow the route of a punitive expedition that Col. José Antonio Vizcarra had led against the Navajos in 1821. Thus, the region west of Santa Fe and Albuquerque was not unknown to Mexicans and Americans, but no graphic images of it existed in print. Simpson's *Journal* of the expedition, published in 1850, would give the American reading public its first detailed look at the marvels of the new country, as seen largely through the eyes of Richard Kern.[17]

On August 16, three days after Simpson put the finishing touches on his report of the Fort Smith to Santa Fe route, Colonel Washington's com-

mand moved out of Santa Fe. Richard Kern left Santa Fe a day behind the main party and traveled with the pack animals. "Many of the mules being wild much trouble ensued," he noted in a diary that he kept on the expedition and from which Lieutenant Simpson would borrow liberally in preparing his report.[18]

Straight ahead, as one travels south from Santa Fe over level country, the rugged Ortiz Mountains rise abruptly from the high plains. The Cerrillos hills are visible in the foreground, and the mass of the Sandia Mountains looms behind. Busy with wild mules and hurrying to catch up with the main party, Kern apparently had no time to sketch the scene, but his brother had done so, apparently the day before. Based on Ned's sketch, Dick would later do a polished drawing entitled *View of the Placer or Gold Mountain, and Sandia Mountain.* Vigorous mining activity in the "Placer or Gold Mountain," as they called the Ortiz Mountains, made it "famous," according to Simpson. A lithograph of the Kerns' drawing would become the first illustration in Simpson's *Journal* (fig. 28). In this view, the Kerns placed another cross along the roadside and outlined vividly what Dick termed the "frightful precipices and pointed peaks" of the Ortiz Mountains. The brothers rendered the scene with reasonable fidelity, but the collaboration may have contributed to their distortion of the Cerrillos hills and the contours of the Ortiz Mountains.[19]

Two days of travel down the Río Santa

Fig. 28. *View of the Placer or Gold Mountain, and Sandia Mountain from Santa Fe.* Lithograph based on a wash drawing by Richard H. Kern from a field sketch by Edward M. Kern. James H. Simpson, *Journal of a Military Reconnaissance . . . to the Navajo Country in 1849* (Washington, D.C., 1850). For the drawing, see fig. 142.

Fe into the Rio Grande Valley brought Richard Kern and the wild mules to the "small but very clean and neat" Pueblo of Santo Domingo. There the party forded the Rio Grande and camped. Kern made detailed notes describing the architecture of the pueblo and the dress of residents. The place seemed exotic. "It is harvest time," he wrote, "& the Indians are carrying their wheat in bundles on their heads to the thrashing place and singing their wild songs—in the foreground wagons, spaniards mules & americans."[20] Kern apparently did no sketching here, but his notes might have been designed to refresh his memory later on.

Sunday afternoon, August 19, Kern caught up with Simpson, his brother, and the rest of the main party at Jémez Pueblo. He probably arrived too late to watch an Indian ceremonial that the explorers called the Green Corn Dance, but he heard about it from Ned, who

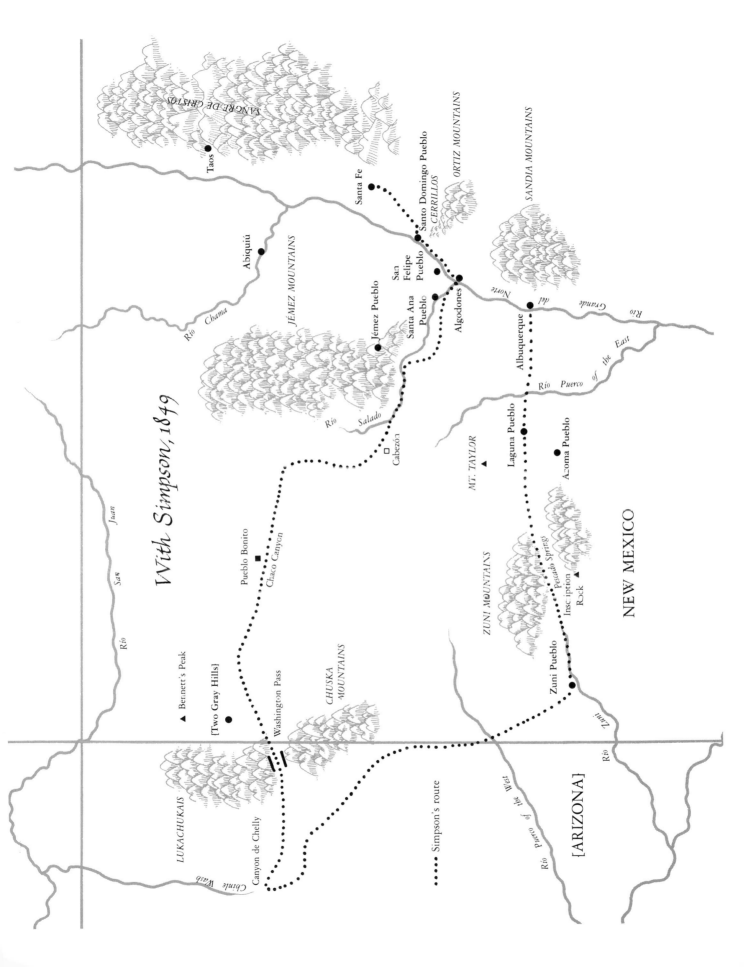

Fig. 29. *Hos-ta, (the Lightning). Governor of the Pueblo of Jémez. Aug. 20.* Watercolor by Richard H. Kern. Courtesy, Academy of Natural Sciences of Philadelphia.

Fig. 30. *Whar-te, (The Industrious Woman). Wife of the Governor of Jémez. Aug. 20th.* Watercolor by Richard H. Kern. Courtesy, Academy of Natural Sciences of Philadelphia.

had climbed atop one of the flat-roofed buildings to view the entire proceedings and make a sketch (fig. 139).[21]

Colonel Washington's entire command rested at Jémez for the next two days, preparing pack mules and waiting for Pueblo Indian militia to join them. Kern used the time to do a re-

markable number of sketches and watercolors. He acquainted himself with the governor of Jémez, Hosta, and his wife, Wharte, and did dignified watercolors of each—*Hos-ta, (The Lightning),* "in his war costume," and *Whar-te, (The Industrious Woman),* "in her best attire, with some of the accessories of

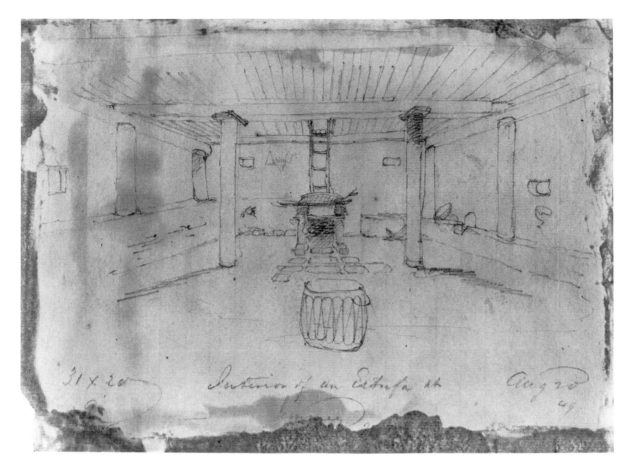

Fig. 31. *Interior of an Estufa at Jemez, Aug 20, 49.* Sketch by Richard H. Kern. Courtesy, Bushnell Collection, Peabody Museum of Archaeology and Ethnology, Harvard University.

their way of life" (figs. 29 and 30). A few years later, a copy of Simpson's report with its colored lithograph of Kern's full-length portrait of Hosta made its way to New Mexico. "Old Hoosta of Jamez [sic] has seen his portrait in Simpson's report and appears highly delighted," a friend told Richard Kern.[22]

Hosta would accompany the expedition into Navajo country, where Simpson would describe him as "one of the finest looking and most intelligent Pueblo Indians I have seen, and on account of his vivacity and offhand graciousness, is quite a favorite among us."[23]

Perhaps through the aid of Hosta,

Fig. 32. *Copies of Paintings Upon the Walls of an Estufa at Jémez. N⁰ 3, Aug. 20.*
Chromolithograph based on a watercolor by Richard H. Kern. James H. Simpson, *Journal of a Military Reconnaissance . . . to the Navajo Country in 1849* (Washington, D.C., 1850).

Kern had the rare privilege of visiting a ceremonial chamber at Jémez. He called it an *"estufa,"* after the Spanish term, but they are known commonly today by the Hopi word *kiva*. Kern did a rough pencil sketch of the interior of the kiva (fig. 31), and must have spent considerable time doing the five watercolors he entitled *Copies of Paintings upon the Walls of an Estufa at Jémez.* Simpson praised Kern's watercolors of the drawings on the kiva walls as "an exact picture . . . both as regards details of form and color, and also as respects the dingy, smoky complexion of the walls upon which they are painted."[24] Lithographs of Kern's five watercolors accompanied Simpson's *Journal,* and seem to represent the earliest detailed renderings of kiva wall paintings in any of the pueblos of New Mexico (fig. 32). Richard Kern's pioneering work has extended our knowledge about the continuity of kiva wall painting, for images much like those that Kern saw were still being painted on a kiva wall in

Jémez in the 1920s. Indeed, few Anglo-Americans since Kern have had both the access and the artistic skill to depict kiva wall murals.[25]

Richard Kern had enjoyed a very productive day in Jémez, and his output was further increased by the Kern brothers' habit of exchanging sketches. While Dick had worked in Jémez that day, Ned had accompanied Simpson on a side trip about a dozen miles up the Jémez River to see some hot springs, then called Ojo Caliente and today called Jémez Springs. Ned had sketched the springs and the nearby ruins of a mission at the abandoned pueblo of Giusewa. Dick took Ned's sketches of these places he had never seen and, perhaps with Ned occasionally looking over his shoulder, made them into polished drawings (figs. 33 and 34).[26]

The next afternoon, August 21, Hosta squired Simpson, Capt. Henry Linn Dodge, and the two Kern brothers through the pueblo's Catholic church. Afterward, reflecting the coexistence of two religions among the Pueblos, Hosta took the visitors to see a kiva. Dick filled several pages in his notebook with Hosta's stories about Pueblo religion, religious symbols, history, and customs. Hosta told his guests that when he was governor of Jémez in 1824, Indians from the beleaguered pueblo of Pecos, who have "different customs but the same language," asked for permission to resettle at Jémez. The last of the Pecos did abandon their pueblo and move to Jémez in 1838. Either Dick or Ned did a pen-and-ink portrait of

one of them, *Wash-u-hos-te, (Big White Bead)* (fig. 35).[27]

Hosta also told the visitors that the kivas were "the same as used by Montezuma," and of Montezuma's great power, such as building a house in an hour and harvesting corn in the morning that he had planted just the night before. These tales about Montezuma were probably not efforts to deceive gullible visitors. Legends of Montezuma as an epic figure entered Pueblo mythology early, possibly antedating the arrival of Spaniards in the region, and Hosta was merely repeating well-known traditions. Richard Kern was not the first Anglo-American, nor would he be the last, to believe that Montezuma once ranged among the Pueblos.[28]

Before the explorers left Jémez, Kern drew two panoramic views of the pueblo. For one of these sketches, he scrambled up a high ridge to the east, where he could look over the pueblo rooftops to the Jémez Mountains to the west. This sketch became the basis of a published lithograph, *Pueblo of Jémez from the East* (figs. 36 and 137), that gave the American public one of its first views of a New Mexico pueblo.[29]

On August 22, the troops were ready to move westward. The pause at Jémez had been necessary for the men to transfer supplies from wagons to pack mules, for the wagons had begun to break down on the rough road up to Jémez and it was clear that they could not go much farther. The delay had also enabled volunteers from several Indian pueblos to

Fig. 33. *The Ojo Caliente twelve Miles Above Jémez.* Drawing by Richard H. Kern from a sketch by Edward M. Kern. Courtesy, Academy of Natural Sciences of Philadelphia.

Fig. 34. *Ruins of a Roman Catholic Church near the Ojo Caliente twelve miles above Jémez.* Wash drawing by Richard H. Kern from a sketch by Edward M. Kern. Courtesy, Academy of Natural Sciences of Philadelphia.

join them. Pueblo Indians made valuable soldiers and had a long tradition of military campaigns against Navajos, who pillaged their crops and livestock. When Colonel Washington's entire force assembled, it would number nearly four hundred. That included Mexican militia from Abiquiú under Capt. John Chapman, the same officer who had tried to help the Kerns retrieve Ben's body and their property.[30]

The omissions in Richard Kern's diary suggest that he had little interest in military matters, but Indians did fascinate him. He drew a sketch of *Ow-te-wa,* from the pueblo of Santa Ana (fig. 37), who would be "elected captain" of the Pueblo volunteers, and he listened to more tales of Montezuma, including a tradition among the elders at Santo Domingo Pueblo "that those who were to deliver them from the Spaniards would come from the east and they regard the white men as being their deliverers and in some way connected with Montezuma."[31] When he found himself at the great Anasazi ruins in Chaco Canyon, later that month, it was easy for Richard Kern to imagine that he was walking among Aztec ruins.

In the sandy country of canyons, plateaus, and mesas to the west of the Jémez Mountains, Kern saw sights that must have amazed a young man from Philadelphia: "springs impregnated with soda & streams with salt" and "arches columns & ravins." Two days out of Jémez, Cabezón became visible, a great volcanic plug rising out of the Puerco Valley to the south. Kern described it as a "rock which bears some resem-

Fig. 35. *Wash-U-Hos-te (Big White Bead), a Pecos Indian.* Lithograph based on a drawing by either Richard or Edward Kern. James H. Simpson, *Journal of a Military Reconnaissance . . . to the Navajo Country in 1849* (Washington, D.C., 1850).

blance to a dome, & appears to be about 1500 feet & about 1000 in diameter." At that, he underestimated, for Cabezón is actually 2,160 feet high and 1,400 feet in diameter. The next day, just before they crossed the Puerco, he did a sketch of Cabezón that evokes its height more powerfully than does his verbal description. Cabezón remained a prominent landmark as the expedi-

Fig. 36. *Pueblo of Jémez from the East, Aug. 20.* Lithograph based on a drawing by Richard H. Kern. James H. Simpson, *Journal of a Military Reconnaissance . . . to the Navajo Country in 1849* (Washington, D.C., 1850). For the drawing, see fig. 137.

tion moved westward (fig. 38). The sight of it at the first rays of dawn one day led Simpson to extoll "its towering sublimity . . . I thought I had never seen anything more beautiful and at the same time more grand."[32]

Beyond the Puerco, "a miserable dirty & little stream of brackish water," they entered Copa Canyon with its "very singularly shaped rocks . . . resembling an immense vase sitting on a pedestal." Every day seemed to bring new, extraordinary sights. On Sunday, August 26, Kern saw petrified wood for the first time, and sketched and measured one upright trunk and another "lying & as if split in two by an axe . . . chips lying about" (fig. 39).[33]

Late in the day they struck the Chaco River; as they came over a rise, Kern

Fig. 37. *Ow-te-wa (Captain),
ExGouvernor of Santa Ana.*
Lithograph of a drawing by
Edward M. Kern, based on a
sketch by Richard H. Kern
James H. Simpson, *Journal of
a Military Reconnaissance . . .
to the Navajo Country in 1849*
(Washington, D.C., 1850).

Fig. 38. *Cerro de la Cabeza in the Valley of the Rio Puerco. View taken three miles west of
Camp 6, Aug. 25.* Wash drawing by Richard H. Kern. Courtesy, Academy of
Natural Sciences of Philadelphia.

Fig. 39. *Elevation and Cross Section of a Petrified Stump. . . .* Chromolithograph based on a watercolor by Richard H. Kern. James H. Simpson, *Journal of a Military Reconnaissance . . . to the Navajo Country in 1849* (Washington, D.C., 1850).

said, they "came in sight of the Aztec Pueblo de Raton or Pueblo Grande standing on a hill a prominent and lonely object." What Kern termed an Aztec pueblo was the easternmost ruin of what had once been a series of fabulous, multistoried apartment buildings strung out along the Chaco. The largest of these structures contained some eight hundred rooms. The imposing pueblos were built, in the main, between A.D. 1030 and 1125, several centuries before the Aztecs came to power in Mexico. Archaeologists have adopted the Navajo word *Anazasi,* or ancient ones, to identify the builders, who represented a mixture of desert traditions and who might have had contact with the great civilizations of Mesoamerica. The Anazasi probably abandoned their fortress-like apartments between A.D. 1150 and 1300, as environmental changes made it difficult to sustain life in the region. They apparently scattered in all directions, some settling on the Hopi mesa to the west, others going to Zuni and Acoma, and still others moving into the Rio Grande Valley, where their descendants would become known to the first Europeans as Pueblos.[34]

Simpson's Indian and Mexican guides each had a different name for the ruins that lay at the eastern gateway to Chaco Canyon. Hosta knew them as the Pueblo de Ratones, or town of rats; others called them the Pueblo de Montezuma, or Pueblo Grande. Simpson finally settled upon the name Pueblo Pintado, suggested by an old Mexican guide, Rafael Carravahal, who had joined the expe-

Fig. 40. *North West View of the Ruins of the Pueblo Pintado in the Valley of the Rio Chaco. Aug. 26. Nº 1.* Lithograph based on a wash drawing by Richard H. Kern. James H. Simpson, *Journal of a Military Reconnaissance . . . to the Navajo Country in 1849* (Washington, D.C., 1850). For the drawing, see fig. 141.

dition at his village of San Ysidro, on the edge of Navajo country, and who apparently knew the area well.[35] Thus, the ruins appeared as Pueblo Pintado in Simpson's *Journal* and on Richard Kern's lithographs, and so they have remained until the present day. Indeed, most of the prominent ruins in the Chaco complex derive their present names from those suggested by Carravahal to Simpson.

The expedition made camp that day about a mile from Pueblo Pintado. After dinner, Simpson and his two assistants went to explore the ruins. As the August sun dropped over the barren river plain and the evening became cool on the high desert, the Kerns and Simpson measured Pueblo Pintado inside and out, counted the number of rooms, took compass readings, and wrote detailed descriptions of the woodwork and stonework. Kern also began a wash sketch of the roofless walls of the three-

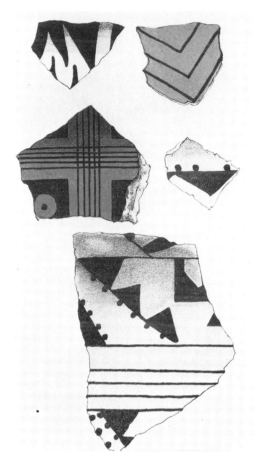

Fig. 41. *Pottery found at the Pueblo Pintado.* Lithograph based on a pen-and-ink drawing by Richard H. Kern. James H. Simpson, *Journal of a Military Reconnaissance . . . to the Navajo Country in 1849* (Washington, D.C., 1850).

Fig. 42. *Hieroglyphics on a Sand Stone Boulder, Near Camp 9.* Chromolithograph based on a watercolor by Richard H. Kern. James H. Simpson, *Journal of a Military Reconnaissance . . . to the Navajo Country in 1849* (Washington, D.C., 1850).

story pueblo, evoking some of the romantic desolation he saw in the scene (fig. 40). "The wolf & lizard & hare are the only inhabitants," he wrote, "& the bright wild flowers fill the open court & halls." Notwithstanding Hosta's assurances that "this pueblo was built by Montezuma and his people when they were on their way from the north toward the south"—an idea Simpson accepted—Kern remained skeptical.[36] "Who built it no one knows," he wrote in his diary. Like modern archaeologists, he saw a link with the modern Pueblos: "there can be no doubt of its having been [built] by a race living here

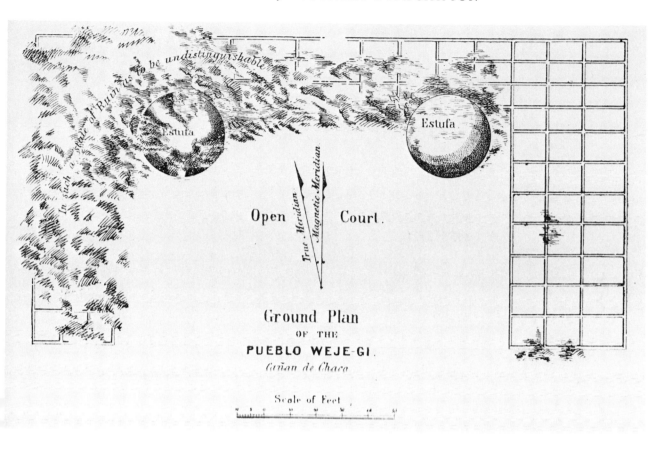

Open Court.

Ground Plan
OF THE
PUEBLO WEJE-GI.
Cañon de Chaco

Scale of Feet

Fig. 43. *Ground Plan of the Pueblo Weje-gi, Cañon de Chaco.* Lithograph based on a pen-and-ink drawing by Richard H. Kern. James H. Simpson, *Journal of a Military Reconnaissance . . . to the Navajo Country in 1849* (Washington, D.C., 1850)

in long past ages—Its style is so different from anything Spanish & so similar to all the Indian Pueblos."

The next morning, August 27, while the main expedition moved down the Chaco, the Kerns and Simpson remained behind to explore Pueblo Pintado further. Richard Kern did a pen-

and-ink drawing of the designs on pot sherds that lay scattered about and perhaps some other sketches as well (fig. 41). Then they hurried on to rejoin the main party. Two miles down the river, they entered Chaco Canyon, from which the river derives its name—*tsékoh* meaning canyon in Navajo. As they

Fig. 44. *Interior of a Room in the North Range of the Pueblo Chetho-Kette (the Rain).* Lithograph of a wash drawing by Richard H. Kern. James H. Simpson, *Journal of a Military Reconnaissance . . . to the Navajo Country in 1849* (Washington, D.C., 1850).

moved through this "immense corridor," Kern saw cliff dwellings along its walls, and massive boulders, some with "hieroglyphics" carved into them. Dick and Ned faithfully recorded some of these petroglyphs (fig. 42). Toward the end of the day, some thirteen miles down the river from Pueblo Pintado, they

came to the ruins of another great apartment house—Pueblo Wijiji. While the troops set up camp in sight of a spectacular butte, known today as Fajada Butte, Kern drew a gound plan and a view of Wijiji (fig. 43).[37]

Now they had entered the part of Chaco Canyon with the greatest concentration of ruins. The next day, while the main expedition moved ahead, Kern and Simpson remained behind once again. Edward had received orders to proceed with the troops and continue his topographic work, but Richard and Simpson were joined by the expedition's doctor, John Fox Hammond, the translator, James L. Collins, the guide Rafael Carravahal, and "an escort of 8 Mexicans."[38] The small band proceeded down the canyon, examining and measuring some of the major sites along the north side, including Pueblo Una Vida, Hungo Pavie, Chetro Ketl, and Pueblo Bonito. All of these names, which are still in use today, were apparently known to Carravahal.

Richard Kern did a prodigious number of sketches that day. He drew ground plans of the four major ruins named above, and did views of Pueblo Una Vida and Pueblo Bonito. He drew the interior of a room at Chetro Ketl, which he described as "in almost perfect state." Its roof was still intact, serving as the floor of the room above, and the walls were still plastered (fig. 44). That day he also drew more pottery, petroglyphs, samples of masonry, a room interior at Pueblo Bonito, and perhaps additional sketches that have not been preserved. Kern also rendered two splendid watercolor recreations of the *Pueblo Hungo Pavie* and *Pueblo Peñasca Blanca,* showing them as they might have looked when Indians occupied them (fig. 45). He imagined these structures with uninterrupted outer walls and terraced inner walls. "Mr. R. H. Kern was the

first to suggest," Simpson wrote, "that these pueblos were terraced on their inner or court side."[39] Modern archaeologists would agree.

In addition to his formal drawing that day, Kern also joined Lieutenant Simpson in scratching his name and the date into the soft plaster wall of a room at Pueblo Bonito. The photographer William Henry Jackson reported seeing the graffiti there in 1877, "as plainly as if done but a few days previously."[40]

Although they had but a day and a half to examine these ruins, and were forced to many of the lesser sites, Simpson and Richard Kern had accomplished a great deal. They were the first Americans to record a visit to Chaco, and William Henry Jackson was correct when he wrote nearly three decades later that the Simpson report "contained the first detailed and authentic account ever published of these wonderful ruins, and it has been up to this time the only source of information."[41] Beginning with Jackson, other visitors wrote detailed descriptions of the Chaco ruins that easily exceeded the brief survey by Simpson and Kern, but Simpson's *Journal* and Richard's often-reproduced drawings have remained valuable to archaeologists in the twentieth century as a basis for determining changes. The historian William Goetzmann has termed the Simpson-Kern report on Chaco "a spectacular contribution to scientific knowledge."[42]

Kern, Simpson, and their companions paid a price for their curiosity that August day in Chaco. At five o'clock,

Fig. 45. *Pueblo Peñasca Blanca. Chaco Cañon, N.M.* Watercolor (above), with sketch on back side (below), by Richard H. Kern. Courtesy, Berry-Hill Galleries Inc., New York.

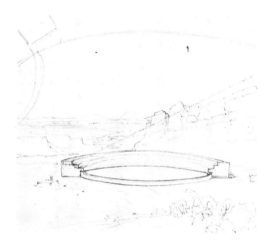

they stopped working and rode hard to catch up with the main party, as they had done the day before. Although they rode fifteen miles, and continued until well after dark, they failed to find Colonel Washington's command, which had left the canyon to take a shortcut. The weary scientists had to spend an uncomfortable night without their regular supper—their horseblankets substituting for bedding and their "saddles serving as pillows."[43] Fortunately, their Mexican escort had brought

Fig. 46. *Natural Sand Stone Formations, Aug. 29. About six miles east of Camp 11.* Watercolor by Richard H. Kern. Courtesy, Academy of Natural Sciences of Philadelphia.

along provisions and furnished food for dinner and for breakfast the next morning.

They rode all of the next day, August 29, to catch the main party. About six miles out of camp, they passed through extraordinary rock formations, which Kern described as "the most curious hills we had yet seen. Mounds, vases, columns, temples, tables, domes, & every form imaginable. . . . The trail wound over these and in some places [I] had to lead my horse—a frightful abyss some hundred feet in depth yawned beneath." Kern did a watercolor of some of these *Natural Stone Formations*, making them look unnaturally like buildings and towers (fig. 46).[44]

Isolated from the main force, and well into Navajo country, the explorers' apprehension grew. They supposed, Simpson said, that hostile Navajo spies were also dogging their trail. Late in the day, as the army's encampment came into view, so did a group of Indians. Simpson's small escort "brandished their

Fig. 47. *Peaks of Los Ojos Calientes, as seen between Camps 11 and 12—Aug.* Lithograph based on a wash drawing by Richard H. Kern. James H. Simpson, *Journal of a Military Reconnaissance . . . to the Navajo Country in 1849* (Washington, D.C., 1850). For the drawing, see fig. 138.

arms and shouted most valiantly," Kern wrote with sarcasm. He mocked one Mexican, who "seemed particularly brave & to have centered in himself all the courage of Santa Anna & the sublime Mexican Republic." No attack came, but they received a last minute scare "when within a mile of camp a large band of Indians appeared to be coming between us & it & we came in at a round gallop." They had caught up with Colonel Washington in the Chusca Valley, some forty miles beyond Chaco Canyon. Navajos milled around the camp, angry that three of their number had been taken prisoner and that the troops had raided a cornfield to feed their animals.

It was the first of several days of close encounters with potentially hostile Navajos that must have included some frightening moments for an artist from Philadelphia. The next day, August 30, they traveled fifteen miles with "multitudes of Indians around us." Preparing for the worst, Colonel Washington ordered several mountain howitzers removed from the pack mules and readied for action. Despite the tension, Kern did a wash of the stunning *Peaks of Los Ojos Calientes*, known today as Bennett's Peak, with "several Navajos in costume being exhibited in the foreground, gazing at the troops in the distance beyond" (fig. 47).[45] When they stopped to make camp in the Chusca Valley on the north fork of Tunicha Creek, not far from the present Two Gray Hills trading post, Navajos surrounded their camp and some leaders came into parley with Colonel Washington. Kern may have been close enough to hear the conversation. According to Kern, the Navajo leaders asked Washington "if we were friends why did we take their corn?" They would not promise to meet at Canyon de Chelly, where Washington wanted to hold a council, and they "disavowed all connections with those [Navajos] beyond the Mountains . . . but agreed to come in council tomorrow at 12 oclk & make peace."

As promised, Navajos returned the next day. Several of their leaders, including one Narbona, met with Colonel Washington and agreed to send representatives to Chelly. Then, as talks were breaking up, an ugly incident occurred that left Narbona dead and would have far ranging consequences for Na-

vajo-American relations. As Dick described it,

> The council was dissolved, when a Spaniard [one of the New Mexican militia] said a horse had been stolen from him some time ago—the horse was among the Navajoes & he could identify him. The Col. ordered the horse to be given up—The Mexican advanced to get him, when Narbona said Something in Navajoe & the horseman rode off—Col. W. gave the word to fire—the guard did so & at the first shot the Indians broke & fled up a ravine. . . . The six pounder was fired 3 times at them, and a force sent in pursuit—Narbona the head chief was shot in 4 or 5 places & Scalped.

A white-haired, slender man, whom Simpson thought to be about eighty years old, Narbona had been a principal headman and an advocate of peace among the Chusca Navajos since 1833, at least. Moreover, he had advocated friendship with the "new men," as he called Americans. With his death, an important voice of moderation was silenced. "Just before his death," Dick and Ned teamed up to draw a profile of *Narbona, Head Chief of the Navajos*, suggestive of a kindly and handsome figure (fig. 48).[46]

All accounts, including Kern's, suggest that the Navajos did nothing to provoke the attack in which Narbona was killed, but Kern made no moral judgment in his diary about the events of the day and expressed no regrets over Narbona's death. Nearly a year later, however, Dick did express a different kind of regret over the incident, in a letter to his friend Dr. Samuel George Morton in Philadelphia:

NARBONA

Fig. 48. *Narbona, Head Chief of the Navajos.*
Aug. 31. Wash drawing by Edward M. Kern
from a sketch by Richard H. Kern.
Courtesy, Academy of Natural Sciences of
Philadelphia.

I very much regret that I had not pro-
cured Narbona's cranium, as I think he
had the finest head I ever saw on an Indian. He was killed in our skirmish with
the Navajoes in the Tunicha Valley, but
the excitement drove everything else out
of my mind. He was the head chief of
the Nation, and had been a wise man
and great warrior. His frame was immense—I should think his height near
6ft 6in. He was near 90 years old when
killed.[47]

In search of a theory for the origin
of the races of mankind, Morton had
long studied human crania. The leading physical anthropologist of his day,
Morton had argued in his landmark
work, *Crania Americana* (1839), that
the American Indian represented a dis-
tinct race, separate from other races of
man. By 1847 Morton had assembled
a collection of over four hundred Indian
crania, and one Navajo skull may have
seemed insignificant to him. Nonetheless, Kern was eager to please his patron
and would soon have the opportunity
to send another Indian cranium to Morton.[48]

For the next six days, Colonel Washington's troops feared an ambush as they
moved toward Canyon de Chelly. Ner-
vous and prepared to fight, they climbed
over boulders and through ponderosa
pines, toward the Chusca Mountains
and Washington Pass, named by Simpson in honor of Colonel Washington.
Here, Richard Kern noted, was "the
most dangerous place & where a fight
was expected. . . . At nearly every point
stones can be rolled from above on the
passers by" (fig. 49).[49] Although Navajo

Fig. 49. *Pass Washington, Tune-Cha Mountains. Sept. 2.* Wash drawing by Richard H. Kern. Courtesy, Academy of Natural Sciences of Philadelphia.

scouts kept watch on their movements, an attack never came. On September 5, as they neared the entrance to Canyon de Chelly, Simpson, the two Kerns, Colonel Washington, and a few others took an early morning side trip—"a pleasant ride of 5 miles through pines, pinon & cedar forests"—to get a view into the canyon. The immensity of Chelly, whose name in Navajo, *tséyi,* means "between the rocks," must have seemed overwhelming to Dick. Its "sheer precipices of about 1000 feet—the stream winding through seemed like a small thread" (fig. 50).[50]

Just before sundown on September

97

Fig. 50. *View of the Cañon de Chelly Near its Head, five miles south west of Camp 17. Sept. 5.* Wash drawing by Richard H. Kern. Courtesy, Academy of Natural Sciences of Philadelphia.

26, after covering twenty-six miles with little water and much sagebrush, they reached their objective. At the entrance to Canyon de Chelly, "where the Indian settlements are," Kern saw small groups of Navajos all around. Some of the Navajo hogans were in flames as they approached, and Kern speculated the Indians had burned them "as signals, before the command appeared in sight." It may be, however, that unbeknown to Kern, Colonel Washington had ordered an advance party to do the burnings.[51]

Washington's command made camp at the mouth of the canyon, with "everything prepared in case of an attack." Just as at Washington Pass, an attack never came. Instead, the following morning two Navajo leaders came into camp. One, Mariano Martínez, was introduced to Colonel Washington as "the principal chief of the Navajos," according to Simpson. Martínez expressed willingness to return stolen livestock, to turn over captives, and to sign a treaty of peace. Two days later, Martínez returned with a token number of stock, three Mexican captives, and Chapitone, headman of a group of Navajo known as San Juan. On a knoll near present-day Thunderbird Ranch, they talked. Then, with Richard Kern acting as one of the official witnesses, Martínez and Chapitone signed a treaty as representatives of the "Navajo Tribe of Indians." In this one-sided document, which the U.S. Senate would later ratify, the two Indian leaders acknowledged that the Treaty of Guadalupe Hidalgo, which ended the Mexican War, had placed them under United States jurisdiction and that "perpetual peace and friendship shall exist."[52]

It is clear in retrospect that the treaty of September 9 was a farce. Martínez was not the "principal chief" of the Navajos, and the so-called tribe did not exist as a single political entity or have one leader. Nearly all of the Navajo headmen had ignored Colonel Washington's demand that they meet him at Chelly. Indeed, following Narbona's murder, Washington could hardly expect the Chusca Navajo to honor their

agreement to send representatives. Martínez and Chapitone were apparently doing what they thought best to get rid of the unwelcome visitors without bloodshed. Meanwhile, in revenge for Narbona's death, near Chaco Canyon some Navajos murdered an American courier who had been carrying mail to Colonel Washington. And Navajo attacks on the New Mexico settlements would soon resume.[53]

If Richard Kern had any reservations about the treaty, he kept them to himself. His brief journal entry for that day says only that "the treaty was made & signed & the trading commenced." Apparently a Hopi Indian with fine looking facial features, who was among the Navajo, held greater interest for the Philadelphia artist. This was Yellow Wolf, whose portrait Ned sketched that day (fig. 51). Simpson ethnocentrically paid Yellow Wolf the dubious compliment of possessing "the air and manner of a well-bred, vivacious American gentleman, and the only thing Indian in his appearance was his complexion."[54] In what would seem an extraordinary coincidence, the Hopi told Richard Kern that he remembered Old Bill Williams, whose wanderings had taken him through Arizona.[55] For his part, Kern probably told Yellow Wolf of the tragic deaths of Old Bill and Doc Kern.

While the negotiators discussed the treaty that day, Richard Kern made sketches of the two Navajo leaders, Mariano Martínez and Chapitone; Ned later polished those sketches into fine

Fig. 51. (Above, left.) *Che-ki-wat-te-wa ("Yellow Wolf"), a Moqui. Sept. 8th.* Lithograph based on a wash drawing by Edward M. Kern. James H. Simpson, *Journal of a Military Reconnaissance . . . to the Navajo Country in 1849* (Washington, D.C., 1850).

Fig. 52. (Above, right.) *Mariano Martinez, Chief of the Navajo Indians. Sept. 8th.* Wash drawing by Edward M. Kern from a sketch by Richard H. Kern. Courtesy, Academy of Natural Sciences of Philadelphia.

Fig. 53. (Below, right.) *Chapaton, Chief of the S. Juan Navajos. Sept. 8th.* Wash drawing by Edward M. Kern from a sketch by Richard H. Kern. Courtesy, Academy of Natural Sciences of Philadelphia.

Fig. 54. *Navajo Costume.* Unsigned watercolor, apparently
by Richard H. Kern. Courtesy, Academy of Natural Sciences
of Philadelphia. See, also, figs. 134 and 140.

head-and-shoulder profiles (figs. 52 and 53). The Kerns depicted Martínez in what appears to be an improbable jacket, but Simpson's verbal description of Martínez's outfit corroborates the Kern drawings: "a sky-blue blanket great-coat, apparently of American manufac-ture and not unlike my own; a tarpaulin hat of rather narrow brim and semi-spherical crown."[56] Similarly, Dick's full-length portrait, *Navajo Costume* (fig. 54), looks highly unrealistic when com-pared with standards of Navajo dress later in the nineteenth century. Navajo styles changed dramatically, however, after the Indians' exposure to American fabrics and fashions during their tragic captivity at Bosque Redondo, 1863–68. Kern's rendering of this warrior's costume squares with other contemporary descriptions, even to the feathered helmet, which Navajos reportedly made from heads of mountain lions or other fierce animals.[57] The accuracy of the Kerns' likenesses of the facial features of figures such as Martínez, Chapitone, Hosta, and Narbona cannot be evaluated, however, for they are the only images we have.

In addition to these sketches of individual Navajos, Richard Kern also gave Americans their first view of Canyon de Chelly and its extraordinary cliff dwellings. On September 8, the day before the treaty was signed, Simpson, the two Kerns, Dr. Hammond, James Collins (the translator), a few officers, and a military escort of some sixty men had entered the canyon. With awesome, beautiful sandstone cliffs rising at times nearly parallel on either side of them, they rode along the well-watered valley floor, passing hogans, cornfields, peach orchards, and uninhabited cliff dwellings built by the "ancient ones." Meeting no resistance, they went over nine miles into the canyon, "& it became wilder at every turn," Kern wrote. At a point some eight miles up the canyon, he made a sketch that effectively suggests how the high, sheer walls block out much of the sun (fig. 55). He also did sketches of Canyon de Chelly's largest and best preserved cliff-house ruins, today called White House, with "stupendous rocks in rear and overhanging them," and of pottery found at that site (fig. 56).[58]

Colonel Washington's command did not tarry at Chelly. Rumor of an Apache raid at Zuni—a rumor probably started by Navajos eager to get rid of their guests—sent the expedition back toward Santa Fe by way of Zuni on the morning after the treaty was signed. As they traveled through a variety of landforms, including pine forests and meadows, Richard Kern continued to sketch and to comment on the rock formations in this fantastic new country. One red sandstone summit put the whimsical Pennsylvania artist "in mind of Wm Penn with his broad brimmed beaver [hat] & inflated by a hearty meal."

The sixth day out of Chelly, Saturday, September 15, they rode into the valley of the Río de Zuni, passing the Zuni Buttes on their west. When Coronado first saw these people in 1540, they occupied six villages, but after the Pueblo Revolt of 1680 they occupied only the single town of Zuni, the site of old Háloma, where they remain today. As they approached Zuni, Kern noted, "a deputation headed by the governor & alcalde came to receive the Col." Then, as they rode toward the pueblo with their new hosts, "the chief discharged his rifle and . . . an ambuscade opened on us and the field was in a moment covered with red devils yelling and dancing." It was a sham fight, for the amusement of the visitors, and Colonel Washington's Pueblo vol-

Fig. 55. *Cañon of Chelly, eight miles above the mouth. Sept. 8.* Wash drawing by Richard H. Kern. Courtesy, Academy of Natural Sciences of Philadelphia.

Fig. 56. *Ruins of an Old Pueblo in the Cañon of Chelly. Sept. 8.* Wash drawing by Richard H. Kern. Courtesy, Academy of Natural Sciences of Philadelphia.

Fig. 57. *Pueblo of Zuñi. Sept. 15th.* Wash drawing by Richard H. Kern. Courtesy, Academy of Natural Sciences of Philadelphia.

unteers joined in with enthusiasm.

The rumor of an attack on Zuni by Apaches proved false, but a recent altercation with a Navajo provided Kern with another opportunity to secure a cranium for Dr. Morton. With Dr. Hammond and another companion, Kern "went after supper . . . to procure the head of a Navajoe who had been found near this place trying to steal and was killed by the inhabitants." They "separated the head from the body, and

brought it into camp," about 10:30 that night. Later, Dr. Lewis A. Edwards, an assistant army surgeon in Santa Fe, would bleach the skull and plan to deliver it to Dr. Morton.[59]

Although they remained at Zuni for only one night, Simpson's report on the pueblo was the best written in English up to that time. Kern did a view of *Pueblo of Zuni* (fig. 57) that historian C. Gregory Crampton says "may very well have been the first graphic ever

Fig. 58. *North Face of Inscription Rock. Sept. 17.* Wash drawing by Richard H. Kern. Courtesy, Academy of Natural Sciences of Philadelphia.

made of the pueblo," and "given the popularity of Simpson's narrative, it may have had some impact in creating a popular image of the Zuni Pueblo." Although he distorted the large mesa known as Corn Mountain, or Towayalane to the Zunis, Kern's drawing of the pueblo and its church seems quite accurate. Two years later, Kern would return to Zuni to make a remarkable series of drawings.[60]

On Monday, September 16, the command made a "short march of 13 miles and camped at Pescado Springs near the Río del Pescado. Nearby, "nearly level with the ground," were the ruins of what Kern called Old Zuni. Dick would later argue that Old Zuni was the site of Coronado's famed Cíbola.[61] At Cíbola in 1540, Spaniards and Pueblos had first encountered one another, but Kern knew little about such matters in 1849. Simpson had a few books with him, such as Gregg's *Com-*

merce of the Prairies, Prescott's *History of Mexico,* and John T. Hughes's semifanciful *Doniphan's Expedition,* but they shed little light on the ruins the explorers encountered.[62] The next day, Kern was to see one of the most remarkable historical sites in America—one that apparently excited his curiosity and prompted him to comb historical records when he returned to Santa Fe.

The day began routinely, with the usual seven o'clock departure from camp. Along the trail, several miles up the Río Pescado, they met a "Mr. Lewis," who traded with the Navajos and knew the country well. Lewis, Simpson said, offered "his services as guide to a rock upon the face of which were, according to his repeated assertions, half an acre of inscriptions, many of them very beautiful, and upon its summit some ruins of a very extraordinary character." Receiving permission from Colonel Washington to explore the place, Simpson set out with Lewis, a camphand, and with Richard Kern, whom Simpson described as "ever zealous in an enterprise of this kind."[63]

Their destination was El Morro, whose name in Spanish literally means large, round rock. El Morro rises prominently amid pines and red bluffs near the Continental Divide, and has also been known by the name that Simpson bestowed upon it—Inscription Rock (fig. 58). The gigantic promontory, with a natural basin of rainwater at its base, served both as a landmark and a dependable source of water for travelers. Beginning at least as early as 1605, with Juan de

Oñate, hundreds of Hispanic wayfarers had camped nearby and incised their names on the smooth sandstone cliffs (fig. 59).

With Lewis as their guide, Simpson and Kern were among the first Americans to see the "written rocks," as Kern called them, and the first to record the most prominent inscriptions.[64] From noon to sunset, Simpson and his assistant laboriously made facsimiles of the Spanish names and dates contained on the cliffsides. In the evening, Lewis led them up a well-worn trail to the top of the rock, to inspect the ruins of "the old Pueblo of Moro." With stunning views in all directions, Kern worked in the twilight to sketch a plan of the pueblos, which he found "so ruinous, that it is difficult to distinguish much more than the outline." He also drew some of the potsherds they found strewn on the ground in abundance.

That night, so excited that he slept poorly, Simpson awoke at three o'clock and hurried breakfast along, "in order that by daylight we might be ready to continue our labors upon the inscriptions."[65] Accompanied by birdsong, they set to work at the light of day to continue copying. Altogether, they recorded some forty inscriptions, nearly all Spanish names and dates. As finally drawn by Kern, and rendered by the lithographer, these appeared on ten plates in Simpson's published report, along with English translations. Here, however, Simpson and Kern had ventured into an area where their ambition exceeded their talent. They knew little

Fig. 59. *Spring at Inscription Rock.* Watercolor by Richard H. Kern. Courtesy, Academy of Natural Sciences of Philadelphia.

Spanish or local history, and as Charles Lummis put it, "nothing whatever of Spanish writing and cryptography of the seventeenth and eighteenth centuries."[66] The result was a number of seriously flawed "facsimiles." Notwithstanding errors in transcription, for the rest of the century the Simpson-Kern drawings remained the most complete published inventory of the historic graffiti on El Morro, and they remain of value even today, because weather and vandals have effaced many of the original inscriptions (fig. 60).[67]

Somehow, Kern also found time to copy a number of Indian petroglyphs and to do three splendid views of El Morro itself.[68] Just before they finished their work that morning, he made a deep incision on the north face of the rock: "Lt. J. H. Simpson U.S.A. & R. H. Kern Artist, visited and copied these inscriptions, September 17th 18th 1849." His inscription can still be read there today, at what is now El Morro National Monument (fig. 61).[69]

By eight o'clock in the morning they had packed up their instruments and camping equipment and were ready to rejoin Colonel Washington's command. Since he had left his instruments with the troops, the indefatigable Simpson was eager to catch the main party by nightfall in order to continue his "succession of astronomical positions."[70] Simpson and Kern crossed the Zuni Mountains and the continental divide, where the artist was charmed by the "fine grass" and "wild flowers all over—white oak & pine abundant."

From "the summit of Zuni Pass," Kern did a sketch of a prominent peak to the northeast that Simpson thought "one of the finest mountain peaks I have seen in this country." Although the mountain already had several names—Navajos knew it as "Big, Tall Mountain," or "Turquoise Mountains," and Mexicans called it "Little Onion"—Simpson renamed it in honor of President Zachary Taylor: "standing within the domain which has been so recently the theater of his sagacity and prowess, it exists, not inappropriately, an ever-enduring monument to his patriotism and integrity."[71] One of New Mexico's better known landmarks, Mount Taylor still bears the name Simpson gave it. Kern's drawing of *Mount Taylor from the Summit of the Zuni Pass* (fig. 62) is a reasonable likeness.

Descending the Zuni Mountains and crossing a part of the great lava beds to the east, they caught up with the troops at a spring near present-day San Rafael, just after nightfall. Three more days of travel brought them through Laguna Pueblo, where "drying boiled corn & chile colorado" hung on the adobe walls in the autumn sun. Here, from the south side of the San José River, Kern drew what may be the earliest sketch of this Indian town (fig. 112).[72]

Beyond Laguna they crossed the "perfectly dry" Río Puerco, where cottonwoods had not yet changed to their fall colors, then continued to the Rio Grande at Atrisco, just across from Albuquerque, where they made camp a little after sundown on September 21.

Fig. 60. *Inscriptions on North face of Inscription Rock*. Wash drawing by Richard H. Kern. Courtesy, Academy of Natural Sciences of Philadelphia.

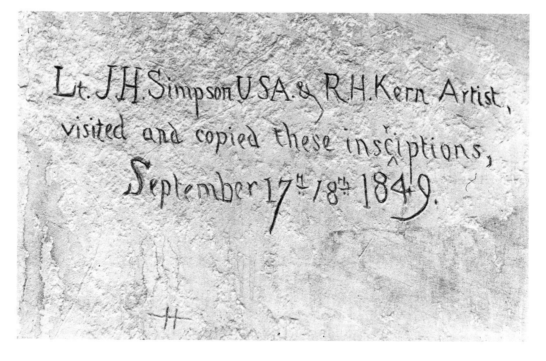

Fig. 61. Richard Kern's 1849 inscription at El Morro. Photograph by George Grant, 1929. Courtesy of the United States National Park Service, Western Archeological and Conservation Center, Tucson, Arizona.

Fig. 62. *Mount Taylor from the summit of the Zuñi Pass. Sept. 18th.* Wash drawing by Richard H. Kern. Courtesy, Academy of Natural Sciences of Philadelphia.

Here the expedition ended. Richard Kern jotted the last entry in his diary, and the men found their way back to Santa Fe in small groups.

But the work of the expedition had not yet ended for the Kern brothers. They remained in Santa Fe on Simpson's payroll until the day after Christmas, 1849.[73] Ned completed the map that would accompany Simpson's report, and Ned and Dick put their field sketches into more polished form for the lithographer.[74] Dick recopied his sketches with considerable accuracy, adding detail and embellishment. To provide a sense of scale to some of his landscapes, Dick added figures of soldiers or Indians, as in his redrawing of *Pueblo Pintado* or of the *Peaks of Los Ojos Calientes*. Some of the new drawings were done in watercolor, others in washes or pen-and-ink. A few field sketches, such as views of *Albuquerque, Bernalillo,* and the *Pueblo of San Felipe,* apparently were not converted into finished drawings. Paper must have remained scarce in Santa Fe; the brothers redrew their sketches on thick paper, thin paper, wallpaper, and even on the back of what appears to be an advertisement. Cutting his paper by hand, Dick prepared most of his drawings on sheets of roughly the same size. Perhaps to save paper, these were small (about $4^{1}/_{4}'' \times 7^{1}/_{4}''$).

Although the Kerns finished their work on December 26, Simpson kept their drawings and map with him in Santa Fe until April, when he could be assured of a military convoy to get them safely across the Plains. When he sent the Kerns' drawings east with his final report that April, Simpson praised the brothers "for the kind, zealous, and effective manner in which they ever were found ready to co-operate with me."[75]

Published in 1850 as a government document, in an edition of three thousand copies, Simpson's *Journal of a Military Reconnaissance from Santa Fé, New Mexico, to the Navajo Country* gave the American reading public its first authentic glimpse of the people, landscape, and antiquities in a remote corner of the country recently wrested from Mexico. Copies of the report found their way into the hands of leading scientists of the day, such as Benjamin Silliman and Ephraim George Squier, and it would influence subsequent exploration and understanding of the region.[76]

The Kerns' contributions to the *Journal* were considerable. The intellectual companionship of the brothers, one historian has suggested, may have stimulated Simpson to write an outstanding report. More concretely, Edward's maps were the first detailed charts of the Navajo country, and the seventy-two lithographs that illustrated the *Journal* represented the first printed graphic images of the region west of Santa Fe and Albuquerque. Fifty-seven of the plates were attributed to Richard; two were attributed to Edward; seven were the combined efforts of the brothers; and six were unsigned, but probably Richard's work.[77]

These lithographs of the Kerns' drawings enhanced Simpson's *Journal* considerably, especially since twenty-two of the seventy-two lithographs were in color, and a dozen were toned. In 1850, chromolithography was still a novelty, and it was almost unheard of in government reports.[78] Kern's work had been sent back to his hometown of Philadelphia, where one of the nation's leading lithographers, Peter S. Duval, did all of the prints—both those in black-and-white and in color. That same year, Duval had also done the lithographs of the two Kern drawings that accompanied Simpson's report on the route from Fort Smith, Arkansas, to Santa Fe.

French-born and French-trained, Duval was proprietor of the largest, most prestigious and innovative lithography firm in Philadelphia—a city which could boast of some of America's finest lithographers. A pioneer in color printing, Duval had been experimenting with chromolithography since the 1840s. The process involved printing images from multiple stones, each inked with a separate color. In efficiency, if not in beauty, the technique represented a clear advance over hand-colored prints. Duval won prizes for his color work in 1849 and 1850 but, like other American lithographers, he was not yet skilled at blending colors. Kern may have been displeased that the prints lacked the subtle tones of his watercolors, but the new technology might have appealed to some readers. In addition to printing from several colored stones, Duval applied still another new technique to the lithographs that accompanied Simpson's report. Duval printed them on a steam-powered press that he had installed in 1849, the first in Philadelphia. Each of the prints bears his proud advertisement: "P.S. Duval's Steam Lith. Press." Whatever their defects, Duval's lithographs were done cheaply and quickly enough to please his federal patrons, who awarded him another government contract in 1851 to do some of the plates for Henry Schoolcraft's monumental work on American Indians.[79]

The first edition of the *Journal* sold out quickly and Simpson arranged for a private printing, done in Philadelphia in 1852. Complete with the same maps and lithographs as the 1850 edition, the handsomely bound new printing, made in the Kerns' hometown, must have been a source of satisfaction to the two brothers.[80]

Richard Kern was clearly pleased with

the information contained in the report and his assessment of Simpson's work was on the mark:

> I was with him all the time, and whatever is in his report is correct, his information having been drawn from the Indians themselves. His report contains an immense amount of information on all subjects bearing on the country. The knowledge of the existence of the ruins of those old Pueblos at Chelly, and his descriptions of them must throw great light on the history of the early Indians of this country, aided as it will be by the traditions of the present race. Those inscriptions we copied will also add information to the Spanish period as they record the passing by of numerous men of rank and station.[81]

The Navajo expedition launched Lieutenant Simpson on a brilliant ten-year career, which would take him "over more of the western country" than any other member of the United State Corps of Topographical Engineers.[82] The Navajo expedition also started Richard Kern on a career as an artist and scientist in the Southwest. His association with the bookish, inquisitive, and well-informed Simpson, whose work he respected, apparently taught him a great deal. Moreover, visits to Indian pueblos, abandoned cities, and to the exotic Inscription Rock aroused Kern's curiosity to learn more about the new country. Plans to return to Philadelphia evaporated in the dry mountain air around Santa Fe, as the Kern brothers looked for ways to put their talents to work in New Mexico.

-4-
Pocketed in New Mexico

INADVERTENTLY, THE KERNS had stumbled into an extraordinary environment—intense light, ever-changing colors, mountains and mesas, and exotic Indian and Hispanic subjects. Beginning in the 1880s and continuing up to the present day, the Santa Fe and Taos areas have proved irresistible to artists.[1] For the Kerns, however, these were still rude, dangerous communities that could not support an artist, much less a pair of them. For the next year and a half the brothers would make New Mexico their home, working at odd jobs or seeking employment. For Edward, who may have been ill, this stint in New Mexico seems to have been artistically unproductive.[2] Richard, too, seems to have done little finished drawing, but the months in New Mexico were a time of intense work and travel that saw him achieve competence and reputation as a mapmaker and as a spe-

cialist in the geography and ethnology of the Southwest.

Employment with Simpson had no sooner ended than Richard Kern was off on another trip, this time to Chihuahua City. Edward Kern stayed behind. Richard made this journey with William C. Skinner, a merchant, attorney, and aspiring politician, who probably had business in Chihuahua. Kern may have been in Skinner's employ, but more likely he went along as a tourist. Kern carried a letter of introduction describing him as an artist who "travels for pleasure." Written by his friend Dr. Lewis A. Edwards, the army surgeon in Santa Fe who had bleached an Indian cranium for Dr. Morton, the letter recommended Kern to a fellow American physician in Chihuahua.[3]

Their route went through dangerous country, but Kern and Skinner broke no new ground; they followed the much-used Camino Real all the way to Chihuahua. Large trading caravans with wheeled vehicles had used this trail for two and a half centuries, but Kern and Skinner probably traveled on horseback. They made very good time—in a month they made a round-trip journey of twelve hundred miles. Kern and Skinner left Santa Fe on December 29, winding their way down rocky hills and canyons to the Rio Grande, then following the road on the east side of the river through towns such as Algodones, Albuquerque, Peralta, Casa Colorado, and La Joya. This area of New Mexico, known as the Río Abajo, had a character of its own. Large estates of wealthy merchant families, such as the Chavezes and Oteros, covered the bottomlands where the valley widened. For Kern these large, privately held ranchos contrasted sharply with the communal villages of Río Arriba, as the more mountainous region north of Santa Fe was called. At Peralta Kern found the houses "neater and cleaner" than any in the north. Here he met Antonio José Otero, whom Kearny had appointed to the New Mexico Supreme Court. Kern described him as "a jolly, fat, thick-set, clever, laughing man."[4]

As was his habit, Kern made numerous sketches along the way. Sixty have survived in one sketchbook, many of them topographic. Kern was impressed with the wide expanse of the Rio Grande, its inviting groves of cottonwoods, and the splendid views of mountains "high and bold." He found the towns picturesque, but noted that in "all New Mexican towns the distant view is the best as it swallows all the dirt and misery." In the town of Pareda, Kern did several sketches, one of which became the basis of a watercolor that he probably completed a few years later. A small town on the east side of the river, across and a few miles upstream from Socorro, Pareda is no longer on the map. When Kern passed through Pareda on January 2, 1850, he noted: "a fine view of the valley is here obtained as well as of the mountains to the northwest." Kern's small watercolor, *Pareda* (plate 6), emphasizes the setting rather than the town. His soft green tones evoke the summertime colors of cottonwoods and fields in the river bottom and contrast with the sandy, mesquite-covered mesas nearby. In the 1840s Pareda was built around a plaza, boasted a shoemaker and perhaps other tradespeople, and seems to have prospered. Lt. James Abert went out of his way to go there for supplies in the winter of 1846 and was "struck with the kindness of the good people here." He stayed with don Miguel Baca, who "had a Yankee clock in his house." Today the modern highway runs on the other side of the river; the town has languished.[5]

On January 3, Kern and Skinner left the hospitable valley of the Rio Grande behind. Five days of travel had brought them 180 miles from Santa Fe to the campground of Fray Cristóbal, at the northern edge of the forbidding Jornada del Muerto. "This place is very dangerous on account of the Indians,"

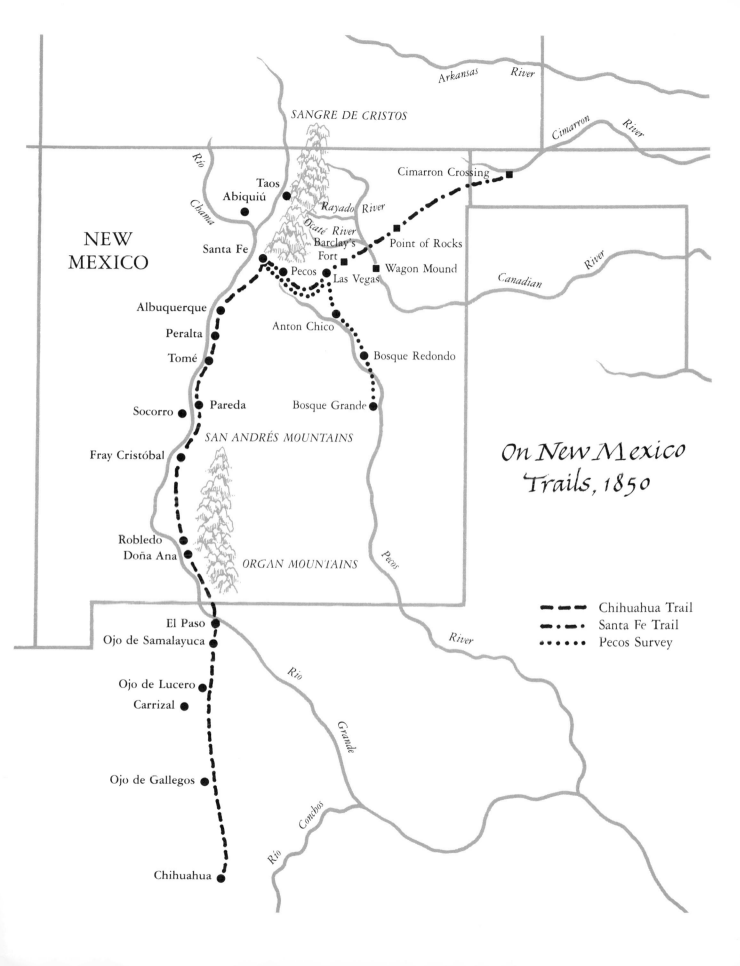

Arkansas *River*

Cimarron *River*

SANGRE DE CRISTOS

Taos
Abiquiú

Río

Chama

Cimarron Crossing

NEW
MEXICO

Santa Fe

Rayado River

Ocaté River

Barclay's
Fort

Point of Rocks

Pecos
Las Vegas

Wagon Mound

Canadian

River

Albuquerque

Peralta

Tomé

Anton Chico

Bosque Redondo

Pareda

SAN ANDRÉS MOUNTAINS

Socorro

On New Mexico
Trails, 1850

Bosque Grande

Fray Cristóbal

Robledo
Doña Ana

ORGAN MOUNTAINS

Pecos

El Paso

Ojo de Samalayuca

River

Ojo de Lucero

Carrizal

Río

— — — Chihuahua Trail
—·—·— Santa Fe Trail
········· Pecos Survey

Grande

Ojo de Gallegos

Conchos

Río

Chihuahua

Kern wrote in his diary, "and . . . there is more or less uncertainty of finding water on the Jornado [sic]." Without pausing to rest for a day or two at Fray Cristóbal, as many travelers did, Kern and Skinner plunged into the desert, traveling mostly at night to conserve water. Two days later they emerged safely from the Jornada and returned to the Rio Grande, which they followed south through towns such as Robledo, Doña Ana, and Frontera. Kern continued to sketch along the way.

On January 6, nine days and about 330 miles from Santa Fe, they crossed the river to El Paso, today's Ciudad Juárez. Kern drew a number of El Paso scenes, including the interior of a home and the mission of Nuestra Señora de Guadalupe, founded in 1659. But Skinner apparently had no time to linger. The next day, January 7, they resumed their journey. They stopped at the popular springs along the Chihuahua Trail, such as Ojo de Samalyuca and Ojo de Lucero, and passed through the garrison town of Carrizal (fig. 63). Kern drew a quick sketch of the decaying presidio, built in 1773, and dismissed the declining town with a few words: "cholera, poverty, and former wealth."[6] Some 170 miles south of El Paso, on January 10, Skinner and Kern came upon the scene of a tragedy at Ojo de Gallego. As they approached the spring, Kern saw a wagon train drawn in a circle and "men with their arms & on the look out." Indians had killed the leader of the train, Edward S. Thwait, and a "Spaniard." The body of the

"Spaniard" was being laid to rest as Kern and Skinner arrived. Moved by the scene, Kern copied into his sketchbook what might have been the inscription from Thwait's grave: "To the memory of Edwd. S. Thwait / Murdered by the Apaches." On his return to Santa Fe some weeks later, Kern learned that wolves had dug up the fresh graves.

Skinner and Kern moved on, doubtless more apprehensive, but certainly grateful that they had not crossed paths with the Apaches who attacked Thwait's party. One hundred miles beyond Ojo de Gallegos, a journey of two or three days at the rate that Skinner and Kern were traveling, they reached their destination, Ciudad de Chihuahua, the most impressive city Kern had yet seen in Mexico. They stayed in Chihuahua for a few days, and Kern took advantage of the time to draw.

The most impressive building in Chihuahua was the cathedral, with its carved facade and tall bell towers built from the wealth of nearby silver mines. Kern's favorite building, however, was a more melancholy structure, the unfinished stone church of what he called the "old College of the Jesuits." Jesuits had built the Colegio de Nuestra Señora de Loreto to teach Tarahumara linguistics to missionaries and to train neophyte assistants. A number of buildings had been completed when the Jesuits were expelled from Mexico in 1767, but the chapel of the college had never been finished. After the expulsion of the Jesuits, the government acquired the buildings, planning to use them

Fig. 63. *El Presidio at Carrizal, Jan. 9, 1850.* Field sketch by Richard H. Kern. Courtesy, Fred W. Cron.

for a school, a hospital, a jail, and a military chapel. As a jail, the old college acquired notoriety. In 1811 it received a prisoner, Father Miguel Hidalgo, whose subsequent fame as the Father of Mexican Independence gave the building a measure of immortality. The rebel priest had been captured en route to Texas in 1811 and taken to Chihuahua, where he was incarcerated in the old colegio, executed in its courtyard, and decapitated. In Kern's day, visitors were taken to a small monument to his memory that marked the spot. Three decades after Hidalgo's execution, the gloomy compound housed another notorious group of prisoners— Texans from the so-called Texan-Santa Fe expedition, who had been captured in New Mexico and marched to Mexico

Fig. 64. Untitled watercolors, apparently of the chapel of the Jesuit College in Chihuahua.
Courtesy, Fred W. Cron.

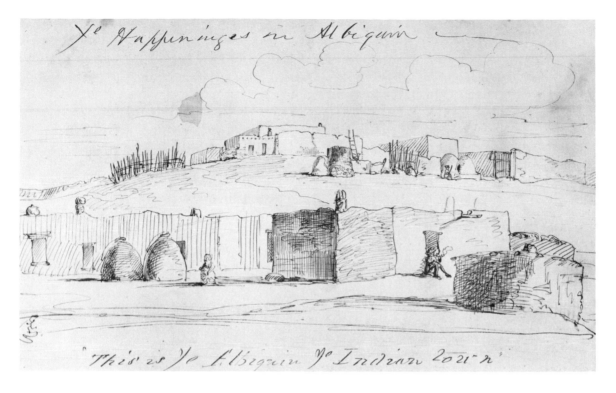

Fig. 65. *This is Ye Abiquiu, Ye Indian Town.* Drawing by Edward M. Kern, 1850. Courtesy, Fred W. Cron.

City by way of Chihuahua. Kern probably knew of these events, and the building's story as well as its romantic, dilapidated condition may have prompted him to do several watercolors. The best of the group is the *Interior of the Jesuit College, Chihuahua,* with part of its roof open to the sky (plate 7). Two of Kern's other watercolors apparently depict the exterior of this same stone building (fig. 64). Today the ruins of the Jesuit College are gone; state and federal buildings occupy the site. The cell in which Hidalgo reportedly was held has been preserved in the basement of the federal building, the Palacio Federal. It is a tourist attraction and the only vestige of the old Jesuit College. Richard Kern's watercolors may be the only extant images of the interior and exterior of the chapel in the old colegio.[7]

On January 19, Kern made more sketches in the city, then he and Skinner started back to Santa Fe. They returned even more quickly than they had come. By January 24 they had covered the 250 miles to El Paso. Three days later, on January 27, they had crossed the Jornada del Muerto and made camp at Valverde, about 175 miles above El Paso. On February 1, they rode into Santa Fe. Edward Kern was not there to greet them. As Dick later told a friend, "Ned had gone to a frontier town, having a good situation in the Quarter Master Dept." About the first of February, Ned started work as a forage master in the Army Quartermaster Corps at a military post in Abiquiú, a village on the Chama River some forty-five miles to the northwest of Santa Fe (fig. 65). He remained in that position for nearly a year and a half, until June 1851.[8]

The trip to Chihuahua had introduced Richard Kern to new corners of New Mexico and old Mexico, but had not solved his most pressing problem: how to support himself in Santa Fe. Even the tools of the artist's trade remained in short supply in this provincial capital. Thus, when Richard learned that William Skinner planned a short trip to the East Coast, he wrote to his older brother, John, to send materials from Philadelphia to him and Ned. John gathered together pens, pencils, and paper to give to Skinner, who planned to visit him at the brothers' studio on Filbert Street. John Kern could not find the lithographic pens his brother wanted, but he did send an item Dick had not requested: "a few crow quills . . . which I find sometimes useful." Lonesome,

perhaps, for the familiar sights of home, Dick had asked for flower seeds, and John sent larkspur, along with instructions for getting young plants through the winter. John's shipment to Santa Fe included a comb, sent by a friend: "He says he knows your antipathy to its use, but trusts it may gain you favor in the eyes of the senoritas."[9]

If Dick ever used the comb or found time for young ladies, no record remains. He must have had many lonely moments, however. "Call me not lonely!" began a poem scribbled in one of Richard's sketchbooks from this year:

> To me blossom mid the wreath
> whose buds have perished
> send some bright dream
> of love without its strife.[10]

And another verse, written in the same sketchbook, spoke of deliverance:

> There came to him many a maiden
> Whose eyes had forgot to shine;
> And widows, with grief overladen
> For a draught of his sleepy wine.
>   Hurrah &c.
> The scholar left all his learning
> The Poet his fancied woes;
> And the Beauty her bloom returning
> Like life to the fading rose.
>   Hurrah &c.

As Edward Kern had discovered, in New Mexico the United States Army held the key to employment for men with the Kerns' background and talents. In order to maintain the province and protect it from depredations of Navajos, Utes, and Apaches, the Army spent some three million dollars a year in New Mexico. This sum represented about 8 percent of the cash in circulation. The army also provided opportunities for civilian employment because it was shorthanded. Only a thousand or so troops had been assigned to New Mexico in 1850, and they were spread thinly throughout the vast territory.[11]

Whether by chance or by design, Richard Kern cultivated the officers, merchants, and would-be politicians who had the means to advance his career. Most of his closest acquaintances supported the presence of the military in New Mexico and wanted it to continue to play a large role in local government. Known collectively as the territorial, or American, party, these people favored territorial government rather than statehood for New Mexico. They believed correctly that territorial status would keep federal dollars and patronage flowing westward over the Santa Fe Trail. Moreover, with political appointments emanating from Washington, political power would remain in the hands of the territory's Anglo-American minority. Statehood, on the other hand, would open the way for the Hispanic majority to seize political power.[12]

Many members of the American party viewed the New Mexicans as incompetent to govern themselves as a state, an opinion Kern apparently shared. "The wise people here," he wrote sarcastically, "have formed themselves into a state government, and will soon be knocking at a door that *should* be closed against them."[13] Those who took this stance probably found their resolve

stiffened by the knowledge that statehood would permit New Mexico's overwhelmingly Hispanic majority to elect its own officials and to exercise control of the budget and patronage of the state.

Political stakes were high, then, in the rough-and-tumble arena of New Mexico politics, and so were political tensions. In the fall of 1849, as Kern was returning from the Navajo country, the leader of the statehood faction, Richard H. Weightman, publicly impugned the integrity of the head of the territorial group, Judge Joab Houghton, and questioned his ability to adjudicate fairly. Houghton responded by challenging Weightman to a duel. Amazingly, both survived, but their mutual enmity endured. Kern and his friends took Houghton's side, and remained on it. "Weightman is an ambitious little fellow," James Simpson told Kern, "but his name is a misnomer with regard to his merits."[14]

Among the members of the territorial faction with whom Kern associated were the group's tacit leader, Joab Houghton, a college-educated New Yorker with no legal training, who served as chief justice of New Mexico for five years after his appointment by Kearny in 1846; Charles Blumner, the territorial treasurer; James L. Collins, a prominent merchant and occasional editor and part owner of the Santa Fe *Gazette,* who had served as translator on the 1849 Navajo expedition, where he and Kern followed the same paths; William C. Skinner, a merchant, attorney, delegate to New Mexico's first constitutional convention in the fall of 1849 and the man with whom Kern traveled to Chihuahua; William S. Messervy, a merchant elected in 1850 as New Mexico's first representative to Congress, and whose knowledge of New Mexico Kern found very extensive; and Captain Alexander W. Reynolds, assistant army quartermaster and sometime acting quartermaster for the post in Santa Fe. Reynolds, whose position gave him discretion to spend a good many federal dollars, would be the American party's candidate for territorial delegate to Congress in 1851.[15]

While Kern cultivated those who could help him, he also associated with what appears to have been a fun-loving, irreverent group of young men. Many of them formed an Odd Fellows Lodge, partied, drank, and boasted of real or imagined liaisons with Indian and Mexican women. One of his closest friends, a twenty-four-year-old merchant from New York named Horace L. Dickinson, chided Kern for contracting the "inflamatory *two step.*" A local Indian agent, Dickinson said, had come down with the same illness, "caused by the exposure to the cold, bugs, lice, & squaws, very dangerous antagonists sometimes." After Richard Kern had left Santa Fe, Dickinson wrote to him: "Your old washerwoman has had a baby, legal father known, real father unknown—funny ain't it."[16]

Kern and his iconoclastic friends used humor and ridicule to cope with their new environment. They referred to the local paper, the Santa Fe *Gazette,* as the

"Santa Fe Emetic," terming its editor "Squire Collins," and its opinions "twaddle." They also bestowed nicknames upon the most influential people in the territory. They adopted local usage and referred to Governor James S. Calhoun and Indian agent John Greiner as "Tata," a word by which very young New Mexican children address their parents. Charles Blumner, the territorial treasurer, became "Prussian Blue," and one officer, probably the military store keeper Captain William R. Shoemaker, was dubbed "Capt. Shoeboots."[17]

The local Hispanic population also came under their attack. In anger, Horace Dickinson referred to them as "G-d d-d *Greasers.*" In his correspondence with the Kerns, Dickinson rarely mentions the New Mexicans except to condemn their supposed immorality, as in the case of one "Mexy" who shot another. This occurred, Dickinson said, because "although the husband has delivered over his wife to the embraces of other men, several times before, he did not like that she should do it of her own accord & so shot the same man in the head that helped her."[18] Richard Kern may have shared Dickinson's contempt for Mexicans, as many Americans did at the time of the Mexican War. Although Kern drew a number of sketches of Indians, none of his extant drawings or paintings depict Mexicans as more than stick figures, added to a scene to provide a sense of scale.

Kern probably also shared Dickinson's jaundiced view of the ability of the U.S. Army to bring Indians under control in New Mexico. "The Indians commit their usual depradations [*sic*], murder more than ever," Kern told a friend in Philadelphia, notwithstanding the presence of five or six hundred infantrymen sent from Washington.[19] After Kern left New Mexico, Dickinson sent him a cynical report on Indian strategy: "Tata Governador just made the usual winter peace with the Utahs. . . . I suppose the peace will last as long as usual . . . 'till the snow goes off." A few months later, Dickinson told Ned Kern that many of his military friends had been dispersed around the territory, "cocked up in some little fort and ordered to look sharp for injins, which of course they don't do, fools if they did."[20]

If Kern lacked confidence in the army's ability to quell Indian disturbances, he nonetheless found the army of immense value in providing him with employment. Containing Indians required that the military know the local terrain, the best routes into Indian territory, and the finest sites for fortifications. This required maps, but the U.S. government had little cartographic information about New Mexico. Indeed, in the summer of 1848, months after the signing of the Treaty of Guadalupe Hidalgo, the American secretary of state could not find a single map of New Mexico in Washington.[21] So the army needed maps of New Mexico, and the making of maps required a draftsman. In this capacity, Richard Kern began to find work.

In March of 1850 Kern found short-term employment with Capt. Henry Bethel Judd. On March 15 Judd led a party of troops out of Las Vegas to make a quick reconnaissance of the Pecos River. Below the town of Anton Chico the Pecos flowed through high, grass-covered plains where no permanent settlements existed in 1850. Judd was assigned to locate the best routes for wagons along the river, and to find sites that had ample wood and water. He followed the southeasterly meanderings of the Pecos through places known to Mexican buffalo hunters and Indian traders by such tantalizing names such as the Cañada de Juan de Dios, the Arroyo de las Carretas, Spy Peak, and Navajo Crossing. On March 23, 8 days and 192 miles out of Las Vegas, they reached the Bosque Grande. About 50 miles south of Bosque Redondo, where Ft. Sumner would be founded in 1862, the wooded bottomlands of the Bosque Grande extended some 15 miles along the river at a width of 8 to 10 miles. Judd led his command to the southern end of the bosque, camped for the night, then headed back the following day, returning to Las Vegas as quickly as he had come.[22]

Kern's task on the Judd expedition was to survey and draw the area. Kern had apparently learned the skills of map making from his brother Ned and from Lieutenant Simpson. Kern carefully mapped Judd's route, both coming and going, indicating distances, place names, camp sites, and places where wood and water were scarce or plentiful. In ad-

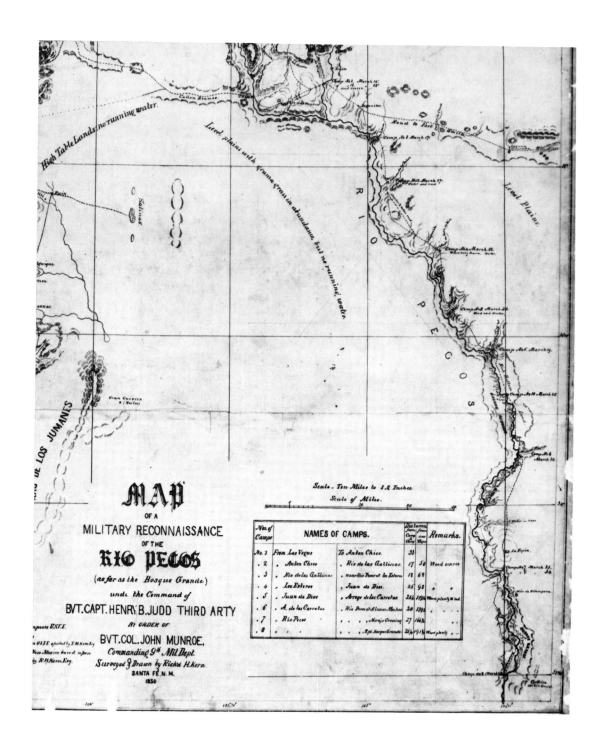

Fig. 66. Detail of the manuscript "Map of a Military Reconnaissance of the Rio Pecos," drawn in Richard H. Kern's hand. Courtesy, Cartographic and Architectural Branch, National Archives and Records Service.

dition to drawing the results of his own survey of the Pecos and its topography, Kern incorporated into his map the previous surveys of the Rio Grande basin by Abert, Peck, Simpson, and Edward Kern. The result was a comprehensive map of eastern New Mexico from the Rio Grande to the Pecos, "the best that had yet been made" (fig. 66).[23] Kern produced this ambitious map for the use of Col. John Munroe, who headed the military department of New Mexico, at no cost to the Topographical Bureau. Simpson recognized the value of the map and in late June employed Kern "at a small compensation" to make a duplicate of the map for the bureau.[24] Kern finished work on the copy by late August or early September.

Completing the maps of the Pecos survey kept Kern "constantly employed," as he put it, well into the summer of 1850—except when new opportunities to explore presented themselves.[25] In May he took a few weeks away from his work to accompany Simpson on a dangerous survey of the lower reaches of the Santa Fe Trail. Simpson had received orders to reconnoiter the eastern slope of the Sangre de Cristos between the Ocaté and Rayado rivers and to locate a site for a military post. When Kern and Simpson reached Las Vegas, on May 21, they learned that Indians, apparently Jicarilla Apaches and Utes, had attacked a wagon train bringing mail in from the United States. Ten men had died. A group of traders heading eastward over

the trail had come upon the scene of the tragedy, near Wagon Mound. Too frightened to continue on, the traders had returned to Las Vegas with some of the mail and had asked for a military escort. A contingent of troops under Lt. Ambrose Burnside, which had been assigned to Simpson's survey, was diverted into this more pressing business. Burnside received orders to accompany the traders as far as the Cimarron crossing of the Santa Fe Trail and to stop along the way at Wagon Mound to investigate the murders. For the moment, Simpson had to abandon his survey, but he decided to make the trip with Burnside, and Kern went along. "Lieut. Simpson having concluded to go also, why here I am," Kern explained many weary days later in a letter written from the "Crossing of the Cimarron, 230 miles from Santa Fe."[26]

Richard Kern's account of the tragedy at Wagon Mound, which he termed "the most daring murder ever committed by the Indians" along the trail, was published in the Philadelphia *Public Ledger* on July 2, 1850. Eleven men had died. The bodies of most of the victims, Kern wrote, "had been eaten by the wolves and ravens." The military escort buried the remains in a single grave and burned the wagons. After leaving this grisly scene, Burnside's command came across a group of buffalo hunters, or *ciboleros,* made up of "Spaniards and Pueblo Indians," according to Kern. The Americans suspected the ciboleros of having perpetrated the attack and Kern, feisty in his correspondence if not in actuality, boasted: "We wished for some pretext to attack the party, and though they were five times our number we would have made short work of it."

After seeing the traders safely to the Cimarron, the escort headed back toward Las Vegas, pausing at the crossing of the Ocaté for Simpson and Kern to carry out their survey. Simpson's reconnaissance of this area was one of several that preceded the establishment of Fort Union, near present-day Las Vegas, the following year. Simpson filed no formal report, however, so Kern's contribution to the survey is not clear. As was his custom, however, Kern sketched along the way. One sketch from this trip, *Ruins of Old Pecos, June 14, 1850,* later appeared in Henry Schoolcraft's *Indian Tribes of the United States* (fig. 110). It must have been with some sense of relief that Kern returned safely to Santa Fe from the Indian country on June 15.[27]

Three weeks later, on July 6, Kern left Santa Fe again with Simpson, this time heading south. Simpson's mission was to measure the distance from Santa Fe to Doña Ana, a village where a military post had been established the year before, just north of present Las Cruces. The party made its way to Doña Ana by following the eastern bank of the Rio Grande, on the same road that Kern had taken to Chihuahua in January. Simpson measured distances from town to town and place to place with a "viameter," a reasonably accurate device that marked off 272 miles between Santa Fe

and Doña Ana. From Doña Ana, Simpson and Kern apparently returned directly to Santa Fe, retracing their steps over the Jornada, then crossing the Rio Grande near Socorro and measuring the distance along the west side of the river.[28]

Kern's duties on this trip are not known, but he continued to fill his sketchbooks with drawings. As usual, these were mostly topographic views of stopping points along the way, such as Pareda, Fray Cristóbal, and Doña Ana, or of impressive mountains, such as the Organos. When colors seemed unusual, Kern took notes as a reminder. On an untitled scene of mountains, horses, and an adobe with fence, he wrote: "all in deep shade except the mountains/ mount are purplish green—upper rocks purple—lower yellowish." Kern continued to find Indians a subject of interest. He did two portrait sketches entitled *Sacramento Apache.* He also continued to draw structures. His sketch of the *Church at Tomé* (fig. 67), done on July 8, is the earliest known view of that church, then nearly one hundred years old and remodeled frequently since Kern's day. The present church does not resemble the structure that Kern saw, but Kern's sketch will be invaluable if the church is ever restored again. At Doña Ana, Kern met Lt. John Trevitt and copied a drawing that Trevitt had done of the Mission of Concepción near San Antonio, Texas. In this case, Kern noted on the drawing, "from a sketch by Lt. Trevitt, USA." This copy, however, suggests the possibility that other sketches made by Kern and by other

Church at Tomé July 8 1850

Fig. 67. *Church at Tomé, July 8, 1850.* Field sketch by Richard H. Kern. Courtesy, Fred W. Cron.

expeditionary artists as well, may be of scenes that they had not seen first-hand.[29]

By August of 1850, with another trip down the Chihuahua Trail behind him, Richard Kern could boast of knowing the Rio Grande valley from southern Colorado down to El Paso, and of having traveled west of the valley into the Navajo country with Simpson, and out on the high plains to the northeast with Simpson and to the southwest

with Judd. For an American, Kern possessed rare, firsthand knowledge of newly acquired New Mexico. That knowledge, together with his proven skills as a mapmaker, would make Kern invaluable to the new chief of the Topographical Engineers in the territory, Lt. John Grubb Parke.

On September 10, Kern went to work for Lieutenant Parke. Parke had arrived in Santa Fe on July 12 and had soon succeeded Simpson as the sole topographical engineer in the Department of New Mexico. For months, Simpson had pleaded with his boss in Washington, Col. John J. Abert, to allow him to return east to his young wife, in Buffalo, New York. She, in turn, had pleaded with Abert to transfer her husband closer to home. These letters fell on deaf ears until Simpson came down with a serious throat infection and the post surgeon recommended a six-month medical leave. Lieutenant Parke took over Simpson's duties on August 21, and Simpson headed out over the Santa Fe Trail, measuring distances all the way to Ft. Leavenworth.[30]

Like Kern, Parke was a native of Philadelphia. He had graduated from West Point in 1845, second in his class, and had received an appointment as brevet lieutenant in the Topographical Engineers in July 1849. The next year found him in New Mexico, admitting his inexperience to his boss, Colonel Abert. The presence in Santa Fe of Richard Kern, with the skills of a draftsman and substantial field experience, seemed like a godsend to the young lieutenant—especially when Col. John Munroe ordered Parke to make a map of territory he hardly knew. "To assist me in it I was recommended to engage the services of Mr. Kern both in account of his extensive knowledge of this country, and his also being a good topographer," Parke reported to Abert. Parke hired Kern at three dollars a day, and over the next year Kern drew two important maps under Parke's supervision.[31]

One of Kern's assignments under Parke was to produce an improved version of the map of the Navajo country that Edward Kern had made for Lieutenant Simpson in 1849. Parke and Kern gathered information from a variety of sources, including testimony from the "old guide" Rafael Carravajal, who had led Simpson to Canyon de Chelly. This new map was intended to aid Colonel Monroe, who planned to launch an offensive against the Navajos in the spring of 1851 to force them to adhere to the treaty that Mariano Martínez and Chapitone had signed in 1849. The map, completed by March 7, 1851, showed six major routes that an invading force could take to reach Canyon de Chelly. It also told which of those routes were practical for wagons, identified camp sites with dependable grass and water, and indicated where Navajos planted crops, so that the army could destroy them. Monroe's expedition never left that spring, but in August when Colonel Edwin Vose Sumner replaced Monroe, he carried out the planned invasion of the Navajo country. Sumner probably took with him the map that Parke and Kern had prepared; he took Parke and Kern along with him as well.[32]

By April 24, 1851, the team of Parke and Kern had completed another project, two drawings of a monumental five-by-seven-foot "Map of the Territory of New Mexico" that superseded all previous maps of the region. Kern did the drawing and assisted Parke in compiling the data. At a scale of ten miles to the inch, the map ranged from the Colorado River in the west, which then formed the boundary between New Mexico and California, east to the high plains, where the Santa Fe and the Canadian River trails entered New Mexico. To the north, the map embraced the Pikes Peak country of Colorado and the southern part of the newly created Utah Territory. To the south, it extended into Mexico, well below El Paso, Cooke's Wagon Road, and the Gila River route to California.[33]

Parke and Kern explicitly credited the makers of previous maps for much of their information. Their authorities included Edward Kern's 1849 map of the Navajo country and the surveys of the Rio Pecos and the Jornada del Muerto that Richard Kern himself had done the previous year. But Parke and Kern went beyond creating a composite of previous maps. They also gathered fresh data from men who knew the mountains and deserts, such as Antoine Leroux, Ceran St. Vrain, and John Hatcher, and from Kern's talks with the late Bill Williams. In addition, the Parke-Kern map benefited from the first-hand knowledge of Richard and his brother Edward. Through informants, then, Parke and Kern were able to supply names even to places on the map that they labeled "Unexplored." Carl Wheat, the foremost authority on the mapping of the West, has commented that "the names along the upper Grand River, and in the valley at the head of the Rio Grande del Norte, are remarkable in that they here appear so early (fig. 68)."[34] One pass in southern Colorado, for ex-

ample, appeared on the Parke-Kern map as "Leroux Pass." In Washington, D.C., a couple of years later, Leroux commented that "this Pass is laid down on a map I saw in the War Office, made by Lieut. Parke and Mr. R. H. Kern, and is there named after me, because I gave Lieut. Parke information about it."[35]

Because of his extensive field experience and contacts in New Mexico, Kern's role in making the map exceeded that of a draftsman and he was proud of his work. As he told a friend, "I was . . . ordered to compile a map of New Mexico which I did and made two copies of it about 7 feet by 6 ft— No one else could have done this for none other possessed the data."[36] Parke acknowledged Kern's work by indicating on the map itself that he was both "assisted" by Kern and that the map was "drawn" by Kern. Colonel Munroe, who apparently had recommended Kern to Lieutenant Parke, thought Kern deserved more credit. Munroe ordered that the title of the map be changed to read: "Compiled & drawn by Mr. R. H. Kern under the direction of Lt. J. G. Parke." Parke protested the alteration, which he termed "wholly unjust to myself and unwarranted." Parke's original wording prevailed (fig. 69).[37]

By order of the U.S. Senate, March 15, 1852, the Parke-Kern map was printed. The New York firm of J. & D. Major, which won the bid, completed the job in early June 1852, reproducing the map on a reduced scale of twenty-six miles to the inch, but still in a large

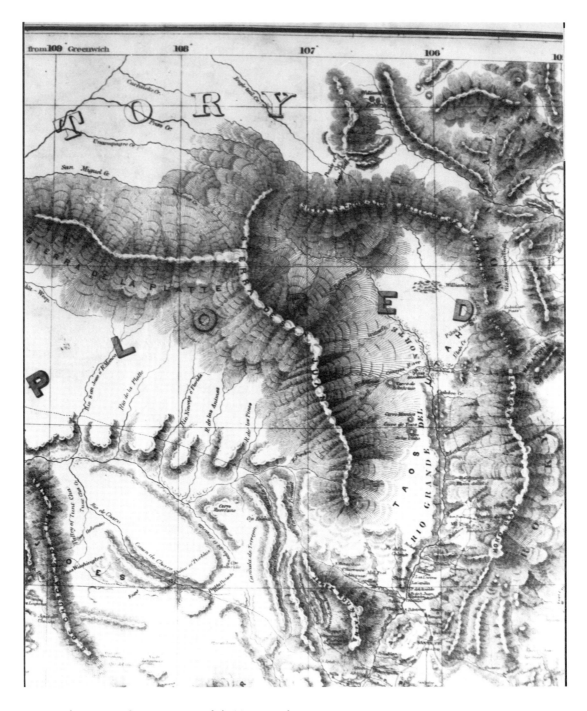

Fig. 68. Detail from the *Map of the Territory of New Mexico*. Courtesy, Cartographic and Architectural Branch, National Archives and Records Service, Washington, D.C.

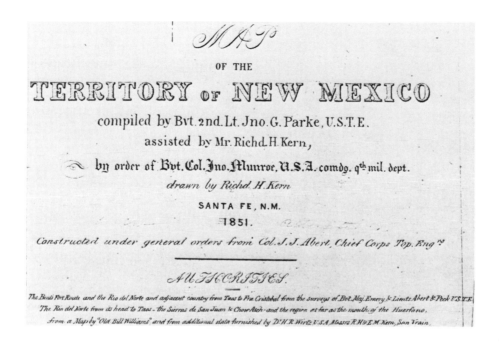

Fig. 69. Detail from the *Map of the Territory of New Mexico*. Courtesy, Cartographic and Architectural Branch, National Archives and Records Service, Washington, D.C.

format (thirty-three by twenty-four inches). Richard Kern, who was in Washington at the time, may have seen the newly published map. Majors apparently printed 3,750 copies, of which 100 went to the Topographical Bureau, 100 to the War Department, and 100 to Parke. The Senate retained the remainder. The maps no sooner arrived at the offices of the Topographical Bureau than its chief, Colonel Abert, sent copies to the commanders of all eleven military posts in New Mexico, and to the post in El Paso, Texas.[38]

The Parke-Kern map of the Territory of New Mexico would stand for the rest of the decade as the most comprehensive and dependable rendering of the newly acquired lands between the Pecos and the Colorado. From this pioneering cartography, historian Frank McNitt has noted, "came later maps that charted military expeditions, directed emigrant trains on their southern routes to Los Angeles, and eventually aided in the selection of Indian reservations, a transcontinental railroad, and the first non-Spanish occupation of land westward from the Rio Grande for one thousand miles."[39] Like his drawings, Kern's map remains valuable yet today. It records long-forgotten place names and trails of the era, and enables us to understand the cartographic perceptions of Kern's generation. For those reasons, the lithograph of the Parke-Kern map of 1851 has been reproduced in books, and it still remains in print.[40]

Valuable as it might have been, mapmaking was not sufficient to make ends meet. In mid-September 1850, a week after he started working for Parke, Kern had taken a second job as a clerk and storekeeper in the U.S. Army Clothing Depot at Santa Fe. He held that position, which paid fifty dollars per month, from Sept. 17, 1850 through May 31, 1851.[41] Although his work had nothing to do with art or science, it apparently was agreeable. Kern's friend, Simpson, who had returned home to Buffalo, expressed pleasure at learning that Kern had landed the job: "I should think such a position the most desirable one you can have in the [Quartermaster] Department." Simpson knew Kern's boss, Captain Langdon Cheves Easton, and told Kern "the Captain is so considerate & judicious, I should think you would not only get along pleasantly with him but that you would be likely to retain the situation at least as long as he should be in charge, and you desired to remain."[42]

Although he held two jobs, Kern still found it difficult to support himself in Santa Fe. His brother was in

Abiquiú, and Dick lived alone. To cut down on expenses, he joined a small group of men who shared meals. From his wife's home in Buffalo, Simpson commiserated: "I regret to learn that you have had so much trouble in getting with a mess, and that when you wrote it was so small," Simpson wrote to Kern. "I know how economically I was obliged to live in Santa Fe."[43]

While he worked as a supply clerk for the Quartermaster and as a draftsman for Lieutenant Parke, Richard Kern also pursued his interests in the natural sciences. He had never recovered the collection of birds that he had gathered while traveling with Frémont, but he began again. Within a year he had assembled "a large botannical & entomological collection," which he sent east in 1850.[44] He probably intended this latest collection to go to the Philadelphia Academy of Natural Sciences, for he continued to correspond with its most illustrious member, Dr. Samuel George Morton, and with its curator, Dr. Joseph Leidy.[45] Dr. Morton, for whom Kern had obtained the skull of a Navajo, soon became the beneficiary of the skull of a Jicarilla Apache, also thanks to Kern. The unfortunate Apache was killed on July 4, 1850 while attempting to escape from the guard house in Santa Fe, and Dr. Edwards, the post surgeon, "secured the cranium" for Morton. Upon his return to Philadelphia, early in 1852, Kern personally presented a number of specimens from New Mexico to the Academy of Natural Sciences, including beetles, cockroaches, crickets, grasshoppers, centipedes, millipedes, scorpions, and the cranium of a coyote. These may have come from the collection that Kern assembled in 1850, or perhaps from a subsequent collection.[46]

In addition, Kern indulged new interests in ethnology and archaeology. The New Mexico pueblos, the great ruins at Chaco and Chelley, and the extraordinary inscriptions on El Morro had excited his curiosity about New Mexico Indians and early Spanish exploration. There were few published sources, however, to which he could turn for answers. "We are entirely destitute of books of references," Kern told Dr. Morton, "and if we wish to judge of the truth of things by comparison we cannot do so for this reason." Kern did, however, have access to a few books through Simpson, and he borrowed others from acquaintances such as Spruce Baird, a self-educated attorney from Texas who had recently settled in Albuquerque.[47]

Josiah Gregg's *Commerce of the Prairies*, published in 1844 and based on several visits to Santa Fe between 1831 and 1840, Kern judged "the most reliable work on this country, yet what he says in regard to the Pueblo Indians is very incorrect." *Adventures in Mexico and the Rocky Mountains* (1847), the work of the English traveler George Frederick Ruxton who journeyed through New Mexico in 1846, Kern thought "makes a horrid jumble" of the Pueblos "and excuses all inaccuracies by saying he lost all his notes whilst crossing the

Arkansas." Lieutenant William H. Emory's *Notes of a Military Reconnoissance* [sic] (1848) said little about the Pueblos and "I think shows he was not capable of judging, when he calls part of the ruins of Old Pecos, 'Ruins of Pecos Aztek Church.'" Kern aimed his harshest words, however, at young Lt. James W. Abert, who had shared a mess with Edward Kern on Frémont's third expedition and whose report of a tour through New Mexico in 1846–47 was published in 1848. Kern mocked Abert's prose: "Judging by Lt Aberts Report on N. Mexico," Kern wrote, "one must come to the conclusion that his mind never grasped any idea beyond that connected with 'the sweet warbler of the woods.' The insipidity and trashiness in his report would make him an excellent contractor for the furnishing of milk man's milk."[48]

It is difficult to understand Kern's unduly harsh judgment of Abert's fine report. Perhaps Kern felt a twinge of envy or annoyance that the young lieutenant's father, Col. John J. Abert, who had headed the Corps of Topographical Engineers since its founding in 1838, had seen to it that his son received choice appointments since his graduation from West Point in 1842. Ironically, the high sounding phrases to which Kern objected, such as "the woods rejoiced with the voice of the mocking bird," were probably not written by Abert. They do not appear in his original account, but were probably added later to achieve the style that passed in that day for elegance.[49]

Much of the information that Kern sought could not be found in books. Like American officials in Santa Fe who wanted information about the newly acquired province, Kern turned to the old Spanish and Mexican archives. Among other documents, Kern found a diary of Diego de Vargas, the reconqueror of New Mexico, who chronicled a visit to Zuni in 1692. The Vargas diary corroborated the date of an inscription that Kern had copied from the walls of El Morro, and made a profound impression on him. "This work should be translated and published: it is in good repair, and written in a beautiful style, and its historical value must be evident to all," Kern told Morton; the Vargas journal was finally translated into English nearly a century later, in 1940. Even after Kern left Santa Fe permanently, his friend Horace Dickinson continued to visit the archives and make tracings for him of the signatures of prominent figures such as Juan de Oñate and Antonio de Otermín.[50] In the East, Kern would continue his study of Southwestern antiquities, quickly becoming a recognized authority.

Until recently, our knowledge of Richard Kern's artistic production during his years in New Mexico was limited to the lithographs published in the Simpson report and reproductions of some of his work in Henry Schoolcraft's multivolume series on *Indian Tribes.* From private collections, however, a number of Kern's original drawings of New Mexico subjects have come to light. These offer fresh insights into Kern as an artist, and provide us with unique glimpses into a vanished world. For example, a scrapbook of drawings by the Kern brothers, which is presently in a private collection, contains a beautiful sketch by Richard Kern of *La Iglesia de Nuestra Señora de Guadalupe* (fig. 70). Drawn on May 14, 1850, this is apparently the earliest known image of the Church of Guadalupe and shows long-forgotten architectural details. Built between 1795 and 1803 as an auxiliary to the main parish church, it still stands on its original location on Agua Fria Street. It was freshly restored as a bicentennial project in 1976.[51] Another collection has yielded a sketch of Alexander Barclay's well-known trading post on the Santa Fe Trail. Richard Kern had drawn Barclay's Fort at the request of its owner, but Barclay felt that the sketch did not adequately portray the fort and its surroundings, and so made his own watercolor to send to his family in England.[52]

Of the recently discovered work done by Kern in New Mexico, the most pleasing to the eye are five watercolors in the Kern album at the Amon Carter Museum. Two of these watercolors, as we have seen, were scenes from his trip to Chihuahua—*Pareda* and the *Jesuit College* (plates 6 and 7). Three other watercolors in the album are of scenes from Santa Fe and environs. The first of the three, done in 1849 perhaps after his return from the Navajo expedition, is of the greatest historical interest. It is a rare view of Santa Fe's old parish church, the *parroquia,* and the adjacent

Fig. 70. *La Iglesia de Nuestra Señora de Guadalupe, Santa Fé, N.M., May 14, 1850.* Wash drawing by Richard H. Kern. Courtesy, Fred W. Cron.

home of the vicar, Juan Felipe Ortiz, with its fine portal (plate 8). A night-time scene done in somber, gray-blue tones, Kern's *Parroquia* may have reflected his mood. Certainly it is one of the most sympathetic and accurate renderings of the old church, and adds to our knowledge of the parroquia's ap-

pearance at the end of the Mexican era.

Prior to the discovery of the Kern sketchbook, only two other drawings of the parroquia from these years were known to exist: an engraving based on a drawing by Lt. J. W. Abert, and an anonymous, undated sketch, apparently by an American soldier. The latter

Fig. 71. *Fort Marcy and the Parroquia, Santa Fe.* Engraving based on a drawing made in 1846 by J. W. Abert. *Report of Lieut. J. W. Abert of His Examination of New Mexico* (Washington, D.C., 1848).

shows a crenelated roofline on the parroquia; the Abert engraving does not. The Kern watercolor settles the question. The parroquia did not have crenelations at the time of the American conquest of Santa Fe—they were added a few years later. Kern also shows a window on the south side of the tran- sept. Although such a window does not appear in the Abert engraving, it seems likely that it was there. When Abert stepped inside the parroquia, in 1846, "from a high window a flood of crimson light, tinged by the curtain it passed through, poured down upon the altar." Such a window would usually be placed on the south side of the transept in order to admit the most light. Compared to the Abert engraving (fig. 71), in which the parroquia appears to have the straight, plumbed lines of a New England schoolhouse, Kern's watercolor more accurately suggests undulating adobe walls. The three crosses, however, probably did not lean as much as Kern has portrayed them. Kern occasionally drew expressive, leaning crosses in a way that suggests a mannerism rather than an effort at portraying reality. Curiously, Kern omitted the public clock that Abert placed between the two bell towers. If the clock was still there in 1849, when Kern drew the building, he has hidden it in the shadows, hoping perhaps to make the building seem older and more romantic.[53]

Kern's melancholy view of the parroquia takes on a special importance and poignancy in light of the building's subsequent demise. A quarter century after Kern did his painting, the French-born Archbishop Jean Baptiste Lamy began construction of the walls of the great "Midi romanesque" cathedral that still dominates Santa Fe today. The walls of the new cathedral went up around the old parish church, literally enveloping it. Meanwhile, the parroquia continued to be used until the cathedral was nearly complete. Then workman demolished the old structure and hauled the rubble out of the interior of the new cathedral.

In addition to his view of the parroquia, Kern's sketchbook contained two watercolors of scenes in the Sangre de Cristos, to the east of Santa Fe. One is entitled *From Near the Summit of "Kern's Peak," Rocky Mts Near Santa Fe, N.M., Sept. 1850, [Looking North]* (plate 9). Despite its clear title, the exact place that inspired this scene is difficult, if not impossible, to identify. Kern's Peak appears on no contemporary maps, nor did Kern place it on any of the maps he drew for the Topographical Bureau. This study of diagonal lines, with its strong juxtaposition of light and dark, may have been an idealized view. The drawing was probably inspired by a trip into the Sangre de Cristos in search of a specimen of the "fish with legs" that had excited the interest of J. J. Abert when Simpson first reported seeing it the year before. Lieutenant Parke had learned that these creatures lived "in a mountain lake," believed to be the source of the Santa Fe River—probably Santa Fe Lake, on the south side of Lake Peak (12,409') at the headwaters of the Santa Fe River. "A party was formed to make it a visit," Parke told Abert, "and after a day's hard riding over exceedingly rough ground, and climbing rugged, trailless mountains . . . we succeeded in finding this beautiful sheet of water." They also found two specimens of the fish with legs," which Parke sent to Abert.[54]

Another watercolor inspired by a trip into the Sangre de Cristos is a warm, idyllic, late afternoon view, *New Mexican Aqueduct. Santa Fe Creek, New Mexico, 1851* (plate 10).[55] Both the *Aqueduct* and *Kern's Peak* seem to capture the essence of the places they portray, but as with his view of the Taos valley, Kern appears to have taken considerable liberties with topography in order to improve the composition and dramatic quality of the scenes.

Richard Kern did other sketches and paintings during his residence in Santa Fe, apparently including portraits of Indians. These may be irretrievably lost, or they may surface one day in a private collection.[56]

His varied interests must have kept him occupied in Santa Fe, but a restless Richard Kern continued to look for better opportunities. As usual, opportunity for an ambitious artist in the West seemed linked to the activities of the United States government. In January, 1851, Kern wrote to one Charles A. Hoppin, whom he had met the previous summer in Doña Ana, and asked Hoppin to recommend him to John Russell Bartlett, who had just begun to survey the U.S.-Mexican boundary. "I am busy on another map, 8 × 6 feet," Kern told Hoppin, "besides computing the square miles in each county for the census marshall & making a rough map for the head [quartermaster]." Kern said that he could get letters of reference "from every officer in the territory from Col. Munro down," and specifically mentioned one Moss, of Bartlett's staff, and Maj. Henry L. Kendrick, who had been with Kern on the Navajo expedition. Hoppin recommended Kern to Bartlett with enthusiasm: "Kern is an artist of no little merit," he told Bartlett. "He sketches

with great rapidity & accuracy & some of the specimens of his coloring I have seen have given me a very favorable opinion of his talent."[57]

Whether because of his connections or his talent, Kern soon received an offer from Bartlett to work as a draftsman for the Boundary Commission. But when the offer arrived, Kern felt obliged to decline "unwillingly," as he put it. He still had work to complete for Parke, referring apparently to the large map of New Mexico. That work, he told Bartlett, would "preclude the possibility of my joining you in time to be of much service this spring." Kern then went on at considerable length to recommend his brother, outlining Ned's experience with Frémont and Simpson, and offering a generous evaluation. Kern described Ned as "my superior in topographical drawing and portrait painting, and my equal in other departments of the art."[58] Kern also asked the army paymaster in Santa Fe to write to Bartlett on Ned's behalf.[59]

Edward Kern may have grown restless working for the Quartermaster Corps in Abiquiú, but an offer from Bartlett either did not come through or Ned declined it. He remained in Abiquiú until June, 1851. That month, at the first session of the territorial legislature, Spruce Baird, who had been corresponding with Dick about New Mexico's antiquities, nominated Ned for the position of "engrossing-and-enrolling clerk" of the territorial House of Representatives. Ned won the job unanimously. He moved back to Santa

Fe and worked well into July, lettering legislative bills.[60]

Summer of 1851 brought an end to the Kerns' stay in New Mexico, but the brothers left in different directions. About the first of August, Ned headed east over the Santa Fe Trail with Capt. John Pope, who had replaced Lieutenant Parke as head of the Topographical Bureau in the territory. Assigned to find a more direct route from Santa Fe to Fort Leavenworth, Missouri, Pope hired Ned as the expedition's topographer. Ned had vague plans to return to Santa Fe, or perhaps he would go to work for James Simpson, who was now surveying roads in Minnesota. First, however, he went home. Ned was back in Philadelphia by October 1.[61]

On August 13, two weeks after Ned left Santa Fe for the East, Richard Kern left for the Pacific. His way would also be paid by the Topographical Bureau. Believing, apparently, that either he or Ned would be returning to Santa Fe, Dick left brushes, paints, and canvas behind, but apparently left New Mexico with little reluctance. As his friend Simpson later characterized the situation, "you must have felt that . . . you had had for several years been pocketed in New Mexico & at last got out only as it were with the skin of your teeth."[62] Richard Kern would never see Santa Fe again.

-5-
With Sitgreaves to the Pacific, 1851

IN AUGUST 1851, an opportunity arose for Richard Kern to join another government survey party, this time under Capt. Lorenzo Sitgreaves of the Corps of Topographical Engineers. With Sitgreaves, Kern would leave New Mexico at government expense and finally reach the Pacific—the destination that had eluded him when he started west with Frémont two years before. From the Pacific, Kern planned to return to Philadelphia by sea. First, however, he had to make his way across a poorly charted region of canyons, deserts, mesas, and mountains, inhabited by hostile Indians. For a person of Kern's tastes, the prospect of such an adventure must have been as exciting as thoughts of returning home. Kern left Santa Fe, his friend Horace Dickinson reported, "charging in buckram or buckskin rather, with the prospect of an agreeable time."[1] Dickinson's playful reference to buckram, a cloth used commonly to bind

books, might have been a reference to the volumes that the studious Kern was taking along.

Like three of Kern's previous bosses, Simpson, Judd, and Parke, Lorenzo Sitgreaves had studied at the United States Military Academy at West Point. He had graduated in 1832 (twenty-fifth in a class of forty-five) and entered the newly created Topographical Corps six years later, as a second lieutenant. With other topographers, Sitgreaves had seen action in Mexico during the recent war. He had marched with troops under Gen. John E. Wool from San Antonio into northeastern Mexico in the fall of 1846, and helped map the route and the region. In February 1847, he had fought at the pivotal battle of Buena Vista, where American forces defeated Santa Anna, and had been promoted to brevet captain for gallantry and meritorious conduct. Following the war, Sitgreaves's service in the Corps included heading a team to survey the boundaries of the Creek nation in Indian territory. Kern's new boss, then, had ample field experience as well as the best available training.[2]

In Washington, D.C., in November 1850, Sitgreaves had received orders from J. J. Abert, head of the Topographical Bureau, to report to Santa Fe and organize an "exploring expedition." Abert had assigned Lieutenant Parke to assist Sitgreaves and had told Sitgreaves that "Mr. Kerns [sic], now at Santa Fé in the employ of Lieut. Parke, will be a valuable assistant from his experience on such expeditions, and from his talent in sketching." Following standard practice, whatever drawings Kern did would become the property of the federal government. Orders in hand, Sitgreaves had made his way to New Mexico by way of New Orleans, Galveston, San Antonio, and El Paso. By July 30, if not before, he was in Santa Fe where Parke and Kern went to work under his command.[3]

Sitgreaves's instructions were brief but clear. Abert had understood from "good authority" that the Zuni River flowed westward into the Colorado River. Sitgreaves was to pick up the Zuni River at Zuni Pueblo, to which point Lieutenant Simpson had already explored, then follow the Zuni to the Colorado and continue down that river to its mouth on the Gulf of California. In case Abert's good authority turned out to be wrong, and the Zuni did "not empty into the Colorado but into the Gila," Sitgreaves was to proceed overland and locate the "best and most direct way to the Colorado." This would take the expedition across what is now central Arizona (then part of New Mexico Territory), through an area that Spanish explorers knew, but which appeared as a void on most contemporary maps.[4]

Abert's good authority was almost certainly James H. Simpson. At the end of his 1849 journal, Simpson had urged that the Topographical Corps determine the feasibility of opening a wagon route from Zuni to Los Angeles or San Diego. A trail due west of Zuni, Simpson had argued, would be several hundred miles shorter than both the Gila River route, which Philip St. George Cooke had charted during the Mexican War, and the Old Spanish Trail, which looped north through southern Utah to skirt the Grand Canyon.[5]

Upon arrival at Santa Fe, Sitgreaves must have learned that although Simpson's general plan was sound, he was wrong in one particular. The Zuni River did not flow into the Colorado, as Simpson had supposed, but rather into the Río Colorado Chiquito, or Little Colorado. In constructing their map of New Mexico Territory, completed that spring, Parke and Kern had learned of Simpson's error. One of the sources of the new information was Antoine Leroux, a former trapper whom Mexicans called Joaquín—a name that Americans twisted, somewhat phonetically, into Watkin. Born in St. Louis of French-Spanish parents, and a resident of New Mexico since at least as early as 1824,

Joaquín Leroux probably knew the country west of Santa Fe as well as any white man. By 1846, when Philip St. George Cooke hired him to guide the Mormon Batallion to California, contemporaries already regarded Leroux as "one of the most famous mountain men."[6]

The Zuni River would not do, Leroux said, but he told Kern of a stream called Bill Williams Fork, whose headwaters he represented as not far from the Little Colorado and that flowed southwesterly into the "Big Colorado."[7] Following Leroux's advice, the Parke-Kern map of 1851 showed a clear and seemingly easy route across Arizona by way of the Little Colorado and Williams Fork. Along these rivers, Kern had written: "Proposed Waggon Road from the Pueblo de Zuñi to the Spanish Trail," crediting Simpson with the idea for such a road. In reality, neither the Little Colorado nor Williams Fork was as long as Leroux had led the mapmakers to believe. Sitgreaves would encounter terrible, waterless stretches, but he would also have the dubious satisfaction of seeing Leroux acknowledge his errors, for he hired him to serve as guide for the expedition.

Leroux, Parke, Kern, and Dr. Samuel Washington Woodhouse, who served as the expedition's "physician and naturalist," comprised the principle members of Sitgreaves's expedition. Sitgreaves also hired five American and ten Mexican *arrieros*, or muleteers, to take charge of supplies and equipment.

When this small band set out from Santa Fe, on August 13, it had a more substantial military escort than planned. Col. Edwin Vose Sumner, a tough, abrasive, fifty-five-year-old veteran known to his men as "Bull-Head Sumner," had arrived in New Mexico in mid-July with orders to chastise troublesome Indians and to build military posts closer to them. Within a month after his arrival, Sumner was ready to march against the Navajos with the largest force since Col. John Washington had invaded the Navajo country in 1849. Sumner had ordered Sitgreaves to delay his own departure so that the two might travel together as far as their routes coincided. Sitgreaves had obliged. He had been convinced that he could not safely perform his mission without a military escort, but this military escort proved both an asset and a liability.[8] "Everybody hates old Sumner and all are afraid of him," Richard Kern confided to his brother. "Old Bull," as Kern called Sumner, "does not seem to have too much sense."[9]

The topographers and the army moved slowly southward to Albuquerque where they left the Rio Grande and headed west. Colonel Sumner, who would apparently be following the map of the Navajo country that Parke and Kern had prepared the previous spring, sought Kern's advice: "Old Bull has had several talks with me," Dick told Ned, "and says he will be very thankful for any information I can impart. I told how he ought to march and when [to] camp and he seemed for a wonder to coincide with me."[10]

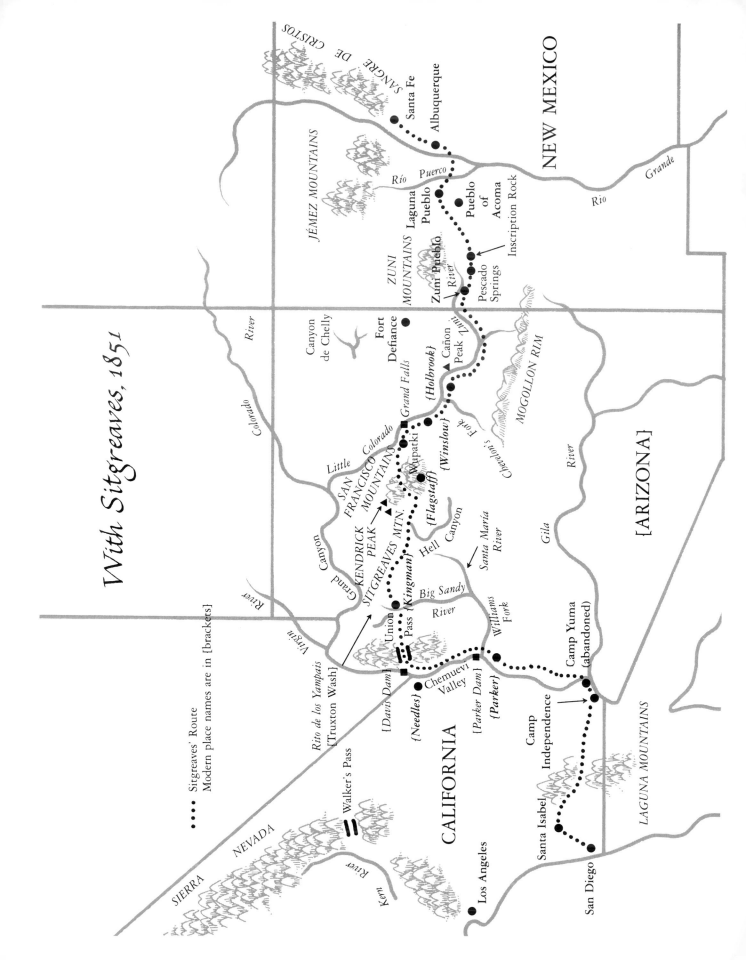

With Sitgreaves, 1851

NEW MEXICO

[ARIZONA]

CALIFORNIA

NEVADA

SANGRE DE CRISTOS

JÉMEZ MOUNTAINS

Santa Fe
Albuquerque

Río Puerco

Río Grande

Río Grande

Laguna Pueblo

Pueblo of Acoma

Inscription Rock

ZUNI MOUNTAINS

Zuni Pueblo

Pescado Springs

Zuni River

Canyon de Chelly

Fort Defiance

Cañon Peak Zuni

MOGOLLON RIM

{Holbrook}

Grand Falls

{Winslow}

Chevelon's Fork

Little Colorado River

SAN FRANCISCO MOUNTAINS

Wupatki

{Flagstaff}

KENDRICK PEAK

SITGREAVES MTN.

Colorado River

Grand Canyon

Hell Canyon

Santa María River

Gila River

Big Sandy River

Union Pass
{Kingman}

Williams Fork

Camp Yuma (abandoned)

[Davis Dam]

{Needles}

Chemuevi Valley

[Parker Dam]

{Parker}

Camp Independence

Virgin River

Rito de los Yampais
[Truxton Wash]

Walker's Pass

SIERRA

Kern River

Santa Isabel

LAGUNA MOUNTAINS

Los Angeles

San Diego

• Sitgreaves' Route
Modern place names are in [brackets]

Two days west of Albuquerque, August 23, brought them to Laguna, where they camped for a few days to the east of the pueblo. While there, Kern took advantage of the opportunity to see and sketch one of the great sights in the Southwest, the nearby Pueblo of Acoma, then some 650 years old, partly hidden and nearly impregnable atop a 350-foot mesa.[11] On August 25, a three-hour ride from Laguna brought Kern, Parke, Woodhouse, Maj. Henry Lane Kendrick, and a small escort within sight of the mesa. They tried to ascend one side of the great rock, where the Acomans had cut foot holes, but hampered by boots and spurs, the Americans had to turn back after climbing 100 feet. The Acomans, who "travel over this way with the same facility as on level ground greeted our defeat . . . with a hearty laugh," Kern said.[12] The Americans retreated and scrambled to the top of the mesa over an easier trail.

With its huge church, orderly houses, and "air of oldness," the "Sky City" appealed to Kern. The Americans stayed at Acoma for only two hours, during which time Kern apparently made sketches that became the basis of three watercolors. One watercolor shows the *Rock and Pueblo of Acoma* as it is approached from the north-northeast (plate 11). In this watercolor, Kern captured the general contours of the mesa top and evoked the solid face that the three-story, thousand-foot-long apartment complex showed to the outside world. He failed, however, to suggest the height

of the structure (three stories), and he exaggerated the size of the selenite windows that opened into rooms on the pueblo's upper floors. In the field sketch upon which the watercolor is based, Kern more accurately conveyed the size of the pueblo in relation to the mesa. Kern later recopied his field sketch for Henry Schoolcraft, who published it in his monumental reference work on the American Indian (fig. 109).[13]

Another of Kern's watercolors of Acoma shows the trail that he probably climbed, known as Burro Trail, Horse Trail, or Padre's Trail. It begins on the west side and swings around the mesa, approaching the top from the south-southwest, through spectacular formations in the red sandstone caprock (plate 12). In Kern's day this was the most gradual ascent. Today a paved road leads to the mesa top, and the old Burro Trail is closed to outsiders because the Acomans regard the ground it occupies as sacred. Kern's third watercolor offers a handsome view through an archway in the red sandstone at the bottom of the west side of the mesa, where Burro Trail begins (plate 13). As he did so often, Kern placed a few people in the scene to add interest and to suggest the enormity of the rocks.

Kern was not the first American artist to draw Acoma. Lt. J. W. Abert of the topographical engineers had sketched it in 1846, and lithographs based on his sketches had already appeared in a government report by 1848 (fig. 72). Kern was familiar with the Abert re-

Fig. 72. *Acoma no. 3.* Lithograph based on a drawing by James W. Abert. *Report of Lieut. J. W. Abert of His Examination of New Mexico* (Washington, D.C., 1848). (Compare with Richard Kern's *Acoma,* plate 12.)

port, and Abert's perspective might have influenced Kern to draw two views that were remarkably similar to his.[14]

From Laguna, Sumner and Sitgreaves proceeded toward Zuni over a route just south of the trail Kern had followed in 1849. Sumner took a new road, Kern said, built by Pueblos from Zuni, Acoma, and Laguna for the visit of Bishop José Antonio Laureano de Zubiría in 1850, and called the Camino del Obispo. It took them through lava fields, over the pine-forested Zuni Mountains, and past Inscription Rock, where the ever-inquisitive Kern paused to explore the box canyon in the heart of the great peñol. On the north side of the rock, about three feet from where he had chiseled his name in 1849, he carved "R. H. Kern/ Aug. 29/ 1851." Then, on the northeast face of El Morro, along with Sitgreaves and Woodhouse, Kern scratched his name into the rock a third time.[15]

The next day the journey continued without incident, but that evening, on the Ojo del Río Pescado, just a day out of Zuni, the camp was thrown into panic. "Our chief arriero Joaquin came into camp," Kern wrote in his journal, "and said the Navajos had ran off all our mules except two. Here was a row. Old Bull had the assembly blown, and all the animals were picketed within the command." The next morning, however, they managed to retrieve most of the animals. Wolves, rather than Navajos, had apparently spooked the herders, who had hurried toward camp and let the mules wander off.[16]

On August 31 they pushed on to the edge of Zuni, then entered the pueblo the next day. Sumner remained at Zuni for only a few hours, long enough to meet with Indian leaders, then headed north "to give the Navajos the devil," as Kern put it. Instead, the Navajos bedeviled Sumner. Although he managed to march into Canyon de Chelly, Sumner failed to "chastise" the Navajos. To his annoyance, the Indians refused to fight directly, but wounded and intimidated his men with guerrilla tactics. Alarmed by the implications of what seemed to be thousands of campfires on the rim of Canyon de Chelly, Sumner silently retreated from the canyon in the dead of night. By October 1, the tough-talking colonel was back in Albuquerque, his major accomplishment having been the establishment of a military post, Fort Defiance, isolated in the heart of Navajo country.[17]

While Sumner pursued the Navajos in vain, a frustrated Sitgreaves lost valuable time and rations waiting at Zuni for a military escort. Sumner had assigned Maj. Henry Lane Kendrick, with thirty artillerymen, to accompany Sitgreaves to the Colorado. Kendrick knew the country as well as any officer, having served in Colonel Washington's 1849 Navajo expedition, where he and Kern apparently had come into frequent contact. The two shared an interest in science. Following his graduation from West Point in 1835, Kendrick had stayed on at the Academy as professor of chemistry, mineralogy, and geology, until he was called into active service

by the outbreak of war with Mexico. Before the escort could join Sitgreaves, however, Kendrick had orders to help establish the new post at Fort Defiance. Thus, instead of leaving Zuni on September 5, as planned, the explorers waited at Zuni for Kendrick's return.[18]

During the delay at Zuni, Kern tried to take care of unfinished business back in Santa Fe. He asked Horace Dickinson to run some errands that included delivering a message to his landlady, collecting $102 from the territorial treasurer, Charles Blummer, and looking for a misplaced sketchbook. Dickinson searched Kern's usual haunts in Santa Fe, but to no avail. Later that fall the sketchbook turned up in Jacob Spiegelberg's store, where "some of his clerks, thinking it some book of the store, laid it away."[19] Joe Ellis found it and sent it on to Philadelphia. Dick also wrote from Zuni to the Indian agent in Santa Fe, John Greiner, asking him to try to locate the bodies of his brother and Old Bill Williams, to give them a decent burial, and to recover the Kerns' missing property. Dick had "got well acquainted" with Greiner in Santa Fe, and thought him "a fine old sensible fellow."[20] Notwithstanding Dick's confidence in him, Greiner was unable to go up the Rio Grande that fall, for lack of a military escort. In the winter Greiner became ill and still could not make the trip, but he told Kern that he hoped to go in the spring.[21]

The delay at Zuni also gave Kern an opportunity to sketch. Several lithographs based on Kern's drawings at Zuni

Fig. 73. *Buffalo Dance, Pueblo de Zuñi, N.M.* Lithograph based on a drawing by Richard H. Kern. Lorenzo Sitgreaves, *Report of an Expedition down the Zuni and Colorado Rivers* (Washington, D.C., 1853).

that autumn constitute some of his best known work, and are of historical and ethnographical as well as of artistic interest.

Three of the lithographs of Kern's drawings show Zunis performing what Kern called the Buffalo Dance—known today as the Tablita Dance and named for the small, decorated boards, or *tablas*, the women dancers wore on their heads. Kern's is the first, and perhaps the only, artist's depiction of this seldom-performed dance (figs. 73, 74, 75).[22] Although his rendering (or the

Fig. 74. *Zuñi Indian (Buffalo Dance).* Lithograph based on a drawing by Richard H. Kern. Lorenzo Sitgreaves, *Report of an Expedition down the Zuni and Colorado Rivers* (Washington, D.C., 1853).

Fig. 75. *Zuñi Indian Woman (Buffalo Dance).* Lithograph based on a drawing by Richard H. Kern. Lorenzo Sitgreaves, *Report of an Expedition down the Zuni and Colorado Rivers* (Washington, D.C., 1853).

lithographer's) of the human form was clumsy, Kern paid considerable attention to the details of Zuni costumes and accoutrements. In his diary and in his sketchbook, for example, Kern drew preliminary studies of the poses of male and female dancers, together with de-tails of their different wrist bands and headdresses, noting the colors and materials of which they were made (fig. 76). A comparison of Kern's verbal description of the dancers with the three lithographs based on his sketches further demonstrates Kern's attention to

Fig. 76. Field sketches of Zuni dancers. Richard H. Kern. Courtesy, Fred W. Cron.

detail and suggests why his work is valued by ethnologists.[23]

Kern witnessed the Tablita Dance on Sunday, September 7, and wrote the following in his diary:

Today the expected dances came off. The day of Col. Sumner's arrival they had the same dance, but as Pablo Pino, the governor, could not witness it, he ordered them to make the dance over for him, and this was the day solicited. There was a sort of east and west end rivalry, or rather a contest between that part of the Pueblo living in front of the church and that living in the rear. The former danced the San Domingo dance. The males were naked except from the middle to the knees and this covering consisted of scarfs and other woolen fabric of Moqui [Hopi] manufacture. Many of them had the skin of the silver fox dangling behind. Pine or cedar tufts were fastened about the waist, and above the elbow. The body & legs were smeared with yellow or pink earth. Some had hands impressed on the bodies. The hair was unbound from the usual queue and suffered to fall over the back & shoulders. It was most frequently cut into three ridges or layers—and yellow dyed feathers fastened to the crown of the head. Red and white beads were strung around the neck and different colored yarn also. In the right hand a gourd with seed or small stones was held, and in the left some twigs of pine. The gourds were shaken briskly. . . .

The women were dressed in their usual every day dress of the black woolen but . . . each one had a white tilma joined at[?] corners on the left breast, and allowed to fall as gracefully as it could over either arm. Corral [sic] beads and yarn were around the neck, whilst they had[?] to each wrist a bunch of yarn. Some wore moccasins & some were barefooted, but

all had tops worked with porcupine quills. The head dress was the funniest of all and was called the tabla or board. It consisted of a thin plane piece of wood about a foot in height and 3 or 4 inches wider than the head with a circular place cut in the bottom for the head to fit on. It was painted all in colors but mostly blue, white & red & the tops hacked into different forms. Some had birds on top and some crosses[?] and spears cut out of the wood. Below this was a tuft of yellow feathers then[?] to this were a quantity of part[?] colored ribbons.

Three other lithographs based on sketches Kern did at Zuni show Pueblos at work: a man weaving (fig. 77), four women grinding corn (fig. 78), and two men at the forge (fig. 79). In all of these representations, Kern seemed concerned with depicting the details of daily life, such as clothing styles, pottery, baskets, wall adornments, and architectural detail. Kern's view of two apron-clad smiths is unique in this regard, constituting, according to one study, "our only pictoral representation of a blacksmith shop furnished with Spanish equipment."[24] Kern's blacksmith drawing is also of historical value as the sole piece of documentary evidence that smiths worked at Zuni at this early date.

Kern did other sketches at Zuni that never found their way into Sitgreaves's report.[25] Some of them remain in Kern's sketchbooks and others are lost, but Kern's wash drawings of anthropomorphic and zoomorphic water jars were preserved and rendered into lithographs for Henry Schoolcraft's report

Fig. 77. *Indian Weaving (Pueblo Zuñi).* Lithograph based on a drawing by Richard H. Kern. Lorenzo Sitgreaves, *Report of an Expedition down the Zuni and Colorado Rivers* (Washington, D.C., 1853). Kern's field sketch is fig. 144.

Fig. 78. *Women Grinding Corn.* Lithograph based on a drawing by Richard H. Kern. Lorenzo Sitgreaves, *Report of an Expedition down the Zuni and Colorado Rivers* (Washington, D.C., 1853).

Fig. 79. *Indian Blacksmith Shop (Pueblo Zuñi).* Lithograph based on a drawing by Richard H. Kern. Lorenzo Sitgreaves, *Report of an Expedition down the Zuni and Colorado Rivers* (Washington, D.C., 1853). For Kern's field sketches, see figs. 145 and 146.

on American Indians (fig. 117). The Schoolcraft report also contained a splendid view of Zuni by Seth Eastman, based upon a sketch that Kern drew "from the southeastern angle of the plaza in which the church is situated" (fig. 116).[26]

One of the finest pieces of work that Kern did at Zuni has never before been published or exhibited; this watercolor constitutes the only known view of the interior of the Zuni chapel prior to its deterioration in the last century (plate 14). Kern mistitled his work the *Iglesia de San Miguel,* instead of Guadalupe, but his painting conforms in general to a disparaging verbal description of the church's interior made by Lieutenant Simpson in 1849: "A miserable painting of *Nuestra Señora de Guadalupe* and a couple of statues garnish the walls back of the chancel. The walls elsewhere are perfectly bare."[27] Zuni had no resident priest, and visiting priests

Fig. 80. Field sketch of the archangels Michael (with shield) and Gabriel (with fish). Richard H. Kern. Courtesy, Fred W. Cron.

Fig. 81. Field sketch of the altar screen at Zuni. Pencil and watercolor by Richard H. Kern. Courtesy, Fred W. Cron.

performed services very infrequently. In the intervals between those visits, the Zunis apparently maintained the chapel's interior, apparently leaving a colorful cloth on the altar, unless Kern added it to his painting for artistic effect. Six years after Kern's visit to Zuni, Edward Fitzgerald Beale passed through the pueblo and found the church in ruins, "but a picture over the altar attracted our attention from the beauty of four small medallion paintings in each corner, which were very beautifully done. After much rubbing off the mud and dust we made out that it was painted by Miguel somebody in 1701."[28]

Kern's beautiful watercolor focuses on the carved and painted baroque wooden altar screen that frames the Virgin of Guadalupe, whose form he only suggests. Kern did not attempt to sketch the statues of the archangels Michael and Gabriel, which flanked the Virgin, although he did field sketches of them (fig. 80), as well as of the altar screen (fig. 81). Kern's heretofore unknown field sketches of the altar screen and the archangels are "of major documentary value," according to a leading authority on the religious art of New Mexico. The statues of the archangels, carved by the celebrated Bernardo Miera y Pacheco, have survived, but have been damaged. Kern's field sketches show how they once looked. San Miguel is now missing the wings and arms that Kern depicts. Kern's watercolor field sketch of the altar screen, or *retablo,* is of interest for several reasons. It shows, for example, the archangel Gabriel standing

free in front of the carved column, or *estipite,* rather than in a niche customarily constructed for that purpose. This suggests that the archangels were reused from an earlier retablo, and that the new altar screen was not designed to accommodate them.[29]

From what appears at first to be an improbable source in the roof, light bathes the altar in Kern's watercolor of the interior of the chapel at Zuni. The source of light was in fact a transverse clerestory window, located between two levels of the roof of the nave. According to one historian,

> nowhere was this feature developed so fully or used so effectively as in the missions of New Mexico . . . the effect was more than satisfactory. It was theatrical. Peering down the long tunnellike nave from the doorway, the viewer focused immediately on the stream of light descending like the Dove. . . .[30]

By September 20, the military escort of thirty artillerymen under Major Kendrick had returned from the Navajo country and the expedition could get underway, but an accident had befallen Dr. Woodhouse that caused further delay.[31] Woodhouse, who served as both naturalist and physician for the expedition, had been bitten on a finger of his left hand while trying to capture a rattlesnake a couple of miles from Zuni, on September 17. The physician tried to heal himself with the standard remedy. He applied a ligature, lacerated the wound, and sucked out the venom. Meanwhile, Kern had learned about the accident and had traveled out from Zuni

Fig. 82. Samuel Washington Woodhouse, M.D., dressed in buckskin pants, ca. 1852. Photograph. Courtesy, Museum of Northern Arizona, Flagstaff.

to find Woodhouse. Kern recommended a stronger cure, telling Woodhouse to "try the western remedy; that is to say, to get drunk." This, Woodhouse said, was a treatment "I had often heard of, and, determined to try its efficacy."[32] By the time that he reached Zuni, Woodhouse had downed a half pint of whiskey (presumably delivered by Kern), along with some strong ammonia water, but "it took a quart of fourth-proof brandy, besides the whiskey, to produce intoxication." Whether because of, or in spite of, the "Western remedy," Woodhouse recovered. He had to keep his arm in a sling until mid-November, however, and the loss of the use of one hand limited his ability to gather specimens. For that, he depended heavily upon his trail companions, Kern probably among them.[33]

Kern and Woodhouse seem to have become friends on this expedition. The two men shared a common background and interests. Like Kern, Woodhouse came from Philadelphia and was also a member of the Academy of Natural Sciences (fig. 82). Membership in that small circle of men with scientific interests had probably brought them together in Philadelphia. If not, they had certainly become acquainted in Santa Fe. By the time he arrived in Santa Fe, Woodhouse, like Kern, was a veteran western traveler. He had served under Sitgreaves as physician and naturalist on a survey of the Creek boundary in Oklahoma, in 1849, and on a subsequent government expedition in Texas.[34]

By September 24, Woodhouse had

recovered enough to travel, and the Sit-greaves expedition officially got under-way. It would prove more perilous than anyone had imagined. Two months later, with two men dead, two men wounded, their food gone, and most of their mules lost, the bedraggled remnants of the expedition would stagger into a small military post near Yuma on the lower Colorado River. But the reconnaissance that would end so badly began auspi-ciously, with the men in high spirits. Woodhouse noted in his diary that they had pitched their tents right in the Pueblo:

> Much rejoiced were we all to leave this dirty place and once more to get on the road where we could breathe the fresh air, for living in an Indian pueblo is any-thing but agreeable. The atmosphere is strongly impregnated with all kinds [of] nauseous perfumes.[35]

Kern himself wrote from Zuni to a friend that his duty with Sitgreaves was "very pleasant; serving in the field being much more congenial to my semi savage hab-its than living in a civilized commu-nity."[36]

On mule back, the party moved out from Zuni over a much-used trail that followed the Zuni River through corn-fields and peach orchards. Just as he had done on the Frémont expedition, Kern kept a sketchbook and made daily entries in a diary, often describing the route and the day's activities in greater detail than Sitgreaves would do in his published report.[37] Four day's travel brought them to the Little Colorado on September 27. Near camp that after-noon, "in a beautiful little canyon," Kern sketched two members of the expedi-tion posing atop what Kern called Ler-oux Island in the middle of the Little Colorado (fig. 83), where the river flowed through "a broad bottom about half a mile wide & filled with rushes."[38]

At the Little Colorado they left the well-marked trail they had been fol-lowing, for it turned southerly toward the Salt River. With Leroux and some Mexican arrieros guiding him, Sit-greaves continued westward, following the Little Colorado. It was tough going. At times the river disappeared into steep-walled canyons they could not follow, and there always seemed to be another arroyo or stream to cross—sometimes rocky and sometimes sandy, but always requiring the monotonous yet taxing efforts to move animals up hill and down hill, up and down. Kern's terse journal entry of September 30 suggests the na-ture of travel on a day in which they covered eleven miles. On this day, as he would on other occasions, Kern went ahead of the main party with the guide, Antoine Leroux:

> Left at 7:30 with Leroux. Passed small rocky arroyo and at 8:50 descended into bottom near pile of rocks . . . passed fine spring, the spring jumping down the big rocks to our left. Bottom good & hemmed in on north by rocky hills jutting out into it in rocky points of red & white sandstone. At 9:15 came to bad arroyo. At 10:10 passed little point and bore toward dark line of timber. The river some little distance to the left enters quite a cañon of white sand stone. After trav-

Fig. 83. *Leroux Island—Little Colorado River, near Camp 4.* Lithograph based on a drawing by Richard H. Kern. Lorenzo Sitgreaves, *Report of an Expedition down the Zuni and Colorado Rivers* (Washington, D.C., 1853).

eling along the edge until 11:10 and not finding a place to descend we bore more to the n.w. and at 11:45 crossed the river . . . the banks steep. River bottom hard & rocky, water pleasant tasted but red in color—passed over top of cañon and at 1:35 descended into hollow & made camp . . . we are hemmed in all around by rocky hills.

From camp that afternoon, Kern sketched "the solitary cone of Cañon Peak—a lovely looking object having none of its kind near" (fig. 84). Cañon Peak, which had served as a landmark

for the party for several days, is about a dozen miles southeast of modern Holbrook, and is today called Woodruff Butte.[39]

For the next few days they followed the Little Colorado westward. The view from high ridges revealed the winding river stretched before them, its course "strongly marked by its skirts of cotton[wood] trees," beginning to turn yellow with the first chill of autumn. To the south, Kern noted, "way off in the distance and barely distinguishable

Fig. 84. *Cañon Peak from Camp 7.* Lithograph based on a drawing by Richard H. Kern. Lorenzo Sitgreaves, *Report of an Expedition down the Zuni and Colorado Rivers* (Washington, D.C., 1853).

from the haze was the long and many peaked range of the big Mogoyone," the Mogollon Rim, that stretches across some two hundred miles of today's eastern Arizona (fig. 85). Ahead of them, on the far horizon, San Francisco Mountain could be seen, "looming up nearly due west and so far off that it seemed like a dream," Kern wrote in his diary on October 1. By the end of the next day, the dream became sufficiently real for Kern to sketch the *Valley of the Little Colorado River, and San Francisco Moun-*

tain (fig. 86). The mountain, which Kern correctly described as "extremely symetrical [*sic*]," drew closer every day.

Depending on conditions, they traveled ten to fifteen miles a day, making camp by midday at watering places along the river. On October 2, for example, they camped on Chevelon's Fork, named for "a trapper who poisoned himself . . . by eating wild parsnip." Kern, who apparently picked this story up from Leroux, said that Chevelon had been buried up the fork at the foot of Chevelon

Fig. 85. *Sierra Mogollon from near Camp 4.* Lithograph based on a drawing by Richard H. Kern. Lorenzo Sitgreaves, *Report of an Expedition down the Zuni and Colorado Rivers* (Washington, D.C., 1853).

Butte. The next day they found another good campsite, on Big Dry Fork (today's East Clear Creek), which Kern described as "Full of water."

Day after day as they pushed west, the artist doubled as scientist. Although Sitgreaves described Kern as the expedition's "draughtsman," Kern was much more than that. In a letter to a friend, Kern characterized his position as that of an assistant engineer, and he did not exaggerate when he told his brother, "I am astronomer and obser-

vation star selector for the Expedition."[40] To carry out these tasks, Kern had to read instruments whose use he might have learned on the Navajo expedition. With a sextant, an undependable pocket chronometer, a box chronometer that stopped from time to time, and trigonometic formulas that he had practiced using in Santa Fe, Kern calculated the latitude and longitude along the way. He also determined altitudes, directions, and distances, and made detailed drawings of the moun-

Fig. 86. *Valley of the Little Colorado River, and San Francisco Mountain*, lithograph based on a drawing by Richard H. Kern. Lorenzo Sitgreaves, *Report of an Expedition down the Zuni and Colorado Rivers* (Washington, D.C., 1853).

tains, valleys, and camping places along the route. Now a veteran mapmaker, Kern would use his field notes to draw the map that would accompany Sitgreaves's final report.[41] In addition to his topographical work, Kern also served as the expedition's meteorologist. Daily he recorded the temperature, described weather conditions and clouds, and measured the atmospheric pressure with two aneroid barometers.[42] He also made pencil and pen-and-ink sketches of a number of Indian petroglyphs along the

Little Colorado. These did not appear as illustrations for Sitgreaves's report, but Kern would later put them to good use.[43]

Kern continued to collect specimens of flora and fauna, as he had done on the Frémont expedition, but the extent of his collecting is not clear. We do know that upon return home he donated an example of a new species of squirrel, found on San Francisco Mountain, in central Arizona, to the Philadelphia Academy of Natural Sciences.[44]

Kern probably also assisted the expedition's physician and naturalist, Samuel Washington Woodhouse, in gathering specimens of plants and animals. Despite his injured hand, Woodhouse managed to collect an impressive number of specimens, including some species that he regarded as new—a squirrel, two birds, two types of pouched rats, and several reptiles. Richard Kern's drawings of a few of these animals would appear in Sitgreaves's published *Report*.[45]

As the nights grew colder and the pack mules more weary and saddlesore, a week of travel brought the expedition to Grand Falls, about sixteen miles northwest of present-day Sunrise, Arizona. Although Sitgreaves is sometimes credited with discovering Grand Falls, it seems clear from Kern's diary that the Mexican arrieros already knew of their existence. Moreover, Joe Walker had passed by the falls earlier that year and had told Kern about them. Kern, however, drew the first known sketch of what he termed the *Cascade of the Little Colorado* (fig. 87), when he rode out from camp at dawn on October 8 to see them. "It is a stupendous sight," he wrote in his diary. "First come the rapids (as though like an animal it was preparing for a jump by preparatory runs), then a leap of about 40 feet another gathering up and the last leap of fifty feet. . . . Below the fall the river goes into an immense canyon." Actually, the Grand Falls are higher than Kern supposed, dropping a total of 185 feet, or nearly 20 feet more than Niagara Falls. Kern was fortunate to see them at all. Except in the rainy season of late summer, the falls are usually dry.[46]

Downstream from Grand Falls, Sitgreaves learned from Leroux, the Little Colorado flowed into the Grand Canyon. To proceed farther along the Little Colorado seemed both hazardous and foolhardy, for supplies were running low and their progress would surely be impaired in the deep canyons. Thus, Sitgreaves decided to take Leroux's advice to strike out to the west, hoping to hit the Colorado beyond the Grand Canyon and then backtrack upriver.

Beyond the Little Colorado the high plateau country became parched, so Sitgreaves headed toward the north slope of San Francisco Mountain, above present Flagstaff, in the hope of finding water. For several days they encountered the ruins of multistoried houses, similar, Kern thought, to those he had seen at Chaco. In some places pot sherds lay scattered on the surface of the ground. Today, the best known of these ruins is the great three-story apartment structure called Wupatki, which gave its name to a national monument created in 1924. Although the Sitgreaves expedition is credited with the discovery of this important archaeological site, Spanish explorers, Mexican traders, and American trappers had surely visited the ruins. Kern, however, was the first to depict them. His drawing, simply entitled *Ruined Pueblos* (fig. 88), approximates a portion of the major ruin at today's Wupatki National Monu-

Fig. 87. Untitled drawing of Grand Falls. Richard H. Kern, 1851. Courtesy, Fred W. Cron. Reproduced as a lithograph entitled *Cascade of the Little Colorado River, near Camp 13,* in Lorenzo Sitgreaves, *Report of an Expedition down the Zuni and Colorado Rivers* (Washington, D.C., 1853). See fig. 135.

ment. Lonely and forlorn atop a rocky knoll, the red sandstone ruins are all that remain of a community of Indians known to archaeologists as Sinagua, who abandoned their villages in the thirteenth century. Kern's hunch that "the desertion of their Pueblos can be accounted for by the failure of the water in that vicinity," remains the most plausible explanation. There is no evi-dence that Kern measured and sketched floor plans at Wupatki, as he had done at Chaco two years before.[47]

As Sitgreaves pushed toward San Francisco Mountain, he sent Leroux ahead to scout for a watering place. Leroux found water, but he also found Indians—either "Tontos or Yampais," Kern reported. The Indians, who had been gathering piñón nuts, fled at the

Fig. 88. Untitled drawing of ruins at Wupatki. Richard H. Kern. Courtesy, Fred W. Cron. Reproduced as a lithograph entitled *Ruined Pueblos,* in Lorenzo Sitgreaves, *Report of an Expedition down the Zuni and Colorado Rivers* (Washington, D.C., 1853). See fig. 143.

sight of the strangers. Leroux then permitted the Mexicans who were with him to enter the Indians' abandoned camp and take baskets, mescal (probably the sweet, bread-like roasted roots of the agave), bread made from mesquite beans, "and other things as trophies." Sitgreaves apparently reprimanded Leroux for allowing this to happen; for a while thereafter the American intruders attempted to treat Indians with greater courtesy.

Not wanting to challenge Indians for control of the watering place Leroux had found, Sitgreaves instead ordered that the mules, who had gone without water for two days, be sent back to the Little Colorado. They returned that same evening, October 10, well watered and bearing kegs and rubber bags full of

Fig. 89. *View Looking West, from Camp 16.* Lithograph based on a drawing by Richard H. Kern. Lorenzo Sitgreaves, *Report of an Expedition down the Zuni and Colorado Rivers* (Washington, D.C., 1853).

water. The next morning the expedition pushed on, climbing the northern flanks of San Francisco Mountain (fig. 89), under a brilliant autumn sky, through groves of quaking aspen. "Their white trunks and yellowed leaves," Kern exclaimed, "gave one an idea of a newly whitewashed room—so light everything seemed." Two waterless days along the western slope of the mountain brought them to a spring near present Flagstaff, known today as Leroux

Springs.[48] Here they halted for two more days, to rest the mules and reshoe them. On October 15, they resumed travel, but had to stop again for four days when an arriero, Inocencio Valdez, became ill, apparently as a result of a blow delivered in a fight with a man named Ortega. Valdez's condition deteriorated steadily, and on October 20 he died and was buried at sunset.[49]

Gloom settled over the camp. In addition to the death of Valdez, "Old Juan de Dios" was missing and presumed dead. He had failed to return from a hunting trip, and Kern imagined that either a bear had killed Old Juan or that he was murdered by Yampais, "skulking behind trees and grasping him as he passed by and then killing him." To add to the gloom, Sitgreaves had taken advantage of the delay to do an inventory of provisions and found that they had enough to last only another twenty-five days. One man dead, another missing, and the prospect of running out of food—the situation apparently reminded Kern of the Frémont disaster. "The feelings of old times came over me," he confided to his diary the evening that Valdez died. Juan de Dios turned up near camp the next day, but there would soon be other reasons to remind Kern of old times.

On October 21 they continued moving westward toward the Big Colorado, into a country that Kern said "is very appropriately called by the trappers 'hell,' on account of its volcanic rock, & numerous deep & rugged cañons. . . ." From their campsite that evening, "on a kind of peninsula about 1½ miles wide & bounded on 3 sides by two immense cañons," Kern made a sketch of one of those canyons—probably what is today called Sycamore Canyon (fig. 90).[50] As he did from time to time, Kern took notes in his diary that would help him paint the scene at a later date:

> The view only towards the South is worth looking at. There an immense cañon stretches out towards the San Francisco River, and bounded by distant Mts. The effect was very fine, the west side in deep blue shade with sharp jutty points—on the east side the sunlight fell on a rich compound of bright yellow [illegible] a green, carmine & gray. . . .

That evening Kern also drew what Sitgreaves called "a singular cedar . . . with wide-spreading branches, and the bark, several inches thick, is corrugated" (fig. 91).

After three days of travel, by the afternoon of October 23, they had left the mountainous country and had entered an area of high, dry tablelands. Now behind them, San Francisco Mountain "loomed up almost as blue-symetric [sic] as when we first saw it," Kern noted. They made camp that afternoon on a stream that Leroux identified as Williams Fork, and that appeared by that name on the Parke-Kern map of 1851. "The branch receives its name from Old Bill Williams," Kern recorded in his diary. "Leroux says he met him at the mouth . . . in 1837. Old Bill had travelled down it in 3 days & then in 3 more had struck over to the Colorado." Bill Williams Fork, or Bill Williams River, remains on maps today, but it was not as lengthy a stream as Kern supposed. On the map that accompanied Sitgreaves's report, Kern put the headwaters of Williams Fork within forty miles of present-day Flagstaff, with its source in Bill Williams Mountain (a name that first appears on the Sitgreaves map and that has endured to this day). In actuality, Williams Fork is much shorter, originating some thirty miles from the Colorado,

Fig 90. *View of Canon near Camp 39 {19}*. Lithograph based on a drawing by Richard H. Kern. Lorenzo Sitgreaves, *Report of an Expedition down the Zuni and Colorado Rivers* (Washington, D.C., 1853).

at the confluence of the Big Sandy and the Santa Maria, and entering the Colorado just above today's Parker Dam.

On October 23, then, Leroux was mistaken in assuming they had reached Bill Williams Fork, whose name Kern helped preserve for posterity. Instead, the explorers were on the spring-fed upper end of Hell Canyon, just south of Bill Williams Mountain. Their error in placing Williams Fork too far east would cause some confusion for the next group to make a reconnaissance of the area.[51]

Sitgreaves hoped to explore up the Colorado River. When the stream he believed to be Williams Fork led him toward the southwest, he left it and continued west by northwest, hoping to strike the Colorado near the Grand Canyon. Once away from the river, however, water was scarce.

On October 27, they "struck an In-

Fig. 91. *Juniperus Plochyderma (Rough Barked Cedar), (Torrey) Camp 19.* Lithograph based on a drawing by Richard H. Kern. Lorenzo Sitgreaves, *Report of an Expedition down the Zuni and Colorado Rivers* (Washington, D.C., 1853).

dian trail with fresh moccasin tracks," Kern noted, and "then came suddenly upon a lodge of Yampais." This was as close as the main party had come to Indians since leaving Zuni, but Kern had no reason for apprehension. The Indians—apparently women, children, and an elderly man—ran at the sight of the intruders (fig. 92). Leroux and Juan de Dios seized the old man and forced him to lead the party's mules to

water. Kern, in the meantime, entered the Indians' camp:

> They left everything—having not yet recovered from their fright. They had arrows, bows, straw baskets (waterproof), metates, antelope heads, antelope skins, seed of the Belle Dame[?], mezcal, tools for making arrows, arrow points, paints &c, &c.

As he often did, Kern took careful notes and made some sketches, apparently to jog his memory at a later date. He displayed no illusions, however, about the "noble savage." Quite the contrary, as this notation from his diary indicates:

> [The Yampais] were extraordinary looking objects—small in stature—the old man with a remnant of red paint on his idiotic face and no covering but the breech clout. The woman was a disgusting looking beast. Any mop was well combed in comparison to her hair and the upper part of her face painted black. She had on the remnant of a navajo blanket and altogether they approach more the Ourang Ourang [orangutan] than any of the genus homo I have seen.

The Yampais of whom Kern wrote so disparagingly were probably Havasupai, a group of Yuman-speaking Pai people who planted, hunted, and gathered crops seasonally over a large area of the Colorado Plateau. Their contact with Spanish-Mexicans had been infrequent, and usually indirect. Although American trappers and Mexican traders had moved through the Havasupai territory, in the 1820s and 1830s, the Sitgreaves expedition was the first to record an encounter with these Indians or to describe them. A lithograph in Sitgreaves' published report, based on a drawing by Richard Kern, provided the American public with the first graphic image of these remarkable people, who live today at the bottom of the Grand Canyon, on a 518–acre reservation (fig. 93).[52]

The springs near the Yampais camp were poor. The Americans spent part

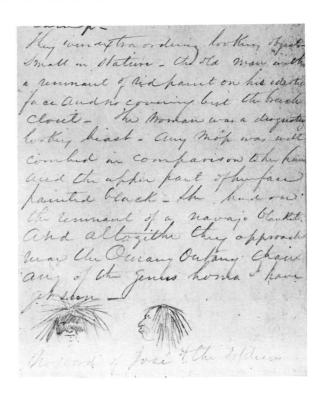

Fig. 92. Field sketch of "Yampais" Indians. Richard H. Kern. Diary, entry of October 27, 1851. Courtesy, Huntington Library.

Fig. 93. *Yampai Indians.* Lithograph based on a drawing by Richard H. Kern. Lorenzo Sitgreaves, *Report of an Expedition down the Zuni and Colorado Rivers* (Washington, D.C., 1853).

of October 28 trying to find enough water for their mules and hoping for rain. Clouds had appeared daily, but disappointed them. "It seems impossible for it to rain in this miserable country where every thing appears to be your enemy and is armed with a thorn or a poisonous sting," Dr. Woodhouse lamented in his diary.[53] Failing to find water, they pushed on, sending Leroux ahead to scout. "Should Leroux return without news of water, the prospect ahead is bad enough. We will have to leave everything," Kern noted, "take the strongest mules to pack provisions and try it afoot." But Leroux brought back good news. Yampais told him of water ahead, and two days later, on October 30, the expedition made camp near a stream lined with cottonwoods that Kern called the "Rito de los Yampais" (fig. 94). Today it bears a more prosaic name—Truxton Wash.

Here, on November 1, they met the first resistance from Indians. "A little after breakfast," according to Kern, "the guard brought in an Indian, one of a party of four that was skulking about the camp." The Indian identified himself as a "Cosnino," probably a name for another group of Pai people, members of the Cerbat or Walapai Mountain band.[54] As the captive began reluctantly to give information to the Americans, an altercation ensued, involving his three companions. One Indian was wounded, but all escaped. The fray left the Americans feeling less charitable toward Indians. When the expedition set out again, on Sunday morning, November 2, they butchered one of the mules killed in the scuffle and left the meat behind in their camp, along with biscuits. These had "plenty of arsenic in them in hopes that some of the Indians may get them," Kern noted matter-of-factly in his diary.

If the arsenic had any ill effect, it was not on the Indians they encountered the next day. A little after noon, while climbing a small range, Kern, Sitgreaves, and Woodhouse had stopped at a spring to rest. Then, as Woodhouse told it, they heard "a shrill yell followed by the report of a rifle." Woodhouse turned to Sitgreaves to ask about the noise, "when Mr. Kern saw Mr. Leroux coming and exclaimed Watkin [Leroux] is shot."[55] As Kern recalled in his diary, "I saw Leroux running down from some rocks to the north, his rifle on his shoulder and [an] arrow in his hand." Leroux, who had gone ahead to scout, had walked into an ambush. He had suffered a glancing wound to the head, but another arrow had penetrated

Fig. 94. *On El Rito de los Yampais.* Sketch by Richard H. Kern. Diary, entry of October 31, 1851. Courtesy, Huntington Library.

173

Fig. 95. *Cosnina Indians.* Lithograph based on a drawing by Richard H. Kern. Lorenzo
Sitgreaves, *Report of an Expedition down the Zuni and Colorado Rivers* (Washington, D.C., 1853).

his forearm and left him disabled for the remainder of the journey. The arrowhead was imbedded so deeply in the bone that Dr. Woodhouse bent his forceps trying to extract it.[56] But Leroux had saved the expedition, in Kern's opinion:

> Had not Leroux drawn them from their abuscade, we might have received considerable damage from them as we not knowing of their proximity, would not have been as cautious, and they could easily have picked off the struggling men & mules. He hastened the crisis and saved us.

The Indians, perhaps of the same group that had been in their camp two days before, continued to threaten and taunt them, but did not attack the main party. Sometime during these encounters, Kern did a sketch of three *Cosnina Indians,* armed with bows and arrows, poised beside an ocotillo—the first known drawing of these Pai people (fig. 95).

Shaken and apprehensive, the ex-

Fig. 96. *Mountain Pass, Near Camp 31.* Lithograph based on a drawing by Richard H. Kern. Lorenzo Sitgreaves, *Report of an Expedition down the Zuni and Colorado Rivers* (Washington, D.C., 1853).

plorers continued on through the parched, rugged country (fig. 96). Two days after Leroux was wounded, on November 5, they crossed Union Pass through the Black Mountains, and the Colorado River finally came into view. "Balboa at his first sight of the Pacific," Kern exclaimed, "did not experience greater pleasure than our party—for we had a certainty of life for our mules. All cause of anxiety on account of water immediately vanished and three hearty cheers were given." Kern confided to his diary, however, that he was not as excited as some members of the party, for he had never doubted that they would soon reach the Colorado: "as Leroux said *positively* we would find it where we did, I knew such must be the case, for I never felt my confidence in his knowledge and judgment diminish." From the summit where they first saw the river, Kern did a dramatic sketch that he entitled *First View of the Big Colorado*

Fig. 97. *First View of the Big Colorado River from summit of mountain between Camps 31 and 32.* Lithograph based on a drawing by Richard H. Kern. Lorenzo Sitgreaves, *Report of an Expedition down the Zuni and Colorado Rivers* (Washington, D.C., 1853).

River (fig. 97). Before the day ended, they had made the rugged descent of the mountain and camped on the river, apparently near what is today Davis Dam, on the Nevada-Arizona border. While they spent a day resting their animals, Kern measured the width and depth of the river.

From this point, Sitgreaves's original plans called for the party to ascend the Colorado to the Grand Canyon, and to locate the mouth of the Virgin River.

But the mules were already exhausted and supplies were running low. The men had been on reduced rations for several days.[57] Instead of going north, then, Sitgreaves decided to turn south, toward a military post at the Yuma crossing of the Colorado, near the mouth of the Gila River, that they desperately hoped would still be there. Over the next twenty-four days they covered 243 anxious miles along the eastern side of the Colorado, sometimes passing through thick underbrush along the riverbottom and other times crossing through barren, rugged mountains. In addition to the natural obstacles that took a terrible toll on their mules, the tribes along the Colorado also let the visitors know that they were unwelcome.

Signs of Indian hostility appeared the first morning they started south. They had advanced only a few hundred yards from camp when they saw what Kern described as "a large and fresh drawing in the ground, which clearly said we must retrace our steps or they would kill us."

This ominous sign notwithstanding, the first Indians they encountered were friendly Mohaves, a Yuman-speaking group that had come, Kern said, to trade their pumpkins, beans, and corn. At least as early as 1604, Mohaves had had direct but infrequent contact with Spaniards, and since the 1820s Mexican traders and American trappers had passed through the Mohave Valley. None of these visitors left detailed descriptions, however, and anthropologists have wondered about the extent of Hispanic influence on Mohave culture by the time of the American takeover in 1848. Kern's notes suggest the existence of considerable Mexican and American influence in this remote area by the autumn of 1851. He noted that some of the Mohaves rode "beautiful California ponies." Instead of stirrups, they managed the animals with "a broad plait of rope, passing around the belly." Kern described one Mohave as looking "quite

fanciful, with a pair of goggles, Mexican soldier's jacket, and breech clout." Antoine Leroux, who had visited the Mohaves in 1837, remembered on his earlier visit that most of the men wore breechclouts made of willow bark, but now most were made of cloth. In general, Kern said, "their manner indicated they were quite used to Americans."[58]

The first graphic image of the Mohaves available to the public came from Richard Kern's pen, and appeared as a lithograph in Sitgreaves's *Report* (fig. 98).[59] The handsome appearance of the Mohaves in this drawing reflects Kern's high opinion of them, and conformed to his verbal description of the Mohave men as the largest "race" he had ever seen. They were "not only very tall but well formed," making the Yampais look "like pigmies in comparison."

Their hair is plaited in separate plaits & falls about half way between the shoulder & small of the back. They all had the breech clout. . . . This is the only article of clothing worn. . . . Some tattoo their faces & breasts in thin lines or dots; black paint is the most used and red is the only other color. . . . Some of them wear beads & pearls in the ear & nose and have buckskin cut in thongs and hung around the neck. The left or bow arm on many is guarded with leather ornamented with buttons & buckskin strap.

Kern described the Mohave women as

short and fat, and wear an apron of willow bark which is held around the middle by a piece of woolen fabric exposed in front but hidden behind by the apron

Fig. 98. *Mohave Indians, Big Colorado River, N.M.* Lithograph based on a drawing by Richard H. Kern. Lorenzo Sitgreaves, *Report of an Expedition down the Zuni and Colorado Rivers* (Washington, D.C., 1853).

falling over it. Their hair is worn shorter than the men's and some have their chins tattooed. They are very well developed, too.

For two days after their first encounter with Mohaves on the morning of November 7, relations between the two groups remained amicable. Some Mohaves served as guides, and others followed the strangers down the river, gathering in their camp in the evenings to trade. On November 9, Kern was awakened about four o'clock in the

morning, by a light rain. He rose, washed, and started to tie up his bedroll, when he heard Dr. Woodhouse yell, "Look out they are throwing their arrows in here, for I have one in my leg." Kern and other Americans went for their guns and returned the fire until the Mohaves stopped. "On returning to finish tying my bed," Kern laconically notes in his diary, "I found an arrow in it."

Kern conjectured that the Mohaves were angry because they had been forcibly evicted from the Americans' camp the evening before. Perhaps he was right; a few years after Sitgreaves's visit, one Mohave retained a vivid impression of the way Americans treated them: "The whites, when you come near them, push you away; they kick you. A woman, if she is kicked, cries."[60]

Kern was probably correct, too, in suggesting that the Indians "might easily have wiped us out." But luck was on the Americans' side. With arrows occasionally flying at them, Sitgreaves' party broke camp that morning and moved south for six days, traveling unmolested from the area of present-day Needles through the Chemehuevi Valley to the mouth of Bill Williams Fork, near today's Parker.

Along the way, on November 11, Kern did two sketches that evoke the inhospitable, mountainous terrain *On the Big Colorado River* (figs. 99 and 100). Both scenes appear to have been drawn in Blankenship Valley, just south of Mohave Rock. A prominent landmark, the rock appears bathed in light, on the right-hand side of the view Kern entitled *On the Big Colorado River near Camp 37. Looking North* (fig. 100). Today much of Mohave Rock is under the waters of Lake Havasu, created by the construction of Parker Dam. Kern's other view, from the same place, looks southwestward toward Blankenship Bend and the Chemehuevi Mountains of California (fig. 99). Beyond the bend, Sitgreaves's party would enter the Chemehuevi Valley.[61]

The going had become exceedingly rough. Kern considered one hill they ascended "perhaps the most difficult place we have encountered." At times, Sitgreaves wrote, they had to leave the river and take "long detours over naked cliffs of extreme acclivity," where they had to use ropes to pull their mules up and chip out stepping places in the rocks for the animals. On one occasion they watched horrified as a mule plunged to its death.[62]

They crossed Williams Fork on November 15, then the next day met a group of Quechans, another of the Yuman-speaking Colorado River tribes. One of the Quechans spoke "excellent Spanish." He knew of the American military post at the Yuma crossing and offered to guide them. Here Kern's diary ends abruptly, although he continued to sketch, to record latitude, longitude, and meteorological data for another week, and to take chronometer readings for two more weeks.[63]

Sitgreaves's report also becomes very terse at this point, reflecting perhaps the grim conditions under which they traveled for the next two weeks. Rations had finally given out, and the men were reduced to killing and eating their pack mules. Eating nothing but mule meat, "without condiments of any kind," caused most of the men, including Richard Kern, to suffer from diarrhea, Dr. Woodhouse reported. Some of the men also began to show symptoms of scurvy.[64] Without the mules, Sitgreaves said, they could no longer carry "the spare saddles, blankets, tents, ammunition, books, and whatever was not

Fig. 99. *On the Big Colorado River near Camp 37*. Lithograph based on a drawing by Richard H. Kern. Lorenzo Sitgreaves, *Report of an Expedition down the Zuni and Colorado Rivers* (Washington, D.C., 1853).

absolutely essential to our safety," and so destroyed them.[65] Among the books that Woodhouse had to discard were reference volumes on medicine, fauna, geology, mineralogy, and a Spanish dictionary. To his annoyance, Woodhouse also had to dispose of some of his birdshot to lighten the load.[66]

Tragedy and anxiety added to their suffering. A group of Quechans attacked the explorers on November 17,

clubbing to death one of the military escort, a Private Jones. The reason for this attack is not clear, but it is certain that the Quechans had had their fill of outsiders. Since 1849, hordes of California-bound gold seekers from Mexico and the United States had passed through Quechan lands, stealing crops or letting their animals trample and feed in the fields. Indians, in turn, had stolen from the travelers, and minor incidents

Fig. 100. *On the Big Colorado near Camp 37. Looking North.* Lithograph based on a drawing by Richard H. Kern. Lorenzo Sitgreaves, *Report of an Expedition down the Zuni and Colorado Rivers* (Washington, D.C., 1853).

had frequently erupted into violence. By the fall of 1851, when Sitgreaves's men entered their lands, the Quechans had joined in a plan to unite with neighboring tribes to expel all Americans from southern California. The Quechans did not take the offensive against Sitgreaves again, but signal fires reminded the Americans of the Indians' presence and kept the weakened party apprehensive. Moreover, the explorers remained uncertain as to what would await them at the mouth of the Gila. Should the military post no longer be there, Dr. Woodhouse wrote, "we will be in a sad condition."[67]

On November 29, Sitgreaves reached the mouth of the Gila, but Camp Yuma, which had stood on a bluff on the Colorado River across from the mouth of the Gila, had been abandoned. The post had been established the previous year, in November 1850, to protect immigrants at the essential Yuma crossing of the Colorado. It had proved very expensive, however, to supply the garrison from San Diego, 210 miles away over mountains and desert, or via the treacherous Colorado River. In June, prior to Sitgreaves's arrival, the costly post had been abandoned and the garrison had moved to the mountain community of Santa Ysabel. Meanwhile, First Lt. Thomas W. Sweeny, with a detachment of ten men, had been left behind to protect immigrants. Sweeny had established his command at a private ferry crossing, about six miles below the mouth of the Gila, in a thicket of mesquite on the west bank of the Colorado. Free of the commanding officer he despised, Capt. Samuel P. Heintzelman, Sweeny had named his new post Camp Independence.[68]

From a Mexican they met near the mouth of the Gila, Sitgreaves's party learned that Sweeny had moved the post down river. Sitgreaves and his men removed their pants and shoes, waded across the Gila, redressed, and hiked on until they came in sight of Camp Independence at a bend in the Colorado. A surf boat was sent across the river to pick them up. Before crossing, Kern made the only extant sketch of Sweeny's Camp, with its picket stockade and the promontory called Pilot Knob in the background (fig. 101). Kern mistitled the drawing *Camp Yuma,* and subsequent writers have mistaken the drawing for the upstream site of Camp Yuma—the site of the notorious Fort

Yuma, from its reestablishment in 1852 until 1885.[69]

The Sitgreaves expedition reached Camp Independence on November 30, at a critical juncture; the officers there expected an attack at any moment. From its inception in June, the ten-man post had occupied an untenable position, as Lieutenant Sweeny had explained despondently in a letter to his wife: "to be stationed here with ten men on this desolate spot, surrounded by hostile tribes, who neither want the will nor power, to annihilate us at any time . . . this is what I did not conceive of even in a dream."[70] The situation became especially precarious when the Yuma post became the focal point of an effort by Antonio Garra, a Cupeño chief, to unite the southern California mountain and river tribes with Mexicans, to drive the Americans out. "The first step in Garra's strategy," according to one historian's analysis, "was the destruction of Camp Independence."[71]

A few weeks before Kern's arrival at the camp, on November 11, a group of Indians including Garra had attempted to seize the post. Sweeny's defense with a howitzer, and the coincidental arrival of reinforcements the following day, saved the Americans, but harrassment continued and the officers decided they could not hold out. The addition of the nearly fifty hungry men with Sitgreaves and Kendrick, on November 30, and the arrival of reinforcements from San Diego, on December 3, put too great a strain on the post's chronically limited supplies. On

Fig. 101. *Camp Yuma. Big Colorado Below the Mouth of the Gila.* Lithograph based on a drawing by Richard H. Kern. Lorenzo Sitgreaves, *Report of an Expedition down the Zuni and Colorado Rivers* (Washington, D.C., 1853).

December 6, the military abandoned Camp Independence, marching some one hundred strong toward San Diego. They followed a well-worn and littered immigrant trail through the valleys of Carrizo, Vallecito, and San Felipe creeks, up the dry, rocky east slope of the Laguna Mountains. Through pine forest, with snow on the ground, they crossed over the divide and made their way to the Indian village of Santa Ysabel.[72]

Although they were no longer traveling in uncharted territory, they still feared for their lives. The Garra uprising had spread into the mountains behind San Diego; blood had been shed and buildings burned at Warner's Ranch, near Santa Ysabel. Rumors abounded. Indian signal fires lighted the sky along the route and Kern and his companions had good reason to be "a little timid" about an Indian attack, as Lieutenant

Sweeny put it. Indeed, one day out of Yuma they had buried the flesh-stripped bones of four men recently killed by Indians. But the Indians made no attempt to assault the large, well armed force.[73]

On the morning of December 18, just as the Pacific mail steamer was leaving the harbor, Sitgreaves's little band reached San Diego—"the termination of our overland journey which to us has been . . . one of much anxiety and constant suspense."[74] The sense of relief among the men was palpable. In the plaza of the old Mexican center of town, people gathered around the explorers, eager for news about the Indian country. Sitgreaves and his companions obliged, Dr. Woodhouse said, yet "nothing would do but that we must take a toddy with them." A few drinks later, "we went to the Post Office and enquired for letters but Mr. Kern was the only fortunate one amongst us." From the adobe old town section of San Diego, the explorers continued to nearby new town, with its wood-frame buildings. Here they dined with American officers and were quartered in a "very nice" two-story house while they awaited a vessel that would carry them back to the states.

Thus, three years after starting west with Frémont, Richard Kern reached the Pacific. This last leg of the journey with Sitgreaves had been difficult, but Kern was apparently no worse for the wear. The day of his arrival in San Diego, he ran into George McKinstry, a friend of his brother. In a letter to Edward Kern, back in Philadelphia, McKinstry reported on Dick's health and made light of the arduous trip: "I will not go into a history of his agreeable trip over the desert," McKinstry wrote with irony. "Suffice it to say he came in fat and saucy having been well fed on mule beef and roasted Jack Ass."[75]

By their own reckoning, the members of the Sitgreaves expedition had covered 658 miles from Zuni to the Yuma post, where the expedition had officially ended. With considerable help from their guides, the topographers and the artist had made the first reconnaissance over much of what would soon become known as the 35th parallel route to the Pacific. Two years later, another member of the U.S. Corps of Topographical Engineers, Amiel Weeks Whipple, surveyed much of the same route with an eye toward its use for a transcontinental railroad. Sitgreaves's report was not published in time to be of use, but Whipple took along a tracing of the map that Richard Kern had drawn of Sitgreaves's route.[76] Kern, as we shall see, became a staunch advocate of the 35th parallel route as the most satisfactory way to the Pacific. The first railroad to the Pacific did not, of course, follow the 35th parallel, but by the 1880s the Atlantic & Pacific Railroad, a subsidiary of the Atchison, Topeka, & Santa Fe Railway, had laid tracks across central Arizona, closely following Sitgreaves's route as far as Kingman. The highway that would enter American folklore as Route 66 (today's Interstate 40) would also parallel Sitgreaves's route, connecting towns that had sprung up along the way, such as Holbrook, Winslow, Flagstaff, Williams, and Kingman.[77]

Today, leaders of the Sitgreaves expedition are remembered in place names in Arizona. Sitgreaves National Forest sprawls through parts of three Arizona counties, above the Mogollon Rim. A low mountain pass along the Colorado River and a peak northeast of Williams also bear Sitgreaves's name. Nearby, another peak commemorates the name of Kendrick, head of the military escort. Near Flagstaff, Leroux Springs recalls the name of the mountain man and guide.[78]

No names remain on the land to honor the expedition's draftsman, but Kern's contributions to the dissemination of the findings of the expedition were considerable. When Sitgreaves's *Report* appeared in print in 1853, it contained Kern's "Tables of Distances, Geographic Positions, and Meteorological Observations," and a large, foldout map drawn by Kern. Carl Wheat has characterized Kern's map of Sitgreaves's route as "a monumental achievement . . . generally correct and exceedingly well done."[79] Sitgreaves's *Report* also contained twenty-three lithographs of people and places, prepared from drawings by Kern. The work of the lithographer, James Ackerman of New York, was stiffer and less attractive than the plates that P. S. Duval of Philadelphia had prepared for Simpson's report, but all were tinted and all offered views that the American public had never seen before, including those of Indians

previously unknown to American ethnologists.[80]

Kern also prepared drawings to accompany the descriptions of mammals, birds, and reptiles contained in the report. Among the plates attributed directly to him were drawings of four mammals, one bird, and eight reptiles. Apparently made from specimens brought back to Philadelphia, these drawings exhibit Kern's customary attention to detail, as exemplified by his drawings of the new species of squirrel, found on San Francisco Mountain in Arizona (fig. 102). Dr. Woodhouse named the squirrel Sciurus Abertii, "in honor of Col. J. J. Abert, Chief of the Corps of Topographical Engineers, to whose exertions science is so much indebted."[81] Edward Kern also did some drawings (two mammals and one bird) for Dr. Woodhouse's section of the report; Woodhouse publicly expressed his appreciation to both Kern brothers "for their praiseworthy drawings, which have required time and minute study of nature."[82]

Richard Kern's graphic contributions to the *Report* take on a special significance in light of the brevity of Sitgreaves's verbal narrative of the expedition, which amounts to only seventeen pages. Sitgreaves had found the country along the route "barren, and without general interest," and had noted that "I can add very little to the information afforded by the map," which Kern had drawn.[83]

For Richard Kern, the Sitgreaves expedition did more than get him to the

Fig. 102. *Sciurus Aberti (Woodhouse).* Lithograph based on a drawing by Richard H. Kern. Lorenzo Sitgreaves, *Report of an Expedition down the Zuni and Colorado Rivers* (Washington, D.C., 1853).

Pacific. Coupled with the work that he had already done for Simpson, Judd, and Parke, it helped establish his reputation as one of the nation's authorities on the topography of the southwestern United States—a man whose knowledge and special skills would be in demand as Congress began to seek ways to improve transportation and communication from the East across the continent to the newly acquired Pacific Coast.

-6-
Chief of Roads: Washington, 1852-1853

EXPLORATION BEHIND HIM and the Christmas holidays approaching, Richard Kern's thoughts must have turned toward home. His wanderings had kept him away from family, friends, and studio for over three years. Little wonder, then, that he planned to return home from San Diego in the quickest and surest way. Together with Sitgreaves, Kendrick, Parke, and Woodhouse, Kern planned to take passage to San Francisco, then connect with one of the Pacific mail steamers that plied the sea lanes between San Francisco and Panama City twice a month.

Lodged in a comfortable house in San Diego's New Town, Kern spent a few rainy days putting his gear in order. He hoped to ship out on the *Sea Bird,* due in on Christmas, but the vessel did not arrive that day or in the days that followed. While waiting, Kern and Dr. Woodhouse amused themselves by exploring the old Mexican section of town,

and by calling on the wife and sister of one of the American officers and on a woman whom Woodhouse described as the "belle of San Diego."[1]

On December 28, apparently growing impatient with the wait, Kern and Woodhouse moved into a barracks on the beach with Lieutenant Sweeny and some of his men. There, at La Playa, they would be closer at hand when a vessel arrived. They could "take passage for home without delay," as Sweeny explained in a letter to his wife in New York. Sweeny must have been wistful contemplating the explorers' departures, knowing that he would be assigned back to the lonely desert post at Yuma. Kern and his companions promised, however, to visit Mrs. Sweeny in New York, where she had given birth to a daughter whom Sweeny had not yet seen.[2]

From La Playa, Kern kept a watch on the bay, eager for the arrival of a

San Francisco-bound vessel. On the clear and pleasant morning of December 30, his efforts were rewarded. After breakfast, Kern, Woodhouse, and Lieutenant Parke climbed the hill behind the beach to watch. At nine o'clock, the smoke of a steamer came into view. It touched land about noon, and turned out to be the *Gold Hunter,* coming from Nicaragua. Kern and his companions sent their baggage out to the ship, but it was badly crowded. They decided not to board and had their baggage taken off. Happily, another ship, the *Northerner* of the Pacific Mail Steamship Company, arrived later that same day, headed north from Panama. It too was crowded, and there was sickness aboard, but Kern and his companions took passage nonetheless. The *Northerner* slipped out of San Diego harbor at ten o'clock on the night of December 30. With only a brief stop in Monterey, to drop off the mail, they arrived in San Francisco two days later, toward midnight of January 1, 1852. The following day, the local paper, the *Daily Alta California,* noted the "arrival of Capt. Sitgreaves' Exploring Party," but the paper did not send a reporter to interview the explorers. Instead, it copied in its entirety an article describing the route and hardships of the expedition, which the San Diego paper had carried a couple of weeks before. In booming and boisterous San Francisco, entrepôt for the forty-niners and their thousands of successors, the arrival of Sitgreaves's party attracted little notice.[3]

For the next two weeks, Kern remained in or around San Francisco. Along with other members of the exploring party, he had checked into the Oriental House, but the hotel's high prices, poor service, and indifferent meals soon drove out Kern and Woodhouse. On January 6, the two took rooms at one dollar a day in the more reasonable and clean Casa Grande, an adobe building on Dupont Street, and contracted for meals at the Jackson Restaurant at fourteen dollars a week. Kern probably spent more time on the street than he did in his room. With Woodhouse, he walked the plank sidewalks of the boom town and admired the substantial new brick and iron buildings that were replacing the wood-frame structures that had gone up in flames when fire destroyed a large portion of the town the previous May. The city's surprisingly large stores, saloons, public buildings, and "forest of masts" in the harbor probably reminded Kern of Philadelphia. At the same time, there were frequent reminders that he was on the West Coast. One Sunday, Kern and Woodhouse joined the throngs of people on the plank toll road that ran out to the old Spanish mission of San Francisco de Asís. "Here," Woodhouse noted in his diary, "we attended a bull fight with which I was rather disgusted."[4] It seems likely that Kern sketched on such occasions, but no drawings from his weeks in California have come to light.[5]

During his stay in California, Richard Kern apparently contacted his old boss, John C. Frémont. Following the terrible disaster in the Rockies in the winter of 1849, Frémont had continued on to California, joined there by his wife, Jessie Benton. In San Francisco, where the couple made their home, Frémont's fortunes had dramatically risen from the nadir of disgrace that had followed his court martial and winter exploring debacle. He had been elected California's first senator, and had served a brief stint in Washington in 1850. Meanwhile, gold had been discovered on the Mariposa grant he had purchased in 1846. Fortune had joined fame; Frémont had become a wealthy man.[6]

Frémont and the Kerns had never made peace. Well after the expedition had ended in tragedy, Dick's brother John reported from Philadelphia that Frémont refused to speak with anyone from Philadelphia who visited him in California, if he knew that "they were acquainted with the Kerns."[7] Whether this report was true or not, some of Frémont's anger toward the Kerns is understandable. Shortly after the disaster, Dick had published in several major newspapers a scathing criticism of Frémont's leadership in 1848–49. Dick had also continued to try to villify Frémont, notwithstanding his professed desire to put the "painful subject" of the Frémont expedition behind him. At Santa Fe, in the fall of 1850, when Dick parted ways with Lt. James Simpson after a year of close collaboration, he gave Simpson a written account of his view of the "disaster in the mountains." Simpson was to carry this east and set the record straight. Simpson read Kern's account through twice.

"Be assured," he told Kern, "that I shall, if occasion requires, avail myself of the facts it gives, to put matters on this subject in their true light."[8]

Remarkably, after two years of what appears to have been animosity on both sides, Kern and Frémont somehow patched up their differences during Kern's brief stay in California. The two may have exchanged notes, but more likely they met in person in San Francisco.[9] Although the circumstances surrounding their communication remain unknown, it is clear that Kern left San Francisco convinced that Frémont had apologized to him. Kern reported this to James Simpson, who responded characteristically with a homily:

I am glad you & Fremont have become reconciled to each other. There can be no doubt but he has done great injustice to individuals in his public career, but the first step toward improvement is to confess error, and as he seems to have done this in your case, there is hope that his experience will not be lost upon him.[10]

The reconciliation seems to have lasted. After Frémont lost his bid for the presidency in 1856, and began to prepare his memoirs, his publisher, George W. Childs of Philadelphia, contacted Edward Kern and asked for his help. Edward offered to provide Frémont with his notes and drawings, and Frémont accepted. "The Col. speaks very kindly of you," Childs told Kern, "and will be glad to do you full credit in the work."[11]

From San Francisco, Kern also wrote

to the congenial Swiss expatriate, John Sutter, whose fort Edward Kern had commanded while with Frémont during the Mexican War. As the owner of the site of the fabulous California gold discovery, Sutter too had grown rich and famous, his name a household word. Dick told Sutter of the disaster in the Rockies with Frémont, and sent news of Ned's activities and whereabouts. Sutter responded quickly, with a warm letter full of news. He had already received an account of the Rocky Mountain disaster from Frémont himself. He lamented that Dick had not come to visit him in person, and recalled the days he had spent with Ned: "How many hearty laughs we had, and enjoyed ourselves in our poor old times." Sutter still hoped that Ned would settle in California. Sutter chronicled at length the activities of each of his children and sent Dick "two of my likenesses, one for yourself and one for my friend your brother," along with wishes for "a speedy and pleasant journey to the Atlantic."[12]

On January 16, as planned, Kern and Sitgreaves shipped out of San Francisco on the *California,* a wooden side-wheel steamer that made regular runs between San Francisco and Panama for the Pacific Mail Steamship Company. With three hundred passengers and 1,450,000 dollars in gold dust, the *California* left the docks at eight o'clock in the morning and steamed through the placid bay, past North Beach and Alcatraz, and through the Golden Gate to the Pacific.[13] Woodhouse, Kendrick, and Parke were not aboard, however.

They had decided to return to the states by way of Mexico. They soon abandoned the plan, however, when they discovered they could not assemble a large enough group to cross Mexico safely. On February 1, they took passage on a ship bound for Nicaragua. While these three debated, Kern and Sitgreaves headed for Panama. With the prevailing currents in their favor, the southward journey along the coasts of the two Californias usually went quickly. If all went well, the *California* would round the tip of Cabo San Lucas and reach Acapulco in eight days.[14]

At Acapulco, a Spanish town since 1532 and Mexico's historic gateway to trade with China and the Phillipines, the *California* stopped to take on fresh water, fruit, and vegetables. Like most visitors to the city, Kern probably roamed the streets, admired the women, and bought fresh fruit at one of the numerous stalls that served fruit-hungry seafarers. He also did some drawing. A watercolor and a sketch of Acapulco have been preserved. The scene that he apparently found of greatest artistic interest was the Fort of San Diego, which guarded the northeast entrance to the harbor. From the opposite shore, Kern did a watercolor of the massive structure, *Fort at Mouth of Harbor of Acapulco, Mex., 1852* (fig. 103). Built in the early 1600s, destroyed in an earthquake, and rebuilt in the late 1700s, the Fort of San Diego serves today as a regional museum. Kern's composition suggests, however, that he was more interested in the setting than

Fig. 103. *Fort at Mouth of Harbor of Acapulco, Mex., 1852.* Watercolor by Richard H. Kern. Courtesy, Amon Carter Museum.

in the structure. He has placed a palm tree in the foreground, perhaps to suggest the tropical ambience, but it is the massive mountains, falling abruptly to the sea, that dominate the scene and still make the greatest impression on those who visit that splendid harbor.[15]

Another week or so out of Acapulco brought the *California* to Panama, a two-century-old tropical city with paved streets and impressive public buildings. "Everything bears the appearance of age," one American traveler said. "It has been built up and worn out."[16]

Crowded with travelers headed for California, the city offered few comforts, but the journey across the sixty-mile-wide isthmus offered even less. Until the completion of a railroad in 1855, travelers like Kern either walked or hired a horse or mule to carry them and their baggage twenty miles to the hill country towns of Cruces or Gorgona, on the Chagres River. At one of those towns they would hire a dugout canoe and boatman to pole them downstream some forty miles to the Atlantic—a journey of several days.

The Chagres River, as one American journalist described it, wound "between walls of foliage that rise from its very surface," with colorful and exotic birds, insects, flowers, and a "splendid overplus of vegetable life."[17] There were no accommodations along the river, although a lucky traveler might rent a hammock under the palm-thatched roof of a bamboo-walled hut. More often they camped out or kept traveling through the night, avoiding the tropical sun. In a well-composed pencil sketch, *On Chagres River,* Kern showed the waterway winding through lush foliage and around a bluff where three small huts stood, dwarfed and lonely under a nighttime sky (fig. 104).

The weather was good and the rainy season had ended when Kern arrived in Panama. Provided he encountered no mishap, a three-day overland journey would have brought him to the town of Chagres, on the left bank of the river's mouth. A sleepy fishing village until the events of 1849 awakened it by dumping thousands of frantic gold seekers upon its beaches, Chagres had undergone a dramatic transformation. Wood-frame hotels and restaurants had risen amid the thatch-roofed huts; Kern and Sitgreaves could wait comfortably for a steamer bound for New York.[18] As in Acapulco, the sight that most aroused Kern's artistic interest was a massive Spanish fortification, Castillo San Lorenzo el Real de Chagres.

Like its Acapulco counterpart, Fort San Lorenzo occupied a spectacular setting. In 1597, a Spanish military engineer had ordered it placed atop eighty-foot sandstone cliffs that rise sharply above the sea, forming a small peninsula at the mouth of the Chagres. The fort had a commanding view of the Caribbean portal to Panama and was the scene of some exciting battles. In 1671, it fell to Henry Morgan's pirates, and was later rebuilt. At the time of Kern's visit, the 250-year-old fort still housed a garrison. Thereafter, the buildings deteriorated under the ravages of tropical rains and humidity. Designated a World Historical Site by the UNESCO Committee of World Patrimony, the fort is currently undergoing restoration. Kern's watercolor, painted from the river's bank, shows the fort's many buildings, roofs still intact, perched above the tree-lined cliffs (fig. 105). Unknown until recently, Kern's watercolor is a rare image of the historic fort at a time when it still functioned.[19]

At Chagres, Kern and Sitgreaves boarded the U.S. Mail Steamer *El Dorado.* After some rough weather in the

Fig. 104. *On Chagres River.* Pencil drawing by Richard H. Kern. Courtesy, Amon Carter Museum.

Caribbean and a stop in Jamaica, the *El Dorado* docked in New York, at eleven o'clock at night on February 16, a month to the day from Kern's departure from San Francisco. From New York, Sitgreaves made his way to Washington and Kern headed home to Philadelphia. By 1852 the crossing of the western mountains and prairies by topographers and pioneers had become so common that journalists took no notice of their return. Even the Wilkes expedition, which circled the globe from 1838 to 1842, was greeted upon return by public apathy. Members of Sitgreaves's expedition could expect no better.

Fig. 105. *Fort San Lorenzo, Mouth of Rio Chagres, New Granada. 1852.* Watercolor by Richard H. Kern. Courtesy, Amon Carter Museum.

Unheralded by the press, Richard Kern returned to Filbert Street.[20]

Home again after a three-year absence, there would be news of friends and family to get caught up on, and reunions with members of his family. "What your joy must have been to even now grasp the hand and kiss the cheek of those you loved most in the world after so long an absence," James Simpson gushed. Simpson could well imagine Dick's homecoming, "for as you know I have had some little experience in matters of this kind."[21]

Simpson had left New Mexico in the late summer of 1850, on a medical leave.

He had traveled over the Santa Fe Trail, then made his way to Buffalo to rejoin his young wife, Jane Champlin. Soon thereafter he had apparently visited Kern's family and friends in Philadelphia, where he had been warmly received and had doubtless brought welcome firsthand news. After his leave expired, Simpson had expected to return to his post in New Mexico, but when he learned that the government was sending Sitgreaves to explore the Zuni River and points beyond, he correctly concluded that it "would be superfluous to have two topographical engineers in New Mexico at the same time." Simpson apparently regretted not returning to New Mexico. He had sent some solicited advice to Sitgreaves and admitted to Kern that "I would have been glad to have had the charge of the survey, and nothing would have afforded me greater satisfaction than to have had you and Parke with me."[22] Instead, Simpson had received orders in the spring of 1851 to report to Minnesota Territory, where he would spend the next five years laying out government roads.

Simpson wanted his New Mexico friends, the Kerns and Lieutenant Parke, with him in Minnesota. He had written to the brothers in Santa Fe to see if they could join him. Dick replied that he was going west with Sitgreaves, but his brother would be heading east and was eager to work with Simpson. Simpson should write to Ned at St. Louis if he still wanted him.[23] Simpson promptly sent a letter to St. Louis, offering Ed-

ward Kern a draftsman's position at three dollars a day, but unbeknown to Simpson, the letter did not reach Edward. By December 1, 1850, Simpson had heard nothing from Ned and wrote again, this time to Dick in Philadelphia: "if your brother has not already started and cannot come immediately," he told Dick, *"I wish you to come on with all dispatch."*[24]

Almost three months later, Richard Kern returned to Philadelphia and replied to Simpson's offer. He expressed interest in the position, but must have wondered if his services were still needed. Moreover, his responsibilities with Sitgreaves had not yet ended. As late as May of 1852, Simpson was still hoping that funds would come through so that he could hire Kern and Parke, but those hopes were not realized. Richard Kern remained in the East that spring.[25]

Kern stayed in the East, but not in Philadelphia. Like many other artists of his day who sought commissions or federal employment, he made a pilgrimage to the nation's capital. Sitgreaves had received permission from the Topographical Corps to keep Kern in his employ, and so he had temporary means of support. By late April, if not before, he had checked into the popular Willard Hotel, on Pennsylvania Avenue and Fourteenth Street near the seat of power, and went to work in a room in the Winder Public Office Building. There, with Sitgreaves and Parke, Kern worked on into the summer and fall to finish the map and sketches that would accompany Sitgreaves's terse report.

Sitgreaves hoped to have the report done by the end of August, but a long delay in the arrival of "objects of natural history" that had been left with the Army Quartermaster in San Francisco, prevented quick completion of the report. The shipment did not reach Washington until late October, and then it had to be described and classified. Some of these items may have been turned over to Kern to draw, stretching out still further his employment with Sitgreaves. In any event, Congress did not authorize publication of Sitgreaves's report until March 3, 1853, and it is possible that Kern never saw it in published form.[26]

Although its cultural life was still primitive compared to that of Philadelphia, the capital held much of interest for an ambitious artist. On the second floor of the War Department building, Kern could see the much-admired Indian portraits by Charles Bird King. He and Ned had probably studied lithographs of those same paintings in Philadelphia, before going West. Kern might also have visited King, Washington's "artist-in-residence," in his spacious studio and gallery on Twelfth Street—a mecca for visiting artists.[27]

During Kern's stay in Washington, construction of the Smithsonian Institution was well underway. Founded in 1846 from the bequest of an Englishman, James Smithson, for the "increase and diffusion of knowledge among men," the structure would house eclectic collections of the natural sciences that Kern found so fascinating. In September 1852,

Kern positioned himself on the Capitol grounds with brush in hand and did a Romantic watercolor of the silhouette of the Smithsonian rising above the treetops to the west (plate 15). Kern's watercolor, *Smithsonian Institute,* is the earliest known drawing of that stately Romanesque building, whose red-brown freestone walls had begun to rise in 1847. By the end of 1849, the structure's east and west wings had opened, but the central part of the building was not ready for occupancy until May 1854, and construction continued into 1857. When Kern outlined the building, then, its central portion and nine towers were not yet complete.[28]

Later on, as the weeks in Washington stretched on into months, Kern also did very polished watercolor vignettes in his sketchbook of scenes around Washington: *Christ Church* in Georgetown (fig. 106), the Alexandria *Aqueduct, Georgetown* (fig. 107), and *The Spring, Kalorama Heights,* located near the neoclassical mansion and estate named Kalorama, meaning "beautiful heights" in Greek (fig. 108). The aqueduct and the spring, which appeared in contemporary guidebooks to Washington in Kern's day, have since been razed.[29]

In his spare time, Dick converted sketches from his travels into finished paintings. In the spring of 1852, he was working on some oils to send to his friend Simpson, apparently of scenes the two had witnessed on the Navajo expedition. In July he was completing "a big landscape," a view from the summit of what he called "Santa Fe Moun-

Fig 106. *Christ Church, Washington, D.C.* Watercolor by Richard H. Kern, May 22, 1853. Courtesy, Amon Carter Museum.

tain."[30] These paintings apparently have not survived, but we do have a view of Pikes Peak that Kern did at this time, romantically entitled *Mon Songe* ("My Dream"). Kern had seen Pikes Peak on his way west in 1848, but if he painted it then his work has been lost. Back East, however, he apparently took a lithograph of a sketch that Frémont had done of Pikes Peak in July 1845 and used it as the basis for a watercolor (plate 16). Kern added a tepee and a considerable amount of snow to the scene, to suggest the way Pikes Peak had appeared in 1848.[31]

Kern also used his spare time to look for another job. His work with Sitgreaves would soon run out, so he began to use his modest political connections to find another position on

1853.

Aqueduct Georgetown, D.C.

Fig. 107. *Aqueduct, Georgetown, D.C.* Watecolor by Richard H. Kern, 1852. Courtesy, Amon Carter Museum.

the government payroll. One contact was Com. Robert F. Stockton, whom Edward Kern had probably known in California. Commodore Stockton had won national attention by taking charge of the conquest of California in the recent war, and by vying for control of the province with Frémont. Since his triumph in California, the ambitious Stockton had resigned his commission in the Navy and had won election as a senator from New Jersey. In the spring of 1852, talk in Washington had it that Stockton would be an ideal presidential candidate. He could be very useful to

the Kerns. "Stockton is out of town," Dick wrote to Ned in early May, "I will of course keep working."[32]

Richard Kern also had his New Mexico connections. Some of his old friends from New Mexico were in Washington that spring, still fighting political battles they had begun in Santa Fe. The cause of statehood for New Mexico had died in the Compromise of 1850, but the proponents of statehood and the defenders of New Mexico's territorial status, with whom Kern identified, continued to struggle for power. In September 1851, after Kern had left

Fig. 108. *The Spring, Kalarama Heights, D.C.* Watercolor by Richard H.
Kern. Courtesy, Amon Carter Museum.

Santa Fe with Sitgreaves, the leader of the statehood faction, Richard Weightman, had won a close election to represent New Mexico Territory as its first delegate to Congress. During the heated political battle, Kern's friend and traveling companion William C. Skinner, the merchant who had visited John Kern in Philadelphia the year before, was murdered in Albuquerque. Along with others of Kern's acquaintances, Skinner had belonged to the Odd Fellows Lodge in Santa Fe, and the Lodge brothers sent one of their own, J. D. Ellis, to Albuquerque to retrieve the body and give it proper burial. Kern probably learned details of the sad affair from his friends in Washington, who had come to protest Weightman's election.[33]

After the votes had been counted in the fall of 1851, Weightman's opponent, A. W. Reynolds, a former army quartermaster of Kern's acquaintance, had charged fraud and formally asked the House of Representatives not to seat Weightman. Members of the territorial faction, who clustered around Joab Houghton, rushed to support Reynolds. Houghton and the Santa Fe merchant James L. Collins, both of whom Kern knew well, wrote a personal letter to President Millard Fillmore, charging Weightman with fraud. Then, when Weightman headed to Washington, members of the Houghton faction followed him there, eager to counteract Weightman's influence and perhaps to secure federal appointments themselves. "They are here," Weightman wrote from Washington in February

1852: "Collins, Reynolds, Houghton, Johnson, Tulles [Tullis], McGrorty and Quinn. They do a great business walking up and down the Avenue."[34]

Richard Kern was probably walking with them. He apparently shared a room with Joab Houghton and must have been close to the heat as old enmities flared up in the nation's capital.[35] Charges and countercharges flew back and forth, some finding their way into the public record. Weightman attacked the Houghton-Reynolds faction in a speech that he reportedly gave in the House of Representatives on March 15, and then had printed as a pamphlet. In reply, Houghton published a pamphlet attacking Weightman. Through all of this, Kern continued to side with Houghton and the territorialists and kept his friend Simpson, still in St. Paul, apprised of the activities of their mutual friends and acquaintances. A reading of Weightman's pamphlet, apparently sent to him by Kern, confirmed Simpson's judgment of Weightman's mediocrity and his inability to lead. "It is he all over—short-sighted, vain, unproductive of any good . . . I never did think him a man of any breadth of mind," Simpson wrote to Kern.[36]

One of Kern's contacts in the spring of 1852 had produced an offer of a job, but it was one that he could afford to refuse. Kern had written to a naval officer of his acquaintance, William N. Jeffers, to see if Com. Matthew C. Perry would need an artist on a forthcoming voyage to Japan. Jeffers spoke with Perry, and his response was probably all too familiar to artists who sought to make a living at their craft. Commodore Perry, Jeffers reported, "says that he wishes very much to obtain a competent artist . . . but that the great difficulty is that he has no appropriation from which to pay such a salary as such a one would desire, unless indeed he would go merely for the adventure." Moreover, since this was a government expedition, Perry had indicated that the artist could not keep his drawings "for private use," but had to turn them over to the government. A small sum was available, however, to cover the artist's expenses. Jeffers invited Kern to join the expedition if these terms were acceptable, but he decided against it. He suggested his brother, instead. "I have written to Jeffers to keep you before Old Perry," Dick told Ned.[37]

Edward Kern followed up on his brother's initiatives, but did not get the job with Perry. The next spring, however, Edward would obtain a position as artist and taxidermist on the North Pacific Exploring Expedition, under Cadwalader Ringgold. That expedition, combined with follow-up studies, would keep Edward on the government payroll for the next seven years and take him across the Pacific on two occasions.[38]

If no new position was forthcoming, Richard Kern expected to leave Washington in August 1852, when he finished working for Sitgreaves. Other opportunities came along, however, and he stayed on. How he supported himself is not certain, but it is clear that he could rely increasingly on his own reputation as an experienced artist, draftsman, and topographer who knew the Southwest as few other Americans did. Indeed, his adventures made him a hero to artists who had not enjoyed his opportunities. In Washington, Dick told Ned, he met "a devilish little miniature painter from Boston," Richard H. Staigg, who "looks at me with veneration because I've seen such places." They had become "great chums." Staigg wanted to paint Kern's portrait in a Western costume.[39]

Late in the year, Kern received an offer from the well-known journalist and archaeologist, Ephraim George Squier, to work on the Nicaragua railroad survey. On a previous visit to Nicaragua, Squier's artist had become homesick. In seeking a heartier type, Squier might have come across Richard Kern's name in his own library, because Squier, like other American scientists, had received a copy of Simpson's report of the Navajo reconnaissance. Squier's offer apparently came at an inopportune moment for Kern, who turned it down with a gracious explanation:

> It will be impossible for me to go with you, as engagements hold me here until March. Could I break these consistently I would, but the party who extended them to me, did it from motives of kindness. I regret very much my inability to accompany you, as all feelings and predilections are in favor of such an expedition—and to me the interest & pleasure would be of more consideration than the pay.[40]

While he worked in Washington, Richard Kern's special knowledge of the Southwest also came to the attention of the well-known ethnologist Henry Rowe Schoolcraft. A veteran explorer and writer, Schoolcraft had received a subsidy from Congress to prepare an encyclopedic account of all aspects of Indian life in the United States. The first volume of Schoolcraft's monumental *Historical and Statistical Information Respecting the History, Condition, and Prospects of the Indian Tribes of the United States . . .* had appeared in 1851, prior to Kern's return to the East, but five more volumes were planned. In the spring of 1853, both Kern brothers became involved in Schoolcraft's project. At Schoolcraft's request, Edward Kern wrote a short piece on "Indian Customs of California," and provided Schoolcraft with at least two drawings of California Indians. Richard Kern's contributions to the Schoolcraft report were more extensive.[41]

Schoolcraft planned to begin volume four with an essay on Coronado's epic exploration of the Southwest. He had access to the account of the expedition's chronicler, Pedro de Castañeda, but most of Castañeda's place names did not correspond to names on contemporary maps. Several years before, in 1848, the problem had perplexed the distinguished statesman and pioneering ethnologist Albert Gallatin and the young Ephraim George Squier. In separate essays, each had attempted to untangle Coronado's route, but neither Gallatin nor Squier knew the region firsthand.

The problem of locating the Seven Cities of Cíbola was especially perplexing. Cíbola, whose allure had first drawn Coronado north from Mexico, seemed to be situated in what Squier referred to as one of the "broad blanks" on contemporary maps—"the region between the Gila and Colorado . . . near the dividing ridge of the continent."[42] Richard Kern, as Schoolcraft knew, was one of the few white Americans who had traveled across the broad blanks, and Schoolcraft turned to him for answers.

About May 12, Kern sent to Schoolcraft a well-documented essay, tracing Coronado's route north from Mexico. The essay, he told Schoolcraft, was based on old Spanish maps, his own personal experience, and Castañeda's frustrating account, which Kern used in a French translation and cited frequently.[43] Kern prefaced his treatise with an apology, explaining that he had done the work "during the intervals between duties somewhat arduous; hence the matter has not been examined as closely as it should have been."[44]

In his essay, and on a neat, uncluttered map drawn to accompany it, Kern projected Coronado's route. He traced the main body of the expedition north from Culiacán through what is now eastern Arizona to "Old Zuñi," which Kern reasoned from Castañeda's description must have been the first city of Cíbola that Coronado encountered. Using his knowledge of Pueblo linguistics as well as of New Mexico's topography, Kern took the Spaniards east

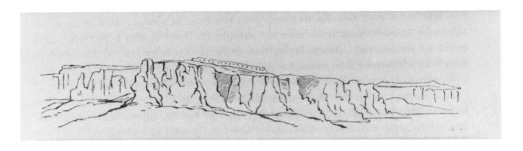

Fig. 109. *Rock of Acuco, or Acoma.* Lithograph based on a line drawing by Richard H. Kern. Henry Schoolcraft, *Indian Tribes,* 6 vols. (Washington, D.C. 1851–57), 4.

Fig. 110. *Cicuyé, or Pecos.* Lithograph based on a line drawing by Richard H. Kern. Henry Schoolcraft, *Indian Tribes,* 6 vols. (Washington, D.C., 1851–57), 4.

Fig. 111. *Old Zuñi, the Cibola of Casteñada {sic}.* Lithograph based on a line drawing by Richard H. Kern. Henry Schoolcraft, *Indian Tribes,* 6 vols. (Washington, D.C., 1851–57), 4.

Fig. 112. *Laguna, Sept. 20, 1849.* Pen-and-ink drawing by Richard H. Kern. Courtesy, Peabody Museum, Harvard University.

through Acoma, across the Rio Grande at Isleta, then out to Pecos Pueblo for his fateful meeting with the Wichita Indian they called the Turk. In attempting to follow Coronado's trail still farther eastward, onto the buffalo plains and to the Turk's beguiling Quivira, Kern became as lost as Coronado had been. Otherwise, he did a creditable job of reconstructing the route of the main party, of several ancillary exploring parties, and of identifying place names.

The problem of identifying the places and paths that Coronado visited would continue to occupy the attention of scholars for the next century, and questions still remain. Even Kern's mentor, James H. Simpson, entered the discussion and wrote a treatise on the sub-

Fig. 113. *Pueblo of Laguna*. Engraving of a drawing by Seth Eastman, based on a sketch by Richard H. Kern. Henry Schoolcraft, *Indian Tribes*, 6 vols. (Washington, D.C., 1851–57), 4.

ject that appeared in the Smithsonian Institution's *Annual Report* of 1869. Simpson agreed with Kern that Cíbola was one of the Zuni villages, but corrected some of Kern's errors and supervised the drawing of a superior map. Some writers did not accept Zuni or its vicinity as Cíbola, and argued for Chaco Canyon or the Hopi villages as more likely sites, but by the end of the last century scholarly consensus supported Kern's position.[45]

To illustrate the article on Coronado, Kern redrew his field sketches of four of the pueblos through which the Coronado party had passed—Zuni, Acoma, Pecos, and Taos. Schoolcraft reproduced three of these simple line drawings without explicit attribution to Kern (figs. 109–11).[46]

Fig. 114. *Estufa or Council Chamber at Jémez.* Wash drawing by Richard H. Kern, 1849. Courtesy, Peabody Museum, Harvard University.

In addition to his work on Coronado, Kern sent several drawings to Schoolcraft that were later redrawn and embellished by Capt. Seth Eastman, whom Schoolcraft had hired as the artist for the series when George Catlin declined to participate. Trained at West Point, where he taught art after graduation, Eastman had substantial experience in the field as an artist and draftsman. Author of a *Treatise on Topographical Drawing* (1837), which Kern might have read, Eastman had worked in Florida, on the Mississippi, and had completed a tour of Texas just prior to going to work for Schoolcraft. Like Kern, Eastman was a documentary artist who placed a premium on accuracy. Judging from

Fig. 115. *Interior of an Estufa*. Engraving of a drawing by Seth Eastman, based on a sketch by Richard H. Kern. Henry Schoolcraft, *Indian Tribes*, 6 vols. (Washington, D.C., 1851–57), 4.

the few examples that remain, Eastman masterfully breathed life and drama into three of Kern's rough sketches of New Mexico Indian pueblos, while remaining true to the details that Kern had provided.[47]

Kern, for example, had sent to Schoolcraft an unfinished wash drawing of the Pueblo of Laguna, as seen from the south, looking across the San José River to the rocky hill on which the pueblo stands (fig. 112). Kern's sketch, apparently done in the field in 1849, remained uncompleted. Across the hills Kern had scrawled "sand & brown," to remind himself, or perhaps someone else, of the color. He had not filled in the sky, nor added figures to provide human interest. This was a clinical sketch, devoid of emotion, and Kern's verbal description suggested that he did not remember Laguna as an attractive place. The surface of the multistory stone buildings, Kern had told Schoolcraft, were "covered with mortar the whole presenting a dirty yellowish aspect."[48] Eastman transformed Kern's prosaic drawing. He bathed the pueblo in the warm dramatic light of the late afternoon sun, placed silhouettes of tranquil Indians in the foreground, and put a cow in the river. The result was a scene of quiet grandeur, a touch of the Hudson River School moved west (fig. 113).[49]

Similarly, Eastman added visual interest and drama to Kern's study of the interior of the kiva at Jémez. In this case, Eastman had two Kern sketches at his disposal, the first a field sketch done in pencil in August 1849 (fig. 31), and the second a more refined wash drawing of the same scene (fig. 114). Eastman added flames to the fireplace, sharpened the viewer's focus on the shaft of light that entered the kiva through the ceiling, and placed robe-covered and feather-bedecked Pueblos in the structure (fig. 115).[50] Eastman also did a drawing of Zuni (fig. 116), based on a Kern sketch that has apparently disappeared.[51]

In addition to the Pueblo scenes that Kern sent to Schoolcraft, he also furnished the ethnologist with a dozen drawings of Indian artifacts: four elaborately designed water jars from Zuni; a Zuni spoon and bowl; anthropomorphic and zoomorphic water jars; and the designs from three Navajo blankets and one Hopi blanket (fig. 117).[52] Always the scientist, Kern accompanied his sketches with verbal descriptions. Of the blankets, for example, Kern wrote: "the white and black portions are the natural colors of the wool—the Blue is made by using Indigo for a dye. The Red is made of Cicenhilos [cochineal] or Bayeta of the Mexicans."[53] Schoolcraft reproduced lithographs of all of these objects in volume four of his series on Indian Tribes, reproducing the blanket designs in color (fig. 118). In addition to drawings of these artifacts, Kern sent to Schoolcraft a number of sketches of Indian petroglyphs, tree carvings, Indian drawings, and a letter explaining their sources.[54]

When the fourth volume of Schoolcraft's Indian Tribes series appeared in 1854, it included Kern's essay and map on Coronado's route, and nearly all of the illustrations that Kern had done for Schoolcraft. Most of the illustrations, however, appeared without attribution to the artist. Had Kern lived long enough to see the volume in print, he might have been annoyed.

At the same time that Schoolcraft called on Kern to illuminate questions regarding the ethnology and topography of the Southwest, politicians had also discovered that Kern possessed unusual knowledge that could help promote a southwestern route for the transcontinental railroad. The acquisition of an American empire on the Pacific, and the westward migration of thousands of gold-seeking Americans

Fig. 116. *Pueblo of Zuñi, New Mexico.* Engraving of a drawing by Seth Eastman, based on a sketch by Richard H. Kern. Henry Schoolcraft, *Indian Tribes,* 6 vols. (Washington, D.C., 1851–57), 4.

to California, had made an iron link between East and West a matter of primary national importance. While the public debated the best route for such a railroad, Congress stood paralyzed. Senators and representatives could not reconcile the national interest with the economic and political benefits that would accrue to their own sections, states, or localities if a transcontinental railroad passed through them. To the head of the Topographical Bureau, Lt. James J. Abert, the answer seemed clear. Abert favored a route that would run

Fig. 117. *Water jar, Zuni* and *Water jug, Zuni.* Wash drawings by Richard H. Kern. Courtesy, Peabody Museum, Harvard University.

through the lower elevations and the benign winters of the Southwest; as early as 1849 he had engineers such as James H. Simpson and Randolph B. Marcy seeking the best trails across the region. But politicians, dazzled by the prospects of vigorous trade and soaring land values in their home districts, could not agree.[55]

Discussions over the railroad route reached a peak in Congress in the winter of 1852–53. A bill to construct a railroad along the 35th parallel route, roughly the line that Sitgreaves had followed in 1851, was introduced by California Senator William M. Gwin. The Senate met as a committee of the whole to consider Gwin's bill, and it monopolized debate throughout the entire session. In the midst of these discussions, in early January of 1853, Gwin asked Richard Kern to report to Congress on the most direct and practical route for a transcontinental railroad. Kern probably welcomed the opportunity. So intense was his interest in trails and transportation that his brother Edward once half-jokingly called him "a sort of Chief of Roads."[56] Richard Kern made maps and calculations and quickly prepared a lengthy report. On January 17, Gwin read Kern's report to the Senate, introducing him as "a gentleman of great experience . . . who was with Colonel Frémont."[57]

Kern argued, as Gwin must have known he would, for the merits of the 35th parallel route. He proposed that such a route begin "near the boundary

of Missouri and Arkansas," then follow the Canadian River west and cross the Rio Grande at Albuquerque. Kern described the terrain from Albuquerque to the Colorado River in detail. His recommended route varied from the trail he had followed with Sitgreaves in 1851, turning south, for example, rather than north of San Francisco Mountain. Like Sitgreaves, Kern had known after the expedition ended that they had not found the ideal route across Arizona, but with some modification the route held considerable promise.[58] Beyond the Colorado River, Kern recommended traveling northeast and crossing the southern Sierra Nevadas into the San Joaquin Valley through Walker's Pass, as his brother had done in 1845. San Diego, which had been Kern's destination with Sitgreaves, had the disadvantage of a "small harbor, sparse population, and rugged back country," offering little to recommend it as the western terminus of the railroad. Where that western terminus should be, Kern diplomatically left to the politicians.

In this well-documented report, Kern said he drew information largely from "my own personal observations . . . the rest is from the most reliable sources." Those sources included James Simpson's report on the Canadian River route; Zebulon Pike's description of a bridge that once crossed the Rio Grande; a conversation with the veteran mountain man Joseph Walker on the best way to reach the pass that bore his name; a letter from Maj. Electus Backus, who

Fig. 118. *Blankets Made by the Pueblo Indians of New Mexico.* Lithograph based on drawings by Richard H. Kern. Henry Schoolcraft, *Indian Tribes,* 6 vols. (Washington, D.C., 1851–57), 4.

had recently returned from New Mexico to Philadelphia with information about a new wagon road from Santa Fe to Fort Defiance; and conversations with his brother.[59]

Kern acknowledged that the construction of a railroad through this arid region would pose "numerous and serious obstacles—the scarcity of timber and water being the principal," but argued that the so-called Albuquerque route avoided the higher elevations and the heavy winter snows of the more northerly alternatives, as well as the sandy deserts of the Gila route to the south. Moreover, Kern asserted, the 35th parallel held the advantage of a central location.

To corroborate Kern's testimony, Senator Gwin called upon a number of other people who knew the area firsthand. The two topographical engineers whom Kern had accompanied across Arizona, Sitgreaves and Parke, warmly endorsed Kern's statement and went on to express confidence in Kern himself. "From Mr. Kern's extensive acquaintance with the country," Sitgreaves said, "I regard him as more competent than any other I know to give an intelligent opinion on the subject." Kern, Parke told Senator Gwin, "has amassed a fund of information about the general features of the country from the valley of the Mississippi river to the Pacific ocean, which is probably unequaled by that of any other individual." The litany of laudatory letters went on, all read into the Congressional Record on January 27.

William S. Messervy, a prominent Santa Fe merchant who was then in the capital, termed Kern "a gentleman of a high order of talent in his profession, and one whose integrity and intelligence recommend his opinions to be received with fullest confidence." Army paymaster and politician Francis A. Cunningham, who had known Kern in Santa Fe, wrote: "I cannot speak too highly of his industry in collecting, and sound judgment in arranging facts bearing on the geography of that Territory."[60]

The "Chief of Roads" had spoken, and his words delighted some of his old Santa Fe cronies. A railroad would bring people to New Mexico, and with people would come profits and perhaps even statehood. The Santa Fe *Gazette* applauded Kern's testimony; New Mexicans, the newspaper editorialized, owed a debt to "our friend R. H. Kern, who was for some years a resident of our territory; he has done us a noble act of kindness for which we trust our citizens will in some appropriate manner express their thanks."[61]

But no one could speak with sufficient authority to convince a majority of congressmen to put aside politics and support the 35th parallel route or any other. In early March, after eight years of intermittent debate, frustrated senators tried to extricate themselves from the seemingly insolvable railroad problem by shifting the question from the political sphere to the realm of science. On March 3, 1853, Congress approved an Army appropriations bill containing an amendment that authorized the secretary of war, Jefferson Davis, to spend up to $150,000 to carry out surveys that would determine "the most practicable and economical route for a railroad from the Mississippi River to the Pacific Ocean."[62] Richard Kern would join one of those surveys, but ironically he would not be assigned to work on the 35th parallel route that he favored. Instead, Davis would send Kern over the central route that had nearly taken his life in 1848. This time the journey would be fatal.

-7-
Martyrs to Physical Science: With Gunnison, 1853

THE PACIFIC RAILROAD surveys offered extraordinary opportunities for scientists and artists, and a stream of applications for employment flowed into Washington. The number was so great, one engineer noted, "that the services of many who had been most highly recommended were necessarily declined."[1] Kern's reputation and experience, however, together with his political influence, assured him a position with one of the surveys.

Congress approved the railroad survey bill on March 3, 1853; in early April, Secretary of War Jefferson Davis, who was in charge of the surveys, began to receive endorsements of Kern from influential people. Lt. Col. Stephen H. Long, a topographical engineer and himself a leader of several significant western expeditions, recommended Kern as "a gentleman and artist well qualified to serve in the capacity of guide, assistant and draughtsman" of one of the survey teams. Long summarized Kern's experiences with Frémont, Simpson, Judd, and Sitgreaves, and applauded Kern's maps. Long had been assigned by the War Department to do a study of the feasibility of a southern route to the Pacific and told Davis: "I have been aided mainly by the items of geographical intelligence kindly imparted by Mr. Kern."[2] In addition to Long's recommendation, Davis received a letter on Kern's behalf from Thomas Hart Benton of Missouri, whose reasons for supporting Kern at this time are not clear. Another letter came from Solon Borland, senator from Arkansas. Kern's knowledge of the country had impressed Borland, and he urged Davis to grant Kern a personal interview.[3]

Sometime in April, Jefferson Davis and Richard Kern met. Since Kern was an outspoken advocate of the 35th parallel route and one of the few Americans who had traversed its westernmost

215

reaches, it seemed likely that Davis would assign Kern to the survey of that route. Kern clearly expected that assignment. Earlier in the month, Lt. Amiel Weeks Whipple of the Topographical Corps arrived in Washington with orders to take charge of the 35th parallel survey. "He came to see me," Kern wrote, "and we immediately made arrangements to go together on the Albuquerque route. He left the city soon after, both being well pleased with our compact."[4]

But the arrangement that Kern and Whipple had made dissolved when Kern met the secretary of war. Col. J. J. Abert had advised Davis that Kern, instead of going with Whipple, should be assigned to the 38th parallel route because, as Kern immodestly and incorrectly explained to an acquaintance, "I was the only person who knew anything of that section of the country."[5] Following Abert's advice, Davis persuaded Kern to take the route he had followed with Frémont in 1848–49. Kern left the meeting satisfied: "Col. Davis had acted most kindly towards me—always heard me patiently and treated me with distinction." The pay, Davis told Kern, "is the highest of all"—$2000 per year and transportation. "I am satisfied," Kern wrote, "not so much with the pay, as with the feeling that my knowledge and services have been appreciated."[6]

Chance, then, put Kern on a survey that he described as "contrary to all my wishes and preconceived ideas," but it was not chance alone.[7] Politics had also

entered into Jefferson Davis's decision, notwithstanding the congressional plan to shift the decision into the seemingly rational sphere of science.

Thomas Hart Benton, thirty years a senator from Missouri until his defeat in the election of 1851, had remained a staunch advocate of the 38th parallel route, with its eastern terminus in Benton's own St. Louis. The Frémont debacle of 1849, spearheaded by Benton, had done nothing to diminish his enthusiasm for a route directly west of St. Louis. Indeed, on March 4, 1851, the day after Congress approved the appropriations bill for the Pacific railroad surveys, Benton drafted a lengthy letter "to the People of Missouri," in which he argued with senatorial eloquence for a survey of what he called the "Central National Highway from the Mississippi to the Pacific." Benton had this letter printed in Washington in the form of a twenty-four-page pamphlet and sent it to various newspapers. He also sent a copy to Jefferson Davis, with a letter urging that John C. Frémont be placed in charge of the survey. Frémont was then in Europe, but Benton had asked his son-in-law to return immediately.[8]

Davis sent Benton an equivocal reply, indicating that he needed more time to study the question. Meanwhile, Benton went into action. He persuaded Edward Fitzgerald Beale, who had just been named superintendent of Indian affairs for California, to proceed to his new post by way of the 38th parallel route. Benton hoped that a successful crossing of the continent by Beale would publicize the route and demonstrate its practicality. To be sure that his efforts did not go unnoticed, Beale invited his cousin, Gwinn Harris Heap, to go along. Heap doubled as journalist and artist on the expedition. His book, *Central Route to the Pacific*, appeared in 1854, with thirteen of his own illustrations.[9]

The Beale-Heap party left Washington on April 20. Twenty days later, on May 10, they started off over the Santa Fe Trail from Westport. Benton personally saw them off, making several rousing speeches along the way. With pride, he called attention to the modest provisions of the party, pointedly noting that "they are not a government party, do not equip at public expense, [and] did not graduate at West Point."[10]

Benton lashed out at the southern, or 32nd parallel route, favored by Jefferson Davis and the Topographical Bureau. Pointing to the Parke-Kern map of the Territory of New Mexico with Simpson's "proposed wagon road" on it, Benton said it "looks like Sonora, and not California, was the destination of the route! It actually runs down southwest within forty miles of that Mexican province, before it turns up northwest, to travel 800 miles to get to San Francisco!" In some places, Benton said, the route passed through shifting sands that would bury a man alive. "Beasts," Benton exclaimed, "have too much sense to go there, but the 'science' of the topographical bureau would put us there."[11]

If Jefferson Davis had been reluctant to survey the 38th parallel route, Ben-

ton's renewed agitation apparently prompted him to go through the motions of making a survey. Or so Davis had intimated to Richard Kern when the two had met in Washington in April. A reconnaissance of the 38th parallel route, Davis had told Kern, would represent "a compromise with Col. Benton, and if the route is found to be impracticable it will stop all cavil on his part, as one or more to whom he has been friendly are on the survey." So Kern was headed toward Zion, as he told an acquaintance, "Old Benton's Zion though and not mine."[12]

Although Davis had decided to launch a government-sponsored survey of the 38th parallel route, he did not put Frémont in charge. When Frémont returned from Europe in the summer, the railroad survey parties had already left. Benton could not be easily defeated, however. Openly suspicious of Davis's objectivity and motives, Benton sponsored a private survey of the 38th parallel, with Frémont at its head. Starting out in October, Frémont would try once again to demonstrate that the San Juan Mountains, which had proved impregnable in 1848–49, could be crossed in winter.[13]

Thus, in addition to the official War Department survey that Kern would accompany, two other expeditions set out over the central route in 1853: Beale in May and Frémont in October. The artist Gwinn Harris Heap accompanied Beale, and the artists F. W. Egloffstein and Solomon Carvalho accompanied Frémont. Beyond the Front Range of the southern Rockies, these artists entered a land largely unknown in American graphic arts. With the exception of lithographs of the Great Salt Lake and environs, published in the report of Howard Stansbury in 1852, the American public had no visual image of the terrain along much of Benton's controversial route.[14] In 1853, then, the artists' reconnaissance of the northern fringe of the Southwest began with Richard Kern once again among the vanguard.

Instead of Frémont, whose antislavery politics were anathema to Davis, the secretary of war put Capt. John Williams Gunnison in charge of the survey of the 38th parallel. A forty-year-old topographical engineer, West Point graduate, and experienced professional, Gunnison had assisted Capt. Howard Stansbury on a reconnaissance of the Great Basin in 1849–50. Gunnison had acquitted himself ably, and had gone beyond his official duties to write a reasonably objective study of *The Mormons . . . Their Rise and Progress, Peculiar Doctrines, Present Condition, and Prospects Derived from Personal Observations*. Published in 1852, this well-received book had brought Gunnison to national attention and probably influenced Davis to appoint him to lead a party headed for Utah.[15] In Milwaukee, on May 6, where he was overseeing harbor improvements, Gunnison received a telegram from J. J. Abert, summoning him to Washington and telling him that he would be taking charge of one of the railroad sur-

veys. Gunnison hastened to Washington where, on May 20, he received his official instructions from Jefferson Davis.[16]

Gunnison's orders required him to direct a survey of a route that would pass through the Rockies by way of the Huerfano River, the San Luis Valley, and Cochetopa Pass or some other appropriate pass, "into the region of Grand and Green rivers," then to the Great Basin and northerly to the Great Salt Lake. Along the way he was to study:

the nature of the rocks and soils; the products of the country, animal, mineral, and vegetable; the resources for supplies of material for the construction and means requisite for the operations of a railway, with a notice of the population, agricultural products, and the habits and languages of the Indian tribes; meteorological and magnetic observations; the hygrometrical and electrical states of the atmosphere, and astronomical observations for determining geographical points.[17]

Gunnison was not to proceed to the Pacific, but to return from Utah by way of South Pass and Fort Laramie. Davis was convinced that "no railway pass could be found north of Kern river, into either the Sacramento or San Joaquin valley." Moreover, he had learned that the Mormons were surveying a railroad route from Salt Lake to Walker's Pass on the 35th parallel. Gunnison, who knew Mormon leaders, was to obtain a copy of their survey and thus connect the 38th parallel and 35th parallel routes in the Sierras.[18]

To carry out this mission, Jefferson Davis assigned Lt. E. G. Beckwith of the third artillery to assist Gunnison, and authorized Gunnison to hire civilian experts, with the approval of the War Department. In addition to Kern, who held the position of topographer and artist, Gunnison's civilian staff would come to include eighteen-year-old James A. Snyder as assistant topographer; Sheppard Homans as astronomer; Frederick Creutzfeldt as botanist; James Schiel, a German scientist from the University of Heidelberg, as "surgeon, geologist, &c.," and Charles Taplin as wagonmaster.[19]

Kern may have helped Gunnison select his staff; he knew both Creutzfeldt and Taplin from the Frémont expedition, where Creutzfeldt had also served as botanist and where Taplin had been a member of Kern's "weak" group that survived the disaster. Kern had received his appointment from Secretary Davis on April 23, two weeks before Gunnison was summoned to Washington, and had probably begun then to line up personnel as well as equipment. As Davis explained to Gunnison on May 24:

> Before it was determined what officer was to take charge of the survey committed to your charge Mr R. H. Kern was appointed an Assistant Engineer, and directed to purchase instruments and make preparations for the expedition. From his long residence in, and acquaintance with the country through which the route will pass, the experience and knowledge of Mr Kern is considered to be very valuable.[20]

Kern seems to have moved swiftly to make preparations. Within a few days of Gunnison's appointment, Kern was ready to leave Washington for St. Louis. On May 12, the St. Louis *Democrat,* an unabashedly pro-Benton newspaper, had reported receiving a letter from Richard Kern announcing that he would be in St. Louis around May 15

> to fit out the government surveying party for the central route. Mr. Kern is an associate in that survey, and will revisit under happier auspices the ground which was so fatal to the little party [under Frémont] in the winter of 1848–49. Thus is fulfilled the promise of the Secretary at [of] War to Col. Benton; and thus will be vindicated the judgment of Frémont in selecting that route by the head of the *Del Norte* as the true one to the Pacific Ocean.[21]

Events did not move along as quickly as Kern thought they would, but by the end of May he was on his way to St. Louis, "made like the great [Henry] Clay," Kern joked, "another martyr to the compromise—mine dwindling down from the whole Union, to old Bullion's [Benton's]." Before he left, Kern visited family and friends in Philadelphia, spending his last evening there at the home of his sister, Mary, and her husband, William Wolfe. The next morning, Wolfe walked Kern to the railroad depot to see him off. Kern left "satisfied, contented, and buoyant in spirit, and pleased with the treatment he had received."[22]

With his assistant, James Snyder, Kern probably traveled by riverboat down the Ohio through Pittsburgh, then took a detour to Chicago, where he was to pick up some scientific instruments and join Gunnison. From Chicago, the three made their way down the Mississippi. They arrived in St. Louis on June 4 or 5, and checked into the Virginia Hotel.[23] James Simpson was in town, and he and Kern enjoyed a brief reunion. They talked over old times in New Mexico and Simpson shared Kern's excitement about the journey ahead: "Kern was all life and animation at the broad prospect before him of extending his explorations," Simpson later recalled, "and of associating his name next [to] those who have contributed to the geographical knowledge of his country."[24]

A couple of days after his arrival, Kern's name appeared in the local press. His involvement in the controversial railroad surveys had brought him more attention than his work as an artist had ever done. Indeed, several weeks before his arrival in St. Louis, one newspaper in that city had identified "Lt. Kern" as the leader of the survey party.[25] On June 7, the St. Louis *Missouri Republican* printed a long summary of a speech that Congressman John S. Phelps had given recently to a large crowd in his hometown of Springfield, in southwestern Missouri. A champion of his own district's interests and a "Judas" to Benton's supporters, Phelps favored the 35th parallel. That route, as Phelps saw it, would pass through Springfield, in southwestern Missouri. Phelps had sought information about the Albuquerque route from knowledgeable men, including Richard Kern, with whom

he had corresponded. In his speech at Springfield, Phelps read extracts from Kern's report to the Senate. Phelps praised Kern's "high character" and told his audience of Kern's "life in the mountains and . . . extensive information on this subject."[26]

The *Missouri Republican* itself expressed less enthusiasm about Kern. In its issue of June 8, the paper credited Kern with being the first to call public attention to the advantages of the 35th parallel route, but implied that Kern's loyalty to the Albuquerque route should preclude him from working on the survey of the 38th parallel: "We have yet to learn that he has abandoned his convictions in regard to the practicability of the Albuquerque route, or the utter impossibility of finding a way suitable anywhere in the neighborhood of the scene of *Frémont*'s disaster."

By June 9, Gunnison had finished purchasing supplies in St. Louis. He shipped them up the Missouri to Westport, Lieutenant Beckwith noted, "in charge of Mr. Kern, who was to transport them to some point suitable for a 'fitting out camp.'" Meanwhile, Gunnison and Beckwith took the steamer *Honduras* up the Missouri to Fort Leavenworth, where they picked up a military escort of thirty mounted riflemen under command of Bvt. Capt. Robert M. Morris. Then Gunnison took a stage to join Kern, who had selected a fine campsite in a grove near a spring about five miles from Westport.[27]

Within a few weeks, they had completed preparations to leave, including testing instruments, purchasing mules and horses, employing additional men, breaking in teams, and preparing nineteen wagons that were to be taken along to test their practicality on the route. It was imperative that the party get off as soon as possible, so that it could complete its work before winter caught them in the mountains. Moreover, the railroad survey bill required the secretary of war to deliver a final report to Congress by the first Monday of February 1854. To the expedition's German geologist, James Schiel, such haste seemed unreasonable. Preparations for such a lengthy expedition should require "considerable time," Schiel wrote, but in characteristic American fashion, he admitted, "everything went swiftly."[28]

Delayed a day by rains that would follow them across the Great Plains, the wagon train, sixty-men strong, set out on the road to Santa Fe on June 23. Three days later, the party divided. While the main group, under Lieutenant Beckwith, continued along the Santa Fe Trail, Gunnison took Kern and a few others to explore an alternate route by way of the Kansas River and its Smoky Hill Fork. On July 12, they rejoined the main group on the Arkansas River at Walnut Creek, near present-day Great Bend, Kansas, and continued to move up the Arkansas. Except for heat, mosquitos, and heavy rains that drenched them and made the crossing of streams difficult, the journey was uneventful.

For Richard Kern, the novelty and exhilaration of travel over western prairies must have been wearing thin. Work that had by now become routine dominated his days. "I am busy from sunrise to 10 P.M.," he reported to a correspondent.[29] If Kern kept a diary and a sketchbook on this trip, as was his usual practice, they have disappeared.

Dramatic changes had occurred on the Great Plains in the five years since Kern first went west. The heavy traffic of forty-niners and those who traveled in their wake had trampled the sea of grass, thinned the buffalo herds, and left a growing number of unmarked graves along the trail. Then, too, American military forces had moved farther west than they had been in 1848. On July 16, Gunnison halted his wagons at a new military post, Fort Atkinson, constructed in 1850 near present-day Dodge City. Two weeks later, on July 29, the wagon train passed by Bent's Fort. A lively gathering place for mountaineers and Indians, and a source of information for Frémont in 1848, the private trading post now lay in ruins: "its adobe walls still stand in part only, with here and there a tower and a chimney," Lieutenant Beckwith wrote.[30] In the summer of 1849, the great migration of California-bound Americans had brought cholera to the Cheyenne and upset the balance of power among William Bent's Indian customers. Bent had gone out of business with a bang: he planted kegs of gunpowder in the rooms of his adobe trading post and then put it to the torch.[31]

Beyond Bent's Fort, Gunnison's instructions called for him to continue

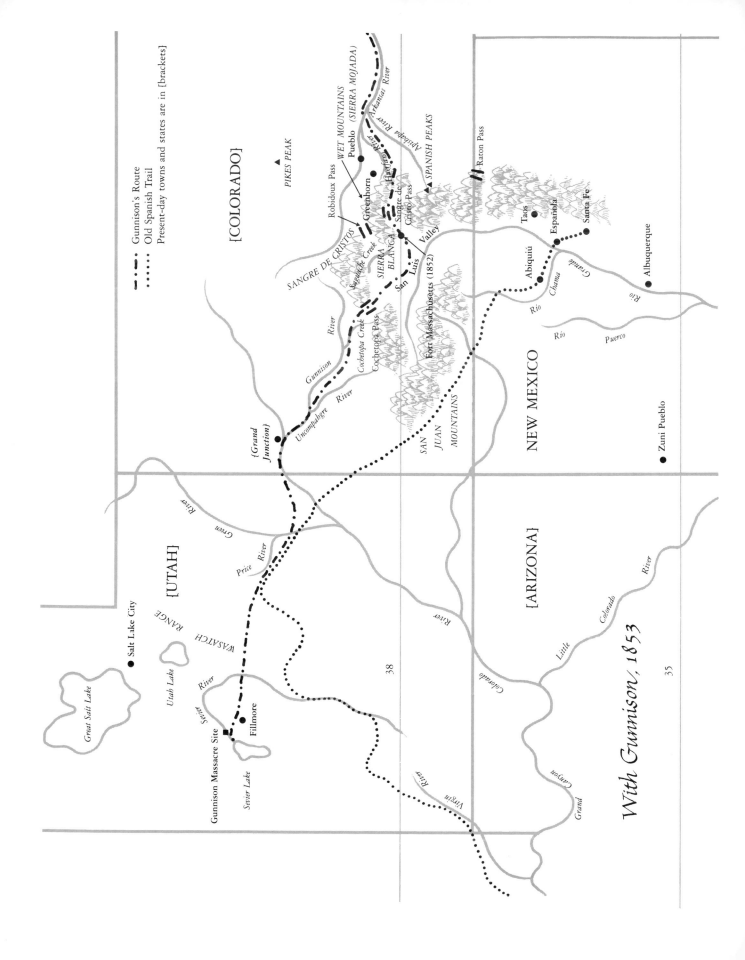

Gunnison's Route
Old Spanish Trail
Present-day towns and states are in [brackets]

[COLORADO]

PIKES PEAK

WET MOUNTAINS (SIERRA MOJADA)
Arkansas River
Huerfano River
Apishapa River
Pueblo
Greenhorn
Robidoux Pass
SPANISH PEAKS
Raton Pass
SANGRE DE CRISTOS
Saguache Creek
Sangre de Cristo Pass
SIERRA BLANCA
San Luis Valley
Taos
Española
Cochetopa Creek
Cochetopa Pass
San Luis
Abiquiú
Santa Fe
Gunnison River
Fort Massachusetts (1852)
Rio Chama
Rio Grande
Albuquerque
Uncompahgre River
SAN JUAN MOUNTAINS
NEW MEXICO
Rio Puerco
{Grand Junction}
Zuni Pueblo

Green River

[UTAH]
Price River
Salt Lake City
Utah Lake
WASATCH RANGE
Sevier River
Fillmore
Gunnison Massacre Site
Sevier Lake
Great Salt Lake

38

[ARIZONA]
Little Colorado River
Colorado River
Virgin River
Grand Canyon

35

With Gunnison, 1853

up the Arkansas to the Huerfano River and to follow that stream into the Sangre de Cristo Mountains. Gunnison mistook the Apishapa River for the Huerfano, however, and followed the Apishapa's southwesterly course for a few days before realizing his mistake. He blamed the error on "those in my command who had been in this country in winter, [and] could not recognize places and streams in a different season."[32] Kern may have been among those whom Gunnison had in mind. Opportunity for help, however, soon presented itself. When the Apishapa crossed a wagon road leading from Raton Pass to the tiny traders' settlements of Greenhorn and Pueblo, Gunnison sent Beckwith into town to obtain a guide.

Hardly into the Front Range of the Rockies and already lost, Gunnison must have known that the real work of the expedition had begun. The route across the Plains was well known, and no one doubted that iron rails could be laid across the gently undulating grasslands. But the defiant mountain and basin country beyond Front Range required careful surveying. This was reflected in the expedition's instructions and in its report. Although Kern probably drew sketches from the time the wagons rolled out of camp near Westport, the first of his drawings to appear in the official published report of the survey, volume two of the *Pacific Railroad Reports*, was a view of the mountains—the Spanish Peaks (fig. 119). While Beckwith had gone in search of a guide, Kern had apparently joined

Gunnison in climbing a ridge where, according to Gunnison, they could see "Pike's Peak to the north, the Spanish Peaks to the south, the Sierra Mojada to the west, and the plains from the Arkansas . . . the finest prospect it has ever fallen to my lot to have seen."[33] It was probably from this spot that Kern sketched the Spanish Peaks, whose Indian name, Wah-to-yah, "Breasts of the World," young Lewis Garrard had brought to the attention of the American reading public in a book by that title published in 1850. A prominent landmark for travelers, the Spanish Peaks had been drawn by Lieutenant Abert in 1846, and by Gwinn Harris Heap a few months before Kern arrived to sketch them. Of the lithographic views available to the public, Kern's had the greatest depth and power.[34]

Kern's view of the *Wah-ha-ta-gas or Spanish Peaks* was the first of a dozen full-page lithographs of his work to appear in the official report of the Gunnison survey. All twelve sketches were redrawn (and doubtless embellished upon) by John Mix Stanley, who prepared them for the lithographer. Since all but one of Kern's original sketches from the expedition are lost, these lithographs of Stanley's renderings of Kern's sketches constitute the major record, albeit a distorted one, of Kern's artistic work on his last reconnaissance.

With the help of Marcelino Baca, an experienced Mexican guide whom Beckwith hired at Greenhorn, the expedition found its way to the Huerfano, then cut a wagon road through dense

Fig. 119. *Wah-ha-ta-gas or Spanish Peaks.* Lithograph of a drawing by John Mix Stanley, based on a sketch by Richard H. Kern. *Reports of Explorations and Surveys . . . for a Railroad from the Mississippi River to the Pacific Ocean,* 13 vols. (Washington, D.C., 1854–1860), 2.

woods up to the summit of Sangre de Cristo Pass, just south of Robidoux Pass, where Frémont had crossed the Sangre de Cristos in 1848.[35] Three of John Mix Stanley's adaptations of Kern's sketches of Sangre de Cristo Pass are included in the *Pacific Railroad Reports.* Kern drew the pass on August 11 (fig. 120). The next day, perhaps, he made a sketch of *Sangre de Cristo Pass, from near the Summit, looking down Gunnison's Creek* (fig. 121). As they descended from the pass, Kern drew still another view, *Sangre de Cristo Pass Looking towards San Luis Valley,* with the Sierra Blanca peaks in the distance (fig. 122). Gwinn Harris Heap

Fig. 120. *View of Sangre de Cristo Pass, Looking northeast from Camp north of Summit, Aug. 11th.* Lithograph of a drawing by John Mix Stanley, based on a sketch by Richard H. Kern. *Reports of Explorations and Surveys . . . for a Railroad from the Mississippi River to the Pacific Ocean,* 13 vols. (Washington, D.C., 1854–1860), 2.

had crossed the pass in early June, but no drawings of it appeared in his book. Lithographs of Kern's sketches were probably the first views of the pass available to the public.

From the top of Sangre de Cristo Pass, on August 12, Kern began to draft a long letter to an acquaintance,

W. B. Phillips of New York City, who professed to be writing a book on the routes to the Pacific. Like Kern, Phillips favored a southern route, but ostensibly for a different reason. Phillips believed that a railroad with a southern terminus would help the South to achieve economic equilibrium with the North,

Fig. 121. *Sangre de Cristo Pass, From near the Summit looking down Gunnison's Creek.* Lithograph of a drawing by John Mix Stanley, based on a sketch by Richard H. Kern. *Reports of Explorations and Surveys . . . for a Railroad from the Mississippi River to the Pacific Ocean,* 13 vols. (Washington, D.C., 1854–1860), 2.

and thereby preserve the union. Kern opened his letter to Phillips with a dramatic image: "Summit of the Rocky Mountains, some five hundred feet above the clouds, and 8,000 above the rest of mankind."[36] The journey thus far, Kern wrote, had only confirmed his conviction that the "Benton Central route," as some called it, was impractical. Kern thought that the grades from the Huerfano to the summit of Sangre de Cristo Pass were too steep. A tunnel, perhaps a mile long, would be required to avoid high elevations, and snow would make the route impassable from December to April.

Strongly partisan, Kern seems to have lost all objectivity on this question. Gunnison himself had a better opinion of this portion of the route, and be-

Fig. 122. *Sangre de Cristo Pass Looking towards San Luis Valley, Sierra Blanca in the distance.* Lithograph of a drawing by John Mix Stanley, based on a sketch by Richard H. Kern. *Reports of Explorations and Surveys . . . for a Railroad from the Mississippi River to the Pacific Ocean,* 13 vols. (Washington, D.C., 1854–1860), 2.

lieved that he had found an easy way across the Sangre de Cristos at a nearby lower elevation.[37] As the expedition's topographer, Kern surely must have discussed this with Gunnison, but he neglected to mention the alternative route. Instead, Kern provided opponents of the 38th parallel route with vivid images. From his perch high above the rest of humanity, Kern described

to Phillips how "it is raining below me, whilst I am catching big hailstones, and some of the higher peaks that are just emerging from the clouds are lined with snow." When Kern's letter was later published, one critic questioned its authenticity. "How can a man catch 'big hail stones' when he is 'five hundred feet *above* the clouds,' . . . except on the hypothesis that it *hails upwards*

Fig. 123. *Fort Massachusetts, At the foot of the Sierra Blanca. Valley of San Luis.* Lithograph of a drawing by John Mix Stanley, based on a sketch by Richard H. Kern. *Reports of Explorations and Surveys . . . for a Railroad from the Mississippi River to the Pacific Ocean,* 13 vols. (Washington, D.C., 1854–1860), 2.

in the Rocky Mountains; or hails downwards so hard that the rebound from rocks below, carries the 'big hailstones' full 'five hundred feet' upwards!" Actually, the phenomenon that Kern describes is possible. While some clouds were below him, hail might well have formed in another cloud layer above.[38]

Descending Sangre de Cristo Creek, Gunnison's party entered the San Luis Valley, a place that must have brought back dismal memories for Richard Kern. Instead of the utter desolation he met there in the winter of 1848–49, however, Kern found a newly constructed military post. Fort Massachusetts had been built the previous summer to protect the settlements of northern New Mexico from Utes and Jicarilla Apaches. Until the creation of Colorado Territory

Fig. 124. *Peaks of the Sierra Blanca, from near Fort Massachusetts.* Lithograph of a drawing by John Mix Stanley, based on a sketch by Richard H. Kern. *Reports of Explorations and Surveys . . . for a Railroad from the Mississippi River to the Pacific Ocean,* 13 vols. (Washington, D.C., 1854–1860), 2.

in 1861, New Mexico had extended north to the 38th parallel and embraced the San Luis Valley.

Kern made one of the two known drawings of Fort Massachusetts, which was abandoned in 1858. He sketched it from its most dramatic angle, with Blanca Peak rising behind it to the northwest (fig. 123). The fort itself occupies the center of Kern's sketch, with the stables visible to the left.[39] From near Fort Massachusetts, Kern also redrew a scene he had painted in 1849— the *Peaks of the Sierra Blanca* (fig. 124), looking much craggier than he had delineated them in his earlier work (see plate 4).

For over a week, the survey party camped on Ute Creek, near the fort. The delay gave Kern an opportunity to complete some correspondence, including the long letter he had begun to write at the summit of Sangre de Cristo Pass. Kern still insisted that the altitude along the route they were following was excessive, and he exclaimed over the cold in August: "I have a fire six feet high in front of my tent. Three blankets and a robe are none too much for comfort."[40]

The need to obtain another guide had occasioned the delay at Fort Massachusetts. Marcelino Baca had fulfilled his contract to lead the surveyors over the Sangre de Cristos, and was heading home to Greenhorn. After getting lost on the Apishapa, Gunnison had come to appreciate what Beckwith termed the "practical lesson in geography gained in the school of the trapper and hunter," so Gunnison sent Beckwith to Taos to hire a guide who knew the country to the west.[41] Beckwith soon returned with three hunters and Antoine Leroux, the veteran trapper who had furnished information to Kern and Parke for their map of New Mexico, and who had led Sitgreaves across Arizona in 1851. Once again, Kern would be following "Watkin" Leroux's lead, but only as far as the Green River crossing of what the Americans called the Spanish Trail, a traders' route that connected Santa Fe and Los Angeles. Leroux had agreed to guide Gunnison to the Green River, in present-day Utah, but no farther. He had to return to Taos to meet Lt. Amiel Whipple, whose survey party Leroux had promised to lead across central Arizona later that fall. Leroux would have

the unique distinction of guiding two of Jefferson Davis's survey parties that year.[42]

On August 23, the expedition set out to skirt the north rim of the San Luis Valley, with Gunnison, Kern, the biologist Creutzfeldt, and others taking a side trip to examine Robidoux Pass. Although the days were oppressively hot, Creutzfeldt remembered very well the snow-bound camp they had made at the edge of the great sand hills five years before.[43]

Beyond Fort Massachusetts, the men began what Gunnison knew would be the most difficult part of the journey. Leroux seemed pessimistic about getting the wagons through. None had ever passed over the Cochetopa route into the Great Basin. "If I get through it will be a triumph," Gunnison had written to his wife.[44] Moreover, the memory of the Frémont disaster remained fresh. At the time of Gunnison's appointment, the Washington correspondent for the Baltimore *Sun* had wondered if Gunnison would be able to cross "the *Jornada del Muertos* or Death Pass, in which so many of Frémont's men perished."[45] As Gunnison's band crossed the San Luis Valley, Lieutenant Beckwith noted, Frémont's tragedy attracted "its full share of attention and comments, some of the gentlemen of our party having participated in that misfortune."[46]

The weather was good and locating the pass proved no problem. Skirting the northern edge of the San Luis Valley, Leroux led Gunnison to the little-traveled north branch of the Old Span-

Fig. 125. *Coo-che-to-pa Pass, View looking up Sahwatch Creek, Sept. 1st.* Lithograph of a drawing by John Mix Stanley, based on a sketch by Richard H. Kern. *Reports of Explorations and Surveys . . . for a Railroad from the Mississippi River to the Pacific Ocean,* 13 vols. (Washington, D.C., 1854–1860), 2.

ish Trail, coming up from Taos and long used by Mexicans heading north to trade with Utes in present-day Colorado and Utah.[47] This variant of the Old Spanish Trail followed Saguache Creek out of the San Luis Valley and over the San Juan Mountains and the Continental Divide by way of Cochetopa Pass—the pass that had eluded Frémont in 1848–49. The map that

Kern had prepared with Lieutenant Parke represented the best chart of this region; now Kern had a chance to see it firsthand. On September 1, he sketched the narrowing valley of the Saguache: *Coo-che-to-pa Pass, View Looking up Sahwatch Creek* (fig. 125). The next day the party reached the summit, after cutting a wagon road through quaking aspen and spruce. The crossing

Fig. 126. *Head of the First Cañon of Grand River, below the Mouth of Coo-che-to-pa Creek, Sept. 7.* Lithograph of a drawing by John Mix Stanley, based on a sketch by Richard H. Kern. *Reports of Explorations and Surveys . . . for a Railroad from the Mississippi River to the Pacific Ocean,* 13 vols. (Washington, D.C., 1854–1860), 2.

of the San Juans over this low pass (10,032 ft.) went smoothly, and by September 6 the surveyors had found their way down the western slope to what they called Grand River, now known as the Gunnison.[48]

The surveyors struck the Gunnison River near the present-day town of Gunnison, and attempted to follow the river westward. But as the river dis-

appeared into the two-thousand-foot-deep gorge of the Black Canyon, they were, Gunnison explained, "forced . . . upon the rocky hills, cut through transversely by creeks, whose gullies were difficult to cross without much labor."[49] With ropes and locked wheels, they coaxed their wagon teams down steep ravines, then whipped them up the other side. Axles cracked under the strain and

Fig. 127. *View of Ordinary Lateral Ravines on Grand River, From Camp Sept.br 3.* Lithograph of a drawing by John Mix Stanley, based on a sketch by Richard H. Kern. *Reports of Explorations and Surveys . . . for a Railroad from the Mississippi River to the Pacific Ocean,* 13 vols. (Washington, D.C., 1854–1860), 2.

the wagons began "to become true invalids," as Creutzfeldt put it. "Two of them made a sumersault today by which they are not essentially improved," he wrote on September 14. Three lithographs of Kern's sketches of this rugged country appeared in the *Pacific Railroad Reports* (figs. 126, 127, 128). Kern's only known field sketch from the expedition was also made along the Gun-

nison—an unfinished view emphasizing topographical detail, showing Black Mesa in the distance, and entitled *Grand River Mesa*.[50]

Once in the valley of the Uncompahgre, the going became easier. Still on the north branch of the Old Spanish Trail, the party descended the Uncompahgre to the Gunnison, then continued downstream along the widening

Fig. 128. *Summit of the Nearest Ridges South of Grand River, Traversed in passing around lateral Cañones 12 O'clock. Sept.bre 12.* Lithograph of a drawing by John Mix Stanley, based on a sketch by Richard H. Kern. *Reports of Explorations and Surveys . . . for a Railroad from the Mississippi River to the Pacific Ocean,* 13 vols. (Washington, D.C., 1854–1860), 2.

valley of the Gunnison to its mouth on the Colorado River, at present-day Grand Junction. From there, Leroux led them westerly along the Colorado to Bitter Creek, near the present Utah-Colorado line. At Bitter Creek, Leroux pointed them west, across the desert plateau country to the main branch of the Spanish Trail. Having fulfilled his contract, Leroux was eager to return to Taos and

his rendezvous with Lieutenant Whipple. On his way back to Taos, where he would later castigate Gunnison for the "miserable organization" of his party and for his failure to take the shortest route or the best pass through the San Juans, Leroux carried Richard Kern's copy of the field map of the expedition's route as far as Bitter Creek. With no attribution to the artist, Kern's copy of

Fig. 129. *View of the Roan or Book Mountains, At the Spanish Trail Ford of Green River, Oct. 1st.* Lithograph of a drawing by John Mix Stanley, based on a sketch by Richard H. Kern. *Reports of Explorations and Surveys . . . for a Railroad from the Mississippi River to the Pacific Ocean*, 13 vols. (Washington, D.C., 1854–1860), 2.

the field map would be published the following year in a report of the secretary of war, Jefferson Davis.[51]

Temporarily without a guide, Gunnison led his entourage into the Mormon country. On the Green River, Kern made a sketch of the historic ford where the Old Spanish Trail crossed the wide, shallow water, with the Roan Cliffs in the background (fig. 129). "Desolate as is the country over which we have passed, and around us," Beckwith wrote that day, "the view is still one of the most beautiful and pleasing I remember to have seen."[52] A few days beyond the Green, on October 1, they made their way over the hills toward Price River, where Kern drew what would be the last of his sketches to be adapted for the *Pacific Railroad Reports,* a view he

Fig. 130. *Rock Hills between Green and White Rivers. Oct.r 2.d, Wahscatch {sic} Mountains in the distance.* Lithograph of a drawing by John Mix Stanley, based on a sketch by Richard H. Kern. *Reports of Explorations and Surveys . . . for a Railroad from the Mississippi River to the Pacific Ocean,* 13 vols. (Washington, D.C., 1854–1860), 2.

entitled *Rock Hills between Green and White Rivers* (fig. 130).

By mid-October, the surveyors had crossed much of Utah. Paralleling the well-worn Spanish Trail, Gunnison's nineteen wagons had made it over the Wasatch Range into the valley of the Sevier River. Now the days and nights grew colder, and it was clear that the season for surveying was nearly over.

Gunnison planned to stop work soon and head north to Salt Lake City to take up winter quarters, as he and Stansbury had done four years earlier. First, however, Gunnison wanted to explore the area around Sevier Lake. To hasten the work, he divided his command. On October 25, Gunnison led a contingent of eleven men, including Richard Kern and the grumbling, dyspeptic Creutzfeldt, south toward the lake. It was a risky decision, as Gunnison knew. A group of California-bound emigrants had passed through the valley some weeks before and had indiscriminately killed some Pahvant Indians, a Ute people, who had come peaceably to trade. The Pahvants would want revenge. In the last letter Gunnison would write to his wife, penned at Manti on October 18, Gunnison reported: "there is a war between the Mormons and the Indians and parties of less than a dozen do not dare to travel. . . . May the favor of Heaven attend us until the work is accomplished."[53]

But Heaven's favor had ceased. On the morning of October 26, as the first rays of the sun came over the mountains, the crack of rifle fire from nearby willows punctuated breakfast. One man was struck down immediately, and the camp was thrown into confusion. Gunnison, according to one account, rushed from his tent unarmed, making signs to the Indians to hold their fire. A volley of arrows cut him down. Kern's life ended quickly, as a well-aimed rifle ball ripped through his chest into his heart. Creutzfeldt, William Potter (the Mormon guide), a camp keeper named John Bellows, and three privates also died in the surprise attack. Four men escaped to tell the story.[54]

Twenty-four hours later, the head of the military escort, Captain Morris, reached the scene, but found no survivors. Indians and wolves had mutilated the bodies; some, Kern's among them, had been stripped of their cloth-ing. Fifteen arrows protruded from Gunnison's body, and his left arm had been severed at the elbow. Both of Creutzfeldt's arms had been cut off. Lacking the proper implements, Capt. Morris left without burying the dead. Over a week later, a group of Mormons sent by Brigham Young arrived to dig the graves. During the interval, wolves had finished their work. The Mormons had the unhappy task of gathering up scattered, nearly fleshless bones. The remains of Gunnison and Potter were taken to nearby Fillmore for burial. The remains of the other men were buried at the site of the attack, one grave for Creutzfeldt, one for Kern, and a common grave for the rest. As the burial party finished its work, angry Pahvants, one of whom wore Kern's cap, rode up and surrounded them. After some discussion, the Pahvants agreed to help the Mormons retrieve some of Gunnison's equipment, and no altercation ensued. Mormons and Pahvants then rode away, leaving Kern and the others in their final resting place, a desolate spot some six miles west of present-day Deseret, Utah.[55]

The stunned survivors of the expedition remembered their last moments with their deceased companions. Sheppard Homans, Gunnison's astronomer, recalled that he usually went on such side trips, not Kern. "In fact, Mr. Kern was so unwell the evening before, that I was requested to be in readiness to take his place, but fortunately for me, he was much better the next morning, as to be able to go."[56] In a more emotional letter, written three days after the killings, Kern's young assistant, James Snyder, lamented: "I am all alone, and have lost one whom I loved dearly, and who had been as a father to me." To his own father, Snyder described his last hours with Richard Kern:

One of the men who escaped has just returned, and brought me a guard that was upon Mr. K's neck, this being the only thing the Indians left upon his person. The night before he left he told me, if he did not return, how to dispose of his books and other articles. His books and paints he wished me to give to his brother N., (now in the Arctic expedition) and his money to his sister. It seems as if every man who was along with him had a presentment of what was to happen. The morning Mr. Kern left he bid me 'good bye,' saying he should not see me again. A tear fell from his eye at the time.

I cannot write more at present, as my feelings are worked up to a high pitch.[57]

When news of the tragedy reached James Simpson in Minnesota, he was doubly grieved, for he had known Gunnison as well as Kern. Deeply moved at the loss of two friends, Simpson wrote a eulogy. The Kern brothers, he said, "were remarkable for their spirit of adventure and geographical enterprise." Both Edward and Richard

proved themselves most eminent artists. They were not only capital sketchers, but were good portrait painters and most excellent topographers. . . . Never can the writer forget the zeal with which they both, but more particularly the deceased, assisted him in the discharge of his public duties; and no one has greater reason

to feel grateful for acts of kindness and generosity shown to him by the deceased, under circumstances when they were truly cordial to his heart, than the undersigned. But both he and Gunnison are gone! . . . May they long be remembered as martyrs to physical science, and their respective relatives not remain long without some substantial token from the Government and Congress that their labors have been appreciated and their memories cherished![58]

Whether Kern's family ever received a "substantial token" is not known. Two of Richard's brothers, John and George, had enough difficulty trying to collect what the government owed Richard at the time of his death. George, who apparently had worked in the United States Appraisers Office of the Port of Philadelphia during all the years his brothers were in the West, opened correspondence with Jefferson Davis on the matter on December 19, 1853. Six months later, in June 1854, John Kern, who still lived at 62 Filbert Street and who was serving as administrator of the estate, was still trying to determine what the government owed his late brother. Nearly a year after Richard's death, in September 1854, the estate remained unsettled. That month John began searching for one of the survivors of the Gunnison expedition who might have Richard's personal effects, hoping that Richard's papers might answer some questions.[59]

A bloodstone ring engraved with a **K**, which Richard had worn at the time of his murder, may have been returned to his family. Indians had removed the ring from Kern's body, but a Mormon Indian agent had recovered it, along with some other equipment taken during the massacre, and had turned those items over to Brigham Young. Several years later, while exploring in the Great Basin, Lt. Simpson heard the story of the bloodstone ring and how it had been delivered to Brigham Young. Simpson wrote to Young, offering to return the ring to Kern's family, with whom Simpson professed to be "intimately acquainted." Young, however, told Simpson that he had given the ring to lieutenants Beckwith and Morris; they presumably returned it to the Kerns.[60]

At the time of Richard's death, Edward Kern was sailing toward the Far East with the North Pacific Expedition, under Commander Cadwalader Ringgold. News of the tragedy probably reached him at Hong Kong. His grief-stricken and angry brother-in-law, William Wolfe, had sent newspaper clippings. Wolfe, who probably reflected the feelings of many members of the family, thought Gunnison "a fool" for risking his life and the lives of his men. In contrast, Richard had behaved nobly by agreeing to go with Gunnison, despite his misgivings, thereby sparing the life of young James Snyder. Richard "is no more," Wolfe wrote. "The Indians done their work effectually, by shooting him through the heart. . . . It is to be hoped therefore he did not suffer, if any but a very short time."[61]

Just as Richard Kern had lived an uncommon life, so he came to an uncommon death, killed in what one his-torian has termed "the worst disaster suffered by the Army in the West up to that time."[62] Indeed, Richard Kern may have been the only artist in American history to be killed by Indians while in the line of duty.

The public was outraged. Some bigots accused Mormons, disguised as Indians, of committing the deed, and the episode contributed to a deterioration of relations between Mormons and the federal government. Most observers, however, including Lieutenant Beckwith, saw no evidence of a Mormon plot. Other angry commentators blamed Indians—all Indians—and took the occasion to rail against federal policies that supposedly protected and coddled them. The St. Louis *Intelligencer* deplored the deaths of "men such as GUNNISON and KERN one of whose lives was worth more to humanity and progress than all the copper-skin devils that skulk and crawl in filth and vermin between the Mississippi River and the Pacific Ocean."[63]

Ironically, the newspapers that carried such stories from coast to coast brought more attention to Kern in death than any of his achievements had earned him during his lifetime. In Philadelphia, where the local press had remained oblivious of his activities, the *Public Ledger* ran a front page story about "Capt." Kern's death. The *Ledger* identified Kern as a native of Philadelphia, noting that he was "a man of fine attainments, a topographical engineer and an artist. His loss will afflict many relatives and personal friends who were warmly attached to him."[64] Perhaps the most rhetorical tribute came from Henry Schoolcraft, who pronounced Kern

one of the most daring, intelligent, experienced, and cultivated pioneers . . . a very superior draftsman, a thorough scholar, and accomplished linguist, and gifted with that sagacity and energy which are so invaluable to those who lead a mountain and frontier life.[65]

It remained for others to complete Kern's work. The Pahvants who took his life had also taken some of his topographical drawings and sketches, but these were soon recovered with the aid of Mormons who traded them back from the Indians for some shirts and blankets.[66] Lieutenant Beckwith, who considered Kern "an accomplished topographer and artist," turned Kern's topographical sketches over to the expedition's astronomer, Sheppard Homans, who used them as the basis for a map of the route.[67] The final drawing of the maps for the published report was rendered by an artist whom Beckwith luckily encountered at Salt Lake.

On March 1, 1854, as Beckwith was preparing to leave winter quarters and resume the survey, two exhausted artists, F. W. Egloffstein and Solomon Nunes Carvalho, made their way into the city. The two had been members of Frémont's late-departing expedition that had followed Gunnison's wagon road west and had suffered terribly through the winter. Too weary to go on to California, the artists had abandoned Frémont and headed to Salt Lake

to recuperate. Beckwith offered them employment. Carvalho declined, but Egloffstein accepted and took Kern's place. It was he who redrew Kern's topographical sketches into the four polished maps that appear in volume eleven of the *Pacific Railroad Reports*. Attributed to "Richard H. Kern, Topographer in the Field," the maps show the route from the western boundary of Missouri to the Wasatch Mountains.[68]

Kern's field sketches were sent back to Washington and placed in the hands of John Mix Stanley, an artist whose experience in New Mexico, California, and Oregon would have won Kern's respect and whom Kern may have known personally. Kern was familiar with the illustrations that Stanley had done for Major Emory's report of his 1846 tour of New Mexico and Arizona, and Kern almost certainly visited Stanley's gallery of Indian paintings that hung in the Smithsonian in 1852 and for many years thereafter. Like Kern, Stanley had painted and worked in Washington in 1852–1853, and had received an appointment as artist on one of the Pacific railroad surveys. Stanley had accompanied Isaac Stevens on the reconnaissance of the northern route, then returned to Washington in early 1854.[69] A year or so later, Stanley redrew a dozen of Kern's sketches for the *Pacific Railroad Reports*. These appeared in volume two of the *Reports*, published in 1855, as large, handsome lithographs, most of them tinted.[70]

Lavishly illustrated in oversize volumes, the *Pacific Railroad Reports* cost

Fig. 131. *Rafting Across Grand River.* Lithograph based on a drawing by Gwinn Harris Heap. Gwinn Harris Heap, *Central Route to the Pacific . . .* (Washington, D.C., 1854).

more to print than the government had spent on the surveys themselves, and they were widely discussed and admired. They put the name of Richard Kern among some of the foremost contemporary artists of the West—men such as John C. Tidball, Gustav Sohon, Frederick W. Egloffstein, Balduin Möllhausen, and Stanley himself. After his death, Kern's work enjoyed its largest distribution—some twenty-one thousand copies of volume two of the *Pacific Railroad Reports* were printed.[71]

The lithographs of the Stanley/Kern sketches that appeared in the *Pacific Railroad Reports,* together with the drawings that Gwinn Harris Heap used to illustrate his *Central Route to the Pacific* (1854), gave the American public the first authentic published views of

Fig. 132. *View on Green River.* Lithograph based on a drawing by Gwinn Harris Heap. Gwinn Harris Heap, *Central Route to the Pacific . . .* (Washington, D.C., 1854).

the 38th parallel route from the Rockies to the Mormon country.[72] The works of Stanley/Kern and Heap nicely complemented one another. Heap drew scenes of some places that Kern ignored, such as the Huerfano River, and Kern drew some places that Heap did not, such as Sangre de Cristo Pass. Where the two drew the same view, their styles also complemented one an-

other. The lithographs of the Stanley/Kern work, clearly superior in quality and craftsmanship to those in Heap's book, possess a formal, majestic, almost transcendent quality. Heap lacked Kern's polish and ability to convey perspective and proportion, but he infused his scenes, such as *Rafting across Grand River* (fig. 131), with human vitality that is lacking in the more classical studies of Stanley and Kern.[73] The contrast is clear in the view that each artist did of the Green River with the Roan Mountains in the background. People in Heap's view are engaged in activity and become central to the subject (fig. 132). The figures in the Stanley/Kern view strike a pose that seems designed to suggest human scale, but not to distract the viewer from the grandeur of nature (see fig. 129).

The two artists who entered the Rockies with Frémont in the fall of 1853, Egloffstein and Carvalho, were destined for disappointment. Frémont never completed his plan to publish an account of his journey, and whatever work Carvalho and Egloffstein did for him was, in the main, lost to contem-poraries. Indeed, the daguerreotypes and drawings done by Carvalho were destroyed in a warehouse fire, although many of the engravings made from the daguerreotypes were saved and used to illustrate Frémont's *Memoirs*, published over three decades later, in 1886.[74] All but one of Kern's original drawings from the Gunnison survey seem to have disappeared. Like much of his work, however, imperfect images of those sketches, redrawn by Stanley, survived through the medium of lithography. These views enlightened Kern's contemporaries and have provided posterity with invaluable glimpses of how one mid-nineteenth-century artist interpreted a remote part of the newly acquired American Southwest.

-8-
Richard Kern in Perspective

TRAGEDY CUT Richard Kern's career short, but he had managed in a few years to leave a remarkable legacy. Kern gave the American public some of the earliest authentic graphic images of Arizona, New Mexico, and southern Colorado and the first views of many of the people and places in the Far Southwest. The earliest published portrayals of Navajo, Zuni, Pai, Mojave, and Pueblo Indians from Jémez, Pecos, and Santa Ana came from his sketches. Richard Kern also provided the public with the first views of what are today some of the most celebrated sites in the region: Chaco Canyon, Canyon de Chelly, Wupatki, and Inscription Rock, as well as the first images of a host of landmarks such as Mount Taylor, the Falls of the Little Colorado, and San Francisco Mountain. In addition to these early images, Kern also drew the best map the region had yet known and contributed to the early study of anthro-pology, archaeology, and history of the Far Southwest. In retrospect it is clear that Richard Kern was one of the most talented and prolific of that small group of artist-explorers who ventured into the dangerous lands beyond the frontier to document the newly acquired territory.

Kern's contemporary expeditionary artists in the Southwest included James W. Abert and John Mix Stanley, who had arrived in the region two years before him; Henry Pratt, John Russell Bartlett, and German-born and trained Arthur Schott, who worked on the U.S.-Mexican boundary surveys; Balduin Möllhausen, another German artist, who accompanied Whipple on the 35th parallel survey in 1853–54 and Ives on the survey of the Colorado River in 1858; Carl Schucard, still another German artist, whose illustrations appeared in A. B. Gray's survey of the 32nd parallel; and Gwinn Harris Heap, Fred-

245

erick W. Egloffstein, and Solomon Carvalho who, as we have seen, worked along the 38th parallel at the same time that Kern did.[1]

In addition to these expeditionary artists, a few other men drew views of the Southwest in the years following the war with Mexico. Some of their sketches, such as those made by soldiers like Pvt. Josiah Rice, or forty-niners like H. M. T. Powell, remained in private journals and had no influence on contemporaries.[2] Other drawings found their way into books and magazines. Lt. George Douglas Brewerton, who had studied drawing at West Point and traveled across the Southwest in 1848, did interesting genre scenes that served as the basis for wood engravings in a series of articles in *Harper's New Monthly Magazine,* beginning in 1853.[3] Watercolor drawings of village and military posts in New Mexico by Brvt. Lt. Col. Joseph Henry Eaton, who was stationed at Fort Defiance in the Navajo country, appeared as engravings in W. W. H. Davis's book, *El Gringo; or, New Mexico and her People,* published in 1857. Fredrick Augustus Percy of El Paso also contributed to Davis's volume, with views of El Paso and Fort Bliss.[4]

In the main, however, the most impressive artistic reportage of the newly acquired Southwest came from government-funded topographic artists such as Richard Kern. These expeditionary artists were assigned to record people, places, flora, and fauna with accuracy, making images to accompany scientific reports. They had little competition from the camera. The daguerreotype had been announced to the world in 1839, and equipment and chemicals had been hauled into the Rockies in the 1840s and 1850s, but the daguerreotype process proved too slow and cumbersome to use efficiently in the field.[5] Its successor, the collodion negative process, was introduced in the 1850s but was slow to win acceptance. When James H. Simpson took photographers and cameras on an expedition into Great Basin in 1859, he found the results disappointing for distant views: "the camera is not adapted to explorations in the field, a good artist, who can sketch readily and accurately, is much to be preferred."[6]

After the Civil War, however, the photographer quickly eclipsed the artist on government-sponsored surveys in the West. Some artists still found employment on special assignments, but technological changes in photography rendered the topographic artist increasingly obsolete. The collodion process enabled photographers to make unlimited numbers of paper prints from glass negatives (the daguerreotypist could make only one image per exposure). Thus, actual photographs instead of printed reproductions could be used in government reports. Perhaps most important, scientists and the general public alike believed that photographs were more objective than drawings.[7]

In presuming the infallibility of the camera, many forgot that the photographer, like the artist, can rearrange a scene, manipulate a subject, or evoke as well as document. As the crusading twentieth-century photographer Lewis Hine put it: "While photographs may not lie, liars may photograph."[8] But whatever its limits, the chemical wizardry of the black box was irresistible. The demand for photographs and stereographs of western scenes soared, and the need for topographic artists diminished. Nonetheless, the work of Kern's generation of artist-explorers has lived on in lithographs and in reproductions of lithographs that have continued to appear in books and magazines up to the present day.

In the nineteenth century, armchair artists often copied the work of their more adventurous counterparts in the West, shamelessly plagiarizing their work as illustrations for books and magazines.[9] Kern was among those artists who received the high compliment of imitation. Perhaps the first artist to plagiarize one of Kern's drawings was Frederick Augustus Percy of El Paso. In 1854, Percy prepared a newsletter illustrated with four watercolors. Two were profiles of Indians taken without acknowledgment from James H. Simpson's *Journal* of the Navajo expedition. One of these Indians was a leader of Santa Ana Pueblo, *Ow-te-wa* (fig. 37), sketched by Richard Kern and drawn by Edward Kern. Percy made a watercolor copy of this Pueblo Indian, *Ow-te-ow-ka,* identifying him as *Chief of the Dog Cañon Indians,* and claiming to have drawn his portrait from life (fig. 133). Similarly, Percy turned a Kern portrait of a Pecos Indian into *the late celebrated*

Fig. 133. *Portrait from Life of the Chief of the Dog-Cañon Indians. From life by the "Ancient Briton." Ow-te-ow-ka. Big White Bead.* Watercolor by Frederick Augustus Percy, in Rex W. Strickland, *El Paso in 1854* (El Paso, 1969). Courtesy, Texas Western Press, El Paso. Compare with fig. 37.

Fig. 134. *Navajo in War Costume*. Engraving by Theodore Rabuski. *Harper's New Monthly Magazine* (April 1854). Compare with fig. 140.

chief of the tribe of Mescalera Apaches, taken from life by the Artist.[10]

Percy's manuscript newsletter, prepared in 1854, did not find its way into print for over one hundred years. The first published borrowing of Kern's drawings probably appeared in *Harper's New Monthly Magazine* in 1854. As illustrations for George Douglas Brewerton's "Incidents of Travel in New Mexico," *Harper's* reproduced a number of woodcuts based on drawings attributed to one Rabuske. The artist, who was almost certainly the Polish-born Theodore Rabuski, probably never saw the Southwest. Instead, often without acknowledging his sources, Rabuski copied illustrations from Josiah Gregg's *Commerce of the Prairies*, Col. W. H. Emory's *Notes of a Military Reconnoissance* [*sic*], and Lt. James Simpson's *Journal*. From the latter, Rabuski copied Kern's *Navajo Costume* and retitled the engraving *Navajo in War Costume* (fig. 134). Either Rabuski or Brewerton himself also copied the portrait of the Navajo leader *Chapaton*, drawn by Edward Kern from a sketch by Richard (see fig. 53). The artist reversed the image and retitled the drawing *Head of Navajo Indian.* Brewerton acknowledged that he was "indebted to the sketches of Mr. R. H. Kern" for the "original" drawings.[11]

The first published plagiarism of Kern's drawings probably appeared in a work by Abbe Em. Domenech, who never visited most of the places he claimed to have seen during *Seven Years' Residence in the Great Deserts of North*

America. This fraudulent compilation was published in two volumes in London in 1860, followed by a French edition two years later. Fifty-eight woodcuts by A. Joliet enlivened the pages of both editions. Three of Joliet's illustrations were crude copies, with images reversed, of lithographs of Richard Kern's work taken from Simpson's *Journal:* full-length portraits of the Jémez chief Hosta and of the Navajo warrior, and a view of Inscription Rock. Joliet also copied, again in reverse, two of Richard Kern's illustrations from Sitgreaves's *Report:* Sycamore Canyon in Arizona and a view of the Falls of the Little Colorado (fig. 135).[12]

In an era when plagiarism of words was commonplace, there was nothing unusual about the flagrant appropriation of Kern's visual images. American artists and publishers continued to pirate lithographs of Kern's drawings until the end of the century. For example, among the over one hundred engravings that appeared in Samuel Woodworth Cozzens's book *The Marvelous Country: or Three Years in Arizona and Mexico . . .* (1873), eight were based on drawings by Richard Kern.[13] William Thayer's *Marvels of the New West . . . Illustrated with Three Hundred and Seventy-nine Fine Engravings and Maps* (1887), also borrowed liberally from Richard Kern. Thayer even used some of the same plates that had appeared in Cozzens's book.[14] In both cases, the artist remained anonymous. Similarly, when *Harper's Magazine* published an article on "The First Americans" in 1882,

its lead illustration was a slightly modified version of Kern's *Northwest View of the Pueblo Pintado* in Chaco Canyon, with the Romantic addition of long-winged birds silhouetted against the sky (fig. 136). The same article also contained copies of Kern's reconstruction and ground plan of the Chaco Canyon site of Hungo Pavie.[15] A few years later, when Harper & Brothers published *Massacres of the Mountains: A History of the Indian Wars of the Far West,* by J. P. Dunn, Jr., the publishing house went to the magazine files of *Harper's Magazine* and dusted off these same plates. *Massacres of the Mountains* contained the same woodcuts of Kern's work that *Harper's* had used in its 1854 article by Brewerton.[16]

The pattern of reproducing works by early documentary artists such as Kern has continued to the present. With some exceptions, however, contemporary writers and publishers have taken pains to identify the source of their illustrations.[17]

Richard Kern's work has been indispensable for modern writers who have sought illustrations of the Southwest as it looked prior to the widespread use of photography, or for those who have sought the charm and sense of period that lithographs lend to a work. Andrew K. Gregg, who compiled *New Mexico in the 19th Century: A Pictorial History,* reproduced twenty-two drawings by the Kern brothers, nearly all of them by Richard.[18] Similarly, Andrew Wallace relied heavily on Richard Kern for drawings of Indians and scenes

Fig. 135. *Cascade of the Little Colorado River, near Camp. 13.* Lithograph (above) based on a sketch by Richard H. Kern (see fig. 87). Lorenzo Sitgreaves, *Report of an Expedition down the Zuni and Colorado Rivers* (Washington, D.C., 1853). (Below) *Falls of the Colorado Chiquito.* Engraving by A. Joliet. Abbé Em. Domenech, *Seven Years' Residence in the Great Deserts of North America* (London, 1860).

Fig. 136. *Ruins of the Pueblo Pintado. Harper's* (August 1882). Compare with fig. 40.

of the prerailroad era in his *Image of Arizona: Pictures from the Past.*[19]

Illustrations by Richard Kern have seemed indispensable for recent books examining aspects of early exploration of the Southwest. LeRoy Hafen and Ann Hafen's *Old Spanish Trail: Santa Fé to Los Angeles* (1954); Edward S. Wallace, *The Great Reconnaissance* (1955); William Goetzmann's magisterial studies of *Army Exploration in the West* (1959) and *Exploration and Empire* (1967); Henry Savage, Jr., *Discovering America, 1700–1875* (1979); Bertha Dodge's treatise

on the 35th parallel route, *The Road West* (1980); and Frank Schubert's *Vanguard of Expansion: Army Engineers in the Transmississippi West* (1980) have all reproduced lithographs of drawings by Richard Kern.[20] Sketches of Indians have been among the most frequently reproduced of Kern's subjects; anthropologists as well as historians have found them useful.[21] Some of Kern's subjects, such as his views of Santa Fe, Camp Yuma, or the Zuni blacksmiths, are unique. Writers have turned to them again and again, reproducing them in sources as varied as the WPA Writers' guide, *New Mexico* (1940), and the Time-Life volume on *The Spanish West* (1976).[22]

This discussion of some of the sources in which Richard Kern's work has appeared, and continues to appear, is meant to be suggestive rather than exhaustive. It is clear that Kern's images of the Far Southwest have continued to influence visual perceptions of the region, reaching readers who have no acquaintance with the government reports in which the images originally appeared. Perhaps the most curious manifestation of Kern's continuing influence is a painting, *Old Bill Williams at Cochetopa Pass,* by Marjorie Thomas. Thomas used the lithograph of Kern's drawing of Cochetopa Pass from the Gunnison report as background for a portrait of Old Bill. This appeared as the frontispiece in the first edition of Alpheus Favour's biography, *Old Bill Williams* (1936).[23] Thus, Kern's drawing, preserved through the medium of lithography, was transformed into a painting and then into a photograph of that painting.

Few of Kern's contemporaries saw his original watercolor and pencil sketches, but thousands saw lithographic copies of his art. Since these copies have made a large and enduring, if intangible, impact on the popular visual image of the Far Southwest, it seems appropriate to ask how faithful the lithographs were to Kern's originals.

Historians who study the art of America's westward expansion have suggested that lithographers and engravers were responsible for many of the inaccuracies that crop up in drawings by artist-explorers. The biographer Robert Hine argued that Edward Kern's work, like that of most other artists who contributed to government reports, "was to be seen in large part through the dark glass of a lithographer." The lithographers, Hine said, added "Romantic touches," stylizing and exaggerating for effect in the reports of Frémont, Simpson, Sitgreaves, and Emory.[24] Similarly, two art historians have asserted that the sketches of most of the topographic artists "seem to have been transformed in some way and embellished with discursive picturesque detail during their transfer to metal, wood, or stone. In all probability, engravers or lithographers invested these conventional scenes with certain drama and grandeur."[25]

In the case of the southwestern drawings of Richard and Edward Kern, this generalization does not seem valid. The original drawings done by the Kern brothers for Simpson's *Journal,* sixty-nine in all, are in the collections of the Academy of Natural Sciences in Philadelphia. A study of the original work, most of which was Richard's, indicates that with only two exceptions, the lithographic artists employed by Peter Duval of Philadelphia added no embellishments and made no discernible effort to achieve dramatic effects (fig. 137). The small human figures that often appear in the foreground of the lithographs appear in the originals as well

Fig. 137. Compare the lithograph of Kern's *Pueblo of Jémez from the East* (above), in James H. Simpson, *Journal of a Military Reconnaissance . . . to the Navajo Country in 1849* (Washington, D.C., 1850), with his drawing (below). Courtesy, Academy of Natural Sciences of Philadelphia.

(fig. 138). Instead of adding dramatic effect, lithographers sometimes lost it. Where Richard Kern sought to portray the intense light that brings a dramatic incandescence to southwestern landscape, lithographers frequently contented themselves with a bland uniformity of tone.[26]

The lithographers who worked for Duval, like lithographers employed in other leading American firms, were artists themselves. Many had been trained in Europe. The high degree of accuracy with which they copied the Kerns' portraits and intricate designs suggests that these lithographic artists may have used a mechanical aid such as a camera lucida—a device containing a prism that transmits an image onto paper or stone. Or they may have made tracings of the Kerns' drawings; in the main, the size of the originals corresponds to the size of the lithographs.[27]

Duval's lithographers did, however, take liberties with the Kerns' illustrations for Simpson's *Journal* on two occasions, both in drawings that involved the human form. In the often-reproduced watercolor of *The Green Corn Dance of the Jémez Indians,* Edward Kern paid scant attention to anatomy, suggesting rather than delineating the features of the halfdressed male dancers. One of Duval's best lithographers, Paris-trained Christian Schuessele, compensated for what he may have regarded as a deficiency in the original by accentuating the chest, pectoral, and leg muscles of the dancers. What had been lean, impressionistically limned figures in

Ned's drawings, appeared as stocky, muscular Indians in the published version (fig. 139).[28]

Christian Schuessele made even more dramatic changes in his rendering of *Navajo Costume,* apparently drawn in the original by Richard Kern.[29] As its title suggests, the watercolor emphasizes the costume rather than the Navajo. The costume is draped on the unobtrusive figure of a slightly built Indian whose facial features remain vague and who is shown standing stiffly, as if at attention. At the lithographer's hand, the Navajo appears powerfully built, and he is presented in a dramatic pose (fig. 140).

The lithographs of the *Navajo Costume* and *The Green Corn Dance* are exceptions, then, to otherwise faithful representations of Kern's drawings for Simpson's *Journal.* Thus, if a geographical feature such as Fajada Butte appears to be inaccurately portrayed in Simpson's *Journal,* it was not the fault of the lithographer, as one historian has suggested, but rather the fault of the artist.[30]

This is not to imply, however, that lithographic artists produced identical images for Simpson's report. Small differences can be detected in even the best copies of the Kerns' work—compare, for example, the height of the walls in Kern's *Pueblo Pintado* with the lithograph (fig. 141). Some small differences seem deliberate, such as the lithographer's occasional effort to delineate foreground vegetation more precisely than Kern did, or to make the foreground more interesting. Other minor

Fig. 138. Compare the lithograph of Kern's *Peaks of the Ojos Calientes* (above) in James H. Simpson, *Journal of a Military Reconnaissance . . . to the Navajo Country in 1849* (Washington, D.C., 1850), with his drawing (below). Courtesy, Academy of Natural Sciences of Philadelphia.

Fig. 139. *You-Pel-Lay, or the Green Corn Dance of the Jémez Indians. Aug. 19 {1849}.* Watercolor by Edward M. Kern (above), erroneously attributed to Richard H. Kern (courtesy, Academy of Natural Sciences of Philadelphia) and lithograph (below) drawn by Christian Schuessele from that watercolor. James H. Simpson, *Journal of a Military Reconnaissance . . . to the Navajo Country in 1849* (Washington, D.C., 1850).

Fig. 140. *Navajo Costume*. Watercolor apparently by Richard H. Kern (left) (courtesy, Academy of Natural Sciences of Philadelphia), and the lithograph (right) drawn by Christian Schuessele from that watercolor, in James H. Simpson, *Journal of a Military Reconnaissance . . . to the Navajo Country in 1849* (Washington, D.C., 1850).

Fig. 141. *North West View of the Pueblo Pintado.* . . . Wash drawing by Richard H. Kern (courtesy, Academy of Natural Sciences of Philadelphia), and lithograph based on that drawing, in James H. Simpson, *Journal of a Military Reconnaissance . . . to the Navajo Country in 1849* (Washington, D.C., 1850).

changes may be a result of errors, some stemming from the lithographer's lack of familiarity with the southwestern milieu. In the *View of the Placer or Gold Mountains* (fig. 142), for example, the Kerns' original drawing shows a Mexican yoke across the horns of the oxen; the lithographer has omitted this. In the same drawing, the man on the left seems to be wearing a serape, but the lithographer has dressed him in a coat. Similarly, Richard Kern's watercolor *Natural Sand Stone Formations* (fig. 46) shows clumps of grass on the desert floor; but the lithographer has turned the desert into a green lawn. These small errors and discrepancies occur infrequently. In general, the lithographs in the Simpson report are faithful to the original drawings.

The preservation of sixty-nine original Kern sketches from the Navajo expedition make it possible to draw clear conclusions about the accuracy of the lithographs that appear in Simpson's *Journal*. Similar evidence does not exist in sufficient quantity, however, to allow an analysis of the quality of the lithographs published in the reports of the Sitgreaves or Gunnison expeditions.

Several of Kern's original sketches from the Sitgreaves reconnaissance have become available for study. Five of these are large pen-and-ink drawings of landscapes, apparently redrawn from field sketches. Although they may not be the polished drawings that the lithographer copied, they correspond closely to the lithographs and suggest that the lithographers employed by James Ack-

erman of New York copied Kern's landscapes with fidelity (fig. 143).[31] Kern's other extant drawings from the Sitgreaves expedition, however, are rough field sketches, far removed from the polished drawings that Kern would have prepared for the lithographer (fig. 144).[32] A comparison of these rough field sketches with the lithographs therefore tells us little about the accuracy of the lithographer. Kern's sketch of two blacksmiths at Zuni is a good example. His sketch shows a bellows-fed fire in an adobe forge, smoke escaping through a hole in the ceiling, and one smith working with anvil and hammer (fig. 145); it is clearly the basis of the well-known lithograph that appeared in the Sitgreaves report (fig. 79). The historian Robert Hine has suggested that the lithographer was responsible for the difference between the sketch and the original. The lithographer, Hine wrote, "completely changed the perspective, vastly enlarged the room, and clothed the Indians like medieval artisans." It seems unlikely, however, that Kern would have turned his rough field sketches and notebooks over to a lithographer. As he did with the Simpson report, Kern almost certainly made fresh drawings from his field sketches, adding detail and embellishment. Moreover, another Kern sketch of the same blacksmiths, which had been unavailable to Hine, shows more clearly the dress of the blacksmiths and demonstrates that the lithographer did not invent the costumes (fig. 146). If the smiths at Zuni seem to be clothed "like

Fig. 142. *View of the Placer or Gold Mountain.* . . . Wash drawing by Richard H. Kern based on a sketch by Edward M. Kern (courtesy, Academy of Natural Sciences of Philadelphia), and lithograph based on that drawing, in James H. Simpson, *Journal of a Military Reconnaissance . . . to the Navajo Country in 1849* (Washington, D.C., 1850).

Fig. 143. Untitled drawing (above) of Wupatki by Richard H. Kern (courtesy, Fred W. Cron), and lithograph (below) entitled *Ruined Pueblos,* apparently based on that drawing, in Lorenzo Sitgreaves, *Report of an Expedition down the Zuni and Colorado Rivers* (Washington, D.C., 1853).

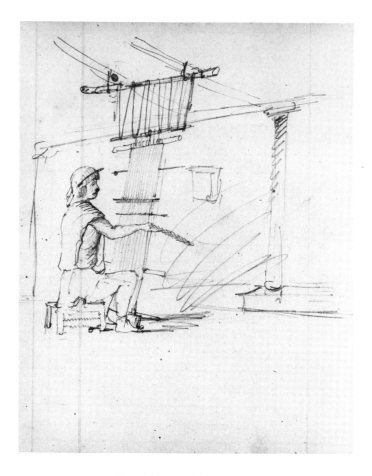

Fig. 144. Field sketch of a weaver at Zuni. Richard H. Kern. Courtesy, Fred W. Cron.

European medieval artisans," Kern himself is responsible. The likelihood is that Kern drew what he saw, and what he saw were either Mexican smiths working at Zuni, or Zunis who had adopted European dress as well as European smithing techniques.[33]

In the case of the Gunnison survey, only one of Kern's original drawings is known to have survived. A rough field sketch, it does not correspond to any of the scenes in the dozen colored lithographs of Kern's work that illustrate the published report.[34] Moreover, Kern's sketches were redrawn by John Mix Stanley before they went to the lithographer. Stanley never visited the places that Kern drew, and he must have relied on Kern's field sketches for topographic detail. Many of the human figures in these illustrations, however, do not appear to be in Kern's style, and were probably added by Stanley or the lithographer. Twice removed from the pen and vision of the artist, the handsome copies of Stanley's rendering of Kern's drawings that appear in the *Pacific Railroad Reports* cannot be relied upon to shed light on the accuracy of the lithographer, much less the accuracy or aesthetics of Richard Kern.

Although we lack more originals by Kern to compare with the lithographs of his work, a comparison of lithographs and originals by other artist-explorers of Kern's era suggests that historians have been too quick to accuse eastern lithographers of adding embellishments, striving for dramatic effects, or copying work inaccurately. Until re-

Fig. 145. Field sketch of a blacksmith shop at Zuni. Richard H. Kern. Courtesy, Fred W. Cron.

cently, original drawings by topographic artists of the Southwest have been either inaccessible or little known, making comparisons difficult. In the last few decades, however, a few more original drawings have become available for study.

The lithographs of the paintings that John Mix Stanley did for Lt. Col. W. H. Emory's *Notes of a Military Recon-* *noissance* [*sic*] (1848) provide a case in point. Robert Taft, writing in the early 1950s, examined the lithographs and surmised that "the lithographer may well have been responsible for the inaccuracies."[35] Taft knew of some original drawings by Stanley in a private collection, but could not examine them. Now eight of Stanley's oils from the Emory expedition have come to light.

Fig. 146. Field sketch of blacksmiths at Zuni. Richard H. Kern. Courtesy, Fred W. Cron.

Four of these were apparently the basis for lithographs published in Emory's *Notes,* and a comparison of the four lithographs with the originals suggests that Taft was wrong.[36] Although the lithographs of these paintings were crudely done, they correspond remarkably well to the originals. The lithographic artist made no effort to add "drama and grandeur" to the scenes, and there is very little evidence of "embellishment with picturesque detail." Stanley had already provided those devices. Compare, for example, Stanley's oil painting of Kearny's dragoons riding in a long column past the Pueblo of San Felipe with the lithograph of the same scene (fig. 147). In this case, the lithograph does not include one of Stanley's romantic embellishments—a flock of birds flying above the mounted column. Ross Calvin, who edited a modern edition of Emory's journal, thought that some of Stanley's drawings were "so inaccurate as to make it clear that the draughtsman never beheld the scenes he was attempting to depict."[37] But Stanley was there; whatever inaccuracies exist in the lithographs appear to be Stanley's rather than the lithographer's.

Similarly, the artists who prepared the woodcuts and exquisite lithographs for John Russell Bartlett's two-volume report on the United States-Mexican boundary survey of 1850–53 lavished attention on accuracy of reproduction. Some of the little-known original drawings of the expedition's artists, Henry C. Pratt, Oscar Bessau, and Bartlett himself, have been reproduced in Rob-

Fig. 147. *San Felipe, New Mexico.* Oil painting (above) by John Mix Stanley, 1846 (courtesy, Stark Museum of Art, Orange, Texas), and lithograph (below) apparently based on that oil painting (W. H. Emory, *Notes of a Military Reconnoissance . . .* [Washington, D.C., 1848]).

ert Hine's splendid study, *Bartlett's West: Drawing the Mexican Boundary,* published in 1968. A comparison of the original work with the illustrations in Bartlett's *Narrative* reveals no embellishments or dramatic flourishes by the copier.[38]

Although original drawings continue to come to light, most of the work prepared for lithographers by ex-peditionary artists in the Southwest has been lost. In some cases, drawings resembling those depicted in lithographs or in engravings have been found, but there is reason to doubt that these are the drawings from which the lithographer worked. For example, at least two watercolors in a sketchbook that Lt. James W. Abert kept on his march west with Kearny in 1846 appear to be the

Fig. 148. *Acoma, N.M.* Watercolor (opposite) by J. W. Abert, 1846 (courtesy, John Howell Books, San Francisco), and lithograph (above) apparently based on that watercolor in *Report of Lieut. J. W. Abert of His Examination of New Mexico* (Washington, D.C., 1848).

basis of lithographs of Acoma and the ruins at Abó, published in Abert's *Report* (fig. 148).[39] It seems unlikely, however, that the lithographer would have worked directly from Abert's sketchbook. More likely, Abert turned those sketches into polished drawings for the lithographer.[40]

In the case of Balduin Möllhausen, most of whose original work done for the Whipple and Ives surveys is also lost, extant drawings resembling lithographs may have been second or third versions of scenes done after Mollhausen returned to Germany and after the lithographs of those scenes had already been published. Two Möllhausen sketches, which apparently served as the basis for wood engravings in the Whipple report, have been preserved. In these cases,

Fig. 149. *Petrified tree near Lithodendron Creek.* Drawing (above) by Balduin Möllhausen, 1854 (courtesy, Oklahoma Historical Society), and lithograph (below), apparently based on that drawing in "Report of Lieutenant A. W. Whipple," in *Reports of Explorations and Surveys . . . for a Railroad from the Mississippi River to the Pacific Ocean,* 13 vols. (Washington, D.C., 1854–60), 2.

the engraver rendered remarkably faithful copies (fig. 149).[41]

In the main, it appears that lithographers and engravers could and did make accurate copies of the work of the earliest topographic artists to enter the Far Southwest. The German artist Arthur Schott complained that the drawings he did for Emory had been copied by a draftsman "who was never out in Texas and can for this reason not be able to finish those sketches as they ought to be done." Nevertheless, Schott admitted that the lithographs were "not bad."[42] There are important exceptions, of course. The startling liberties the lithographer took with Richard Kern's *Navajo Costume* is a case in point. So too are three views of Zuni dancers that appeared in the Sitgreaves report. That the male dancers hold rattles in their left hands, instead of the right, almost certainly resulted from the lithographer's failure to reverse the image on the stone. Kern's preliminary sketches of these dancers all show the rattles in the correct hand. Finally, it must be remembered that variant versions of some lithographs exist, making generalizations perilous.[43] Lithographic artists, however, appear to have aimed at fidelity in making copies for scientific reports. They were encouraged to do so by the "rather high standards of accuracy" of the Topographical Bureau, which frequently sent unfaithful copies back to be redrawn.[44]

In contrast with the high level of accuracy of lithographs in scientific publications, commercial presses may have emphasized style over fidelity. This seems to be the case with engravings, based on sketches attributed to Edward or Richard Kern, done for Frémont's *Memoirs,* published in 1887. Both publisher and author hoped that the lavish volumes would make money. Hence, the engravings had to have popular appeal, transcending the didactic illustrations that had characterized government reports. "By the 1880s," William Goetzmann has written, "the romantic's view of the West had reached a kind of apogee of grandeur."[45] The lush, highly romanticized images of the West done by Thomas Moran, Albert Bierstadt, and others had become authoritative in the public mind, and some of the illustrations in Frémont's *Memoirs* reflected this style. Several of the engravings done for volume two of the *Memoirs* depicted the disastrous expedition of 1848–49 and seem to be based on drawings by either Edward or Richard Kern.[46] The dramatic quality of *Natural Obelisks* (fig. 150), or *In a Canyon of the San Juan Mountains* (fig. 21), exceeded that of most of the work the Kerns had done previously. The engraver probably took considerable liberties with their original sketches.[47]

Much, then, depended on the purposes of the publication for which the engraving or lithograph was prepared, and how well the work to be copied fitted the publisher's purpose and the style of the day. The engraver who did the plates for W. W. H. Davis's *El Gringo; or, New Mexico and Her People* (1857), had to work from the una-

Fig. 150. *Natural Obelisks*. Engraving apparently based on a drawing by either Richard or Edward Kern. Publisher's prospectus for John C. Frémont, *Memoirs of My Life* (Belford, Clarke & Co., 1887). Courtesy, Huntington Library.

dorned wash drawings of Lt. Joseph Henry Eaton. Published by Harper's, *El Gringo* was a commercial venture, but Eaton's drawings gave only a nod to the convention of placing small human figures in a scene to add interest and scale. The engraver filled the void by copying Eaton's drawings faithfully, but added more figures in the foreground than Eaton had done (see fig. 151).[48]

No matter how accurately they copied line and form, however, lithographers could not overcome the limits of their medium. The techniques themselves, and not a lack of artistic proficiency, prevented lithographers and engravers from evoking the vibrancy, charm, and effect of the originals. Although technically correct, prints done for the mass market lacked life and could not replicate the subtleties of drawings done with brush or pencil. The looseness and spontaneity of originals was often lost in tight, tidy copies. Robert Hine, for example, has criticized Kern's *View of Sante Fe and Vicinity from the East* (fig. 27), because he gave the structures "less Spanish feeling than they actually had, injecting a bit too much of Yankee neatness into the scene."[49] Excessive neatness, however, probably came from the lithographer rather than from Kern.

In Kern's day, the technology for reproducing colors was especially deficient. Chromolithography was still in its infancy and could not duplicate the tones or blending of colors of wash drawings. Seth Eastman seems to have been disappointed with the chromo-

lithographs in Schoolcraft's *Indian Tribes of the United States,* and Richard Kern must have felt that the primitive chromos in Simpson's *Journal* did not do justice to his work, either.[50]

Because we have known the work of artist-explorers of the Southwest largely through the imperfect media of lithography and engraving, we have been unable to appreciate the full range of their skills and sensibilities, or to assess their artistic achievements. It may be true, as one historian has put it, that only a few of the expeditionary artists have "produced drawings and watercolors of real beauty."[51] It is also possible that much of the beautiful work of the artist-explorers has been lost and that, as a result, we have underrated documentary artists such as Richard Kern. As more original work by Kern and his contemporaries becomes available, however, our appreciation of their work seems likely to grow.[52]

One important question remains: how accurately did Kern draw what he saw? This question must have engaged the artist himself, for his task on government-sponsored expeditions was essentially reportorial. One contemporary who had watched Kern draw recommended him for a position by explaining that he possessed the essential talent of an expeditionary artist: "He sketches with great rapidity and accuracy."[53] Kern took pride in his accuracy. Describing some portraits of Indians that he had done, Dick told a correspondent that "they are so correct that the Indians them-

selves knew them, even after they had not seen them for two or three months."[54] Kern's experience with Indians in New Mexico was not unique. In 1851, American surveyors passed through a Maricopa Village on the Gila and showed the Indians lithographs of sketches that John Mix Stanley had made there five years before. The Maricopas recognized Stanley's portrait of Juan Antonio, who since had been killed, and the sight of the drawing moved his widow to tears.[55]

A "desire to communicate accurately" was widespread among artists in the West prior to 1890, one specialist on western art has concluded.[56] To achieve accuracy, however, required more than desire; it required skill and knowledge, both of which Kern possessed. He may also have relied upon a camera lucida on some occasions.[57] Whatever the means, Kern achieved remarkable accuracy in *some* of his drawings. One can go today to Acoma or to Jémez with

Fig. 151. *Taos Pueblo, 1855.* Watercolor (opposite) by Joseph Horace Eaton (courtesy, private collection of Gerald Peters, Santa Fe, New Mexico), and lithograph (above) apparently based on that watercolor, entitled *Pueblo of Taos—North Pueblo* (W. W. H. Davis, *El Gringo* (New York: Harper & Bros., 1857).

his drawings in hand, for example, and admire his skill in tracing the contours of mountains and mesas. Kern was also attentive to details of Indian life in both written and visual descriptions. Doubtless he made some errors, but his informative portrayals of Indian costumes and accoutrements, Indian villages, the interior of the kiva at Jémez, the writings on Inscription Rock, and the ruins or ground plans of archaeological sites appear to be correct in the main. Anthropologists and archaeologists have continued to find him dependable.[58]

The former teacher of drawing knew the conventions of his craft—the uses of perspective, composition, light, and color. He understood, for example, the danger of running a horizontal line across a picture, as in his vignette of the Alexandria Aqueduct at Georgetown (fig. 107), where he added strong compensatory vertical lines in the form of trees, clustering them in odd numbers and situating them along the pillars of the aqueduct. Strategically placed, the trees emphasize the form of the aqueduct and do not break the flow of graceful curves.

That Kern did many of his drawings in watercolors also testifies to his artistic skill. An unforgiving medium that does not allow the artist to correct errors as easily as does oil, watercolor may be the most demanding drawing technique. Kern had clearly mastered it.[59]

There were, of course, limits to Kern's ability to draw what he saw, the most serious being his skill at representing the human form. The figure in his *Navajo Costume*, as we have seen, was not fully developed (fig. 54), and lithographs of his drawings of Indian life at Zuni and among several tribes in Arizona show stiff, poorly proportioned figures. Kern must have been aware of his limitations in drawing people; he concentrated on landscapes and antiquities instead of genre.

In portraiture, Kern acknowledged that his brother Edward was his "superior," although he considered the two of them "equal in the other departments of the art."[60] Richard's relative weakness at portraiture probably led the two brothers to collaborate on at least four of the six portraits of Indians prepared for the Simpson report; Edward drew the four portraits from sketches done by Richard.[61] When his brother was not along to help him, Richard may have felt uncomfortable doing portraits. None appear in the Sitgreaves or Gunnison reports.

When the Kern brothers teamed up

to do a drawing, the chances of producing an inaccurate image probably increased. For example, the *View of the Placer or Gold Mountain, and Sandia Mountain from Santa Fe,* was drawn by Richard based on a sketch by Edward (fig. 142). It accurately outlines the Sandia Mountains and what are today called the Ortiz Mountains, but the drawing badly distorts the shapes and sizes of the Cerrillos hills, and the strong diagonal lines running across the Ortiz Mountains make them appear to have been formed by an uplift—a jarring distortion of the way they look in reality. When Richard reworked this drawing, the subject was no longer at hand and he apparently had to supply some of the details from memory or imagination.

Some of the inaccuracies in Richard Kern's work may also be explained by the conditions under which he worked: sketching at night in front of a campfire on the prairies, drawing in subzero temperatures in the Rockies, or scrambling over hills to find an ideal site in the desert heat. Thirst, hunger, mosquitos, bad health, exhaustion, or an Indian arrow in one's bedroll could distract even the most dedicated artist. Little wonder that Kern drew topographical details less precisely on the chilling Frémont expedition than he did in sketching Jémez Pueblo in the autumn. Indeed, Kern's exaggerated vertical walls in Hardscrabble Canyon (plate 1), his careless rendering of the outline of Sierra Blanca (plate 4), his failure to show the depth of the drifting snow on

Proulx' Creek (plate 3), and his mislabeling of some of the scenes in his sketchbook suggest that he did not finish these watercolors of the Frémont expedition in the frozen mountains. He worked either from a very good memory or from ruder sketches now lost.[62]

Like the written word, graphic images do not stand on their own as reliable statements simply because the artist was there. The information contained in paintings, drawings, and lithographs must be submitted to the same scrutiny ordinarily applied to written sources.[63] In the case of landscapes, this may mean comparing the image with the present site. Not to do so can lead to errors. Two writers, for example, mistakenly argue that Kern painted *Pike's Peak* (plate 16) from a site near Pueblo in 1848, then criticize the view as "not altogether true to nature." It seems more likely that Kern painted *Pike's Peak* in Washington D.C. in 1853, from someone else's sketch.[64] The same writers mistakenly take Kern at his word and repeat his mislabeling of *Robidoux' Pass,* which is almost certainly a representation of Hardscrabble Canyon (plate 1).[65] Other writers have confused Kern's mislabeled *Camp Yuma* (fig. 101) with the site of Fort Yuma, although the terrain of the two sites is notably different.[66]

Some of the inaccuracies in Richard Kern's drawings resulted more from artifice than from accident. Kern was not simply what one writer has termed a "topographic workman," trying to achieve "literal representation of the

maximum amount of detail."[67] Although trained as a scientist, he also fell under the influences of the accepted conventions of the artist's craft and the Romanticism of his day. These had a profound influence on his vision of the Far Southwest, and on the accuracy of his images.

When it suited his purposes, Kern artfully altered details of landscapes to make a scene more pleasing aesthetically, while preserving its essential truth. In the interest of what he understood to be good composition, he moved mountains. This is evident in his *View of Santa Fe and Vicinity from the East* (fig. 27). He sketched this scene from a spot near present Gonzales Road, below Cerro Gordo. As background, he took the major topographical features that came within the sweep of his peripheral vision and squeezed them into a narrow compass. The result is a distortion of the topography along the horizon, but a scene of considerable interest and balance. By moving mountains, Kern could frame his view of Santa Fe with the Sandía Mountains to the south and the Jémez to the north. The eye cannot take in this vista without moving, but the artist, by taking some liberties, can place it on a single page. Kern similarly rearranged topography in his watercolor drawing *Valley of Taos, Looking South* (plate 5).

In composing from nature, Kern followed well-established practice, articulated in the popular drawing manuals of his day. Nature, these books argued, could and should be improved upon, not just copied. As John Gadsby Chapman explained it in his elegant manual for would-be artists, the task was to "distill the best from nature," seeking the ideal rather than the unique or momentary.[68] Thomas Cole, the celebrated Romantic landscape artist whose work Kern surely knew, put it more eloquently: "if the imagination is shackled to what the eye sees, seldom will anything great be produced in painting." Cole believed in idealizing a scene by bringing together "the most lovely parts" to form "a whole that shall surpass in effect any picture painted from a single view."[69]

If Richard Kern saw any contradiction between the imperatives of accurate scientific recording and the artistic impulse, or between the scientist's realism and the artist's idealism, his remaining letters and diaries do not reveal his concern. Indeed, he may have felt no tension as a result of these inherent dilemmas, for he painted during what one art historian has described as "a time that sought not only an inner truth but an inner and outer truth that generally managed to have it both ways."[70] Many of Kern's contemporaries believed that nature could be idealized and improved upon through rearrangement, but they also extolled accuracy and precision as artistic virtues.

By altering details to improve composition or perspective, yet retaining verisimilitude, Kern often managed to have it both ways. In drawing the interior of the church at Zuni, for example, he would have found it more difficult to give depth to the scene had he drawn the ceiling beams, or *vigas,* across the narrow width of the nave, as they were in reality (plate 14). Hence, he made them run the length of the building instead of the width—a technique he may also have used with the interior of the kiva at Jémez and a room interior at Chaco Canyon (figs. 31 and 44). Such artistic alterations ordinarily did not effect the essential accuracy of a view. In *Peaks of the Sierra Blanca,* however, Kern, or John Mix Stanley, who reworked his sketch, went too far. This scene survives only as a lithograph in the report of the Gunnison expedition (fig. 124). In this view, trees on a pond lean improbably in opposite directions. Similarly, in his nighttime view of *La Parroquia* in Sante Fe (plate 8), Kern has crosses lean in opposite directions in a manner that seems contrived. In that same scene, light comes from more than one source, a device that enables the viewer to see the padre's house from what should have been a dark shadow.

The interest that artists of Kern's generation had in composing directly from nature reflected the growth of the aesthetics of Romanticism in American art and a shift in popular attitudes toward wilderness. The first Europeans to come to America had regarded wilderness as inhospitable and repulsive. For a people whose idea of beauty in nature had been a well-ordered garden, the chaos of the wilderness seemed ugly and frightening. That the rugged canyons and mountains in the Southwest could be beautiful would have seemed incomprehensible to the minds of sixteenth-century explorers. By the early nineteenth century, however, an often-articulated yet indefinable Romanticism, imported from Europe, had combined with homegrown nationalism to transform wilderness from a liability to an asset in the American mind. While still possessing frightening qualities, wilderness came increasingly to represent a sanctuary from the sordid, corrupt life of cities. In pure nature, unsullied by man, God's power and spiritual truths stood revealed. In wilderness, man might find the "Sublime"—a word which came to mean God resident in nature. Indeed, by mid-century, as one analyst has explained, "ideas of God's nature and God *in* nature" had become "hopelessly entangled," resulting in "a kind of Christianized pantheism."[71] Europeans might possess superior man-made monuments and cultural artifacts, but Americans could boast of wilderness, "fresh, as it were, from the hands of the Creator."[72]

If Richard Kern sought the Sublime, his quest did not lead him to the lofty sentiment of a Thomas Cole or the theatrics of later Romantics such as Albert Bierstadt or Frederic E. Church. Kern worked on a smaller scale, and Romanticism influenced him in quieter ways. Some of his work places him among those early observers of the West, such as Alfred Jacob Miller, George Catlin, and Seth Eastman, who shared what the historian William Goetzmann has termed "the pastoral, elegaic vision."[73]

Indeed, in leaving the comfort of his studio to do plein air sketching in the wilderness, Kern's actions themselves testify to Romantic influence—the quest for "the strange, remote, solitary, and mysterious."[74] As one critic has put it, "the drama of man measured against the awesome untamed expanse of the West provided a subject perfect for the Romantic."[75]

In many of Richard Kern's landscapes, man is measured against nature quite explicitly. Kern frequently employs the convention of placing small stick figures in a scene. These "staffage" elements add human interest and scale. They serve as spectators of southwestern scenery and antiquities, providing the viewer with a sense of the grandeur of nature and inviting the viewer into the scene. In some of Kern's drawings an expressive tree may serve a similar function, acting as a "proxy for man in the landscape."[76]

In general, Kern presents the wilderness as a benign, accessible place for man. He uses the conventional device of framing the foreground with trees or cliffs, lightening the middle distance, and fading out the background to invite the viewer into the scene, as in his picturesque summertime view of *Pareda* (plate 6), or his winter scene *On Proulx' Creek* (plate 3). These are not images of an inhospitable wilderness. Even Kern's watercolors of the disastrous winter in the San Juan Mountains with Frémont do not convey the terror and power of nature's forces unbridled. Indeed, in contrast to the verbal descriptions in his diary and the diaries of his brothers, Richard Kern's graphic images do not show deep snow. Similarly, his views of the Colorado River, where Indians, starvation, and thirst threatened to annihilate the Sitgreaves party, are inviting, almost pastoral scenes reminiscent of that loosely knit group who came to be known as Hudson River artists, with whom Kern was surely familiar (fig. 100).

In the watercolor and pencil drawings now held by the Amon Carter Museum, and which Kern seems to have done for his own pleasure rather than as part of an assignment for an employer, one sees him most clearly moving beyond the documentary task of recording information into the more expressive drawing of the Romantics. His pencil drawing of a waterfall near Taos, for example, has been redrawn from a field sketch and idealized (figs. 23 and 24). *Salto del Rito* does not resemble any waterfalls in the area, then or now, although Kern's field sketch almost certainly represents an actual waterfall, the Salto de Agua near Arroyo Seco. In redrawing his field sketch, Kern has added considerably more water to the falls than one is likely to see in the Taos Valley. Kern has imposed order on the chaotic geography and, in an apparent gesture toward the Sublime, he has conveniently centered a mountain peak and two trees directly above the falls.[77] His watercolors of *Proulx' Creek* and *Kern's Peak* (plates 3 and 9) also appear to be idealized. In the latter scene he experimented with Romantic

conventions—the interplay of jagged shapes, strong light, and dark masses— in a manner that suggests a knowledge of artists such as Thomas Cole.

Many of Kern's landscape drawings in the Amon Carter Museum collection contain structures. In these views, he seems to be measuring the works of man against nature: the town of *Pareda* (plate 6), the *Rock and Pueblo of Acoma* (plate 11), the forts at Acapulco and Chagres (figs. 103 and 105), the *Smithsonian Institute* (plate 15), *Christ Church* (fig. 106), and the *Aqueduct, Georgetown* (fig. 107). In these scenes, Kern shows little interest in depicting architectural detail. He has positioned himself at a considerable distance from his subject, subordinating the structures to nature. Kern's *Smithsonian,* for example, is an organic structure, utterly devoid of detail and presented as a silhouette, along with trees, against the sky. The form of the romanesque building echoes the form of nature's trees. If Kern is measuring man's works against nature in these views, he seems to see no conflict between the two. Like other Americans of his day, Kern may have shared the paradoxical view that wilderness, although it represented the temples of God, could be transformed and humanized through the works of man.[78] The works of man and God become one harmonious whole in these landscapes—the Smithsonian blends into the trees; Pareda is swallowed up by vegetation; Acoma Pueblo merges into the mesa top upon which it stands; and the forts at Acapulco and Chagres blend into the cliffs they are built upon. Sky, trees, mountains, and mesas overwhelm man's work.

In his view of the *Parroquia* of Santa Fe (plate 8), Kern brought a structure into the foreground, but here too he seems uninterested in conveying architectural detail. To the contrary, he seems intent on evoking the mood of the organic adobe mass, rising harmoniously out of the earth at night—an elegaic portrait of mass and shadow in moonlight.

Atop the Parroquia, four crosses tilt in melancholy fashion against the night sky. In 1849, in the months following his brother Benjamin's death, Kern placed crosses in several other drawings. A cross is the main subject of *La Cruz del Muerto* (fig. 22), and crosses appear prominently in his *View of Santa Fe* (fig. 27), *View of the Placer or Gold Mountain* (fig. 142), and his watercolor sketch of *Kern's Peak* (plate 9). These expressive, stylized crosses, which may be anthropomorphic, suggest emotional intensity if not the "Christianized pantheism" characteristic of what one writer has called the "excited spirit" of the Romantics.[79]

In contrast to Kern's drawings of the exteriors of structures, his views of the interiors of the *Jesuit College, Chihuahua* (plate 7) and the *Church of San Miguel, Pueblo of Zuni* (plate 14), appear at first glance to be attempts to convey architectural information. But these drawings, too, show considerable Romantic influence, aiming as much at evoking emotion as recording information. Kern

chose to draw forlorn interiors of abandoned churches, rather than churches that still had resident priests. He uses light and space to create a mood that is at once melancholy yet suggestive of exaltation. The ribbed vaulting of the Jesuit College and the irregular adobe walls of the chapel at Zuni echo forms of nature and convey a sense of energy that transcends the reportorial work of the documentary artist.[80]

Too few of Kern's genre drawings have survived in original form to enable us to generalize with assurance, but his views of Indians appear to be more realistic than romantic. He seems to have shared the interests of many Romantic artists in preserving images of Indians and their artifacts before whites altered their lives, and his full-length portraits of Jémez leader Hos-ta and his wife, Whar-te (figs. 29 and 30), suggest an idealized, serene nobility.[81] But Kern had lost a brother to Indians, lived through one Indian attack on the Colorado River, worried about "skulking" Indians who would ambush a single man, and compared some of the Yampais he saw to apes. The lithograph of his drawings of scrawny Yampais Indians (fig. 93), eking out a living in a harsh land, is the antithesis of Alfred Jacob Miller's dreamy views of Indians in an Arcadian wilderness. Whereas Miller, one historian tells us, "chose his subjects for their beauty or character," Kern did not shirk from drawing Indians he found disgusting.[82] Like many other American scientists of his day, Kern seemed more concerned with the study of archaeology, philology, and physical anthropology (through the collecting of Indian crania), than in the current condition or recent history of living Indians.[83] Perhaps because he held them in contempt and did not regard them as exotic, Kern, like other expeditionary artists, did not draw Mexicans except as staffage elements.

It is not entirely correct, then, to say that Richard Kern and his brother Edward "merely attempted to reproduce their subjects as accurately as the 'eye' of the camera."[84] Like other artist-explorers, such as George Catlin and Karl Bodmer, Richard Kern combined what historian William Goetzmann has described as "a romantic vision of nature with a scientific and ethnological approach."[85] In general, however, Kern kept his emotions in check. Except for some of his watercolor and pencil drawings now held in the Amon Carter Museum, Kern's work is more realistic than romantic, more picturesque than profound. His most unpretentious landscapes, such as *Pike's Peak* (plate 16), reflect the realistic, turn-of-the-century English topographical tradition as reflected in the works of Philadelphia draftsmen such as Charles Willson Peale or the westering Samuel Seymour, rather than the approach of the early Hudson River artists who were Kern's most stylish contemporaries.

By using color washes, Kern also kept himself out of the mainstream of commercial artists. Public acceptance of the medium did not begin to grow until the 1850s and 1860s, and critics ignored it until after the Civil War, regarding it a medium for amateurs. The successful Hudson River artists, such as Thomas Cole and Asher Durand, generally worked in oils. Expeditionary artists, on the other hand, usually preferred to work in watercolors. Available in cakes or in premixed collapsible tubes by the time Kern first went west, watercolors were as portable as oils but dried more rapidly.[86]

The samples of Kern's work that can be seen in the Amon Carter Museum suggest that he did some of his field sketches in transparent watercolors, rather than in gouache or opaque washes. A talented colorist, he applied washes loosely. Browns, greens, and blues predominate, but except for his drawings of the red rocks at Acoma (plates 11, 12, and 13), Kern, like his contemporaries, did not try to capture the vivid colors of the desert Southwest. Perhaps Kern only saw what he was prepared to see from his eastern experience. Or perhaps he shared the reluctance of Lt. James Abert to paint what he saw. "Should a painter, in sketching the landscape, give it the true tone of color," Abert wrote in 1845, "he likely would be censured for exaggeration."[87]

Unlike some of his more successful counterparts in the West, Kern did not live long enough to rework his small sketches and watercolors into showy oils for exhibition. Alfred Jacob Miller, John

Mix Stanley, Balduin Möllhausen, and others survived their western travels and returned to comfortable studios, where they drew inspiration from sketchbooks to produce more painterly, imaginative, and majestic works than they had done in the field.[88] Kern may have done some painting in oils in Santa Fe, and when he returned to Philadelphia and Washington in 1852, he was working on some oils of the Navajo reconnaissance for James Simpson, and on a large canvas of a scene in the mountains near Santa Fe.[89] If they were ever completed, these oils have apparently been lost.

Had he lived longer, aesthetic considerations, revealed so clearly in the album at the Amon Carter Museum, might have come to predominate over the reportorial qualities of Richard Kern's work. But time had run out. Kern died at age thirty-two, before he had time to complete the cycle that he had once described in naturalistic terms to the widow of a good friend:

Life is but a journey. On we travel mid mirth and woe. Time flies along and will not wait or linger on the way. Or as a stream; one moment meandering through gentle slopes, then in eddies playing, or rushing with impetuosity into the great Ocean of Death. The Sun wakes the cheerful day; everything charms; the balmy fragrance of the blossom is spread around, and the merry songsters of the wood attune to peace and harmony. But the tempest bursts and deforms every grace in Nature's fair face; and though it should pass away yet will it be followed by the Ice and Night of the grave. The mystery of Death is as inscrutable as that of existence. Our circle of Light increases, only to be surrounded by a greater circumference of Darkness. Death claims all for his share—he anoints innocence in its playfulness, youth in its panting ambition, manhood in maturity, and old age in decrepitude, resting on crutches and waiting his approach.[90]

List of Illustrations

John Mix Stanley, 1846.

PLATES

Notes

ABBREVIATIONS

FI   Archives of the Franklin Institute, Philadelphia, Pennsylvania

FS   Fort Sutter Papers, Huntington Library, San Marino, California

HEH   Huntington Library, San Marino, California

HM   Huntington Manuscript, Huntington Library, San Marino, California

LS, TB, NARS   Letters Sent, Topographical Bureau of the War Department, National Archives and Records Service, Washington, D.C.

LR, TB, NARS   Letters Received, Topographical Bureau of the War Department, National Archives and Records Service, Washington, D.C.

NARS   National Archives and Records Service, Washington, D.C.

PC   Private Collection of Fred W. Cron and Helen Cron

CHAPTER 1
INTRODUCTION

1. See Lawrence Clark Powell's wry comments on the heart and the heart of hearts of the Southwest in *Southwest Classics: The Creative Literature of the Arid Lands* . . . (Los Angeles: Ward Ritchie, 1974), p. 4.

2. For well-illustrated discussions of the early artists in the West, see John C. Ewers, *Artists of the Old West* (New York: Doubleday & Co., 1965), and Peter Hassrick, *The Way West: Art of the American Frontier* (New York: Harry N. Abrams, 1977). See, too, the tart analysis in Bernard DeVoto, *Across the Wide Missouri* (Boston: Houghton Mifflin, 1947), pp. 391–415. DeVoto argues that few of the published accounts contained accurate images of the West (pp. 396–98).

3. Jeanne Van Nostrand, *The First Hundred*

Years of Painting in California, 1775–1875 (San Francisco: John Howell Books, 1980), pp. 5–19, and George Vancouver, *A Voyage of Discovery* . . . (3 vols.: London: G. G. and J. Robinson and J. Edwards, 1798), vol. 2, facing pp. 10, 440.

4. Artists and amateurs painted scenes and portraits in Texas prior to the 1836 revolt, but little of their work was exhibited or reproduced. See Pauline A. Pinckney, *Painting in Texas: The Nineteenth Century* (Austin: Amon Carter Museum and University of Texas Press, 1967), pp. 3–13. The first printed views of Texas based on firsthand observation seem to have appeared in *A Visit to Texas: Being the Journal of a Traveller through Those Parts Most Interesting to American Settlers.* . . . (New York: Goodrich & Wiley, 1834), facing pp. 38, 46, 61, and 192. For an explanation of why Texas was ignored, see William H. Goetzmann, "Images of Texas," in Becky Duval Reese, *Texas Images and Visions* (Austin: Archer M. Huntington Art Gallery, 1983), p. 16.

5. If such an image exists, it has eluded researchers. See, for example, *The Spanish West* (New York: Time-Life, 1976). The often-reproduced woodcut of a buffalo that first appeared in the account of the Coronado expedition in Francisco López de Gómara, *La historia general de las Indias* (Antwerp: Juan Steelsio, 1554), verso of p. 275, was almost certainly drawn from a verbal account, as Carl Sauer maintains in his *Sixteenth Century North America: The Land and the People as Seen by the Europeans* (Berkeley: University of California Press, 1971), p. 249. Andrew Wallace, *The Image of Arizona: Pictures from the Past* (Albuquerque: University of New Mexico Press, 1971), pp. 3, 99, identifies 1831 as the date of the first published image purporting to be of Arizona. For Spanish scientific terrestial exploration, see Janet Fireman, *The Spanish Royal Corps of Engineers in the Western Borderlands: Instrument of Bourbon Reform, 1764 to 1815* (Glendale, Cal.: Arthur H. Clark Co., 1977).

6. While at Bent's Fort, Barclay made five drawings for his sister that have since been lost.

Some of his watercolors from the early 1850s have survived: George P. Hammond, ed., *Alexander Barclay, Mountain Man* (Denver: Old West Publishing Co., 1976), p. 229, frontispiece, and following pp. vi and 122. Among those English-language accounts that lacked illustrations were: Zebulon Montgomery Pike, *Account of Expeditions* . . . (Philadelphia: C & A Conrad & Co., 1810); the accounts by Augustus Storrs and Alphonso Wetmore, first published in 1825 and reprinted in *Santa Fe Trail, First Reports: 1825* (Houston: Stagecoach Press, 1960); Albert Pike, *Prose Sketches and Poems* . . . (Boston: Light and Horton, 1834); the numerous newspaper articles by Matt Field that appeared in the New Orleans *Picayune* in 1840 and 1841, reprinted in John E. Sunder, ed., *Matt Field on the Santa Fe Trail* (Norman: University of Oklahoma Press, 1960); Thomas Falconer, *Expedition to Santa Fe. An Account of Its Journey from Texas through Mexico* (New Orleans: Office of the Picayune, 1842); Rufus B. Sage, *Scenes in the Rocky Mountains, and in Oregon, California, New Mexico, Texas, and the Grand Prairies* . . . (Philadelphia: Carey & Hart, 1846); and Thomas James, *Three Years among the Indians and the Mexicans* (Waterloo, Ill.: Office of the "War Eagle," 1846). For contemporary imprints by Mexican writers, see some examples in Weber, ed., *Northern Mexico on the Eve of the United States Invasion: Rare Imprints Concerning California, Arizona, New Mexico, and Texas, 1821–1846* (New York: Arno Press, 1976).

7. *The Personal Narrative of James O. Pattie of Kentucky,* Timothy Flint, ed. (Cincinnati: John II. Wood, 1831). The five plates have been reproduced in the edition edited by Milo Milton Quaife (Chicago: Lakeside Press, 1930), but omitted from the "unabridged" reprint published in Philadelphia by J. B. Lippincott, in 1962, with an introduction by William H. Goetzmann. See, too, DeVoto, *Across the Wide Missouri,* p. 398.

8. George Wilkins Kendall, *Narrative of the Texan Santa Fe Expedition* (2 vols., New York: Harper & Bros., 1844).

9. The two Plains scenes are *A Scamper among*

the Buffalo, by J. G. Chapman, and *Incident on the Prairies,* by J. W. Casilear. From Henry George Ward, *Mexico in 1827* (London: H. Colburn, 1828), Kendall's publishers commissioned copies of *Puente Nacional* and *City of Guanajuato.* The British edition of Kendall's *Narrative* (London: David Bogue, 1845), contained the same scenes, but with new engravings that differ in small details from those in the American edition.

10. C. Nebel, *Voyage pittoresque et archéologique dans la partie la plus intéressante du Mexique* (Paris: Moench & Gau, 1836). Nebel's scene, entitled *Poblanas,* contains four people. The two women in the doorway have finer features and are more beguiling than in the engravings in Kendall's work.

For examples of the use of this engraving to illustrate modern works, see John E. Sunder, ed., *Matt Field on the Santa Fe Trail* (Norman: University of Oklahoma Press, 1960), facing p. 258, and David J. Weber, *The Taos Trappers: The Fur Trade in the Far Southwest, 1540–1846* (Norman: University of Oklahoma Press, 1971), following p. 144.

11. Robert Taft, *Artists and Illustrators of the Old West, 1850–1900* (New York: Charles Scribner's Sons, 1953), p. 259. Josiah Gregg, *Commerce of the Prairies: or the Journal of a Santa Fe Trader . . .* (2 vols., New York: Henry G. Langley, 1844). Full-page plates appear as frontispieces to each volume, as well as in vol. 1, facing pp. 102 and 182, and in vol. 2, facing pp. 38 and 230. Half-page engravings appear in vol. 1, pp. 153, 169, 213, 249, and vol. 2, pp. 108, 149. All twelve engravings are reproduced in the best modern edition of *Commerce of the Prairies,* Max L. Moorhead, ed. (Norman: University of Oklahoma Press, 1954), but without the sharpness of the originals.

12. The engraving itself identifies E. Didier as the artist and A. L. Dick as the engraver. They are also credited on the frontispiece to vol. 2, *Indian Alarm on the Cimarron River.* Didier was probably Eugene Didier, a Paris merchant then living in New York, known as a "watercolorist and painter of French scenes."

Archibald L. Dick was a Scottish-born engraver who settled in New York in the early 1830s and established his own business. George C. Groce and David H. Wallace, *The New York Historical Society's Dictionary of Artists in America, 1564–1860* (New Haven: Yale University Press, 1957), pp. 178, 179. Of the ten remaining engravings, three are attributed to "Lossing"— Benjamin John Lossing, who established himself in New York City in 1838. Gregg, *Commerce,* vol. 1, facing p. 182, vol. 2, facing pp. 18, 230; Groce and Wallace, *Dictionary,* p. 404.

Although *Commerce of the Prairies* was published in 1844, Gregg's last trip to Santa Fe had been in 1839, the same year in which Louis Daguerre announced his remarkable discovery to the world. Thus, Gregg probably did not have a daguerreotype camera with him. Had he, or had he supervised the drawings of the artist, he probably would have taken credit for his work, as he did for the preparation of the maps in *Commerce of the Prairies.* See Maurice Garland Fulton, *Diary & Letters of Josiah Gregg* (2 vols., Norman: University of Oklahoma Press, 1941; 1944), 1: 123–58. The earliest known photograph of a New Mexico scene was taken about 1847. Van Deren Coke, *Photography in New Mexico: From the Daguerreotype to the Present* (Albuquerque: University of New Mexico Press, 1979), p. 1.

13. DeVoto, *Across the Wide Missouri,* p. 397.

14. This subject is explored admirably in Ronnie C. Tyler, *The Mexican War: A Lithographic Record* (Austin: Texas State Historical Association, 1973).

15. John T. Hughes, *Doniphan's Expedition . . .* (Cincinnati: J. A. & U. P. James, 1847), pp. v, 35, 38, 78, 121. A brief biographical sketch and a photograph of Maclean appears in William Elsey Connelley, *Doniphan's Expedition . . .* (Topeka, Kansas: Published by the Author, 1907), p. 118; see also pp. 245, 386, 405, 416, 548. Two other accounts of travel in New Mexico appeared in 1847 but did not contain illustrations: Benjamin Franklin Taylor, ed., *Short Ravelings from a Long Yarn, or*

Camp March Sketches of the Santa Fe Trail; from the Notes of Richard L. Wilson (Chicago: Geer & Wilson, Daily Journal Office, 1847), and George Frederick Ruxton, *Adventures in Mexico and the Rocky Mountains* (London: John Murray, 1847).

16. See, for example, Samuel E. Chamberlain, *My Confession,* Roger Butterfield, ed. (New York: Harper & Brothers, 1956); John Francis McDermott, ed., "Alfred S. Waugh's 'Desultory Wanderings' in the Years 1845–46," *Bulletin of the Missouri Historical Society,* 8 (April 1951): 347–65; and Paul Horgan, *Lamy of Santa Fe: His Life and Times* (New York: Farrar, Straus and Giroux, 1975), facing p. 140.

17. Citations to all three editions of the *Notes,* and an evaluation of them, may be found in the modern reprint, edited by Ross Calvin, *Lieutenant Emory Reports:* (Albuquerque: University of New Mexico Press, 1951), pp. 1–16.

18. Taft, *Artists and Illustrators,* pp. 1–21, summarizes Stanley's career.

19. Abert's *Examination* is most conveniently available in a modern facsimile of the House version: *Abert's New Mexico Report, 1846–'47* (Albuquerque: Horn & Wallace, 1962), which includes all of the illustrations as well as the text. Anyone utilizing this volume should also consult *Western America in 1846–1847: The Original Travel Diary of Lieutenant J. W. Abert . . .* John Galvin, ed. (San Francisco: John Howell, Books, 1966), containing Abert's unexpurgated field diary. For evidence that Abert did these drawings, compare the watercolor of Abó in Galvin, ed., *Western America,* p. 53, with the lithograph of Abó on p. 111 of Abert's *New Mexico Report.* In the summer of 1845, Abert had made a reconnaissance from Bent's Fort into New Mexico over Raton Pass and east to St. Louis by way of the Canadian River. On that trip he did not visit any of the New Mexico settlements, but he did some handsome watercolors of Indian life on the Plains and of Bent's Fort. Discovered by John Galvin, these watercolors are reproduced in Galvin, ed., *Through the Country of the Comanche Indians . . . 1845* (San Francisco: John Howell Books, 1970).

20. Two other reports of treks through the region appeared in 1848: A. Wislizenus, *Memoir of a Tour to Northern Mexico, Connected with Col. Doniphan's Expedition, in 1846 and 1847,* 30th Cong., 1st sess., Sen. Misc. Doc. 26 (Washington: Tippin & Streeper, Printers, 1848), and Jacob S. Robinson, *Sketches of the Great West: A Journal of the Santa Fe Expedition, under Col. Doniphan, Which Left St. Louis in June, 1846 . . .* (Portsmouth, N.H.: Portsmouth Journal Press, 1848). Both men traveled with Col. Alexander Doniphan, but no illustrations accompanied their work. Unlike Kearny, Doniphan had no member of the Topographical Corps assigned to him.

Along with the artists' reconnaissance, the practice of copying lithographs without attribution had also begun. E. G. Squier, "New Mexico and California," *The American Review: A Whig Journal* (Nov. 1848), pp. 503–28, reproduced Abert's drawing of the pueblo of Santo Domingo and Stanley's sketch of Casa Grande.

21. Larry Curry, *The American West: Painters from Catlin to Russell* (New York: Viking Press and Los Angeles Museum of Art, 1972), p. 14.

22. The first edition of Hine's work was entitled *Edward Kern and American Expansion* (New Haven: Yale University Press, 1962); the 1982 edition was issued by the University of Oklahoma Press. The other book-length biography is a pioneering work, William Joseph Heffernan, *Edward M. Kern: The Travels of an Artist-Explorer* (Bakersfield, Cal.: Kern County Historical Society, 1953).

23. This is evident even in Hine's biography of Edward. Of thirty-six sketches and paintings of the West used by Robert Hine to illustrate the first edition of *Edward Kern,* eleven were by Edward and twenty-two by Richard. In Hine's judgment, three other illustrations could have been done by either brother. In the second edition of the biography, Hine added two more watercolors of southwestern scenes to the illustrations; both were by Richard.

24. Certainly, other collections of which I am unaware may exist, but one Kern drawing that would seem to exist does not. In their

Biographical Encyclopedia of Artists of the American West (Garden City, N.Y.: Doubleday, 1976), p. 263, Peggy Samuels and Harold Samuels say that the estimated price of an eight-by-ten-inch drawing by Kern "showing a view of Fort Smith would be about $600 to $800. at auction in 1976." Kern was never in Fort Smith, however, and Mr. Samuels explains that they were "estimating a price for an imagined subject." Harold Samuels to Weber, Corrales, New Mexico, Aug. 19, 1983.

25. "Exciting New Discovery in the West's Art and History," *Life,* 46 (April 6, 1954): 95–104. Hine, *Edward Kern,* p. 172, reported that the Crons owned seven sketchbooks.

26. Notes by Frank McNitt from a telephone conversation with Fred Cron, Nov. 2, 1962, McNitt Papers, Box 14, file "Kern Brothers," New Mexico State Records Center, Santa Fe.

27. *Handbook of North American Indians,* William C. Sturtevant, ed., vol. 9, *Southwest,* Alfonso Ortiz, ed. (Washington, D.C.: Smithsonian Institution, 1979), pp. 213, 475. Patricia Trenton and Peter H. Hassrick, *The Rocky Mountains: A Vision for Artists in the Nineteenth Century* (Norman: University of Oklahoma Press, 1983), pp. 53, 56, 63, and p. 352, nn. 69, 72, and 73, which suggests the dimensions of the portion of the collection that Trenton examined.

28. Harold McCracken, Cody, Wyoming, Sept. 11, 1980, to Robert Hine. McCracken told Hine that "about 1960–61 . . . here in Cody, I was visited by a young man whose name I do not remember, who was returning to his home in Montana from a trip to Pennsylvania where a grandparent had recently died. . . . he had inherited an album of the small Kern pictures, found in a trunk in the relative's garage." A different version of the provenance of this collection came from Rudolf G. Wunderlich, then president of Kennedy Galleries, who wrote that McCracken "told me specifically that he purchased them from a garage in Philadelphia many years ago from a descendent of Kern. He does not remember what the relationship

was, but there was no question that these were descendents of Kern. I've called him again about this but he has no further information." Wunderlich to Peter Hassrick, New York, October 31, 1975. Both letters are in the Kern file, Registrar's Office, Amon Carter Museum.

29. Some of these drawings have two titles—one written directly on the drawing and another on a gray label. Both titles appear to be in Kern's hand. When two different titles exist, I have chosen the title on the label, for that appears to have been Kern's final choice. For example, Kern had originally identified three of the drawings in Spanish: *Interior del Collegio* [sic] *Viejo de los Jesuitos* (plate 9), *Interior de la Iglesia de San Miguel, Pueblo de Zuni* (plate 14), and *Presidio San Lorenzo* (fig. 105). The titles on the labels are in English. A few of Kern's original titles contain information that does not appear on the captions. In those cases, I have provided the additional information in square brackets. I have also taken the liberty of adding punctuation. The one item not reproduced in this book is a very rough sketch whose difficult-to-read title seems to say *Lake Como,* and probably represents Kern's copy of another artist's drawing of that much-visited lake in northern Italy.

30. Geoffrey Grigson, "Just for the Record," *Country Life,* 174 (December 8, 1983): 1751. Tyler's book was published in New York by Thames and Hudson in 1983. Tyler reproduces three watercolors by Kern: *Robidoux' Pass, La Parroquia,* and *Valley of Taos, Looking South* (pp. 172–73). In another review of Tyler's book, Mark Abley also found Kern's work noteworthy. *London Times Literary Supplement,* March 23, 1984.

31. Paul Murray Kendall, *The Art of Biography* (New York: Norton & Co., 1965), p. xi.

32. Robert V. Hine, foreword to *Sun Chief: The Autobiography of a Hopi Indian,* Leo W. Simmons, ed. (1st ed., 1942; New Haven: Yale University Press, 1971), p. xiv.

33. For a brief discussion of western ambivalence toward the East, see Gene M. Gressley, "Colonialism and the American West," in

Twentieth-Century American West: A Potpourri (Columbia: University of Missouri Press, 1977), pp. 33–47.

34. Barbara Novak, *Nature and Culture: American Landscape and Painting, 1825–1875* (New York: Oxford University Press, 1980), p. 137.

CHAPTER 2
THE DISASTER IN THE MOUNTAINS

1. Robert V. Hine, *In the Shadow of Frémont: Edward Kern and the Art of American Exploration, 1845–1860* (1st ed.; 1962; Norman: University of Oklahoma Press, 1982), pp. 6–7. For Frémont, see the standard biography by Allan Nevins, *Frémont: Pathmaker of the West* (1st ed., 1939; New York: Longmans, Green & Co., 1955), and Ferol Egan's *Frémont, Explorer for A Restless Nation* (Garden City, N.Y.: Doubleday, 1977), which incorporates recent scholarship. The best source of the reports of Frémont's first two expeditions, together with relevant correspondence and scholarly elucidation, is *The Expeditions of John Charles Frémont*, vol. 1, *Travels from 1838 to 1844*, Donald Jackson and Mary Lee Spence, eds. (Urbana: University of Illinois Press, 1970).

2. E. to R. Kern, In camp at head of Boon Crk., June 1845, FS 7. For Chapman, a well-known portrait artist and painter of historical scenes, see Andrew F. Cosentino, *The Paintings of Charles Bird King, 1785–1862* (Washington, D.C.: Smithsonian Institution Press, 1977), pp. 66–69, and Ellwood Parry, *The Image of the Indian and the Black Man in American Art, 1590–1900* (New York: George Braziller, 1974), p. 75.

3. E. to R. Kern, June 1845.

4. Hine, *Edward Kern*, pp. 7–47, recounts Edward's activities with Frémont.

5. R. to E. Kern, Philadelphia, Feb. 10, 1847, FS 117. Richard mentions that the last letter he received from Ned was dated March 31, 1846. Ned had written in July 1846, as

cited below, but that letter had clearly not reached Dick by February 10, 1847.

6. E. to R. Kern, July 29 [?], 1846, HM 20649: This portion of the letter is quoted in Hine, *Edward Kern*, p. 31.

7. Notes copied from the Bible of Richard's older sister, Mary Kern Wolfe, indicate that Dick was born on April 11, 1821. Copy in "Some Kern Notes," by Helen Wolfe, MS, HEH. Unless otherwise noted, these "Notes" serve as the source for statements regarding the Kern family.

8. Neil Harris, *The Artist in American Society: The Formative Years, 1790–1860* (New York: George Braziller, 1966), pp. 109, 276–78.

9. James Thomas Flexner, *That Wilder Image: The Painting of America's Native School from Thomas Cole to Winslow Homer* (1st ed., 1962; New York: Dover Publications, 1970), p. xi. Russell Lynes, *The Art-Makers of Nineteenth Century America* (New York: Atheneum, 1970), p. 211.

10. Peter C. Marzio, *The Art Crusade: An Analysis of American Drawing Manuals, 1820–1860* (Washington, D.C.: Smithsonian Institution Press, 1976), p. 7.

11. An original sketch of the house on Crown Street, drawn by Richard Kern, was in the collection of Miss Helen Wolfe of Washington, D.C. The sketch reproduced here is from HEH and is labeled a "copy." Wolfe, "Some Kern Notes," p. 2. The family moved from 37 Crown Street in 1844.

12. Matthias Shirk Weaver, diary entry, January 2, 1842, Matthias Shirk Weaver Papers, Ohio Historical Society (microfilm edition). Weaver's diary entry of July 7, 1842, suggests that the home had many books. Weaver, who moved to Philadelphia to study art in 1838, was nearly five years older than Richard Kern. Weaver became a lithographer, and his diaries indicate that he knew Benjamin Kern very well, prior to becoming acquainted with Richard. For more on Weaver see Nicholas B. Wainwright, *Philadelphia in the Romantic Age of Lithography* (Philadelphia: Historical Society of Pennsylvania, 1958), pp. 81–82, which also

describes extant examples of Weaver's work.

As deputy collector, John Kern held the second highest position in a seven-person office. *McElroy's Philadelphia Directory for 1842* (Philadelphia: Orrin Rogers, 1842), p. 333.

13. Thomas Coulson, *The Franklin Institute from 1824–1949* (Lancaster, Pa.: Lancaster Press, [1949]), pp. 1–17; Bruce Sinclair, *Philadelphia's Philosopher Mechanics. A History of the Franklin Institute, 1824–1865* (Baltimore: Johns Hopkins Press, 1974), pp. x, 1 39, 120–21. George C. Groce and David H. Wallace, *The New York Historical Society's Dictionary of Artists in America, 1564–1860* (New Haven: Yale University Press, 1957), p. 428.

14. The two oils, exhibited respectively in 1840 and 1841, were entitled *Swedes' Church, Wilmington, Delaware,* and *Muckross Abbey.* See Hine, *Edward Kern,* p. 4, and Anna Wells Rutledge, ed., *Cumulative Record of Exhibition Catalogues: The Pennsylvania Academy of the Fine Arts, 1807–1870* (2 vols., Philadelphia: American Philosophical Society, 1955), p. 113.

15. R. & E. Kern to the Committee on Instruction of the Franklin Institute, Philadelphia, May 13, 1844, in Miscellaneous Records of the Drawing School, Box 3, folder 8, Archives of the Franklin Institute (FI). The eight references the Kerns listed were: Dr. H. S. Patterson, G. R. Gliddon, Dr. Saml. Geo. Morton, W. H. Strickland, Richard Randolph, Alva Mason, Thomas Ryan, and Charles Ryan. Mason apparently died in early March. The articles he left in his classroom were inventoried on March 8, 1844, and sold to William H. Strickland on March 12. On March 11, 1844, William Hamilton told the Committee of Instruction that he had taken their recommendation to have S. Rufus Mason teach the last nine weeks of the late William Mason's course. Committee on Instruction, Drawing School, Box 3, folder 8, Miscellaneous Records, FI. I am grateful to Gladys Breuer, Associate Curator, for making the Institute's archives available to me.

16. Henry S. Patterson, M.D. [to the Committee on Instruction], Philadelphia, May 10,

1844, in Committee on Instruction, Box 2, folder 5, FI.

17. William H. Strickland to R. H. and E. M. Kern, Philadelphia, May 7, 1844, ibid., and Sinclair, *Philadelphia's Philosopher Mechanics,* pp. 34–35.

18. In a letter resigning their position as teachers of drawing to the Institute School, the Kerns refer to "having held the situation four years." R. and E. Kern to the Committee on Instruction, Philadelphia, June 19, 1848, in Committee on Instruction, Box 2, folder 5, FI.

19. *McElroy's Philadelphia Directory for 1845* (Philadelphia: Edward C. & John Biddle, 1845), p. 190. The announcement appeared in the city directories for the last time in 1853, the year of Dick's death.

20. R. to E. Kern, Philadelphia Feb. 10, 1847, FS 117. R. and E. Kern to the Committee on Instruction of the Franklin Institute, Philadelphia, June 19, 1848, Committee on Instruction, Box 2, folder 5, FI. John Kern's name first appears in the city directory as a teacher of drawing at 62 Filbert St. in 1847. While Dick and Ned were listed together, John's name remained apart.

21. Hine, *Kern,* p. 5 n. 4, identified these books, pointing out that Kern's work appeared in them without attribution to the artist.

22. See, for example, "Cerastes Nasicornus," and "Poebrotherium Wilsoni, Leidy," recorded in the Oct. 26, 1848, meeting, in *Proceedings of the Academy of Natural Sciences of Philadelphia,* III, *1846 & 1847* (Philadelphia: Merrihew & Thompson, 1848), following p. 278.

23. Matthias S. Weaver, diary entry of Jan. 7, 1842.

24. "Merycoidodon Culbertsonii. Leidy," reported on at the meeting of the Philadelphia Academy of Natural Sciences, Apr. 25, 1848, *Proceedings of the Academy of Natural Sciences of Philadelphia,* IV, *1848 & 1849* (Philadelphia: Merrihew & Thompson, 1850), following p. 50.

25. Wainwright, *Philadelphia in the Romantic Age of Lithography.*

26. In R. to E. Kern, Philadelphia, Feb. 10, 1847, Dick identifies his students and provides some clues regarding these relationships. For Wilkes and Drayton see William Stanton, *The Great United States Exploring Expedition, 1838–1842* (Berkeley: University of California Press, 1975), pp. 48, 350. For Morton and Gliddon, see William Stanton, *The Leopard's Spots: Scientific Attitudes toward Race in America, 1815–59* (Chicago: University of Chicago Press, 1960), pp. 24–53. R. Kern to S. G. Morton, St. Louis, Sept. 20, 1848, MS, Library Company of Philadelphia, and R. Kern to S. G. Morton, July 3, 1850. Morton's appraisal of the Kerns, and his comments on what they had done for Gliddon, are in Morton to [Board of Instruction, Franklin Institute], Philadelphia, May 13, 1844, Committee on Instruction, Box 2, folder 5, FI. In 1842, Morton had hired Edward to copy by hand a three-hundred-page manuscript of tables, illustrations, and text by Gliddon, "Analecta Hieroglyphica." Edward's copy is in the American Philosophical Society, Philadelphia. Dick may have assisted his younger brother. In any event, in 1843 Matthias Weaver found Richard "at work upon some of Gliddon's plates, the drawing of the Pyramid of Cheops is a good thing." Weaver, diary entry of Sept. 1, 1843.

27. See Stanton, *Leopard's Spots,* p. 27; R. to E. Kern, Philadelphia, Feb. 10, 1847.

28. *Proceedings of the Academy of Natural Sciences of Philadelphia,* III, pp. 213, 269, 299 (May 25, Sept. 28, and Oct. 26, 1847, respectively). The original three-by-five file cards, noting the dates of the brothers' elections to membership, remain in the archives of the Academy. From its founding in 1812 to December 31, 1851, "420 gentlemen and one lady" were elected members. W. S. W. Ruschenberger, *A Notice of the Origin, Progress, and Present Condition of the Academy of Natural Sciences of Philadelphia* (Philadelphia: T. K. and P. G. Collins, 1852), p. 69. A complete list of members appears on pp. 75–78.

29. Frémont's court-martial is treated in many sources, including Nevins, *Frémont,* pp. 333–40. For the fullest account, see Mary Lee Spence and Donald Jackson, eds., *The Expeditions of John Charles Frémont,* vol. 2 and supplement: *The Bear Flag Revolt and the Court-Martial* (Urbana: University of Illinois Press, 1973).

30. "Benton's Essays on the Road to India," in LeRoy R. Hafen and Ann W. Hafen, eds., *Fremont's Fourth Expedition: A Documentary Account of the Disaster of 1848–1849* . . . (Glendale, Cal.: The Arthur H. Clark Co., 1960), p. 279.

31. Hine, *Kern,* pp. 7–8, and R. to E. Kern, Feb. 10, 1847, who mentioned: "Ben returned in the same summer you left, and is much improved in health."

32. R. Kern to S. Morton, St. Louis, Sept. 20, 1848.

33. Fragment of a letter [R. Kern] to My Dear Friend, Pueblo of Zuni, Sept. 20, 1851, PC.

34. Thomas S. Martin, *With Frémont to California and the Southwest, 1845–1849,* Ferol Egan, ed. (Ashland, Ore.: Lewis Osborne, 1975), p. 23.

35. [Kern] to My Dear Friend, Sept. 20, 1851.

36. Ibid.

37. Quoted in Hine, *Kern,* p. 53; Professor Hine kindly made his notes from Mary Kern's album available to me. From those notes I have drawn the title of the poem.

38. Weaver diary entry, May 29, 1841. Sam Bass Warner, Jr., *The Private City: Philadelphia in Three Periods of Its Growth* (Philadelphia: University of Pennsylvania Press, 1968), pp. 49–62.

39. John K. Howat, *The Hudson River and Its Painters* (New York: Viking Press, 1972), provides an able introduction to the subject and a handsome portfolio of color reproductions. The school, which had many antecedents, is usually portrayed as flourishing between 1825 and 1875. Romanticism and Kern are discussed below, in chapter 8. Howat refers to Cole's use of the flute on p. 21. Dick refers to a trip to the White Mountains in the summer of 1846 in a letter, R. to E. Kern, Philadelphia, Feb. 10, 1847, FS 117. His reference to

"Feeling and Thought" is in R. Kern to Eliza B. Weaver, Philadelphia, Dec. 24, 1847, MS, Historical Society of Pennsylvania. The three works by Kern are in PC, as is a pencil sketch, *Lansdown, Sept. 10, 1847.*

40. Roderick Nash, *Wilderness and the American Mind,* (1st ed., 1967; New Haven: Yale University Press, 1982), p. 47. For Ned's unromantic view of Indians, see Hine, *Edward Kern,* pp. 13–14, 29, 44–45.

41. The Peale Museum operated throughout Kern's youth, until it closed its doors in 1849. Walter Faxon, "Relics of Peale's Museum," *Bulletin of the Museum of Comparative Zoology, Harvard College,* 59 (1951): 125, and Charles Coleman Sellers, *Mr. Peale's Museum* . . . (New York: W. W. Norton, 1980), pp. 235–36, 241, 252, 312, 316–17.

42. Harold McCracken, ed., *Catlin's North American Indian Portfolio* [a facsimile] (1st ed., London, 1844; Chicago: Swallow Press, 1970), p. 3.

43. Catlin exhibited his Indian gallery in Philadelphia in July 1838, when Kern was seventeen. William H. Truettner, *The Natural Man Observed: A Study of Catlin's Indian Gallery* (Washington, D.C.: Smithsonian Institution Press, 1979), p. 39.

44. James D. Horan, *The McKenney-Hall Portrait Gallery of American Indians* (New York: Crown Publishers, 1972), p. 23, reproduces the colored plates. The composition of Peter Rindisbacher's *War Dance* (ibid., p. 167) may have served as an inspiration for Ned Kern's *Green Corn Dance of the Jémez Indians* (fig. 139).

45. Address of Frederick Fraley, Oct. 1844, quoted in the *Journal of the Franklin Institute* 9 (1845): 37.

46. William H. Goetzmann and Joseph C. Porter, *The West as Romantic Horizon* (Omaha: Center for Western Studies, Joslyn Art Museum, 1981), p. 16. See also Theodore E. Stebbins, Jr., *American Master Drawings and Watercolors: A History of Works on Paper from Colonial Times to the Present* (New York: Harper & Row, 1976), p. 72.

47. Thoreau's essay on "Walking," quoted by Howard Lamar in his preface to Martha Sandweiss, *Pictures from an Expedition: Early Views of the American West* (New Haven: Yale University Press, 1978), p. 7.

48. These generalizations derive from a number of sources, including E. to R. Kern, Westport, June 19, 1845; R. to E. Kern, Philadelphia, Feb. 10, 1847 (where Dick mentions "They have a dreadful famine in Europe and Mountain Dew has gone up"); and Horace Dickinson to R. Kern, Santa Fe, Nov. 30, 1851, FS 143. Warner, *Philadelphia,* pp. 61–62.

49. R. Kern to Eliza Weaver, Philadelphia, Dec. 24, 1847.

50. Matthias Weaver diary, entry of March 31, 1841. Elsewhere in his diaries, Weaver mentions playing chess with Kern (Kern beat him), playing music in the evening with Kern, and attending lectures at the Wirt Institute, a literary society, where Kern served on the Lecture Committee. Weaver does not explicitly mention Kern attending the theater or serenading, but these were activities in which Weaver engaged, and it seems likely that Kern did too. "Reading, Talking, and smoking with friends," was Weaver's description of his own evening, January 16, 1842, with Dick's brother, Ben.

51. The poem appears on the back cover of Dick's diary of Aug. 13 to Nov. 16, 1851, HM 4277, when he traveled with Sitgreaves:

Gloire trois fois, gloire á Bacchus
Mais quand nous féterons Venus
Chacun fera ce qu'il poura [*sic*]
pour plaire a l'aimable deesse
Ami[?] [de] la jeunesse.

Three-fold glory, glory to Bacchus
But when we celebrate the rites of Venus
Each will do what he can
To please the amiable goddess
Friend of youth.

52. R. Kern to Morton, St. Louis, Sept. 20, 1848, indicates that John Kern will be delivering this letter personally to Morton. R. and E. Kern to the Committee of Instruction, Philadelphia, June 19, 1848.

53. Many sources provide biographical vi-

gnettes of the men and one boy who accompanied Frémont. See, for example, Hafen and Hafen, eds., *Fremont's Fourth Expedition*, pp. 22–25. By the time Frémont entered the mountains, he had lost a few men and added "Old Bill" Williams to bring the party to thirty-three. Mary Lee Spence, editor of vol. 3 of *The Expeditions of John Charles Frémont* (Urbana: University of Illinois Press, forthcoming), finds that sixteen persons had been on earlier Frémont expeditions. I have used Spence's figure, rather than the twenty-one persons suggested by Hafen and Hafen.

54. The original Richard Kern Diary, Oct. 21, 1848 to Feb. 16, 1849 (HM 4273), is transcribed in Hafen and Hafen, eds., *Fremont's Fourth Expedition*, pp. 109–34. All subsequent quotations in this chapter are from this diary, unless otherwise noted. I have supplied punctuation as needed for clarity.

55. Diary of Edward Kern, Nov. 8, 1848, in Hafen and Hafen, eds., *Fremont's Fourth Expedition*, p. 294. I have relied on this diary, along with Ben's diary (see n. 57), to supplement Richard's laconic diary. In addition to the primary sources cited here, I have profited from William Brandon's masterfully written *The Men and the Mountain: Frémont's Fourth Expedition* (New York: William Morrow & Co., 1955), and the brief account in Nevins, *Frémont*, pp. 343–72.

56. See below, n. 93.

57. Benjamin Kern's diary, Oct. 20, 1848, to Jan. 7, 1849, entry of Nov. 8 (HM 4272), and published in Hafen and Hafen, eds., *Fremont's Fourth Expedition*, pp. 79–108.

58. My reasons for suggesting that *Pike's Peak* was drawn in 1853 rather than in 1848 are discussed in chapter 6. Patricia Trenton and Peter H. Hassrick, *The Rocky Mountains: A Vision for Artists in the Nineteenth Century* (Norman: University of Oklahoma Press, 1983), p. 54, attribute it to Nov. 20, 1848.

59. Frémont to Thomas Hart Benton, Camp at Bent's Fort, November 17, 1848, quoted in Hafen and Hafen, eds., *Fremont's Fourth Expedition*, p. 76.

60. Both quotes are from Micajah McGehee, "Narrative," written within ten years of the event and published in two different versions. A composite is in Hafen and Hafen, eds., *Fremont's Fourth Expedition* pp. 143–73; they point out that two other contemporaries, Preuss and Godey, say that "Williams consented readily to go" (p. 146). McGehee is also quoted in Alpheus H. Favour, *Old Bill Williams, Mountain Man* (1st ed., 1936; Norman: University of Oklahoma Press, 1962), p. 180, who provides a detailed account of the expedition from this point on. See, too, the interesting commentary of Janet Lecompte, *Pueblo, Hardscrabble, Greenhorn: The Upper Arkansas, 1832–1856* (Norman: University of Oklahoma Press, 1978), p. 218.

61. Frémont to Benton, Nov. 17, 1848, Camp at Bent's Fort, in Hafen and Hafen, eds., *Fremont's Fourth Expedition*, p. 76.

62. Lecompte, *Pueblo, Hardscrabble, Greenhorn*, p. 219. Favour, *Old Bill Williams*, p. 183.

63. Dick entitled this painting *Robidoux' Pass White Mts, N.M. 1848*, but his watercolor does not resemble that more gradual, open pass. I am indebted to Pat Richmond and Janet Lecompte for identifying the watercolor as more closely resembling Hardscrabble Canyon. Dick and Ben describe this in their diary entries of Nov. 27 (Hafen and Hafen, eds., *Fremont's Fourth Expedition*, pp. 93, 123). Benjamin calls it "cannon of white oak or hard scrabble creek." Dick's understanding of the geography of the area, as revealed on the Parke map of 1851, put Robidoux Pass slicing through a gap between the White Mountains to the north and the Sangre de Cristos to the south. Hence his identification of the "White Mts." Today this would all be part of the larger Sangre de Cristo Range. Trenton and Hassrick, *Rocky Mountains*, p. 54, seem to err in accepting Kern's identification.

64. From this point on, I am following the detailed reconstruction of Frémont's route suggested in Patricia Joy Richmond's unpublished manuscript "The Route of John C. Frémont's Expedition of 1848–1849 into the San Luis

Valley of Colorado." Mrs. Richmond's interpretation of the route differs markedly from that suggested by Brandon, Hafen and Hafen, and Nevins, but she has done extensive fieldwork and has located fresh evidence—including the newly discovered Kern watercolors—that appears conclusive.

65. There is considerable disagreement as to the source of the mistake. Favour, *Old Bill Williams*, pp. 184–85, takes the view that Williams wanted to take a more southerly route and that Frémont objected and put Godey in charge by the time they reached the sand hills. I am not impressed by Favour's evidence. I am following Hafen and Hafen, eds., *Fremont's Fourth Expedition*, pp. 243–44. For a highly unfavorable view of "Old Bill" Williams see Charles Preuss, *Exploring with Frémont: The Private Diaries of Charles Preuss . . .* , Erwin G. Gudde and Elisabeth K. Gudde, trans. and eds. (Norman: University of Oklahoma Press, 1958), pp. 143–45. Nevins, *Frémont*, pp. 357–60, found the evidence inconclusive.

66. Benjamin Kern to Joe, Taos, Feb. 20, 1849, in Hafen and Hafen, eds., *Fremont's Fourth Expedition*, p. 233.

67. Richmond, "The Route of John C. Frémont's Expedition," p. 5.

68. In Preuss, *Exploring*, p. 146 n. 13, editors Gudde and Gudde argue that the party ate mule meat, as McGehee remembered, and that Richard Kern's diary entry was made with irony. Both Dick and Benjamin recorded the elk meat, rice, and coffee dinner, however, and Benjamin was more specific about alcohol.

69. Hine, *Edward Kern*, p. 65. For examples of historians who have criticized Frémont's decisions, see Favour, *Old Bill Williams*, p. 189; Brandon, *The Men and the Mountain*, p. 243; Hafen and Hafen, eds., *Fremont's Fourth Expedition*, p. 246; and Preuss, *Exploring with Frémont*, p. 148 n. 18.

70. This is evident from the "Map of the Territory of New Mexico" by Lt. John G. Parke, 1851, drawn by Richard H. Kern. The spelling of the modern river, town, and county is Saguache, but the mountains today are spelled

Sawatch. Identification of the site of Kern's painting is through the courtesy of Pat Richmond, who says the place "could be the head of Embargo Creek or it could be the rock outcropping on Groundhog Creek about one mile below the camp." Richmond to Weber, Dec. 23, 1982. An unfinished watercolor and pencil sketch, dated Jan. 1, 1849, shows this same scene. Large scrapbook, PC.

71. An English poet, Thomas Hood (1799–1845), was well known for light verse, such as *Faithless Nelly Grey* (1834), and poems of social protest, such as *The Song of the Shirt* (1843). William Rose Benét, *The Reader's Encyclopedia* (2nd ed., New York: Thomas Y. Crowell Co., 1965), p. 476. On this occasion, one suspects that Dick read some light verse.

72. Benjamin recorded this on January 6, and it seems likely to have occurred on more than one occasion.

73. Benjamin records burning books on January 3, and Richard records burning "some of our things" on January 4.

74. Brandon, *The Men and the Mountain*, pp. 245–46. "Whilst with Col. Fremont in 1848, my brother & myself made a large ornithological collection, but circumstances forced me to leave them in the mountains with most of our other effects." R. Kern to J. R. Bartlett, Santa Fe, March 14, 1851, Mexican Boundary Commission Papers of John Russell Bartlett, 1850–1853, vol. 3, no. 146, John Carter Brown Library, Providence, Rhode Island.

75. [E. Kern] to My Dear Sir, Washington, April 30, 1858, PC. In this letter, written perhaps to George Childs and containing information for Frémont, Edward says: "The other sketch 'the point of Rock,' Proulx' Creek was made by my diary Jany 11 1849." At this point, Kern copied the sketch into his letter; it shows one cave very clearly and resembles the watercolor discussed below. Edward goes on to say: "I called the place at the time, the Creek after Proulx, the first of our party who perished, and the Point of Rocks, was so Known among the men, it being a remarkable land mark for any who might return in search of the effects of the

expedition, as there was a large cache near that place."

76. Pat Richmond is familiar with both the Cave Creek and La Garita Creek sites. She believes that Richard Kern mistakenly drew *On Proulx' Creek* from sketches of a similar spot on Cave Creek. On January 7, 1984, Richmond skiied up La Garita Creek to the site of the watercolor *Point of Rocks,* under weather conditions similar to those that Kern had known. The day was warm and the snow deep. I am basing much of the information in this and in the preceding paragraph on Richmond's observations. Richmond to Weber, Crestone, Colorado, January 8, 1984. The existence of the watercolor, *Point of Rocks,* further substantiates Richmond's thesis that Frémont's party descended La Garita Creek to the Rio Grande.

For a discussion of why I believe that Kern completed at a later date the watercolors that are in the album at the Amon Carter Museum, see chapter 8.

77. I have followed the lead of Spence and Jackson, eds., *Expeditions of Frémont,* in spelling "Vinsonhaler," which is often rendered "Vincenthaler." For Stepperfeldt, see below, n. 90. Richard Kern's charge of being deserted by the stronger group is confirmed by Thomas Martin, *With Frémont,* p. 26, who describes how the Vinsonhaler group waited until the weak were asleep, then "crept out of camp and started again."

78. The answer to the question of whether cannibalism occurred may never be found. It is not even clear as to whether Rohrer and Andrews were in the same camp with the rest of the "weak" men when they died. McGehee's recollections vividly place them in that camp, but Kern's diary and his notes made soon afterwards say that the two fell behind and were presumed dead. See Hafen and Hafen, eds., *Fremont's Fourth Expedition,* pp. 131, 163, 260. For the conversation about cannibalism, see McGehee, ibid., pp. 164–65.

79. Edward Kern to Mary, Taos, February 10, 1849, in Hafen and Hafen, eds., *Fremont's Fourth Expedition,* p. 220.

80. Letter to Joe, Taos, February 20, 1849, in Hafen and Hafen, eds., *Fremont's Fourth Expedition,* p. 235. McGehee, ibid., p. 165, mentions the men were snowblinded. They mistook Godey for Frémont at first.

81. This identification comes from Pat Richmond, who says this "is the only place where the mountain is so visible. . . . The peaks [in Kern's watercolor] are probably Blanca Peak, the highest, Ellingwood and Little Bear." Richmond to Weber, June 27, 1982.

82. The three brothers had become separated. Edward Kern had reached Taos by February 10.

83. Benjamin Kern to Joe, Taos, February 20, 1849, in Hafen and Hafen, eds., *Fremont's Fourth Expedition,* p. 236.

84. *Exploration and Empire* (New York: Alfred Knopf, 1966), p. 270, and Frank McNitt, ed., *Navaho Expedition* (Norman: University of Oklahoma Press, 1964), p. xxxii. For a similar judgment, see Favour, *Old Bill Williams,* p. 180. Hafen and Hafen, ed., *Fremont's Fourth Expedition,* p. 39, cite "strong evidence," including Benjamin Kern's letter of February 2, 1849, that King's body was eaten. Names of the dead are listed in Hafen and Hafen, eds., *Fremont's Fourth Expedition,* p. 44.

85. Andrew Rolle, "Exploring an Explorer: Psychohistory and John Charles Frémont," *Pacific Historical Review,* 51 (May 1982): 152.

86. Edward Kern to Mary Wolfe [late February or early March], 1849, in Hafen and Hafen, eds., *Fremont's Fourth Expedition,* pp. 226–27.

87. Godey to John O. Wheeler, Los Angeles, September 12, 1856, published in the New York *Evening Post,* Oct. 30, 1856, and reprinted in Hafen and Hafen, eds., *Fremont's Fourth Expedition,* pp. 263–75. The quotes are from p. 272. Godey also suggested that the subsequent death of Benjamin Kern had "undoubtedly soured the minds" of Dick and Ned (p. 273), but Dick had written his charges against Frémont *prior* to learning of Benjamin's death on March 25, 1849. Ned's letter to Mary, written before he knew of Ben's death, also

reveals considerable bitterness toward Frémont. Ibid., pp. 224–30.

88. Hafen and Hafen, eds., *Fremont's Fourth Expedition*, p. 228. For Frémont's comments about the men's courage, see Hine, *Edward Kern*, p. 63.

89. Rolle, "Exploring an Explorer," pp. 140, 144–45, 151–52, 156, 161–62.

90. The revised diary is signed Richard H. Kern, Rio Hondo [Arroyo Hondo], March 19, 1849, and first appeared in print in May, in the Quincy (Ill.) *Whig*, May 22, 1849. Mary Lee Spence of the University of Illinois graciously furnished me with a copy of this article, and has identified the "Stepperfeldt" of Frémont's Fourth Expedition as John S. Stepperfeldt. I have also consulted a copy of the article that the Philadelphia *Evening Bulletin* reprinted on June 2, 1849, from the Quincy *Whig*. Hafen and Hafen, eds., *Fremont's Fourth Expedition*, pp. 255–61, reprints essentially the same article from the Washington *Daily Union*, July 31, 1856, attributed to the New York *Tribune* of 1849. There are some minor differences between these printings, including typographical errors. Hafen is in error in terming this a "campaign document," and in suggesting that "the altering of the original may have come as a result of the heated Presidential campaign of 1856 (pp. 255–56 nn. 25 and 29). Kern had clearly altered his diary seven years earlier. In his letter to Cathcart, cited below, Kern wrote: "Stepperfeldt started off alone and was picked up on the prairie perfectly crazy; he however got in safe and published Frémont." For Godey, see *Fremont's Fourth Expedition*, pp. 263–75.

91. Copy of a letter from R. Kern to Capt. Cathcart, Santa Fe, Sept. 30, 1849, HM 20657. See also Hine, *Edward Kern*, p. 62.

92. Richard H. Kern to Samuel George Morton, Santa Fe, July 3, 1850, Newberry Library, Chicago, Ill.

93. In addition to the three watercolors reproduced in this chapter, the private collection holds scenes entitled: *Sat, Oct 28, immediately after leaving camp; Bluff on the Smoky Hill, camping ground in distance, Nov. 2, 48; Immediately after crossing Smoky Hill Fork Near Pawnee Village, Nov. 2, 1848; Monday, Nov. 12, 1848, South Side of Arkansas—Morning; Jan. 1, 1849;* and *Point of Rocks, Proulx Creek {ca. Jan. 11, 1849}.* These were done by either Richard or Edward Kern.

94. Kern to Cathcart, Sept. 30, 1849.

95. These are discussed in chapter 8.

CHAPTER 3
TO THE NAVAJO COUNTRY WITH SIMPSON

1. Quotes from Edward Kern to Mary, Taos, February 10, 1849, and "second letter to Mary," ca. late February 1849, in LeRoy R. Hafen and Ann W. Hafen, eds. *Fremont's Fourth Expedition: A Documentary Account of the Disaster of 1848–1849 . . .* (Glendale, Cal.: Arthur H. Clark, 1960), pp. 221, 229. Evidence that all three Kerns planned to return to Philadelphia also appears in a letter of Micajah McGehee to his father in Mississippi, Taos, New Mexico, February 13, 1849. McGehee, who was also with Frémont, identifies the Kerns as "fellow-sufferers and messmates to whom please extend any assistance they may require as I have tendered them the hospitality of your house and my home." FS 124.

2. Doc's departure with Williams occurred after February 20, for on that date he was still in Taos, as evidenced by the letter he wrote to "Joe." In a letter to Mary, Edward Kern wrote, "Doc has returned to the Mountains to try to recover some of our lost property." Hafen and Hafen, eds., *Fremont's Fourth Expedition*, p. 229. Edward's letter is not dated, but must have been written in late February or early March, since he refers to their terrible suffering "a month ago" (ibid., p. 228). Godey rescued them on January 28.

3. Benjamin Kern to "Joe," Taos, February 20, 1849, in Hafen and Hafen, eds., *Fremont's Fourth Expedition*, p. 236.

4. Edward to Mary [ca. late February, 1849], in Hafen and Hafen, eds., *Fremont's Fourth Expedition*, p. 228.

5. Copy of a letter, R. Kern to John Kern, Santa Fe, ca. Sept. 30, 1849, HM 20657. The first quote is from the diary of Matthias Shirk Weaver, July 29, 1841, Ohio Historical Society (microfilm edition).

6. Chapman to Kern, Abiquiú, April 10, 1849, FS 127, quoted in full in Alpheus H. Favour, *Old Bill Williams: Mountain Man* (1st ed., 1836; Norman: University of Oklahoma Press, 1962), pp. 229–30.

7. The most detailed account of this episode, with fresh information and a discussion of sources is in Frank McNitt's introduction to *Navaho Expedition: Journal of a Military Reconnaissance from Santa Fe, New Mexico to the Navaho Country Made in 1849 by Lieutenant James H. Simpson* (Norman: University of Oklahoma Press, 1964), pp. xxxv–xliii. McNitt seems convinced that the muleteers hired by Ben and Old Bill did the killing, but the evidence that McNitt discusses was never convincing to Dick Kern, who as late as 1853 attributed the murder to "members of the band of Taos Utahs." Kern to H. R. Schoolcraft, Washington, March 19, 1853, in Henry Rowe Schoolcraft, *Historical and Statistical Information Respecting the History, Condition, and Prospects of the Indian Tribes of the United States . . .* 6 vols. (Philadelphia: Lippincott, Grambo & Co., 1851–57), 4:253. Evidence against the Mexicans also failed to convince other contemporaries, who continued to blame Utes for the murder. See Lt. Hendixson to Richard or Edward Kern, Abiquiú [April 1849], FS 128, and John Greiner to R. Kern, Santa Fe, written on a letter from Horace Dickinson to R. Kern, January 27, [1852], FS 129.

8. Reported by James S. Calhoun to Orlando Brown, Commissioner of Indian Affairs, Indian Agency, Santa Fe, November 15, 1849, in Annie Heloise Abel, ed., *The Official Correspondence of James S. Calhoun . . .* (Washington, D.C.: Government Printing Office, 1915), p. 77.

9. This was Blanche C. Grant's speculation, in her pioneering history of Taos: "There had been United States Army lieutenants who had made sketches before, notably Douglass [sic]

Brewerton who was here in the summer of 1848, but, as far as now known, the first real artists to come [to Taos] were Edward and Richard Kern . . ." *When Old Trails were New: The Story of Taos* (New York: Press of the Pioneers, 1934), p. 116.

10. The quote is from an editorial in the Santa Fe *Republican*, April 28, 1849, photocopy in the McNitt Papers, New Mexico State Records Center, Santa Fe. See, too, G. Douglas Brewerton, "Incidents of Travel in New Mexico," *Harper's New Monthly Magazine*, 8 (April 1854):579. With Kern's drawings in hand, and with the help of Taos residents such as Helen Blumenschein, Jack Boyer, and Frank Waters, Bill McIntyre and I visited the Salto de Agua and examined the rim of Taos Valley looking for the sites of the Kern drawings. The field sketch of the waterfall is in the scrapbook, PC. Kern's technique is discussed further in chapter 8.

11. McNitt, ed., *Navaho Expedition*, pp. liii–lxi, contains a brief biography and assessment of Simpson. For Marcy's mission, see the summary in W. Eugene Hollon, *Beyond the Cross Timbers: The Travels of Randolph B. Marcy, 1812–1887* (Norman: University of Oklahoma Press, 1955), pp. 56–74. Simpson's *Report of Exploration and Survey of a Route from Fort Smith, Arkansas, to Santa Fe, New Mexico, Made in 1849* (dated August 13, 1849) was published in 1850, 31 Cong., 1 sess., House Exec. Doc. 45.

12. Simpson, *Report*, p. 3; McNitt, ed., *Navaho Expedition*, p. lxii; and Robert V. Hine, *In the Shadow of Frémont: Edward Kern and the Art of American Exploration, 1845–1860* (1st ed., 1962; Norman: University of Oklahoma Press, 1982), p. 71.

13. Abert's interest in the so-called fish may be inferred from Simpson to Abert, Santa Fe, Nov. 29, 1849, LR, TB, NARS, M 506, r. 62, fr. 435. I am grateful to my colleague in biology, Stan Trauth, for identifying the amphibian as one of the genus Ambystoma. Kern's drawing is not sufficiently clear to identify the species, but it is probably A. tigrinum, or the tiger salamander.

14. Robert Taft, *Artists and Illustrators of the*

Old West, 1850–1900 (New York: Charles Scribner's Sons, 1953), p. 259, says this is "probably the illustration for which R. H. Kern is best known." Lt. J. W. Abert did an earlier view of Santa Fe. For the scattered nature of frontier communities such as Santa Fe, see Weber, *The Mexican Frontier, 1821–1846: The American Southwest under Mexico* (Albuquerque: University of New Mexico Press, 1982), p. 229. Kern apparently did not complete his drawing of Santa Fe until October, 1849, for Simpson forwarded it to Abert at the end of that month with the request that it "be filed and considered a part of my report upon the Arkansas route to New Mexico." Simpson to Abert, Santa Fe, Oct. 30, 1849, LR, TB, NARS, M 506, r. 62, frs. 351–53. For further analysis of this lithograph, see chapter 8.

15. Orders of Lieutenant Colonel Washington, Santa Fe, August 14, 1849, in McNitt, ed., *Navaho Expedition*, p. 3.

16. Simpson uses the terms "first" and "second" assistant in McNitt, ed., *Navaho Expedition*, p. 14. The remainder of the quote is from Simpson to John J. Abert, Santa Fe, April 11, 1850, transmitting the *Journal of a Military Reconnaissance from Santa Fé, New Mexico, to the Navajo Country in 1849*, 31st Cong., 1st sess., Sen. Ex. Doc. 64 (Washington, D.C.: 1850), p. 56.

17. Simpson, *Journal*, p. 56. The best and most accessible edition of Simpson's *Journal* is that edited by McNitt, *Navaho Expedition*, but McNitt did not reproduce most of the lithographs and deleted "Simpson's references in his narrative to the numerical sequence of Richard Kern's accompanying drawings" (p. xv). David M. Brugge, *A History of the Chaco Navajos* (Albuquerque: National Park Service, 1980), p. 14.

18. Richard Kern entitled this diary "Notes of a Military Reconnaissance of the Pais de los Navajos in the Months of Aug & Sept 1849," HM 4274. Subsequent quotations, unless otherwise attributed, are to these "Notes."

19. McNitt, ed., *Navaho Expedition*, pp. 6–7, comments on the scene, and Dick describes Placer Mountain in his diary entry of August

18. A note on the drawing indicates that the view was sketched "from Santa Fé" by R. H. Kern "from a Sketch by E. M. Kern." For more on the accuracy of this view see chapter 8.

20. Entry of August 18, in "Notes." His more detailed description of the pueblo has been preserved separately at the Huntington Library (FS 134), and was copied by Simpson "nearly verbatim." McNitt, ed., *Navaho Expedition*, pp. 8–9 n. 2.

21. McNitt, ed., *Navaho Expedition*, pp. 13–14. Kern's plate 6 in Simpson's *Journal* erroneously attributes the *You-Pel-lay*, or the *Green Corn Dance of the Jémez Indians* to R. E. Kern. The original watercolor shows Ned's signature. Joe Sando of Jémez, the leading authority on the history and culture of his pueblo, writes that "the 'U-pe-le' dancers were no doubt [drawn] from memory as sketching and photography is not allowed today." Sando to Weber, Albuquerque, New Mexico, August 31, 1981. Judging from Richard Kern's success in gaining access to the kiva at Jémez, as related below, it seems to me likely that Edward was permitted to draw the dance. The Jémez had probably not developed a policy about drawing at this early date; the Kerns were probably the first artists to use them as subjects.

22. [Horace Dickinson] to R. Kern, Santa Fe, Nov. 30, 1851, FS 143. Hine, *Edward Kern*, illus. 19, and McNitt, *Navajo Wars*, pp. 139–40, speculate that a small sketch of an Indian head in Kern's diary may be that of Hosta, but it bears no close resemblance to the likeness of Hosta in his war costume, nor does the face match Simpson's description: "the handsome, magnanimous Hosta, apparently unconscious of anything distinguishing about him" (*Navaho Expedition*, p. 72).

Kern's original full-length portrait of *Hosta* came under attack in Joe S. Sando, "Jemez Pueblo," in William C. Sturtevant, ed., *Handbook of North American Indians*, vol. 9, *Southwest*, Alfonso Ortiz, ed. (Washington, D.C.: Smithsonian Institution, 1979), p. 425, fig. 4. A caption below the illustration says: "Inaccurate or improbable details in this and other paintings in this series suggest that the painting was not done entirely from life. Painted by Richard H. Kern, allegedly Aug. 19, 1849." Joe Sando, author of the article, told me: "I am not sure who furnished the description for the pictures . . . I suspect it was Bill Sturtevant." Sando goes on to conclude that "Kern probably painted Hosta just the way he was dressed." Sando to Weber, Albuquerque, Aug. 31, 1981. Judging from the care that Richard Kern took to prepare field sketches and verbal descriptions at Zuni in 1851 (see chapter 5), I think that Sando's conclusion in his letter to me is correct and that there are few "inaccurate or improbable details" in the entire series.

23. McNitt, ed., *Navaho Expedition,* p. 24.

24. Simpson, *Journal,* p. 69. This quote does not appear in McNitt, ed., *Navaho Expedition.*

25. The original pencil sketch of the kiva interior, dated August 20, 1849, is in the Peabody Museum of Archaeology and Ethnology, Harvard University, as is a more polished wash drawing, probably of the same view. These were not reproduced for Simpson's *Journal,* but may be seen in Hine, *Edward Kern,* illus. 31 and 32. Seth Eastman did an engraving of Kern's wash drawing, which appears in Schoolcraft, *Indian Tribes,* 4:87. The original watercolors of kiva wall paintings are in ANSP, and lithographs appear as plates 7–11 in Simpson's *Journal.* The plates are analyzed in Watson Smith, *Kiva Mural Decorations at Awatovi and Kawaika-a, with a Survey of Other Wall Paintings in the Pueblo Southwest* (Cambridge, Mass.: Peabody Museum, 1952), pp. 84–88. See, too, McNitt's commentary in *Navaho Expedition,* pp. 20–21 n. 15. It is possible that Kern misdated his five watercolors of kiva wall paintings, and that instead of doing them on August 20, he did them on August 21, when Simpson says the Kerns accompanied him and Hosta on a visit to two kivas. For an example of the continued use of Kern's drawings among anthropologists, see Richard Parmentier, "The Pueblo Mythological Triangle: Poseyemu, Montezuma, and Jesus in the Pueblos," in Sturtevant, ed., *Handbook of North American Indians,* vol. 9, *Southwest,* Alfonso Ortiz, ed., p. 619, fig. 3.

26. The trip to Ojo Caliente is discussed in McNitt, ed., *Navaho Expedition,* pp. 14–18.

27. This drawing is unsigned. For the Pecos' abandonment of their Pueblo, see John L. Kessell, *Kiva, Cross, and Crown: The Pecos Indians and New Mexico, 1540–1840* (Washington, D.C.: National Park Service, 1979), pp. 455–59. Hosta's date of 1824, which he told Kern, may have been incorrect. He was right that the Jémez and Pecos spoke the same language— Towa.

28. Kern's "Notes" on this subject are repeated in part by Simpson, in McNitt, ed., *Navaho Expedition,* pp. 19–24. For good summaries of Montezuma and the Pueblos, see Marc Simmons, *Witchcraft in the Southwest: Spanish and Indian Supernaturalism on the Rio Grande* (Flagstaff, Ariz.: Northland Press, 1974), pp. 127–34, and Parmentier, "Pueblo Mythological Triangle," pp. 617–20.

29. Kern's two field sketches, entitled *Pueblo of Pecos Indians at Jémez from the North* and *Pueblo of Pecos Indians from the East,* dated Aug. 21, 1849, are in the Scrapbook, PC. The latter has been reproduced in *Life,* 46 (April 9, 1959):95, and in Patricia Trenton and Peter H. Hassrick, *The Rocky Mountains: A Vision for Artists in the Nineteenth Century* (Norman: University of Oklahoma Press, 1983), p. 56. When Kern prepared a polished drawing of this latter sketch for the lithographer, he dated it Aug. 20. The lithograph also bears that date.

30. Chapman's militia joined them two days out of Jémez, bringing the total to 395 (McNitt, *Navajo Wars,* p. 140), a number that would be reduced by desertions.

31. Kern, "Diary," entry of August 25. His sketch of "Ow-te-wa," whom he described as a captain and former governor of Santa Ana, appears in Simpson, *Journal,* pl. 13. Simpson, *Journal,* p. 94, says Ow-te-wa was "elected chief" of the Pueblo volunteers.

32. McNitt, ed., *Navaho Expedition,* p. 31.

33. Dick did a watercolor of the "North Wall of the Cañon de la Copa" on August 24. A color lithograph of it appears as plate 16 in Simpson, *Journal.* Color lithographs of his wa-

tercolors of petrified tree stumps appear as plates 18 and 19.

34. Douglas and Barbara Anderson, *Chaco Canyon* (Globe, Ariz.: Southwest Parks and Monuments Association, 1976), is a good, well-illustrated introduction. A fine summary of recent scholarship on the Anazasi, including those at Chaco, is Linda S. Cordell, "Prehistory: Eastern Anasazi," in the *Handbook of North American Indians,* vol. 9, *Southwest,* Alfonso Ortiz, ed. (Washington, D.C.: Smithsonian Institution, 1979), pp. 131–51.

35. McNitt, ed., *Navaho Expedition,* p. 35. McNitt, *Navajo Wars* (Albuquerque: University of New Mexico Press, 1972), p. 240. William H. Goetzmann, *Army Exploration in the American West, 1803–1863* (New Haven: Yale University Press, 1959), p. 240, errs in attributing the name Pueblo Pintado to Hosta. Simpson explicitly credits Carravahal with the name, and says that Hosta called it the Pueblo de Ratones.

36. McNitt, ed., *Navaho Expedition,* p. 38, paraphrases Hosta. Simpson concluded that it was "very probable that not only were the ruins of the Chaco of Aztec origin, but, as far as has been at present discovered, it is not at all unlikely that they, instead of those on or near the Gila, constituted the last resting place of this people before entering upon the conquest of Anahuac," ibid., pp. 55–56.

37. Simpson, *Journal,* plate 22, depicts "Pottery Found at Pueblo Pintado." Plates 23 and 24 depict "Hieroglyphics on a Sand Stone Boulder" (Ned Kern did a sketch of petroglyphs that appear as plate 25). Plates 26 and 27 are the ground plan and view of Wijiji. The ground plans are unsigned, but were probably drawn by Dick.

38. John Fox Hammond, of South Carolina, joined the army as an assistant surgeon in 1847. See John Fox Hammond, *A Surgeon Reports on Socorro, New Mexico, 1852* (Santa Fe: Stagecoach Press, 1966), for a brief biography and a sample of his prose and observations. Collins, a Santa Fe merchant, would become a newspaper editor, superintendent of Indian affairs, and re-

main a friend of Richard Kern.

39. McNitt, ed., *Navaho Expedition,* p. 52. Goetzmann, *Army Exploration,* p. 241, is incorrect in stating that Kern's "reconstructed version of the Pueblo 'Hungo Pavie' embodied Simpson's idea that these pueblos presented one solid wall to the outside on three sides, while the inner side faced a courtyard and was tiered." Simpson explicitly credits Kern with the idea.

40. William Henry Jackson, "Report on the Ancient Ruins Examined in 1875 and 1877: Ruins of the Chaco Cañon, Examined in 1877," *U.S. Geological and Geographical Survey of the Territories,* Tenth Annual Report (Washington, D.C.: 1878), p. 442, quoted in McNitt, ed., *Navaho Expedition,* p. 48.

41. Edgar L. Hewett, *The Chaco Canyon and its Monuments* (Albuquerque: University of New Mexico Press, 1936), p. 151, quoting Jackson's 1878 report. For similar assessments, see David M. Brugge, *A History of the Chaco Navajos* (Albuquerque: National Park Service, 1980), p. 14, and Robert H. Lister and Florence C. Lister, *Chaco Canyon: Archaeologists and Archaeology* (Albuquerque: University of New Mexico Press, 1982), p. 6.

42. Goetzmann, *Army Explorations,* p. 242. Hewett, *Chaco Canyon,* p. 148, comments on the report's enduring value for "comparative study." Hewett termed Abbé Em. Domenech's excursion between 1850 and 1857 "the first scientific reconnaissance" of Chaco, but my reading of Domenech, *Seven Years' Residence in the Great Deserts of North America,* 2 vols. (London: Longman, Green, Longman, and Roberts, 1860), 1:199–200, suggests nothing scientific about Domenech's commentary, and I doubt that he actually visited Chaco. For a delightfully written account of early exploration of the area, see Frank McNitt, *Richard Wetherill: Anasazi* (Albuquerque: University of New Mexico Press, 1957), pp. 118–39. McNitt, *Navajo Wars,* p. 141, judges that Simpson's description of Chaco "mainly accounts for the enduring value of his journal."

43. McNitt, ed., *Navaho Expedition,* p. 57.

44. Dick did a watercolor of the scene en-

titled "Natural Stone Formations" and dated August 29, "about six miles east of Camp 11." Simpson, *Journal*, plate 42.

45. The quote is from Simpson, *Journal*, p. 88. McNitt identifies the modern name in *Navaho Expedition*, p. 62 n. 72. I am following McNitt's *Navajo Wars*, pp. 142–43, for other geographical locations in this paragraph.

46. For descriptions of Narbona, see McNitt, *Navajo Wars*, pp. 110, 146. Simpson, *Journal*, p. 91 says the sketch was done "just before his death."

47. Santa Fe, July 3, 1850, Newberry Library.

48. Curtis M. Hinsley, Jr., *Savages and Scientists: The Smithsonian Institution and the Development of American Anthropology, 1846–1910* (Washington, D.C.: Smithsonian Institution Press, 1981), pp. 25–26. William Stanton, *The Leopard's Spots: Scientific Attitudes toward Race in America, 1815–59* (Chicago: University of Chicago Press, 1960), pp. 27–33. The number of Indian skulls was reported in the *Proceedings of the Academy of Natural Sciences of Philadelphia*, 3, 1846 & 1847 (Philadelphia: Merrihew & Thompson, 1848), p. 213.

49. Kern's wash drawing of *Pass Washington, Tune-Cha Mountains. Sept. 2*, is plate 45, and shows it "looking back," or east (Simpson, *Journal*, p. 94). Plates 46 and 47 were also done en route to Canyon de Chelly. Plate 46, done on Sept. 3, shows a view as they descended the western slope, and plate 47 shows a dike of trap rock, done on Sept. 4 (described in Simpson, *Navaho Expedition*, p. 80).

50. Kern's *View of the Cañon de Chelly near its head*, is actually a view of a branch canyon, Canyon del Muerto. McNitt, ed. *Navaho Expedition*, p. 82 n. 89, p. 24.

51. In McNitt, ed., *Navaho Expedition*, pp. 87, 164, McNitt disagrees with Kern's explanation for the burning. In a later book, *Navajo Wars*, p. 148, McNitt seems less certain.

52. The text of the treaty, its signatories, and its witnesses, is in McNitt, ed., *Navaho Expedition*, pp. 258–61.

53. See McNitt, *Navajo Wars*, especially pp. 148, 154–55.

54. McNitt, ed., *Navaho Expedition*, p. 101.

55. The story is not implausible. Bill Williams may have passed through the Hopi Villages in 1834, on return from a horse-stealing expedition in California, or on some other occasion. Favour, *Old Bill Williams*, p. 113.

56. McNitt, ed., *Navaho Expedition*, pp. 87–88.

57. See McNitt, ed., *Navaho Expedition*, pp. 63, 97, 100, and n. 107; Schoolcraft, *Indian Tribes*, 4:74; and Brugge, *Chaco Navajos*, p. 28. The often-reproduced lithograph of *Navajo Costume* differs markedly from the original, and appears in chapter 8.

58. The quote is from Simpson, *Journal*, p. 104. Hine, *Edward Kern*, plates 26, 27, 28, juxtaposes Kern's watercolor of White House ruin with the lithograph and a modern photograph. McNitt, ed., *Navaho Expedition*, pp. 90–98, recounts the reconnaissance of Chelly in detail.

59. The first quote in this paragraph is from Kern's diary, the second is from his letter to Morton, Santa Fe, July 3, 1850.

60. C. Gregory Crampton, *The Zunis of Cibola* (Salt Lake City: University of Utah Press, 1977), p. 101. Although appreciating its importance as the first graphic image of Zuni, Crampton dismissed it as "a grotesquely distorted view of a part of the pueblo looking east to Corn Mountain . . . of no particular credit to the artist." Upon reflection, however, Crampton has concluded that Kern's drawing of the pueblo was "quite good given the time of his work . . . the key feature, the church, is quite well done." Crampton explained that his original assessment "was probably based on [Kern's] handling of Corn Mountain . . . which has been reduced in size and lacks the distinctive profile so notable and so important to the Zunis. . . . My judgment of Kern's 'Pueblo' is unfair. Corn Mountain *is* distorted." Crampton to Weber, St. George, Utah, Aug. 29, 1982. A comparison of Kern's Corn Mountain with a photograph can be made in Crampton's *Zuni*, or in Eugene Ostroff, *Western Views and Eastern Visions* (Washington, D.C.: Smithsonian Institution, 1981), p. 32. Goetzmann, *Army Ex-*

ploration, p. 242, finds Simpson's the best of any American account.

Kern's *Zuni* represented a quantum leap over the only other drawing of the pueblo, an often-reproduced painting by Jan Mostaert in 1545, who sought to portray Coronado's assault on the pueblo. Van Deren Coke, *Taos and Santa Fe: The Artist's Environment, 1882–1942* (Albuquerque: University of New Mexico Press for the Amon Carter Museum, 1963), p. 11.

61. See chapter 6.

62. Letter to Dr. Morton, Santa Fe, July 3, 1850.

63. Both quotes are from McNitt, ed., *Navaho Expedition,* p. 125.

64. John M. Slater, *El Morro, Inscription Rock, New Mexico: The Rock Itself, the Inscriptions Thereon, and the Travelers Who Made Them* (Los Angeles: Plantin Press, 1961), chronicles all known early-day visitors to the rock.

65. McNitt, ed., *Navaho Expedition,* p. 132.

66. Charles Fletcher Lummis, *Mesa, Cañon and Pueblo* (New York: Appleton-Century, 1938), p. 480. Lummis judges the Kern-Simpson drawings more harshly than do other specialists.

67. Although scientists, such as Bandelier, later copied names from the bluff, the Simpson-Kern drawings were the best published inventory until the appearance in 1905 of Homer E. Hoopes and Henry L. Broomall, "Photographs of Some of the Inscriptions on El Morro, New Mexico, with Translations and Notes," *Proceedings of the Delaware County Institute of Science* [Media, Pennsylvania], 1, no. 1 (1905):13–24 Bandelier, who visited El Morro in 1888, made the point that "names and dates preserved by [Simpson] now are no longer to be found." Adolph F. Bandelier, *Final Report of Investigations among the Indians of the Southwestern United States . . . 1880 to 1885,* 2 vols. (Cambridge, Mass.: University Press, 1890; 1892), 2:330. Bandelier relied heavily upon Simpson's descriptions. See, too, Charles H. Lange, Carroll L. Riley, and Elizabeth M. Lange, eds., *The Southwestern Journals of Adolph F. Bandelier, 1885–1888* (Albuquerque: University of New Mexico Press, 1975), pp. 301–02; 540–41 n. 1101.

68. Kern's three views of El Morro include washes of the *North Face* and *South Face,* both dated September 17, and an undated watercolor: *Spring at Inscription Rock,* which subsequent research has revealed to be a *tinaja,* or tank, holding rain water.

69. McNitt, ed., *Navaho Expedition,* p. 133. I have taken this from a photograph. Kern also carved their names on the south side of El Morro. The National Monument was created in 1906.

70. Ibid., p. 132.

71. Ibid., p. 140. T. M. Pearce, *New Mexico Place Names* (Albuquerque: University of New Mexico Press, 1965), p. 105.

72. The original sketch, dated Sept. 20, 1849, is in the Bushnell Collection. Seth Eastman used it as the basis of a lithograph that appeared in Schoolcraft, *Indian Tribes,* 4:72. The lithograph appears below, in chapter 6, fig. 113.

73. Simpson returned to Santa Fe on Sept. 26 and received orders on Sept. 29 to make a brief reconnaissance of the Mt. Taylor area to look for a site for a military post. By October 10, he was back in Santa Fe, writing a report. McNitt, ed., *Navaho Expedition,* pp. 158, 166, 244–45. Edward or Richard Kern may have accompanied Simpson, but Hine, *Edward Kern,* p. 83, was in error in placing this reconnaissance in early 1850.

74. A few of the original field sketches survive in a scrapbook in PC. These are unsigned but probably by Richard, and include all of the drawings mentioned in this paragraph, as well as other sketches such as *Spring at the Written Rock, Pueblo of Moro, Sept. 17.*

75. To John J. Abert, Chief, Corps of Topographical Engineers, Santa Fe, April 11, 1850, in Simpson, *Journal,* pp. 56–57, and Simpson to Abert, Santa Fe, Jan. 3, 1850, and Feb. 7, 1850, in LR, TB, NARS, M 506, r. 62, frs. 478, 501–2. See also Hine, *Edward Kern,* p. 83.

76. McNitt, ed., *Navaho Expedition,* pp. 174, 218. B. D. Silliman to J. J. Abert, New York, Aug. 4, 1851, and E. G. Squier to Abert, New York, Aug. 3, 1851, in LR, TB, NARS, M 506, r. 63, frs. 306, 308.

77. McNitt, ed., *Navaho Expedition,* p. 239 n. 67, says: "With the exception of a few passages borrowed from Richard's diary, the authorship of the journal is entirely his, but Simpson drew stimulus from the Kerns—evident here but lacking in his other two reports." The attribution of the artist on these lithographs is not always correct. The *Green Corn Dance,* as we have seen, was attributed to Richard in the lithograph but was attributed to Edward on the original. These figures, however, suggest the relative weight of the work by the two brothers.

78. Taft, *Artists and Illustrators of the Old West,* p. 258 n. 17, pp. 282–83 n. 32. Taft incorrectly puts the number of plates at seventy-four. There are seventy-five numbered plates, but three (2, 21, and 39) are missing from each edition. Taft is also incorrect in suggesting that some of the lithography was done by Ackerman of New York. All of the lithographs bear the imprint of P. S. Duval of Philadelphia.

79. For Duval, see Peter C. Marzio, *The Democratic Art: Chromolithography, 1840–1900. Pictures for a 19th-Century America* (Boston: David R. Godine, 1979), pp. 23–27; Harry T. Peters, *America on Stone* (New York: Doubleday, 1931), pp. 163–68; and Nicholas B. Wainwright, *Philadelphia in the Romantic Age of Lithography* (Philadelphia: Historical Society of Pennsylvania, 1958), pp. 30–45, 61–74.

80. James H. Simpson, *Journal of a Military Reconnaissance, from Santa Fé, New Mexico, to the Navajo Country . . .* (Philadelphia: Lippincott, Grambo and Co., 1852). The same plates were used for each edition, except that foldouts of inscription rock were printed on individual pages in the 1852 edition, and there is considerable color variation between the two editions (compare, for example, plates 8 and 64). Plates 2, 21, and 39 are missing from the 1852 edition, as they are from the 1850 edition.

81. Letter to Dr. Morton, Santa Fe, July 3, 1850. See also Goetzmann's overall assessment of the Simpson expedition in *Army Exploration,* pp. 243–44.

82. Goetzmann, *Army Exploration,* p. 403.

CHAPTER 4
POCKETED IN NEW MEXICO

1. See Van Deren Coke, *Taos and Santa Fe: The Artist's Environment, 1882–1942* (Albuquerque: University of New Mexico Press, 1963); Edna Robertson and Sarah Nestor, *Artists of the Canyons and Caminos: Santa Fe, the Early Years* ([Salt Lake City]: Peregrine Smith, 1976); and Kay Allen Reeve, *Santa Fe and Taos, 1898–1942: An American Cultural Center* (El Paso: Texas Western Press, 1982).

2. Robert V. Hine, *In the Shadow of Frémont: Edward Kern and the Art of American Exploration, 1845–1860* (1st ed., 1962; Norman: University of Oklahoma Press, 1982), pp. 84–86, speculates that Edward suffered from epilepsy. A few of his drawings from this period have survived in a sketchbook; see below, n. 8.

3. Lewis A. Edwards to Thomas A. Hereford, M.D., Santa Fe, Dec. 28, 1849, Benjamin D. Wilson Collection, HEH (Benjamin Wilson married Hereford's widow. Since the Lewis letter was found in Wilson's papers, it seems certain that Kern delivered it to Hereford). Simpson to Kern, St. Paul, Minn., Dec. 1, 1851, HM 20644, suggests that Kern and Lewis had been friends in Santa Fe. Firm evidence that Edward was not along is in [Richard Kern] to "My Dear Friend," Zuni, Sept. 20, 1851, PC.

4. This quote and all details concerning this trip to Chihuahua come from Kern's Sketchbook E, PC, which contains about sixty sketches made on the trip, and a diary of portions of the journey. Unless otherwise cited, all quotations from Kern come from this diary. I have added punctuation to some of the quotes. Because particulars of the route have changed, distances cannot be stated with precision. I have made estimates based on the table in Max L. Moorhead, *New Mexico's Royal Road: Trade and Travel on the Chihuahua Trail* (Norman: University of Oklahoma Press, 1958), pp. 107–08. For a good account of the route as Kern must have seen it, see ibid., chapter 5. For the difference between Rio Arriba and Rio Abajo, see Weber, *The Mexican Frontier, 1821–1846:*

The American Southwest under Mexico (Albuquerque: University of New Mexico Press, 1982), pp. 280–82.

5. Two of Kern's sketches of Pareda, dated January 2, are in Sketchbook E, PC. A third sketch, upon which the watercolor is based, is in Sketchbook H, PC. This latter drawing is labeled "Painted for G." Sketchbook H also contains drawings of Acapulco and of the Smithsonian Institution, which Kern used as the basis of the watercolors in the collection of the Amon Carter Museum. It is possible that the sketch of Pareda in Sketchbook H was made in the summer of 1850, on a subsequent trip. Pareda, often spelled "Parida," did not appear on Zebulon Pike's map, but by the 1840s it began to show up on maps. George Wilkins Kendall, *Narrative of an Expedition across the Great South-Western Prairies,* 2 vols. (London: David Bogue, 1845), 1:426. John Galvan, ed., *Western America in 1846–1847: The Original Travel Diary of Lieutenant J. W. Abert* (San Francisco: John Howell Books, 1966), pp. 70–71. See also the maps in each volume. A. Wislizenus, *Memoir of a Tour to Northern Mexico . . . 1846 and 1847* (1st ed., 1848; Albuquerque: Calvin Horn, 1969), p. 36, describes some of the vegetation at Pareda.

6. In this paragraph, I have taken the date of the founding of the Mission of Nuestra Señora de Guadalupe from W. H. Timmons, ed., *Four Centuries at the Pass* (El Paso: 4 Centuries 81 Foundation, 1980), p. 13, and the date of the founding of Carrizal presidio from Max L. Moorhead, *The Presidio* (Norman: University of Oklahoma Press, 1975), p. 70.

7. Josiah Gregg, *Commerce of the Prairies,* Max L. Moorhead, ed. (Norman: University of Oklahoma Press, 1954), pp. 299–301. George W. Kendall, *Narrative of an Expedition,* 2:71–79. Florence C. Lister and Robert H. Lister, *Chihuahua: Storehouse of Storms* (Albuquerque: University of New Mexico Press, 1966), 61, 69–71, 90, 173. Francisco R. Almada, *Resumen de historia del estado de Chihuahua* (México: n.p., 1955), p. 126. Almada, *Diccionario de historia, geografía y biografía chihuahuenses* (2nd ed.; Chihuahua: Universidad de Chihuahua, 1968), pp.

339, 378, 389–90. Hugh M. Hamill, Jr., *The Hidalgo Revolt: Prelude to Mexican Independence* (Gainesville: University of Florida Press, 1966), p. 216. Richard Hancock, *Chihuahua: A Guide to the Wonderful Country* (Norman: International Training Programs, University of Oklahoma, 1978), p. 57.

The uniqueness of Kern's view of the interior of the chapel is attested to by Francisco Almada, dean of historians of the state of Chihuahua. Alberto Chretin to Weber, Chihuahua, November 30, 1982. Two other watercolors of the exterior of a stone mission seem to be of the same chapel (Scrapbook, PC).

8. [R. Kern] to "My Dear Friend," Zuni, Sept. 20, 1851, PC. In this letter, Richard also indicates that he returned to Santa Fe on February 1. Hine, *Edward Kern,* p. 84, puts the beginning of Edward's employment in Abiquiú on July 1, 1850. Two new sources unavailable to Hine establish an earlier date. First, Richard's September 20, 1851 letter from Zuni, cited above; second, Sketchbook B, PC, kept by Edward at Abiquiú is dated February 1, 1850. "It would be grand," historian John L. Kessell has written, "to discover a Kern portfolio of Abiquiú scenes." Kessell, "Sources for the History of a New Mexico Community: Abiquiú," *New Mexico Historical Review* 54 (October 1979):271. If such a portfolio exists, it is not with any of Edward Kern's other papers and drawings in PC. Edward's one surviving Abiquiú sketchbook contains a formula for mixing colors, "Paul Weber's Landscape Palette," and a few sketches entitled, "Ye Happenings in Albiquiu [*sic*]."

9. John Kern to R. and E. Kern, Philadelphia, May 30, 1850, HM 20654. John Kern mentions his plan to send the "packages" with "Skinner," who was then in New York, and that Skinner and "Collins" were expected to visit him in Philadelphia on May 31. Skinner and Collins are almost certainly William C. Skinner and James L. Collins, merchants who headed east over the Santa Fe Trail that March and returned to New Mexico in September. Louise Barry, *The Beginning of the West: Annals of the Kansas Gateway to the American West, 1540–*

1854 (Topeka: Kansas State Historical Society, 1972), pp. 900, 904, 916, 956. Although John's letter is to both Dick and Ned, I am assuming that Dick drafted the request to John in his and Ned's names. Ned was in Abiquiú at the time. Since their days with the Franklin Institute, it was common for Dick to write on behalf of both.

10. Kern wrote several verses of this poem, but they are difficult to read. This and the poem that follows are written in Kern's Sketchbook D, PC, which contains twenty drawings from the summer of 1850.

11. Howard Roberts Lamar, *The Far Southwest, 1846–1912: A Territorial History* (New Haven: Yale University Press, 1966), pp. 95–96. George Archibald McCall, *New Mexico in 1850: A Military View*, Robert W. Frazer, ed. (Norman: University of Oklahoma Press, 1968), p. 34.

12. Robert W. Larson, *New Mexico's Quest for Statehood, 1846–1912* (Albuquerque: University of New Mexico Press, 1968), p. 20. Lamar, *Far Southwest*, pp. 72–82.

13. Kern to Samuel George Morton, Santa Fe, July 3, 1850, Newberry Library, Chicago, Ill.

14. That a Kern-Houghton friendship existed is apparent from the tone of frequent references to Houghton in correspondence between Kern and Simpson. See, for example, Simpson to Kern, Buffalo, November 13, 1850, FS 132, and Simpson to Kern, St. Paul, December 1, 1851, HM 20644. The quote is from the latter. Ralph Emerson Twitchell, *Leading Facts of New Mexico History*, 2 vols. (Cedar Rapids, Iowa: Torch Press, 1912), 2:165–75, 271–72, recounts the duel and provides a brief biography.

15. The list derives from various pieces of correspondence, especially that between the Kerns and Horace Dickinson and James H. Simpson, cited in this chapter and in chapter 5.

16. Quotes are respectively from Dickinson to R. Kern, Santa Fe, Nov. 30 and Oct. 31, 1851, FS 143 and 142. Dickinson names many newly initiated members of the Odd Fellows

Lodge in his November 30 letter. Kern associated with a number of these Odd Fellows, but may not have joined the group because he was preparing to leave New Mexico about the time the lodge was founded. According to David F. Ferguson, Secretary of Santa Fe Lodge no. 2, I.O.O.F., Montezuma Lodge no. 1 was founded in Santa Fe on August 4, 1851, by six people and soon initiated fifty-seven members, but the name of Richard Kern was not among them. Ferguson to Weber, Santa Fe, August 31, 1982. Dickinson is identified in the federal census of 1850, Santa Fe County, sheet 341, Dec. 4, 1850, microfilm copy, Coronado Room, University of New Mexico Library, Albuquerque, New Mexico. On Dec. 7, 1854, Horace L. Dickinson was appointed auditor of public accounts, and served as territorial auditor through 1855. Miscellaneous Records, Appointments, New Mexico State Records Center, Santa Fe.

17. These nicknames appear in Dickinson to R. Kern, cited above, plus Dickinson to E. Kern, Santa Fe, September 10, 1851, FS 141. Some New Mexico Indians called the governor Tata. See Lamar, *Far Southwest*, p. 84.

18. Dickinson to R. Kern, Santa Fe, Oct. 31, 1851. See also Dickinson to E. Kern, Santa Fe, Jan. 27, 1851 [1852], FS 129, for his comments on the funeral of "Madame Toolis" and "putas" of Santa Fe.

19. Kern to Morton, July 3, 1850.

20. Dickinson to R. and E. Kern, Santa Fe, Nov. 30, 1851 and Jan. 21 [1852], respectively.

21. James Buchanan, quoted in McCall, *New Mexico in 1850*, p. 14, wherein editor Frazer discusses the early mapping of New Mexico.

22. Most of the information in this paragraph derives from the Kern map, cited in n. 23, below. The description of Bosque Grande comes from McCall, *New Mexico in 1850*, p. 95. T. M. Pearce, ed., *New Mexico Place Names: A Geographical Dictionary* (Albuquerque: University of New Mexico Press, 1965), p. 19, says that the Bosque Grande was "named by Spanish settlers about 1860." Clearly it was so named much earlier.

23. Carl I. Wheat, *Mapping the Transmississippi West, 1540–1861* 5 vols. in 6 (San Francisco: Institute of Historical Cartography, 1957–63), 3:18.

24. Simpson to J. J. Abert, Santa Fe, July 4, 1850, LR, TB, NARS, M 506, r. 62, frs. 855–57.

Simpson expected to send the Rio Pecos map to J. J. Abert on August 21, but Kern apparently did not complete it on time. A week or so later, Simpson left New Mexico, and Kern forwarded the map to him in Buffalo, New York, from which point Simpson sent it on to Abert in Washington. Simpson to Abert, Santa Fe, August 21, 1850 and Buffalo, October 21, 1850 in LR, TB, NARS, M 506, roll 62, frs. 927–29 and frs. 925, respectively. The map was not published. A manuscript version, apparently in Kern's hand, is in the NARS, Cartographic & Architectural Branch, Office of the Chief of Engineers, RG 77: US 148: "Map of a Military Reconnaissance of the Rio Pecos . . . Surveyed & Drawn by Richard H. Kern, Santa Fe, New Mexico 1850." A facsimile is in Frank McNitt, "Fort Sumner: A Study in Origins," *New Mexico Historical Review,* 45 (April 1970), between pp. 104 and 105.

25. In his letter to Samuel George Morton, Santa Fe, July 3, 1850, Kern says "I have been constantly employed finishing a map of a survey that I made of the Rio Pecos in last March." In his letter to "My Dear Friend," Zuni, Sept. 20, 1851, PC, Kern remembered that he "finished my map in May & just in time to join Lt. Simpson in making a survey of part of the Road to the States."

26. "The Indian Murder at the 'Wagon Mounds,'" by R. H. K., "a gentleman of this city," Philadelphia *Public Ledger,* July 2, 1850, excerpted from a letter dated June 2, 1850, Crossing of the Cimarron, 230 miles from Santa Fe. The tone of this letter suggests that Kern wrote it to a family member or friend, who then sent an excerpt to the press. Simpson to J. J. Abert, Las Vegas, March [May] 22, 1850, LR, TB, NARS, M 506, r. 62, frs. 793–95. Veronica E. Velarde Tiller, *The Jicarilla Apache Tribe: A History, 1846–1970* (Lincoln: University of Nebraska Press, 1983), pp. 34–36.

27. Simpson to Abert, Upper Cimmaron Creek, 276 miles from Santa Fe, June 2, 1850, and Simpson to Abert, Santa Fe, July 4, 1850, in LR, TB, NARS, M 506, r. 62, frs. 799 and 855–57, respectively. Frank McNitt, ed., *Navaho Expedition* (Norman: University of Oklahoma Press, 1964), pp. 228–30, discusses Simpson's survey but does not recognize the misdating of the letter of May 22, 1850. See, too, Leo E. Oliva, *Soldiers on the Santa Fe Trail* (Norman: University of Oklahoma Press, 1967), pp. 104–05, and Kern to Morton, July 3, 1850, for the date of Kern's return. *Ruins of Old Pecos, June 14, 1850* and *On the Ocaté, New Mexico, 1850* are in the Scrapbook, PC. Other Kern sketches from this trip are in Sketchbook D, PC, and include: *From Near the Lam{?} Mill looking West, May 17, 1850;* drawings of a mill and mill stone, dated May 18; *Rabbit Ear; On Rabbit Ear Creek N.M., June 6, '50, Arroyo de Don Carlos; From the Arroyo de Don Carlos;* and *Wagon Mounds from Rock Creek.*

28. For the departure of Simpson and Kern on July 6, see Simpson to Abert, Santa Fe, July 4 and July 6, 1850, in LR, TB, NARS, M 506, r. 62, frs. 855–57 and 874, and Kern to Morton, Santa Fe, July 3, 1850. I have not been able to locate an account of this trip, but Simpson sent tables of distances to Abert accompanying his letter from Santa Fe, August 21, 1850, in LR, TB, NARS, M 506, frs. 936–37. Modern highway maps put the distance from Santa Fe to Doña Ana at 281 miles. Moorhead, *New Mexico's Royal Road,* p. 108.

The possibility exists that Kern returned to Santa Fe by way of the Santa Rita copper mines, near present-day Silver City in southwestern New Mexico. A sketch by an "unknown artist," entitled *Copper Mines, New Mexico,* exists at the Peabody Museum, Harvard University, and has been attributed to either Richard or Edward Kern by Robert Hine, *Edward Kern,* plate 18. This sketch is clearly of Santa Rita, and resembles closely the illustration in John Russell Bartlett, *Personal Narrative of Explorations & Incidents*

. . . , 2 vols. (New York: D. Appleton and Co., 1854), 1:227, entitled *View of the Copper Mines from the South.* The resemblance is so close that I believe the sketch in the Peabody should be attributed to Bartlett or to one of the artists who accompanied him, rather than to either of the Kerns. If the sketch was done by one of the Kerns, however, Richard is the likely artist. Edward's documented travels never took him into southern New Mexico.

29. Richard's sketches from this trip are in sketchbooks C and D, PC, and number a dozen or so (some cannot be clearly identified). Included are drawings of Doña Ana, dated July 19, 1850, and of Albuquerque, dated July 30, 1850, which help to establish the time frame of the reconnaissance. For the church at Tomé, see John L. Kessell, *The Missions of New Mexico Since 1776* (Albuquerque: University of New Mexico Press, 1980), pp. 149–54, and Kessell to Weber, Albuquerque, Nov. 22, 1983. For Lieutenant Trevitt at Doña Ana, see McCall, *New Mexico in 1850,* p. 167.

30. Kern notes: "Commenced Sept. 10, 1850 with Lt. Parkes [*sic*]," in Sketchbook D, PC. McNitt, ed., *Navaho Expedition* pp. 229–32. Simpson to J. J. Abert, August 21, 1850, in LR, TB, NARS, M 506, roll 62, frs. 927–29, and copy of the surgeon's report, August 13, 1852, ibid., frs. 933–4. Simpson's tables of distances along both the mountain branch and the Cimarron route of the Santa Fe Trail accompany his letter to Abert, Buffalo, November 23, 1850, ibid., frs. 948–57. He claimed that his charts were more complete than any previous work of measuring distances between watering places.

31. Parke to J. J. Abert, Santa Fe, Sept. 12, 1850, LS, TB, NARS, M 506, r. 56, frs. 258–59, says "Ed. M. Kern" was recommended to him, but then goes on to describe Richard. In a letter of Oct. 4 to Abert, Parke corrects the error. Ibid., frs. 262–63. Kern was apparently rehired at $3. per day on July 15, 1851. "Report of the number of civilians employed under the Bureau . . . 30th September 1851," LS, TB, NARS, M 66, r. 14, frs. 165–68. See, too, Parke to Abert, Santa Fe, Aug.

22, 1850, LS, TB, NARS, M 506, r. 56, fr. 232, and Francis B. Heitman, *Historical Register . . . ,* 2 vols. (Washington: Government Printing Office, 1903), 1:768.

32. The map is discussed in Frank McNitt, *Navajo Wars: Military Campaigns, Slave Raids, and Reprisals* (Albuquerque: University of New Mexico Press, 1972), pp. 175–76, and in Wheat, *Mapping,* 3:18, 310, 818. On April 1, 1851, Monroe sent a traced copy of the manuscript map to Maj. Gen. R. Jones, Santa Fe, along with a lengthy explanation of various routes into the Navajo country in a report from Parke to Munroe, Santa Fe, March 7, 1851. NARS, RG 94, Records of the Adjutant General's Office, 1780–1917, Letters Recvd., M 161 (1851). "Mr. Richard H. Kern," Parke wrote, "from his experience and knowledge of the Country, acquired during Col. Washington's expedition, has rendered great assistance in collecting the above information."

33. Parke to Abert, Santa Fe, April 24, 1851, LR, TB, NARS, M 506, r. 56, frs. 445–46, announces the completion of the map. In December 1850, Parke and Kern had finished an earlier version of the map for Colonel Munroe and began making a duplicate for the Bureau. As Parke and Kern continued to gather more information, they modified their work substantially. See Parke to Abert, Santa Fe, Dec. 16, 1850; Jan. 30, 1851; Feb. 28, 1851, ibid., frs. 339, 365–66, 387–88, respectively. The map is described, assessed, and reproduced in Wheat, *Mapping,* 3:19–22, 311, but the reduced scale of the reproduction limits its usefulness. The map is also analyzed in McNitt, ed., *Navaho Expedition,* pp. 1, 270–73, and in William H. Goetzmann, *Army Exploration in the American West, 1803–1863* (New Haven: Yale University Press, 1959), pp. 248–49. The original map is in the Cartographic and Architectural Branch, NARS, RG 77: W 4, on two sheets. A reduced-scale lithograph is filed as RG 77: W 7. I am grateful to Robert E. Richardson of the Cartographic and Architectural Branch for providing me with copies.

34. Wheat, *Mapping,* 3:22.

35. Statement of Antoine Leroux, Wash-

ington, March 1, 1853, in Gwinn Harris Heap, *Central Route to the Pacific,* LeRoy R. Hafen and Ann W. Hafen, eds. (Glendale, Cal.: Arthur H. Clark Co., 1957), p. 30. Leroux identified this as Cochetopa Pass. See William Brandon, *The Men and the Mountain: Frémont's Fourth Expedition* (New York: William Morrow, 1955), p. 192, for another explanation. A "controversial letter," purportedly from Leroux to one of the Kerns, dated Don Fernandes de Taos, Aug. 22, 1850, is in FS 130, and reproduced with substantial editorial comment in LeRoy R. Hafen and Ann W. Hafen, eds., *Fremont's Fourth Expedition* (Glendale, Cal.: Arthur H. Clark Co., 1960), pp. 251–53.

36. [R. Kern] to "My Dear Friend," Zuni, Sept. 20, 1851, PC.

37. This dispute arose over the original version of the map when Parke left Santa Fe in November 1850 and put Kern in charge of completing the map. While Parke was away, Colonel Munroe "directed Mr. Kern to alter the title which I had determined on." Parke to Abert, Santa Fe, Dec. 16, 1850, and Parke to Col. W. G. Freeman, Socorro, Dec. 1, 1850, LR, TB, NARS, M 506, r. 56, frs. 339, 342–43.

38. The Senate resolution is missing from the records of the Topographical Bureau, but an index card remains indicating the date of the resolution. LR, TB, NARS, M 506, r. 63, fr. 575. Bid of Selmar Siebert, n. p., n. d., ibid., fr. 594, and J. J. Abert to John Pope, Washington Feb. 9, 1852; Abert to J & D. Major, April 2, May 14, and June 9, 1852; and Abert to Gen. R. Jones, June 9, 1852; and Abert to Dickens, Secretary of the Senate, June 12, 1852. LS, TB, NARS, M 66, roll 14, frs. 107, 143, 184, 200–204.

39. McNitt, ed., *Navaho Expedition,* p. li.

40. See for example, Anne Heloise Abel, ed., *The Official Correspondence of James S. Calhoun . . .* (Washington, D.C.: U.S. Government Printing Office, 1915), and James A. Bennett, *Forts and Forays: A Dragoon in New Mexico, 1850–1856,* ed. by Clinton E. Brooks and Frank D. Reeve (Albuquerque: University of New Mexico Press, 1948), who reproduced

the map in its entirety. Portions of the map also appear as endpapers in Brandon, *The Men and the Mountain,* and as an illustration in Janet Lecompte, *Pueblo, Hardscrabble, Greenhorn: The Upper Arkansas, 1832–1856* (Norman: University of Oklahoma Press, 1978), p. 9. In the summer of 1982, I purchased a facsimile of the original lithograph at the Kit Carson Museum in Taos, New Mexico. The facsimile does not bear the identity of its present-day maker.

41. Reports of persons employed at the Post of Santa Fe, by Captain L. C. Easton, September 1850–May 1851, Records of the Office of the Quartermaster General, Reports of Persons and Articles Hired, NARS, RG 92. This source was called to my attention by Hine, *Edward Kern,* p. 85. Kern notes in his Sketchbook D, PC, that he took this job on September 16.

42. J. H. Simpson to R. Kern, Buffalo, November 13, 1850, FS 132, HEH.

43. Ibid. Ned lived in Abiquiú from July 1850 to June 1851. The federal census of 1850, Santa Fe County, sheet 345, lists Richard H. Kern, "artist," as occupying a single household when he was counted on Dec. 16, 1850.

44. R. Kern to Bartlett, Santa Fe, March 14, 1851, Mexican Boundary Commission Papers of John Russell Bartlett, 1850–1853, vol. 3, p. 146, John Carter Brown Library, Providence, R.I.

45. Kern to Morton July 3, 1850. Other correspondence between Kern and Morton during Kern's stay in Santa Fe has apparently not survived, but the *Proceedings of the Academy of Natural Sciences of Philadelphia,* 4 (Philadelphia: Merrihew & Thompson, 1850), p. 245, indicate that at the November 6, 1849 meeting, "the Recording Secretary read a letter addressed to Dr. Morton, by Richard H. Kern, a member of this institution, dated Santa Fé, New Mexico, 1849, giving an interesting account of his recent Ethnological and Archaeological exploration in New Mexico." Kern to Morton, July 3, 1850, refers to a letter from Morton to Kern, Feb. 18, 1850.

46. July 4 addenda of Kern to Morton, July 3, 1850. *Proceedings of the Academy of Natural Sciences,* 6 (Philadelphia: Merrihew & Thomp-

son, 1854), p. vii, notes: "A collection of Coleoptera, Orthoptera, Myriapoda, Scorpions, & c., from New Mexico; and a cranium of coyote, from the same. Presented by Mr. Richard H. Kern." I suspect that this collection was assembled in New Mexico and shipped east over the Santa Fe Trail and that it stayed in storage until Kern's return. It may, however, have been assembled in 1851 on the Sitgreave's expedition through Arizona, which was then part of New Mexico.

47. Kern to Morton, July 3, 1850. Spruce M. Baird to R. H. Kern, Albuquerque, March 30, 1851, FS 133, mentions loaning Kern "the book you wish," and patronizingly gives Kern advice on how to examine properly the ruins at Chaco Canyon, should Kern return there. For Baird, see Marc Simmons, *Albuquerque: A Narrative History* (Albuquerque: University of New Mexico Press, 1982), pp. 145–46, 156–59. As he completed his report on the Navajo expedition in Santa Fe in 1849–50, Simpson had available to him all of the important books in English on New Mexico, including those by Emory, Gregg, Wislizenus, Hughes, and Abert. McNitt, ed., *Navaho Expedition,* pp. 55–56, 115, 117.

48. All quotes in this paragraph are from Kern to Morton, Santa Fe, July 3, 1850. For Abert, see Goetzmann, *Army Exploration,* pp. 9–10. Abert expressed considerable interest in birds, as well as in other fauna and flora. Posterity has judged the historical value of his report more kindly than did Kern.

49. Galvan, ed., *Western America,* p. 2.

50. Kern to Morton, July 3, 1850. For a brief discussion of the state of knowledge about New Mexico among contemporary Americans, see McCall, *New Mexico in 1850,* pp. 23–24. J. Manuel Espinosa, ed. and trans., *First Expedition of Vargas into New Mexico, 1692* (Albuquerque: University of New Mexico Press, 1940). Dickinson to E. Kern, Santa Fe, Sept. 10, 1851, and Dickinson to R. Kern, Santa Fe, Oct. 31, 1851, FS 141, 142.

51. Kessell, *Missions of New Mexico,* p. 44; L. Bradford Prince, *Spanish Churches of New Mexico* (1st ed., 1915; Glorieta, N.M.: Rio Grande Press, 1977), pp. 120–21. Santa Fe architect Vic Johnson, who worked on the restoration in 1976, notes that Kern's drawing contains previously unknown details, including the cupola and the adobe finials on the tower. Johnson to Weber, telephone conversation, January 16, 1984.

52. Richard Kern's sketch, dated January 1851, is in the Alexander Barclay Papers, Bancroft Library, Berkeley, California, and is reproduced in George P. Hammond, *Alexander Barclay: Mountain Man* (Denver: Fred A. Rosenstock, Old West Publishing Company, 1976), following p. 42. Kern probably did not travel to the site to do the drawing in January 1851, but rather made it from a field sketch done when he was at the fort in the spring of 1850. Edward Kern did a superior drawing of the fort in August 1851. See ibid. and Hine, *Edward Kern, pl. 38.*

53. The anonymous sketch of the Parroquia is reproduced in Paul Horgan, *Lamy of Santa Fe: His Life and Times* (New York: Farrar, Straus, and Giroux, 1975), p. 140, and the engraving, based on what is apparently a no longer extant sketch by Lt. J. W. Abert, appears in the *Report of Lieut. J. W. Abert of His Examination of New Mexico, in the Years 1846–47.* 30th Cong., 1st sess., Sen. Ex. Doc. no. 23 (Washington, D.C.: 1848), reprinted in facsimile as *Abert's New Mexico Report, 1846–47* (Albuquerque: Horn & Wallace, 1962), p. 55. The quote from Abert appears on p. 54. A splendid summary of the building's history is in Kessell, *Missions of New Mexico,* pp. 37–43. Kern's watercolor subtantiates Kessell's thesis that the crenelations were added after the Mexican War, and help to date the anonymous sketch of the Parroquia (which Horgan puts at ca. 1846–1850) to sometime after 1849. For more on Kern's use of crosses, see chapter 8.

54. Parke to Abert, Santa Fe, Oct. 4, 1850, LR, TB, M 506, r. 56, frs. 262–63. Parke does not identify the members of the party, but he had recently employed Kern, expressed respect for Kern's experience in the country, and

knew that Kern had drawn the "fish with legs" for Simpson's report. It seems very likely that he would have invited Kern along, and Kern seemed to relish this kind of excursion, as we have seen. Parke to Abert, Feb. 28, 1851, ibid., fr. 388, reports sending the specimens.

55. This may have been based on a pencil sketch made in April 1851. One pencil sketch, entitled *On the Rio de Santa Fe* and dated April 27, 1851, is in the Scrapbook, PC.

56. Kern had lost a sketchbook before he left New Mexico for the last time, in 1851. His friend Horace Dickinson found it and mailed it to him in Philadelphia (Dickinson to R. Kern, Santa Fe, Nov. 30, 1851). It may be one of the sketchbooks now in PC. Dick may have painted a portrait of Ned while in Santa Fe, for Dickinson wrote to Ned from Santa Fe on Sept. 10, 1851: "I washed your face and hung it up on my table in my room . . ." FS 141. In Washington, D.C., in July 1852, Kern was finishing work on "a big landscape. View from summit of Santa Fe Mt." that does not seem to exist today in any collection open to the public. [R. Kern] to E. Kern, Washington, D.C., July 22, [1852], James W. Eldridge Collection, Box 55, HEH. Kern sent some portraits of Indians to Samuel George Morton, to which he alludes in his letter to Morton of July 3, 1850. Some of those portraits may be copies of those published in Simpson's report.

57. Charles A. Hoppin to Bartlett, quoting Kern, Doña Ana, January 23, 1851, in the Mexican Boundary Commission Papers of John Russell Bartlett, 1850–1853, vol. 3, no. 38. Bartlett arrived in El Paso in November, 1850, and began work in December.

58. Richard Kern to Bartlett, Santa Fe, March 14, 1851, ibid., 3, no. 146.

59. F. A. Cunningham, Paymaster, to John R. Bartlett, Santa Fe, Feb. 16 and March 13, 1851, FS 140, 141.

60. Hine, *Edward Kern*, pp. 84–86.

61. Hine, *Edward Kern*, pp. 86–89. J. J. Abert to Pope, Washington, Sept. 26, 1851, replying to Pope's letter of August 2, 1851. LS, TB, NARS, M 66, r. 14, fr. 42. Ned said

he left Santa Fe on August 1, 1851, in a rough draft of a letter, recipient unknown, Philadelphia, 1851, FS 144. Evidence that Ned planned to return to New Mexico is in H. Dickinson to E. Kern, Santa Fe, Sept. 10, 1851, FS 141, and in R. to E. Kern, Laguna Pueblo, Aug. 24, 1851, FS 131. Simpson understood from Dick that Ned was "very anxious to be with me as draughtsman." Simpson to J. J. Abert, St. Paul, Minn., August 18, 1851, LR, TB, NARS, M 506, r. 63, frs. 312–13.

62. Simpson to R. Kern, St. Paul, May 11, 1852, HM 20643. Horace Dickinson, with whom Dick left them, mentions the paints, brushes, and canvas in a letter to Ned, Santa Fe, Sept. 10, 1851.

CHAPTER 5
WITH SITGREAVES TO THE PACIFIC

1. Horace Dickinson to Ned [Kern], Santa Fe, September 10, 1851, FS 141.

2. Francis B. Heitman, *Historical Register and Dictionary of the United States Army . . . ,* 2 vols. (Washington, D.C.: Government Printing Office, 1903), 1:890; William H. Goetzmann, *Army Exploration in the American West, 1803–1863* (New Haven: Yale University Press, 1959), p. 150; Sitgreaves's report to J. J. Abert of the "marking of the northern and western boundaries of the Creek country" in the summer of 1849, dated Washington, February 14, 1850, is in LS, TB, NARS, M 506, r. 62, frs. 447–54.

3. Abert to Sitgreaves, Washington, Nov. 18, 1850, LS, TB, NARS, M 66, r. 13, pp. 116–17; and Abert to Parke, Nov. 21, 1850, ibid., p. 118. I have reconstructed Sitgreaves's route west from covering letters to accounts that he sent to Abert: New Orleans, Feb. 24; Galveston, March 1; San Antonio, April 5 and May 5; El Paso, June 28; and Santa Fe, July 30, 1851. LR, TB, NARS, M 506, r. 63, frs. 102, 125, 164, 222, 310, 343. Parke's letters to Abert indicate that he was expecting the arrival of Sitgreaves in the spring of 1851, and

Kern apparently knew that he would accompany Sitgreaves even before Sitgreaves reached Santa Fe. In a letter of August 18, 1851, J. H. Simpson wrote to J. J. Abert from St. Paul, Minn. that "Richard, who goes out with Sitgreaves, writes me from Santa Fe, that Edward will leave for St. Louis 1st September." LR, TB, NARS, M 506, r. 63, frs. 312–13. For Simpson to have that news in mid-August, Richard must have written in June or early July. A copy of the diary of Lt. John Grubbe Parke, Aug. 13–Nov. 17, 1851, is at the library of the United States Military Academy, West Point, New York. Professor Andrew Wallace, of Northern Arizona University, plans to publish it.

4. See, for example, Francisco Garcés, *A Record of Travels in Arizona and California, 1775–1776* (San Francisco: John Howell Books, 1965).

5. Frank McNitt, ed., *Navaho Expedition: Journal of a Military Reconnaissance . . . in 1849 by Lieutenant James H. Simpson* (Norman: University of Oklahoma Press, 1964), pp. 160–62, 215 n. 45.

6. Cooke, quoted in Forbes Parkhill, "Antoine Leroux," in LeRoy R. Hafen, ed., *The Mountain Men and the Fur Trade of the Far West*, 10 vols. (Glendale, Cal.: Arthur H. Clark, 1965–1972), 4:177. Parkhill has also written a book-length chronicle of Leroux's life: *The Blazed Trail of Antoine Leroux* (Los Angeles: Westernlore Press, 1965). On their 1851 map, Parke and Kern credit Leroux with providing information for the proposed route from Zuni to the Colorado. For "Watkin," see below, n. 55.

7. Kern apparently talked to Leroux directly. On a small sheet glued into one of his sketchbooks, Kern has written, "Leroux says for a good road follow down the Zuñi to the little red some distance & cross over by San Francisco Mountain to Williams' Fork which gives a good wagon road . . . Grolman and Biggs says same." Sketchbook C, PC. In the late spring, 1851, perhaps after the Parke-Kern map was completed on April 24, Kern talked with Joe Walker about the route. See chapter 6, n. 59.

8. Lorenzo Sitgreaves, *Report of an Expedition down the Zuni and Colorado Rivers*, 32d Cong., 2d sess., Sen. Exec. doc. no. 59 (Washington, D.C.: Robert Armstrong, Public Printer, 1853), pp. 4, 5 (Sitgreaves's *Report* was reprinted in facsimile by Rio Grande Press, Chicago, 1962). Frank McNitt, *Navajo Wars: Military Campaigns and Slave Raids and Repraisals* (Albuquerque: University of New Mexico Press, 1972), pp. 189–94. Sitgreaves to J. J. Abert, Washington, December 20, 1850, LR, TB, NARS, M 506, r. 62, fr. 988.

9. R. Kern to E. Kern, Laguna, August 24, 1851, FS 121.

10. Ibid. For the 1851 map of the Navajo country, see chapter 4.

11. Ward Alan Minge, *Acoma: Pueblo in the Sky* (Albuquerque: University of New Mexico Press, 1976), p. 1.

12. Richard H. Kern, Diary, August 13–November 16, 1851, HM 4277, entry of August 25. Subsequent quotations from Richard Kern, unless otherwise noted, derive from this diary.

13. Henry Rowe Schoolcraft, *Historical and Statistical Information Respecting the History, Condition, and Prospects of the Indian Tribes of the United States . . .*, vols. (Philadelphia: Lippincott, Grambo & Co., 1851–57), 4:26. See p. 39 for identification of this sketch as Kern's. The original field sketch, *Acoma, Aug. 25*, is in the Scrapbook, PC.

14. *Abert's New Mexico Report, 1846–47* (1st ed. 1848; Albuquerque: Horn & Wallace, 1962) contains three views of Acoma, facing pp. 83, 87, and 89. These are reprinted in Minge, *Acoma*, following p. 52. A color reproduction of one of Abert's watercolors appears in the beautiful book *Western America in 1846–1847: The Original Travel Diary of Lieutenant J. W. Abert . . .* John Galvin, ed. (San Francisco: John Howell Books, 1966), following p. 46. Today the Bishop's Road is New Mexico highway 53. See Carol L. Riley and Joni L. Mason, "The Cíbola-Tiguex Route: Continuity and Change in the Southwest," *New Mexico Historical Review* 58 (Oct. 1983):351, 354, 365 n. 19.

15. McNitt, ed., *Navaho Expedition,* p. 133 n. 153.

16. Richard H. Dillon, ed., *Cannoneer in Navajo Country: Journal of Private Josiah M. Rice, 1851* (Denver: Old West Publishing Company, 1970), p. 65, makes light of this episode, indicating that wolves were the culprits. Kern seems to believe that it was Navajos. Since the animals were recovered, I am inclined to side with Private Rice's version.

17. McNitt, *Navajo Wars,* pp. 195–200.

18. By January 1851, Kern knew Kendrick well enough to mention him as one of the officers in New Mexico who would write a letter of recommendation for him: Charles A. Hoppin to J. R. Bartlett, Doña Ana, January 23, 1851, in the Mexican Boundary Commission Papers of John Russell Bartlett, 1850–53, vol. 3, no. 38, John Carter Brown Library, Providence, R.I. Kendrick's obituary, written by a West Point colleague, Samuel E. Tillman, contains a considerable amount of biographical detail: *Col. Henry L. Kendrick, U.S.A.* (New York: E. P. Dutton & Co., 1892), pp. 19–41. Kern mentions the original plan to leave Zuni on September 5 in R. to E. Kern, Laguna, August 24, 1851. McNitt, *Navajo Wars,* pp. 194–95. Dillon, ed., *Cannoneer,* p. 66.

19. Horace Dickinson to R. Kern, November 30, 1851, FS 143. Dickinson says "Jacob's store," which was probably the store of the German Jew Jacob Solomon Spiegelberg, who established a successful store in Santa Fe in 1848, acting as the post sutler for Fort Marcy. William J. Parish, "The German Jew and the Commercial Revolution in Territorial New Mexico, 1850–1900," *New Mexico Historical Review,* 35 (Jan. 1960):9–10.

20. R. Kern to E. Kern, Laguna, August 24, 1851, FS 131.

21. The nature of Kern's correspondence from Zuni can be inferred from letters of Horace Dickinson to R. Kern, Santa Fe, October 31, 1851 and November 30, 1851, FS 142 and 143; Dickinson to E. Kern, Santa Fe, January 27 [1852], FS 129. The latter contains a note from Greiner to Kern. That Kern wrote from Zuni

seems clear from Dickinson's letter of September 10, and from Greiner's reply to Kern. Dickinson apparently erred in his January 27 letter to E. Kern when he said that he had not heard from Dick since he left Laguna.

22. Kern termed this the Buffalo Dance. A specialist in Pueblo ceremonials, Luke Lyon of Los Alamos, New Mexico, identifies it as the seldom-performed Tablita Dance. Lyon says that Kern's is the earliest and perhaps only depiction of the Tablita Dance by an artist, and knows of only one photograph of the dance— no. 4902 in the collection of the Museum of New Mexico, Santa Fe. Lyon to Weber, November 7 and December 14, 1981. The engraver who did the illustrations for Samuel Woodworth Cozzens, *The Marvellous Country* (Boston: Shepard and Gill, 1873), made a poor copy of Kern's rendition of the Tablita Dance (p. 348), curiously mistitling it "The Green Corn Dance"—a title that he took from a dance scene that Edward Kern did at Jémez in 1849 (published in Simpson's report).

23. "Sketches of male and female dancers on facing pages of the artist's sketchbook" appear in the *Handbook of North American Indians,* William C. Sturtevant, ed., vol. 9, *Southwest,* Alfonso Ortiz, ed. (Washington, D.C.: Smithsonian Institution, 1979), p. 475. The sketchbook is in PC.

24. The quote is from Marc Simmons and Frank Turley, *Southwestern Colonial Ironwork: The Spanish Blacksmithing Tradition from Texas to California* (Santa Fe: Museum of New Mexico Press, 1980), p. 38. The authors reproduce the lithograph on p. 39 and also use it as the basis of the jacket. They hypothesize that the smiths were Mexican residents of the pueblo, not Zunis. Simmons had put forth the same argument in an earlier article, "Blacksmithing at Zuni Pueblo," *The Masterkey* 47 (Nov. 1973):155–57, where he also reproduced the Kern lithograph. Willard Walker, "Palowahtiwa and the Economic Redevelopment of Zuni Pueblo," *Ethnohistory* 21 (Winter 1974):68, offers evidence that the smiths were Zuni, and a contemporary Zuni specialist, E. Richard Hart,

Director of the Institute of the American West in Sun Valley, Idaho, agrees that they were Zuni, arguing that "the dress matches the descriptions I've been given by relatives of the blacksmiths at Zuni." Hart to Weber, January 27, 1983.

Two field sketches upon which the lithograph is based are discussed below in chapter 8.

25. Sketchbook A, PC, contains a number of sketches made at Zuni in 1851, including an exterior of the mission chapel, studies of the altar screen in the chapel, and Indian dancers in various poses. Sketchbook F, PC, contains a sketch of the interior of Zuni mission, looking toward the stairway.

26. The original wash drawings of the water jars are in the Bushnell Collection, Peabody Museum, Harvard University, and are reproduced in Schoolcraft, *Indian Tribes,* 4: following p. 434, pl. 38, figs. 2, 7. For the Eastman lithograph, see ibid., pp. 24–25, and Kern describes it in a letter to Schoolcraft, Washington, D.C., April 20, 1853, MS, Schoolcraft Papers, Library of Congress. The whereabouts of the original sketch is unknown. I am presuming that Kern made these undated drawings at Zuni in 1851, when he spent a substantial amount of time there. It is possible, however, that he made them when he passed through Zuni on September 15, 1849, although this seems unlikely since he was only there for an afternoon and evening.

27. McNitt, ed., *Navaho Expedition,* p. 114.

28. The chapel had no resident priest since 1821, according to Louis R. Caywood, *The Restored Mission of Nuestra Señora de Guadalupe de Zuni* (St. Michaels, Ariz.: St. Michael's Press, 1972), p. 11. Edward F. Beale, "Wagon Road from Fort Defiance to the Colorado River," 35th Cong., 1st sess., House Exec. doc. no. 124. Kern also copied the date of 1701 on his sketch of the altar screen, PC. The artist was Miguel Cabrera (1695–1768). Richard E. Ahlborn, Curator, National Museum of American History, Smithsonian Institution, to Weber, January 17, 1984.

29. The quote is from Ahlborn to Weber, January 17, 1984. John L. Kessell, *The Missions of New Mexico Since 1776* (Albuquerque: University of New Mexico Press, 1980), p. 214 n. 4, indicates that in 1789 the Zuni mission inventory listed a "new altar screen, or retablo, gilded and painted." The ornaments that Kern saw on the retablo are now in the Smithsonian (ibid., pp. 213–14 n. 3). The wooden statues of the two archangels are pictured and discussed in E. Boyd, *Popular Arts of Spanish New Mexico* (Santa Fe: Museum of New Mexico Press, 1974), pp. 59, 100–105, and in Richard E. Ahlborn and Harry R. Rubenstein, "Smithsonian Santos: Collecting and the Collection," in Marta Weigle, ed., *Hispanic Arts and Ethnohistory in the Southwest* (Santa Fe: Ancient City Press, 1983), pp. 244–45. Kern's sketchbook A and his Scrapbook, PC, contain studies of the archangels, the altar screen, and a small relief plaque of the sacred heart beneath a crown.

30. Kessell, *Missions of New Mexico,* p. 6. See also George Kubler, *Religious Architecture of New Mexico* (Colorado Springs: Taylor Museum, 1940), p. 67. The presence of the clerestory window at Zuni is confirmed in the *Missions of New Mexico, 1776: A Description by Fray Francisco Atanasio Domínguez,* Eleanor B. Adams and Fray Angélico Chávez, trans. and eds. (Albuquerque: University of New Mexico Press, 1954), pp. 197–98.

31. In a letter to "My Dear Friend," dated Zuni, Sept. 20, 1851, PC, Kern mentions that the escort had returned.

32. Woodhouse describes how he was bitten, the remedies employed, and his recuperation, in his "Medical Report," in Sitgreaves, *Report,* pp. 181–83. The incident occurred on September 17.

33. Woodhouse to Sitgreaves, Philadelphia, Jan. 25, 1853, in Sitgreaves, *Report,* p. 36.

34. Woodhouse was elected to membership in the Academy in November 1845, two years before Kern (*Proceedings,* 2:283). Evidence of the acquaintance of both Kerns with Woodhouse in Santa Fe appears in R. Kern to E. Kern, Laguna, Aug. 24, 1851, FS

131. Glimpses of Woodhouse's travels appear in his reports in Sitgreaves, *Report*, pp. 50, 94, 95, 100, and in Woodhouse's report to Sitgreaves, Philadelphia, Feb. 20, 1850, in LR, TB, NARS, M 506, roll 62, frs. 456–72.

35. Samuel W. Woodhouse, "Diary of an Expedition down the Zuni and Colorado rivers under Capt. L. Sitgreaves, 1851–52," 4 vols., MS, Philadelphia Academy of Natural Sciences. I am indebted to Professor Andrew Wallace of Northern Arizona University for furnishing me with notes from these diaries. As with Kern's diaries, I have corrected obvious errors in punctuation and capitalization.

36. Kern to "My Dear Friend," Zuni, Sept. 20, 1851.

37. Kern, Diary, Aug. 13–Nov. 16, 1851, HM 4277. Twenty of Kern's field sketches from the Sitgreaves expedition are in Sketchbook F, PC. These include some views, such as *Rough Bark Cedar, Camp 19*, that were redrawn as lithographs for the published report. It seems to me that Alpheus H. Favour exaggerated when he said that "the report of the expedition [by Sitgreaves] was practically copied from Kern's diary, to such an extent, in fact, that in places the report and the diary are identical; *Old Bill Williams: Mountain Man* (1st ed., 1936; Norman: University of Oklahoma, 1962), p. 209. The two sources complement one another.

38. *Leroux Island—Little Colorado* appears as plate 8 of Sitgreaves's *Report*. Professor Andrew Wallace, in a letter to Weber, Flagstaff, September 12, 1982, says: "From ground and aerial reconnaissance I am satisfied that there never was an actual island in the Colorado Chiquito as portrayed in Kern's Plate #8. There are several stony hills in the valley south of Sitgreaves' Camp 4, however, and if the surrounding low ground were marshy one might stretch his imagination to call them 'islands.' I have located one such that looks remarkably like the island of Plate #8."

39. Byrd H. Granger, *Will C. Barnes, Arizona Place Names, Revised and Enlarged* (Tucson: University of Arizona Press, 1960), pp. 236, 254. Professor Andrew Wallace identifies Cañon

Peak as Woodruffe Butte, renamed by Mormons who settled there in 1877.

40. R. Kern to E. Kern, Aug. 24, 1851, Camp at Laguna, FS 131. R. Kern to "My Dear Friend," Zuni, Sept. 20, 1851.

41. Map: "Reconnaissance of the Zuni, Little Colorado, and Colorado Rivers. Made in 1851 under the direction of Col. J. J. Abert, Chief of Corps Topographical Engineers by Bvt. Capt. L. Sitgreaves, T. E. Assisted by Lieut. J. G. Parke, T. E., and Mr. R. H. Kern. Drawn by R. H. Kern. 1852."

42. Kern's notes are preserved in three small volumes of "Field Notes," "Measurements of latitude and longitude," and "Barometric and Meteorological Observation," along with thirteen loose pages containing sketch maps of the route. Navy and Old Army Branch, Military Archives Division, NARS. Kern kept meteorological records in a book in which Simpson had begun to make entries in 1845, and that Simpson probably gave to Kern. Tables of geographical positions and meteorological observations, prepared from Kern's field notes, were published in Sitgreaves's *Report*, pp. 24–29. For Sitgreaves's view of the chronometers, see his *Report*, p. 11. The box chronometer he says, stopped on October 13, but Kern's field notes indicate that it started up again and stopped on subsequent occasions as well.

43. Four of these drawings have been preserved in the Bushnell Collection, Peabody Museum, Cambridge, Mass., and lithographs of Kern's drawings were published in Schoolcraft's compendium on the American Indian; see chapter 6.

44. *Proceedings*, VI, p. xxvii, July 13, 1852. For Woodhouse's description of this squirrel, which he named for Col. J. J. Abert, see ibid., pp. 110, 220. See also chapter 4, n. 41.

45. Woodhouse described five of the new species in the *Proceedings of the Academy of Natural Sciences of Philadelphia*, 6:110, 194, 200–203, as well as in Sitgreaves, *Report*. Edward Hallowell's report on "Reptiles," Sitgreaves, *Report*, pp. 107–29, is vague regarding the discoverer of new species of reptiles, but some

may have been found first by Woodhouse—see p. 125, for example.

46. Granger, *Barnes' Arizona Place Names,* p. 72. Kern describes the falls further in a letter to Schoolcraft, quoted in Schoolcraft, *Indian Tribes,* 4:38, n. 7. Kern puts the total height of the cascades at 120 feet and presumes that one of Coronado's lieutenants, García López de Cárdenas, visited the site in 1540 en route to the Grand Canyon. Kern's notes of his conversation with Walker are in Sketchbook C, PC.

47. H. M. Wormington, *Prehistoric Indians of the Southwest* (Denver: Denver Museum of Natural History, 1961), pp. 163–66; Albert H. Schroeder, *Of Men and Volcanoes: The Sinagua of Northern Arizona* (Globe, Ariz.: Southwest Parks and Monuments Association, 1977), pp. 49–56. Andrew Wallace to Weber, Flagstaff, Sept. 12, 1982, says: "I have confirmed that Kern's Plate #12 is a fair likeness of the principal pueblo of the monument now called Wupatki. I have a photograph made from the same vantage point as Kern used." Joseph Walker told Kern about the "ruined towns" that he had visited that spring. Kern Sketchbook C, PC.

48. Leroux Springs apparently received their name in 1853, when Leroux returned to this place with the Whipple survey party. Grant Foreman, ed., *A Pathfinder in the Southwest: The Itinerary of Lieutenant A. W. Whipple during His Exploration for a Railway Route from Fort Smith to Los Angeles in the Years 1853 & 1854* (Norman: University of Oklahoma Press, 1941), p. 167. Granger, *Barnes' Arizona Place Names,* p. 76.

49. Woodhouse's diary reports the time of the burial. Woodhouse reported Valdez's first name as "Enematio," and Kern said it was "Enisencio." Inocencio seems the closest approximation.

50. This lithograph is identified as "View of cañon near camp 39," in Sitgreaves's *Report,* but the order of its appearance (as plate 15), its subject matter, and the lighting that the lithographer sought to convey correlates closely with the information in Kern's diary entry of

October 21, at "camp 19." The typesetter apparently erred in identifying this as camp 39. Andrew Wallace identifies the scene as Sycamore Canyon.

51. The map accompanying the Sitgreaves *Report* was not the first to use the name of Old Bill Williams for this fork, as writers such as Favour, *Old Bill Williams* p. 209, have suggested. The Parke-Kern map, completed by March 1851, showed "Bill Williams' Fork." Leroux, who furnished Parke and Kern with information for the map, passed a name already in use among trappers on to the mapmakers. By placing the name on the map, Kern helped perpetuate the name of "Old Bill," but it does not seem accurate to say that Kern "named the stream," as Robert Hine suggests in *Edward Kern and American Expansion* (New Haven: Yale University Press, 1962), p. 92. Kern, however, may have bestowed the name of Old Bill Williams on the mountain that continues to bear his name, as Favour claims. I am indebted to Andrew Wallace, who has made a ground reconnaissance of this area using Kern's field notes, for identifying the Hell Canyon location.

The analysis in McNitt, ed., *Navaho Expedition,* p. 216, is not convincing. The problem was not so much that "the name on later maps was confused and finally lost," but that Kern was confused about the length of the river and distorted it greatly on both the Parke-Kern map of 1851 and on the map accompanying Sitgreaves's *Report.* For the confusion that this caused Whipple, see Foreman, ed., *Pathfinder,* p. 174.

52. Albert H. Schroeder, "A Study of Yavapai History," in *Yavapai Indians, American Indian Ethnohistory* series, *Indians of the Southwest,* David Agee Horr, ed. (New York: Garland Publishing, 1974), pp. 1–77, identifies these "Yampais" as Yavapai. I am more persuaded, however, by Robert C. Euler, "Havasupai Historical Data," in *Havasupai Indians,* in the above-cited series (New York: Garland Publishing, 1974), pp. 286–87, who argues that these "Yampai" were Havasupai. See also Henry F. Dobyns and Robert C. Euler, *The Havasupai*

People (Phoenix: Indian Tribal Series, 1971), and Stephen Hirst, *Life in a Narrow Place: The Havasupai of the Grand Canyon* (New York: David McKay, 1976).

53. Entry of October 28.

54. While some specialists (see, for example, Foreman, ed., *Pathfinder*, p. 171 n. 12), believe that the term Cosnino referred to the Havasupai, there is considerable disagreement on about which group or groups contemporaries were describing when they used the term. See Robert A. Manners, "Havasupai Indians: An Ethnohistorical Report," in *Havasupai Indians*, pp. 95–122. Henry F. Dobyns and Robert C. Euler, who have made the most careful study of this area, identify the people who shot Leroux as of the Cerbat or Walapai Mountain Band. *The Walapai People* (Phoenix: Indian Tribal Series, 1976), p. 31. See, too, Robert C. Euler, "Walapai Culture-History" (Ph.D. diss., University of New Mexico, 1958), p. 60.

55. The entry in Woodhouse's diary clearly reads "Watkin is shot," but Woodhouse is without a doubt referring to Antoine Leroux. "Watkin" was Woodhouse's phonetic spelling of Joaquín, another name by which Antoine was known. For the use of Joaquín, see LeRoy R. Hafen and Ann W. Hafen, eds., *Fremont's Fourth Expedition* (Glendale, Cal.: Arthur H. Clark, 1960), p. 252 n. 20; for another use of Watkin for Leroux, see J. W. Gunnison to J. J. Abert, Fort Massachusetts, Aug. 22, 1853, in "Report of the Secretary of War," 33rd Cong., 1st sess., Sen. Ex. doc. no. 29, p. 100.

56. Woodhouse's own account of this, in Sitgreaves, *Report*, p. 184, provides more detail and agrees with Kern's (except that Woodhouse specifies that the arrow entered the lower forearm, not the hand as Kern said. The quote from Woodhouse is from his diary, entry of November 3.

57. Sitgreaves, *Report*, p. 17.

58. Kenneth M. Stewart, "The Mohave Indians in Hispanic Times," *The Kiva* 32 (October 1966):29; Stewart, "A Brief History of the Mohave Indians Since 1850," *The Kiva* 34 (April 1969):219–20. For a discussion of bibliography on the Mohaves see Henry F. Dobyns and Robert C. Euler, *Indians of the Southwest: A Critical Bibliography* (Bloomington: Indiana University Press, 1980), pp. 73–75. A. L. Kroeber and C. B. Kroeber, *A Mohave War Reminiscence, 1854–1880, University of California Publications in Anthropology* no. 10, (Berkeley: University of California Press, 1973), pp. 4–5 raise questions regarding cultural change insofar as it affected warfare.

All quotations from Kern regarding the Mohaves come from his diary entry of November 7.

59. David H. Miller, "Balduin Möllhausen: A Prussian's Image of the American West" (Ph.D. diss., University of New Mexico, 1970), p. 248, credits Möllhausen with the first drawing of Mohaves, but Möllhausen did not see these Indians until 1854.

60. The recollection of Chooksa Homar, of a conversation among Mohaves in 1858, in Kroeber & Kroeber, *Mohave War Reminiscence*, p. 12.

61. Once again, I am indebted to Andrew Wallace for providing the location of these drawings. Wallace to Weber, March 25, 1983. The description in Kern's diary of Kern's view downriver from camp on November 11 may be of the scene that appears in fig. 99: "Ahead a small loma [hill] of conglomerate, and on the other side perhaps a wide [river] bottom. The mountain range on the west side is very high and rugged, while a new one begins on the east side. The river is narrow and turns to the west, enters a small cañon of perpendicular walls of conglomerate."

62. The quote from Kern is from his diary entry of November 10. Sitgreaves's quote appears in his *Report*, p. 20.

63. Kern's three books of field notes, as cited in n. 42, above, show that he continued to enter longitude and latitude until Nov. 25; meteorological data until Nov. 26; and daily readings of both chronometers until Nov. 30. A small field sketch, *On el Rio Colorado del Poniente, Nov. 16, 1851* is in the Scrapbook, PC.

64. S. W. Woodhouse, "Medical Report,"

in Sitgreaves, *Report,* p. 184, and the last page of vol. 4 of the Woodhouse Diary, which mentions Kern suffering from diarrhea on Nov. 25.

65. Sitgreaves, *Report,* p. 20.

66. Woodhouse diary, entries of Nov. 12 and Nov. 22.

67. The best account of events in this region just prior to the arrival of Sitgreaves is Jack D. Forbes, *Warriors of the Colorado: The Yumas of the Quechan Nation and Their Neighbors* (Norman: University of Oklahoma Press, 1965), pp. 297–329. Sitgreaves, *Report,* pp. 19–20, and San Diego *Herald,* December 18, 1851. The Woodhouse quote is from his diary, entry of Nov. 23. Woodhouse is the best source for the last weeks of the expedition.

68. Robert W. Frazer, "Camp Yuma—1852," *Southern California Quarterly* 52 (June 1970):170–71; Arthur Woodward, ed., *Journal of Lt. Thomas Sweeny, 1849–1853* (Los Angeles: Westernlore Press, 1956), pp. 54–55; and Clifford E. Trafzer, *Yuma: Frontier Crossing of the Far Southwest* (Wichita: Western Heritage Books, 1980), p. 54. For the subsequent history of Fort Yuma, see Ray Brandes, *Frontier Military Posts of Arizona* (Globe, Ariz.: Dale Stuart King, 1960), pp. 81–86.

69. See, for example, Woodward, ed., *Journal of Lt. Thomas Sweeny,* facing p. 48, who titles the lithograph: "Earliest View of Camp Yuma," and Trafzer, *Yuma,* p. 56, and Andrew Wallace, *The Image of Arizona: Pictures from the Past* (Albuquerque: University of New Mexico Press, 1971), p. 98. In letters to Weber of June 29, 1982, and July 5, 1982, Professor Trafzer, of Washington State University, and Harvey Johnson, of Yuma, both of whom know the area well, indicate that Kern's drawing of Pilot Knob is quite recognizable, although "the Knob looks much different today due to the blasting that took place . . . when the Southern Pacific used the rock from the mountain to fill a man-made cut in the Colorado" (Trafzer to Weber). For a good early view of Fort Yuma, see John Russell Bartlett, *Personal Narrative* . . . , 2 vols. (New York: D. Appleton, 1854), 1, frontispiece, which shows a very different place from that which Kern sketched.

70. Quoted in Robert Glass Cleland, "An Exile on the Colorado," *Westerners Brand Book, Los Angeles Corral,* no. 6 (Los Angeles: Los Angeles Westerners, 1956), p. 20.

71. George Harwood Phillips, *Chiefs and Challengers: Indian Resistance and Cooperation in Southern California* (Berkeley: University of California Press, 1975), p. 76.

72. Dr. Woodhouse outlines the route in Sitgreaves, *Report,* p. 40. For the surprising amount of traffic and litter along this relatively young trail, see Diana Elaine Lindsay, *Our Historic Desert: The Story of Anza-Borrego Desert* (San Diego: Copley Books, 1973), pp. 59–61.

73. Phillips, *Chiefs and Challengers,* pp. 77–86; Frazer, "Camp Yuma," p. 172; San Diego *Herald,* December 18, 1851. More details of the march can be found in letters from Thomas Sweeny to his wife, Ellen Swain, dated Dec. 25, 1851, and Jan. 16, 1852, and in a manuscript copy of Sweeny's journal that varies from the version edited by Arthur Woodward. The above are in the HEH. Woodhouse's unpublished diary provides the most detail, and the most dependable date of the party's arrival.

74. This, and all other quotes in this paragraph, derives from the entry of Dec. 18, 1851, in the Woodhouse diaries.

75. George McKinstry to Edward Kern, San Diego, December 23, 1851, FS 122. For Ned's relationship to McKinstry, see Hine, *Edward Kern,* p. 42.

76. Reference to the sketch of Kern's map is in Foreman, ed., *Pathfinder,* p. 113. Foreman maintained that Whipple had a copy of Sitgreaves's report (pp. 149–50 n. 2), but he appears to be in error. Similarly, David Conrad, "The Whipple Expedition in Arizona, 1853–1854," *Arizona and the West* 11 (Summer 1969):p. 154, states that Whipple "had read carefully the account of Captain Lorenzo Sitgreaves." If so, Whipple read it in manuscript form in Washington. Instead of having Sitgreaves's report to guide him, Whipple depended on Leroux, who was along again as a guide, and on the Kern map. First, there would have been no reason for the Topographical Bureau to send Whipple a tracing of Kern's map if it were

already available in printed form. Second, toward the end of the expedition, on March 9, 1854, Whipple says: "with regard to the navigation of the Colorado river, the report of Capt. Sitgreaves will probably be explicit," presumably because Whipple had not yet seen Sitgreaves's report (Foreman, ed., *Pathfinder,* p. 257). I am indebted to Andrew Wallace for help in clarifying this question. The artist on the Whipple expedition, Balduin Möllhausen, seems to have had access to a copy of the Sitgreaves *Report* (as well as to Simpson's report), but he probably obtained these after the expedition completed its work. Möllhausen makes no reference to Kern: *Diary of a Journey from the Mississippi to the Coasts of the Pacific with a United States Government Expedition,* Mrs. Percy Sinnett, trans., 2 vols. (London: Longman, Brown, Green . . . , 1858), 1:352; 2:24, 69, 71–73, 128, 131, 166–67, 176.

77. For the significance of the Sitgreaves expedition relative to other exploration of the era, see William H. Goetzmann, *Army Exploration in the American West, 1803–1863* (New Haven: Yale University Press, 1959), pp. 244–46, and Goetzmann, *Exploration and Empire: The Explorer and the Scientist in the Winning of the American West* (New York: Alfred A. Knopf, 1967), pp. 275–76, 327. A history of the 35th parallel route that emphasizes narrative over accuracy and analysis is Bertha S. Dodge, *The Road West: Saga of the 35th Parallel* (Albuquerque: University of New Mexico Press, 1980). Many writers have noted that the Santa Fe railroad followed the Sitgreaves route. See, for example, Carl I. Wheat, *Mapping the Transmississippi West,* vol. 3, *From the Mexican War to the Boundary Surveys, 1846–1854* (San Francisco: Institute of Historical Cartography 1959), p. 24.

78. For more precise locations and etymologies, see Granger, *Barnes' Arizona Place Names.* McNitt, ed., *Navaho Expedition,* p. 216, says that Kern named Kendrick and Sitgreaves peaks, but he appears to be in error. The names do not appear in Sitgreaves's *Report,* nor on Kern's map. It seems more likely that the names were first bestowed by the Whipple expedition in 1853. See Foreman, ed., *Pathfinder,* pp. 174,

175 n. 16. Möllhausen, *Diary,* 2:163, also credits the Whipple expedition with naming "Mount Sitgreaves," and both "Mt. Kendrick" and "Mt. Sitgreaves" make their first cartographic appearance on the geological map accompanying Whipple's "Report of Exploration for a Railway Route near the Thirty-fifth Parallel . . . ," in vol. 3 of *Reports of Explorations and Surveys to Ascertain the Most Practicable and Economical Route for a Railroad . . . 1853–54* (Washington, D.C.: Beverley Tucker, 1856).

79. "Reconnaissance of the Zuñi, Little Colorado and Colorado Rivers. Made in 1851 under the direction of Col. J. J. Abert, Chief of Corps Topographical Engineers, by Bvt. Capt. L. Sitgreaves, T.E. Assisted by Lieut. J. G. Parke, T.E. and Mr. M. H. Kern {*sic*}. Drawn by R. H. Kern, 1852." Carl Wheat, *Mapping the Transmississippi West,* 5 vols. in 6 (San Francisco: Institute of Historical Cartography, 1957–63) 3:24.

80. The plates are numbered 1–24, but plate 14 is missing in all printings. For James Ackerman, see Harry T. Peters, *America on Stone* (New York: Doubleday, 1931), p. 72, and Peter C. Marzio, *The Democratic Art: Chromolithography, 1840–1900. Pictures for a 19th-Century America* (Boston: David R. Godine and the Amon Carter Museum of Western Art, 1979), pp. 30–31. Ackerman also worked on the Schoolcraft report. Marzio discusses the difference between a tinted lithograph and a toned lithograph on p. 9.

81. "Mammals," by Woodhouse, in Sitgreaves, *Report,* p. 54.

82. Woodhouse to Sitgreaves, January 25, 1853, in Sitgreaves, *Report,* p. 40.

83. Sitgreaves, *Report,* p. 5.

CHAPTER 6
CHIEF OF ROADS

1. Samuel W. Woodhouse, "Diary of an Expedition down the Zuni and Colorado rivers under Capt. L. Sitgreaves, 1851–1852," 4 vols., MS, Philadelphia Academy of Natural Sciences, entry of December 23, 1851. I have

relied heavily on Woodhouse's diary for events in San Diego and San Francisco. The officer whose wife they called on was Capt. Delozier Davidson, who had headed the party of reinforcements sent to Fort Yuma.

2. Thomas Sweeny to his wife [Ellen Swain], San Diego, Dec. 25, 1851, and Jan. 16, 1852, Sweeny Papers, SW 850 (nos. 28, 29), HEH.

3. Woodhouse, "Diary," recounts the details of the trip to San Francisco on the *Northerner*. The San Diego *Herald*, January 5, 1852, mistakenly indicated that the party had left on the *Gold Hunter*. The evening edition of the San Francisco *Daily Alta California*, January 2, 1852, put the arrival of the *Northerner* at ten o'clock at night on Jan. 1. Dr. Woodhouse noted in his diary that they arrived at midnight.

4. Woodhouse, "Diary," entry of Jan. 4, 1852. These paragraphs are drawn almost entirely from Woodhouse's impressions of San Francisco, corroborated by Roger W. Lotchin, *San Francisco, 1846–1856: From Hamlet to City* (New York: Oxford University Press, 1974).

5. One apparent exception is a sketch of Indian petroglyphs "found on the trunk of a cottonwood tree in the valley of King's river, California," drawn by Richard Kern and printed in Henry Rowe Schoolcraft, *Indian Tribes of the United States*, 6 vols. (Philadelphia: Lippincott, Grambo & Co., 1851–1857), vol. 4, following p. 252, pl. 33, fig. A, and Kern to Schoolcraft, Washington, D.C., March 19, 1853, ibid., p. 253. This drawing, however, is Richard's good copy of a drawing made in 1846 by Edward Kern as he and some companions traveled north from what came to be called the Kern River, in search of Frémont. Ned's original wash drawing, unsigned but entitled *Indian Drawing on a Cottonwood at Camp, Jany 26, '46, on King's River—Cal.*, is in the scrapbook, PC. A pen-and-ink copy, signed by R. H. Kern, is in the Bushnell Collection, Peabody Museum, Harvard University.

6. Allan Nevins, *Frémont: Pathmarker of the West* (2nd edition, London: Longman's, 1955), pp. 369–401.

7. J. Kern to R. and E. Kern, Philadelphia,

May 30, 1850, HM 20654. John also accused Frémont of stealing letters and packages that he had sent to his brothers "Care of Col. Frémont." Adding to John's suspicions about Frémont was a letter John received from Christina King, Georgetown, May 14, 1850, PC. Christina King, the mother of Henry King, had been trying to obtain the journal of her dead son: "my husband has been several times with him [Frémont] but I am not satisfied with what he says."

8. Simpson to R. Kern, Fort Leavenworth, Oct. 9, 1850, HM 20646. Kern's reference to the "painful subject" is from his letter to Dr. Morton, quoted more fully in chapter 2, n. 92.

9. I am indebted to Mary Lee Spence, of the University of Illinois, who kindly furnished me with copies of letters from Frémont to George Wright and to David Hoffman, dated from San Francisco, Dec. 26, 1851, and Jan. 15, 1852, respectively. Frémont appears to have been in San Francisco during the time of Kern's stay there.

10. J. H. Simpson to R. Kern, Saint Paul, May 11, 1852, HM 20643.

11. George W. Childs to [E.] Kern, Philadelphia, Dec. 26, 1857, PC. A fragment of a letter from Edward, dated April 30, 1858, PC, and addressed to someone in Washington, seems to contain information for Frémont. Edward talks about the description of Sutter's farm that he had promised to send, of a sketch of *The Head of Kern's River* ("the Col. already has that"), and of another sketch, *The Point of Rock, Proulx' Creek*. See also Donald Jackson and Mary Lee Spence, eds., *The Expeditions of John Charles Frémont*, vol. 1: *Travels from 1838 to 1844* (Urbana: University of Illinois Press, 1970), pp. xxxiii–xxxiv.

12. Sutter's letter, written from Hock Farm, January 10, 1852, was in response to Dick's letter of Jan. 6, HM 20647. In 1855, after Dick's death, Ned was in San Francisco, where he received a warm invitation from Sutter to visit him in Sacramento: "When you are here we go and see my Portrait made by Mr. Jewitt, for which the Legislature paid the artist $2500—

you see that I am worth something. I have the honor to be in company with our great Washington & Henry Clay." Sutter to E. M. Kern, Sacramento City, Oct. 19, 1855, PC.

13. San Francisco *Daily Alta California* of Jan. 15 and Jan. 16, 1852, notes the departure of the *California* on Jan. 16; Woodhouse, "Diary," undated entry of ca. Jan. 16, 1852, mentions that Kern and Sitgreaves left on the *California* at 8:00 A.M. on Jan. 15.

14. Woodhouse, "Diary," entries of Jan. 7, Jan. 24, and Feb. 1, 1852. For background information, I have relied upon John Haskell Kemble's classic study, *The Panama Route, 1848–1869* (Berkeley: University of California Press, 1943). Oscar Lewis, *Sea Routes to the Gold Fields: The Migration by Water to California in 1849–1852* (1st ed., 1949; New York: Ballantine Books, 1971), provides vivid descriptions.

15. For a contemporary account of a visit to Acapulco see *Three Years in California: William Perkins' Journal of Life at Sonora, 1849–1852,* Dale L. Morgan and James R. Scobie, eds. (Berkeley: University of California Press, 1964), pp. 338–61. José Gorbea Trueba, *El fuerto de San Diego en Acapulco, Gro.* (Mexico: Instituto Nacional de Antropología e Historia, 1960). The pencil sketch from which Kern made his watercolor of the fort is in Sketchbook H, PC.

16. Charles William Churchill, *Fortunes Are for the Few: Letters of a Forty-niner,* Duane A. Smith and David J. Weber, eds. (San Diego: San Diego Historical Society, 1977), p. 32.

17. Bayard Taylor, *Eldorado or Adventures in the Path of Empire,* intro. by Robert Glass Cleland (New York: Alfred A. Knopf, 1949), p. 13. For a scholarly discussion of the isthmanian crossing, see Kemble, *Panama Route,* pp. 166–99.

18. My comments on the good weather derive from the *New York Daily Times,* Feb. 17, 1852, and the transformation of Chagres can be seen by comparing Churchill, *Fortunes Are for the Few,* p. 30, and a letter from "M.," Chagres, Feb. 20, 1852, to *The Panama Star,* Feb. 26, 1852.

19. The best summary of the history of Fort

San Lorenzo is probably Richard B. Chardkoff, "Fort San Lorenzo," *Americas* (Feb. 1970), pp. 2–8. Katie Wingenbach, "Architect leads Ft. San Lorenzo Restoration Effort," *Southern Command News,* U.S. Armed Forces (Jan. 14, 1983), p. 11, reports on current restoration efforts. I am grateful to Oakah L. Jones of Purdue University, a long-time resident of the Canal Zone, for his comments on the significance of this watercolor (Jones to Weber, Sept. 13, 1982), and to Nan S. Chong, Panama Collection Librarian, Panama Canal Commission, who provided me with current information and other historical sketches of the fort. Mrs. Chong knew of no other watercolor of the fort from that era (Chong to Weber, Feb. 8, 1983).

20. *New York Daily Times,* Feb. 17, 1852, announces the arrival of the vessel and contains a passenger list. A check of the Philadelphia *Public Ledger,* Feb. 17 through March 16, 1852; *Cummings' (Philadelphia) Evening Bulletin,* Feb. 17–28, 1852; and the *New York Daily Times,* Feb. 17–20, 1852, reveals no mention of Kern's or Sitgreaves' accomplishments. For Wilkes, see William Stanton, *The Great United States Exploring Expedition* (Berkeley: University of California Press, 1975), p. 282.

21. Simpson to R. Kern, St. Paul, May 11, 1852, HM 20643.

22. Simpson to R. H. Kern, St. Paul, Dec. 1, 1851, HM 20644. Simpson to Kern, Buffalo, Nov. 13, 1850, FS 132, in which Simpson gives advice to Sitgreaves. Simpson's career following the Navajo expedition is outlined in McNitt, ed., *Navaho Expedition,* pp. 227–41.

23. Simpson to J. J. Abert, St. Paul, Minn., LR, TB, NARS, M 506, r. 63, frs. 312–13.

24. Simpson to R. H. Kern, St. Paul, Dec. 1, 1851. E. Kern to Simpson, Philadelphia, November 13, 1851, FS 145; Simpson to E. Kern, St. Paul, September 15, 1851, containing a fragment of a letter from [R. Kern] to Ned, [Washington, D.C.], July 22, [1852], in the James W. Eldridge Collection, Box 55, HEH. On both occasions when Simpson wrote to the Kerns, he did not have appropriations to hire a draftsman. For example, on Jan. 14,

1852, over a month after writing to ask Dick to come immediately, Simpson wrote to his boss, J. J. Abert: "I would also respectfully request if Mr. Edward M. Kern has not already left Philadelphia to join me (of which Mr. Richard H. Kern will inform you on his arrival from the Pacific), and [if] additional appropriations should be granted for the roads, that Mr. R. H. Kern on the completion of his duties with Sitgreaves be requested to join me instead of his brother." LR, TB, NARS, 506, r. 63, fr. 534.

25. I have not been able to locate R. Kern's reply to Simpson, but presume it to have been a letter of Feb. 27, 1852, to which Simpson alludes in Simpson to R. Kern, St. Paul, May 11, 1852, HM 20643.

26. J. H. Abert to Sitgreaves, Washington, March 10, 1852. LS, TB, NARS, M 66, r. 14, fr. 127. Evidence that Kern stayed at Willard's Hotel is cited below, n. 37. R. Kern to Spencer Baird, Washington, May 23 [1852], Spencer Baird, Assistant Secretary, Smithsonian Institution, Incoming Corres., vol. 6, p. 40, Smithsonian Institution Archives. Fragment of a letter, [R.] to E. Kern, [Washington, D.C., July 22, [1852]. Sitgreaves to Abert, Washington, Nov. 18, 1852, LR, TB, NARS, M 506, r. 63, fr. 1200. *Congressional Globe,* 32nd Cong., 2nd sess. (March 3, 1853), p. 1108. On June 15, 1853, Abert wrote to A. Dickins, Secretary of the Senate, from Washington, June 15, 1853, that the Topographical Bureau had not yet received copies of Sitgreaves' report (LS, TB, NARS, M 66, r. 16, p. 149). By that time Kern was in St. Louis, heading west with Gunnison. Unless a copy of the report overtook him, he probably did not live to see it.

27. Andrew F. Constentino, *The Paintings of Charles Bird King, 1785-1862* (Washington, D.C.: Smithsonian Institution Press, 1977), pp. 37-42, 57-60.

28. Paul H. Oehser, *Sons of Science: The Story of the Smithsonian Institution and Its Leaders* (New York: Henry Schuman, 1949), pp. 38-39. William R. Massa, Jr., Assistant Archivist, Smithsonian Institution Archives, to Weber,

Sept. 3, 1982, identifies a photograph, ca. 1850, that probably antedated the Kern watercolor and reports that: "James Goode, Curator of the Smithsonian Building, indicated that Kern's is the earliest painting that he ever heard of, although there are probably some earlier works done in other media." The pencil sketch from which Kern made his watercolor of the Smithsonian is in Sketchbook H, PC. For "Romantic," see chapter 8.

29. See James M. Goode, *Capital Losses: A Cultural History of Washington's Destroyed Buildings* (Washington: Smithsonian Institution Press, 1979), pp. 29-31, 408-09. The Alexandria Aqueduct, later known as Aqueduct Bridge, was built in 1833 and razed in 1933. It stood just to the west of the present Key Bridge. Kalorama, built in 1807 and razed in 1889, was at the present S and 23rd streets, N.W. There were two Christ Churches in Washington in 1853. Kern's watercolor seems to be of the Georgetown church, which was rebuilt in 1867. Elizabeth J. Miller and Elizabeth Shepard, both of the Columbia Historical Society, provided me with welcome help in making these identifications.

30. J. H. Simpson to R. Kern, St. Paul, May 11, 1852, HM 20643. Fragment of a letter, [R.] to E. Kern, [Washington, D.C.], July 22, [1852].

31. The inscription below the watercolor, in red ink and apparently in Kern's hand, reads: "Pike's Peak. 1848/'Mon Songe.'" The watercolor itself is signed "R. H. Kern, 1853." Patricia Trenton and Peter H. Hassrick, *The Rocky Mountains: A Vision for Artists in the Nineteenth Century* (Norman: University of Oklahoma Press, 1983), p. 54, are probably in error in stating that "we can assume that" Richard Kern did this watercolor on Nov. 20, 1848. As they point out, "the picture is not altogether true to nature," but that is probably because Kern did not draw this picture of Pikes Peak from near Pueblo, as they argue. The profile of the peak and the artist's proximity to it suggest that it was drawn from a place that came to be called Jimmy Camp, a popular oasis for trav-

elers about ten miles east of Colorado Springs (Janet Lecompte to Weber, June 12 and July 6, 1982). Following the Arkansas River west in 1848 and again in 1853, Dick never saw Pikes Peak from Jimmy Camp, so it seems likely that his watercolor was based on Frémont's similar drawing, or perhaps on a drawing by Ned that is now lost. Donald Jackson and Mary Lee Spence, eds. *The Expeditions of John Charles Frémont,* vol. 1: *Travels from 1838 to 1844* (Urbana: University of Illinois Press, 1970), pp. 441–42; 444.

32. R. to E. Kern, Washington, May 2, 1852, HM 20710. [Samuel J. Bayard], *A Sketch of the Life of Commodore Robert F. Stockton* (New York: Derby & Jackson, 1856), pp. 183–88.

33. Robert W. Larson, *New Mexico's Quest for Statehood, 1846–1912* (Albuquerque: University of New Mexico Press, 1968), pp. 66–67. [Horace Dickinson] to R. Kern, Santa Fe, Oct. 31, 1851, FS 142, refers to Skinner as "our friend."

34. Quoted in Larson, *New Mexico's Quest for Statehood,* p. 69.

35. That Houghton and Kern shared a room is implied in Simpson's remark to Kern, "How are you and Houghton living?" St. Paul, May 11, 1852. Evidence of Dick's association with Collins and Houghton while in Washington appears in [R.] to E. Kern, [Washington], July 22 [1852]. See also E. Kern to James Collins, April 21, 1852, cited in Larson, *New Mexico's Quest for Statehood,* p. 320 n. 29.

36. Simpson to Kern, St. Paul, May 11, 1852. For Weightman's motives in issuing this pamphlet, which he had translated into Spanish, see his letter to Miguel Pino and Hilario Gonzales, Washington, March 20, 1852, in Ralph Emerson Twitchell, *The History of the Military Occupation of the Territory of New Mexico from 1846 to 1851* (Denver: Smith-Brooks Co., 1909), pp. 386–91. For full citations to these pamphlets and the historical context, see Larson, *New Mexico's Quest for Statehood,* chapt. 5, and pp. 374, 377.

37. Wm. N. Jeffers to R. H. Kern, Navy Yard, Charleston [?], Mass. April 28, 1852,

addressed to Kern at "Willards Hotel, Washington." Dick forwarded this letter to Ned on May 1, penciling a message on the same sheets. HM 20710.

38. Robert V. Hine, *In the Shadow of Frémont: Edward Kern and the Art of American Exploration, 1845–1860* (1st ed., 1962; Norman: University of Oklahoma Press, 1982), pp. 95, 99–145.

39. R. to E. Kern, Washington, May 2, 1852. The English-born Richard M. Staigg (1817–1881) had migrated to America with his family in 1837 and made Boston his home. George C. Groce and David H. Wallace, *The New York Historical Society's Dictionary of Artists in America, 1564–1860* (New Haven: Yale University Press, 1957), p. 598.

40. R. Kern to E. G. Squier, Washington, Jan. 1, 1853, in response to a letter from Squier of Dec. 29, 1852, Library of Congress, Manuscript Division. Called to my attention by Hine, *Edward Kern,* p. 96. Squier had received a copy of the Simpson report upon its publication directly from J. J. Abert, and told Abert: "It is a most interesting and valuable paper, and of no little importance to me in the investigations with which I am occupied." New York, August 3, 1851, in LR, TB, NARS, M 506, r. 62, fr. 308. For Squier's trips to Nicaragua, see Daniel E. Alleger's introduction to Samuel A. Bard [Ephraim George Squier], *Waikna; Adventures on the Mosquito Shore. A Facsimile of the 1855 Edition* (Gainesville: University of Florida Press, 1965), pp. xiii–xiv.

41. E. Kern to Schoolcraft, Philadelphia, March 1853, in *Indian Tribes,* 5:649–50. For a brief description of Schoolcraft's achievements, see Henry Savage, Jr., *Discovering America, 1700–1875* (New York: Harper & Row, 1979), pp. 229–33.

42. E. G. Squier, "New Mexico and California. *The Ancient Monuments, and the Aboriginal, Semi-civilized Nations . . . with an Abstract of the Early Spanish Explorations and Conquests in those Regions . . .*"(pamphlet reprinted from *The American Review* for November 1848), p. 18. Albert Gallatin, "Ancient Semi-Civilization of

New Mexico Rio Gila, and Its Vicinity," *Transactions of the American Ethnological Society*, 2, no. V (1848), pp. liii–xcvii. Gallatin was eager for firsthand knowledge of the field. See his letter of October 1, 1847, to Emory, in W. H. Emory, *Notes of a Military Reconnoissance from Fort Leavenworth, in Missouri to San Diego, in California . . .* 30th Cong., 1st sess., Sen. Exec. Doc. 7 (Washington, D.C.: Wendell and Van Benthysen, 1848), pp. 127–30.

43. Until George Parker Winship translated it in "The Coronado Expedition, 1540–1542," *Fourteenth Annual Report of the Bureau of Ethnology, 1892–93* (Washington, D.C.: Government Printing Office, 1896), pp. 339–613, the only printed version of the Castañeda account was in Henri Ternaux-Compans, *Voyages, relations et mémoires originaux pour servir a l'histoire de la découverte de l'Amérique*, 20 vols. Paris: Arthus Bertrand, 1837–41) 9:1–246. This was the source used by Schoolcraft and must have been the source used by Kern. Among Kern's papers (FS 136) is a translation of the notes of Fray Pedro Font's account of his 1775 visit to Casa Grande on the Gila, which appears as Appendix VII, ibid., pp. 383–86. The translation is not written in Kern's hand.

44. The quote is from a rough draft of the essay, Kern to Schoolcraft, Washington, May 10, 1853, FS 135. Kern wrote another draft, dated May 12, 1853 (FS 136), but the May 10 draft is the more polished version. Neither manuscript is complete. The only finished copy probably went to Schoolcraft, who published it in the fourth volume of *Indian Tribes* (1854), pp. 32–39.

45. J. H. Simpson, "Coronado's March in Search of the 'Seven Cities of Cíbola,' and Discussion of Their Probable Locations," *Annual Report of the Smithsonian Institution, 1869* (Washington, D.C.: 1871), reprinted as a separate pamphlet (Washington, D.C.: 1884). Simpson refers to the Chaco theory of Lewis Morgan on p. 22, and Schoolcraft, *Indian Tribes*, 4:87, refers to Gallatin's argument that Cíbola was one of the Hopi villages. The discussion has come to center on which of several Zuni villages

was Cíbola. Kern's "Old Zuñi," the ruins known to Bandelier as Héshota Izina, are no longer a serious contender. The ruins of Hawikuh, located some fifteen miles southwest of Zuni, are the generally accepted site. For a summary of some of the literature after Kern's time, see Madeleine Turrell Rodack's introduction to *Adolph F. Bandelier's The Discovery of New Mexico by the Franciscan Monk Friar Marcos de Niza in 1539*, trans. and ed. by Rodack (Tucson: University of Arizona Press, 1981), pp. 34–36, 91. The debate on the location of Cíbola began earlier than Rodack presumes. For current thinking about Coronado's route and a listing of principal sources, see Carl Ortwin Sauer, *Sixteenth Century North America* (Berkeley: University of California Press, 1971), pp. 130–51. For the most recent examination of Coronado's route through Texas, see J. W. Williams, *Old Texas Trails*, Kenneth F. Neighbors, ed. (Burnet, Tex.: Eakin Press, 1979), pp. 44–76.

46. *Indian Tribes*, 4:26, 29, 40. Evidence that Kern sent the four sketches to Schoolcraft appears in vol. 4, p. 39. Two of Kern's original field sketches, from which he copied the drawings for Schoolcraft, are in the Scrapbook, PC: *Ruins of Old Pecos, June 14, 1850*, and *Acoma, Aug. 25* [1851].

47. For Eastman, see John F. McDermott, *Seth Eastman: Pictorial Historian of the Indian* (Norman: University of Oklahoma Press, 1961), pp. 21, 63, 80–84, and McDermott, ed. *Seth Eastman's Mississippi: A Lost Portfolio Recovered* (Urbana: University of Illinois Press, 1973); and *A Seth Eastman Sketchbook, 1848–1849*, intro. by Lois Brukhalter (Austin: University of Texas Press, 1961).

48. Kern to Schoolcraft, Washington, April 20, 1853, Library of Congress.

49. Kern's unfinished sketch, dated Sept. 20, 1849, is in the Bushnell Collection, Peabody Museum, Harvard University. (David Bushnell acquired this and other Kern drawings from Eastman's granddaughter, a Mrs. Forrest). The steel engraving of Eastman's redrawing of that scene is in Schoolcraft, *Indian Tribes*, 4, facing p. 72: "Drawn by Captn. S.

Eastman from a sketch by R. H. Kern."

50. Kern's original sketches are in the Bushnell Collection. A steel engraving of the Eastman drawing appears in Schoolcraft, *Indian Tribes*, 4, facing p. 86.

51. Schoolcraft, *Indian Tribes*, 4, facing p. 24.

52. The original wash drawings of the spoon and two of the water jars, one "intended to represent a mexican on horseback" and the other "the representation of a bear" (according to Kern to Schoolcraft, Washington, April 20, 1853), are in the Bushnell Collection. They appear in *Indian Tribes*, 4, facing p. 434, as nos. 2 and 7 on pl. 38. All eight pieces of pottery on pl. 38 are from Kern sketches, and appear there without attribution. The blanket designs, which also appear without attribution, face p. 436.

53. R. Kern to Schoolcraft, Washington, April 20, 1853.

54. *Indian Tribes*, 4:253, reproduces a letter from R. Kern to Schoolcraft, Washington, March 19, 1853, in which Kern explains the sources of the drawings that appear on plates 33, 34, and 35, following p. 252. The original sketches are in the Bushnell Collection.

55. George L. Albright, *Official Explorations for Pacific Railroads, 1853–1855* (Berkeley: University of California Press, 1921), pp. 10–32; William H. Goetzmann, *Exploration and Empire* (New York: Alfred A. Knopf, 1967), pp. 270–72; Goetzmann, *Army Exploration in the American West, 1803–1863* (New Haven: Yale University Press, 1959), pp. 262–64, 295–96.

56. E. to R. Kern, Sand Creek, 22 miles north of the Arkansas, Aug. 22, 1851, HEH, HM 4276. The full quote says, "(being a sort of Chief of Roads & Sakies) particularly the sakies)." Ned was apparently referring to Dick's interest in irrigation as well as roads. Sakie is a variant spelling of sakia, a waterwheel used in North Africa for drawing water for irrigation. *The Oxford English Dictionary*, 13 vols. (Oxford: Clarendon Press, 1933), 9:45.

57. Dick's calculations and manuscript maps are in FS 154, 155, 156, and 157. A manuscript version of his report is R. Kern to Gwin, Philadelphia, Jan. 10, 1853, FS 158. The published version appeared in the *Congressional Globe*, 32nd Cong., 2nd sess. (Jan. 17 and 18, 1853), pp. 320–21. Kern says that he wrote this in reply to Gwin's request of Jan. 4. On Jan. 3, however, Kern apparently wrote to E. Backus in Philadelphia for information on the road from Fort Defiance to the Hopi villages. Backus to Kern, Philadelphia, Jan. 5, 1853, FS 153.

58. Kern suggested to Simpson, in a letter of either Feb. 27 or April 24, 1852, that the Sitgreaves route was not suitable for a railroad. See Simpson to Kern, St. Paul, May 11, 1852, HM 20643.

59. Walker, whom historians have known as Joseph Reddeford Walker but whose name was actually Joseph Rutherford Walker, discovered the pass in 1834. Walker had used the pass in 1851, following the 35th parallel route from Los Angeles, months ahead of Sitgreaves. Walker was in Santa Fe by late spring of 1851. Bil Gilbert, *Westering Man: The Life of Joseph Walker, Master of the Frontier* (New York: Atheneum, 1983), pp. 7, 144, 236–40. Kern talked with Walker in Santa Fe and took notes on Walker's route, tipping them into his sketchbook with sealing wax and noting: "Got this from Old Joe in Santa Fe in 1851." Kern's notes from his conversation with Walker (heretofore unknown to historians) are of value as one of the only descriptions of Walker's journey (Sketchbook C, PC):

> Joe Walker's Route—crossed the Big Colorado at mouth of Virgin—Sandy comes in opposite—Big Cañon ends 3 miles above—followed up Sandy & struck out east—country level and good traveling—found wood, grass & water—crossed little Red at full struck little red two days below—followed up to fall—found plenty of ruined towns—from little red to Moqui about 40 miles—good road & water & grass—water in spring from Moqui villages inland crossing Navajo country to the Gallo [*sic*]—Moquis said Navajos were at war with Americans—turned down to Zuñi and then to Albuquerque—says Zuni Mt. is only difficult part of the road—the rest [word illeg.] with

wood, grass & water—road is the best between Ca. & N.M. he ever traveled—no obstacle at all to a railroad—Says Sandy or Williams Fork can be traveled with wagons and then up the Mohave.

In March 1853, Joseph Rutherford Walker issued his own public statement about the advantage of Walker's Pass, to the California state legistature. See Pat Adler and Walt Wheelock, *Walker's R.R. Routes—1853* (Glendale, Cal: La Siesta Press, 1965).

60. All of these letters, sent to Gwin from Washington, D.C., and dated respectively Jan. 24, Jan. 23, Jan. 22, and Jan. 24, 1853, appear in the *Congressional Globe,* 32nd Cong., 2nd sess. (Jan. 27, 1853), p. 422. In addition, Gwin read letters from E. Backus, Washington, Jan. 24, and John S. Jones, Washington, Jan. 23, who also praised Kern's report.

61. Issue of March 26, 1853, quoted in Hine, *Edward Kern,* p. 93. See also "Emigracion" in the *Gazette* of Feb. 19, 1853, p. 5, and the "Correspondence" column of the issue of May 20, 1853. The latter reference is through the courtesy of Orlando Romero, Museum of New Mexico.

62. Quoted in full in Albright, *Official Explorations for Pacific Railroad Routes,* p. 38. Robert R. Russel, *Improvement of Communication with the Pacific Coast as an Issue in American Politics, 1783–1864* (Cedar Rapids, Iowa: Torch Press, 1948), pp. 95–109, provides the most detailed discussion of the debate in the short session of the 32nd Congress.

CHAPTER 7
MARTYRS TO PHYSICAL SCIENCE

1. Amiel W. Whipple, quoted in William H. Goetzmann, *Army Exploration in the American West, 1803–1863* (New Haven: Yale University Press, 1959), p. 307.

2. Long to Davis, Washington, April 1, 1853, in Office of Explorations and Surveys,

Applications for Employment, 1853–1860, NARS, RG 48, Box 6, Binder 1. I am indebted to Frank Schubert, Historical Division of the Office of the Chief of Engineers, Department of the Army, and to Richard Beidleman of Colorado College, for facilitating my use of this archive. Professor Beidleman had been through these materials in search of information concerning Frederick Creutzfeldt, and he generously made transcripts of documents available to me, which I checked against the originals. For Long's activities at this time, see Richard G. Wood, *Stephen Harriman Long, 1784–1865* (Glendale, Cal.: Arthur H. Clark Co., 1966), pp. 234–35.

3. A notation of the receipt of letters by Benton and Borland, dated April 8 and 12, respectively, and both introducing Richard Kern, is recorded under the date of April 22 (nos. 72 and 73), Secretary of War, Register of Letters Received, NARS, M 22, r. 76. Benton's letter is not in the file of letters received by the War Department. Borland's letter is in the Office of Explorations and Surveys, Applications for Employment, 1853–1860, NARS, RG 48, Box 6, Binder 1. Here, too, I am grateful for Professor Beidleman's leads.

4. R. H. Kern to J. S. Phelps, Pittsburgh, May 29, 1853, Western Americana Collection, Yale University.

5. Ibid.

6. Ibid.

7. Ibid.

8. Benton's letter of March 4, 1851, is quoted in full in LeRoy R. Hafen and Ann W. Hafen, eds., *Central Route to the Pacific by Gwinn Harris Heap* (Glendale, Cal., Arthur H. Clark Co., 1957), pp. 24–56. For the correspondence between Benton and Davis, ibid., pp. 283–86.

9. The book, together with all illustrations, is reprinted in Hafen and Hafen, eds., *Central Route.*

10. Benton's speeches of May 6 and 7, 1853, quoted in Hafen and Hafen, eds., *Central Route,* p. 59. The introduction to this volume explains the background of the Beale expedition and contains Heap's account, from which I have

taken the dates the expedition departed (p. 80).

11. The two quotes derive from Benton's speeches, quoted ibid., pp. 62 and 63, respectively.

12. The quotes are both from Kern to Phelps, Pittsburgh, May 29, 1853. See also Goetzmann, *Army Exploration,* pp. 298, 302.

13. The story of Frémont's fifth expedition is told in Allan Nevins, *Frémont: Pathmarker of the West* (New York: Longmans, Green and Co., 1955), pp. 408–20, and in Ferol Egan, *Frémont: Explorer for a Restless Nation* (Garden City, New York: Doubleday & Co., 1977), pp. 491–504.

14. Thirty-five plates based on drawings by F. R. Grist and John Hudson appear in Howard Stansbury, *Exploration and Survey of the Great Salt Lake of Utah* (Philadelphia: Lippincott, Grambo & Co., 1852). Some of John Hudson's original drawings have been reproduced in Brigham D. Madsen, ed., *A Forty-Niner in Utah: With the Stansbury Exploration of Great Salt Lake; Letters and Journal of John Hudson, 1848–50* (Salt Lake: University of Utah Library, 1981).

15. For background on Gunnison see Nolie Mumey, *John Williams Gunnison (1812–1853): The Last of the Western Explorers . . .* (Denver: Artcraft Press, 1955), pp. 7–30.

16. On May 2, Abert ordered Gunnison to "repair without delay to St. Louis Mo. & there await further orders," but the next day Abert changed his mind and sent Gunnison a telegram ordering him to Washington "to take charge of one of the parties on Survey of Pacific Road route." LS, TB, NARS, M 66, r. 16, pp. 28, 43. Gunnison received the telegram on May 6 and had arrived in Washington by May 20, if not before. Gunnison to Abert, Milwaukee, May 7, 1853, and Gunnison to Abert, May 20, 1853, in LR, TB, NARS, M 506, r. 24, frs. 290, 299. Gunnison may have arrived in Washington by May 10, for Davis was able to announce on that date that Gunnison was in charge of one of the surveys. Davis to Hon. S. Clemens, Washington, May 10, 1853, War Dept., Secretary's Office, LS, Military Affairs, NARS, M 6, r. 34, p. 265.

17. Davis to Gunnison, War Dept., May 20, 1853, in "Report of the Secretary of War," Washington, Dec. 1, 1853, 33rd Cong., 1st sess., Sen. Ex. Doc. no. 1 (Washington, D.C.: Robert Armstrong, Printer, 1853), pp. 57–58.

18. "Report of the Secretary of War," Dec. 1, 1853, p. 20.

19. E. G. Beckwith, "Report of Explorations for a Route for the Pacific Railroad, by Capt. J. W. Gunnison," in *Reports of Explorations and Surveys to Ascertain the Most Practicable and Economical Route for a Railroad from the Mississippi River to the Pacific Ocean . . . ,* 13 vols. (Washington, D.C.: Beverley Tucker, Printer, 1854–60), 2:12. These volumes are generally cited as the *Pacific Railroad Reports.* Creutzfeldt's German manuscript and a typed English translation, "Memorandum of Mr. Kreuzfeldt [sic]," June 18–Oct. 24, 1853, is in the Smithsonian Institution Archives, Record Unit 7157, and provides a valuable supplement to Beckwith's account. Called to my attention by Frank N. Schubert, *Vanguard of Expansion: Army Engineers in the Trans-Mississippi West, 1819–1879* (Washington, D.C.: Dept. of the Army, 1980).

20. War Dept., Secretary's Office, LS, Military Affairs, NARS, M 6, r. 34, p. 287. Reference courtesy of Richard Beidleman. In this letter, Davis confirms Kern's salary at $2,000 per year and mentions April 23 as the date of Kern's appointment.

21. St. Louis *Democrat,* May 12, 1853. Reprinted in the Santa Fe Weekly *Gazette,* July 9, 1853; the latter reference courtesy of Marc Simmons. Kern to Schoolcraft, Washington, May 12, 1853, "I expect to leave in a few days to visit New Mexico." Quoted in Henry Rowe Schoolcraft, *Historical and Statistical Information Respecting the History, Condition, and Prospects of the Indian Tribes of the United States . . . ,* 6 vols. (Philadelphia: Lippincott, Grambo & Co., 1851–57), 4:39. Since New Mexico extended north to the 38th parallel in 1853 and included the San Luis Valley and part of the central route, Kern might have been telling Schoolcraft that he was leaving with Gunnison.

22. The first quote in this paragraph is from

Kern to Phelps, Pittsburgh, May 29, 1853. The second quote is from W. B. Wolfe to E. Kern, Philadelphia, Dec. 21, 1853, PC. Dick was apparently still in Washington as late as May 22, for he put that date on his watercolor of Christ's Church.

23. Gunnison to Kern, May 25, 1853, HM 21349. Kern to Schoolcraft, Akron, Ohio, May 31, 1853, HM 20655. The St. Louis *Missouri Republican,* June 6, 1853, noted the arrival of Gunnison, Kern, and J. A. "Favor" [Snyder], all of the Topographical Engineers, "yesterday"—a Sunday. The June 8 issue of the *Republican* indicated that the group had been in St. Louis since the previous Saturday—June 4. The June 6 reference is courtesy of Richard Beidleman.

24. [James H. Simpson], "The Late Captain John W. Gunnison and his Assistant, Richard H. Kern," Dec. 20, 1853, reprinted in the *National Intelligencer,* Jan. 24, 1854, from a Minnesota newspaper and signed "S."

25. St. Louis *Democrat,* May 19, 1853.

26. St. Louis *Missouri Republican,* June 7, 1853, reprinting an article from the *Springfield Advertiser* of June 1, 1853, reporting on a speech that Phelps had given on May 28. Kern to Phelps, Pittsburgh, May 29, 1853. For Phelps, see Robert Russel, *Improvement of Communication with the Pacific Coast as an Issue in American Politics, 1783–1864* (Cedar Rapids, Iowa: Torch Press, 1948), pp. 43, 112, 113. The pro-Benton St. Louis *Democrat* attacked Phelps with special vigor. The reference to "Judas" is from the issue of May 16, 1853.

27. The quote is from Beckwith, "Report," p. 11. Unless otherwise noted, my account of Gunnison's expedition is based on Beckwith's account. Gunnison to his wife and to his mother, June 9 and June 12, Gunnison Collection, HEH.

28. Jacob H. Schiel, *Journey through the Rocky Mountains and the Humboldt Mountains to the Pacific,* Thomas N. Bonner, ed. and trans. (Norman: University of Oklahoma Press, 1959), p. 6. Schiel's work appeared originally in German, in 1859. Although Bonner does not acknowledge them, two earlier translations exist:

Frederick W. Bachmann and William Swilling Wallace, trans. and eds., *The Land Between: Dr. James Schiel's Account of the Gunnison-Beckwith Expedition into the West, 1853–1854* (Los Angeles: Westernlore Press, 1957), and a translation by Maria Williams that appeared in Mumey, *Gunnison,* pp. 55–111, in 1955. Schiel may have joined the party in St. Louis, as implied in the St. Louis *Missouri Republican,* June 9, 1853.

29. Kern to Phillips, Aug. 12 and 21, 1853, reprinted in the St. Louis *Missouri Republican,* Jan. 23, 1854.

30. Beckwith, "Report," p. 28.

31. David Lavender, *Bent's Fort* (Garden City, New York: Doubleday, 1954), pp. 312–17. Some specialists have doubted that Bent committed this act, but the evidence seems conclusive. See Louisa Ward Arps, "From Trading Post to Melted Adobe, 1849–1920," *Colorado Magazine* 54 (Fall 1977):29–31, who surveyed the literature and concluded that "William Bent only partially destroyed his fort" (p. 31 n. 1). For Fort Atkinson, see Robert W. Frazer, *Forts of the West* . . . (Norman: University of Oklahoma Press, 1965), p. 50.

32. Gunnison to J. Davis, Near Fort Massachusetts, Aug. 22, 1853, in "Report of the Secretary of War," Washington, Dec. 1, 1853, p. 99.

33. Beckwith, "Report," p. 34.

34. *Abert's Mexico Report, 1846–'47* (Albuquerque: Horn & Wallace, 1962), p. 24. Hafen and Hafen, eds., *Central Route,* p. 104. Lewis H. Garrard, *Wah-to-yah, and the Taos Trail* . . . (Cincinnati: H. W. Derby & Co., 1850), which contained no illustrations.

35. For the identity of Baca, see Janet Lecompte, *Pueblo, Hardscrabble, Greenhorn: The Upper Arkansas, 1832–1856* (Norman: University of Oklahoma Press, 1978), p. 230.

36. Kern to Phillips, Aug. 12 & 21, 1853, reprinted in the New York *Herald,* Jan. 11, 1854, and in the St. Louis *Missouri Republican,* Jan. 23, 1854. A covering letter, from W. B. Phillips, 35 Wall St., N.Y., Jan. 3, 1854, indicates that Kern's letter was a private com-

munication sent to him "to assist me in my investigation for the purpose of writing a treatise on the subject of a Pacific Railroad." Phillips's letter was reproduced more fully by the *Herald.*

37. Gunnison to Davis, Near Fort Massachusetts, Aug. 22, 1853. For a reference to the "Benton Central" see the St. Louis *Missouri Republican,* June 8 1853.

38. *Liberty Weekly Tribune,* Missouri, Feb. 3, 1854. For this reference I am indebted to James W. Goodrich, Associate Director of the State Historical Society of Missouri. The possibility that Kern's letter to Phillips was a forgery cannot be completely dismissed, for the original does not exist. If it is a forgery, it was elaborately done and has the ring of authenticity. For a meteorological explanation, I am indebted to my colleague Alan McDonald, Chair of the Department of Physics.

39. For Fort Massachusetts see Frazer, *Forts of the West,* p. 40, and Fraser, ed., *Mansfield on the Condition of Western Forts, 1853–54* (Norman: University of Oklahoma Press, 1963), pp. 17–19. Mansfield's ground plan of the fort appears as plate F.

Another contemporary drawing of Fort Massachusetts appeared in DeWitt C. Peters, *Pioneer Life and Frontier Adventures . . . Kit Carson and his Companions* (1st ed. under a different title, 1858; Boston: Estes and Lauriat, 1880), p. 485. Peters, an army surgeon, was in the San Luis Valley in 1855 (Harvey Lewis Carter, 'Dear Old Kit': *The Historical Christopher Carson* [Norman: University of Oklahoma Press, 1968], p. 15), and the illustration is probably based on an original sketch. LeRoy Hafen found the Peters's drawing superior to Kern's, which he termed "a side view, dim and unrevealing." See M. L. Crimmins, "Fort Massachusetts, First U.S. Military Post in Colorado," *Colorado Magazine* 14 (July 1937):132 n. 1.

40. Kern to Phillips, Aug. 12 and 21, 1853.

41. Beckwith, "Report," p. 39.

42. Forbes Parkhill, *The Blazed Trail of Antoine Leroux* (Los Angeles: Westernlore Press, 1965), pp. 167–92.

43. Creutzfeldt, "Memorandum," Aug. 24 and 25, 1853.

44. Gunnison to his wife, n.d. [Fort Massachusetts], quoted in Mumey, *Gunnison,* p. 45. Creutzfeldt, "Memorandum," Aug. 21, 1853.

45. Quoted in the St. Louis *Democrat,* May 20, 1853.

46. Beckwith, "Report," p. 44.

47. LeRoy R. Hafen and Ann W. Hafen, *Old Spanish Trail: Santa Fé to Los Angeles* (Glendale, Cal.: Arthur H. Clark Co., 1954), p. 303. Leland Hargrave Creer traced the general route of the expedition in "The Explorations of Gunnison and Beckwith in Colorado and Utah, 1853," *Colorado Magazine* 6 (January 1929):184–92. A more detailed tracing of Gunnison's route through Utah, based on on-site inspection, is C. Gregory Crampton, "Utah's Spanish Trail," *Utah Historical Quarterly* 47 (Fall 1979):371–78.

48. Mumey, *Gunnison,* p. 48 n. 103, credits Colorado Governor William Gilpin for renaming the river in 1861.

49. Gunnison to Abert, Grand River, Utah, Sept. 20, 1853, in "Report to the Secretary of War," Dec. 1, 1853, p. 101.

50. A reproduction of this unsigned sketch appears in Patricia Trenton and Peter H. Hassrick, *The Rocky Mountains: A Vision for Artists in the Nineteenth Century* (Norman: University of Oklahoma Press, 1983), plate 26 (see also pp. 74, 75). The sketch is in PC.

51. Gunnison to J. J. Abert, Bitter Creek, Utah, Sept. 23, 1853, in "Report to the Secretary of War," Dec. 1, 1853, pp. 101, 103, and foldout map. The map ends at Camp 72, on Bitter Creek, at the point where Gunnison drafted the above letter, so it appears to be the same map to which Gunnison refers. Letter from James H. Quinn to Col. Benton, Taos, Oct. 27, 1853, containing the "Proceedings of a Public Meeting at Taos," held on Oct. 22, 1853, with Antoine Leroux presiding. Printed in the *National Intelligencer* (Washington, D.C.), Dec. 5, 1853.

52. Beckwith, "Report," p. 62.

53. Quoted in Mumey, *Gunnison*, p. 52. Josiah F. Gibbs, "Gunnison Massacre—1853," *Utah Historical Quarterly* 1 (July 1928):67–75, contains Gibbs's summary of an interview with one of the Indians who attacked the Gunnison party and who explains their motives. The best account of events leading up to the massacre is David H. Miller, "The Impact of the Gunnison Massacre on Mormon-Federal Relations: Colonel Edward Jenner Steptoe's Command in Utah Territory, 1854–1855" (M.A. thesis, University of Utah, 1968), pp. 27–57, who explains why Gunnison might have felt secure from attack. The "war between the Mormons and the Indians," to which Gunnison alluded, is treated in Howard A. Christy, "The Walker War: Defense and Conciliation as Strategy," *Utah Historical Quarterly* 47 (Fall 1979):395–420.

54. Beckwith, "Report," pp. 73–74. A letter from two of Captain Morris's men, Alexander and Richard Moran, to their father, dated Utah Territory, Oct. 29, 1853, appeared in the *Detroit Advertiser* and provides further details, some contradicting other sources. Kern, the Mormans reported, received "one ball through his heart." Gunnison Collection, HEH. Sheppard Homans, letter of Oct. 28, 1853, *New York Daily Times,* Dec. 12, 1853, also reported that "Mr. Kern was shot directly through the heart." Article called to my attention by David Miller.

55. Mumey, *Gunnison,* devotes a chapter to the massacre and includes Morris' reports of Oct. 29 and Nov. 9 (pp. 115–16) and a first-hand account of the Mormon effort at burial (pp. 117–18). Evidence that Kern's body was stripped of its clothing is in the letter of James Snyder to his father, cited below, n. 57. The location of the massacre is in Gibbs, "Gunnison Massacre," p. 69. The number and occupants of the graves come from Brigham Young to George Kern, May 31, 1854, cited in Miller, "Impact of the Gunnison Massacre," p. 71. The Indian wearing Kern's cap was reported in the testimony of George Block, cited in Miller, p. 72. A letter from a merchant in Salt Lake City, dated Oct. 30, 1853, published in the St. Louis *Missouri Republican,* Dec. 6, 1853, said both of Kern's arms had been cut off, but the author had probably confused Kern with Creutzfeldt. Mumey, *Gunnison*, p. 128.

56. *New York Daily Times,* Dec. 12, 1853.

57. James A. Snyder to Capt. M. Snyder, published in the Washington, D.C., *National Intelligencer,* Dec. 10, 1853, in the St. Louis *Evening News,* Dec. 19, 1853, and reprinted in Mumey, *Gunnison,* pp. 130–31.

58. "The Late Captain John W. Gunnison and his Assistant, Richard H. Kern," reprinted in the *National Intelligencer,* Jan. 24, 1854, from a Minnesota newspaper, signed "S." and dated Dec. 20, 1853. The author is clearly James H. Simpson.

59. Kern's family and friends probably learned of his death on Dec. 2, when the *Philadelphia Evening Bulletin* carried stories of the tragedy from the *New York Herald* and the *New York Courier,* datelined Washington D.C., Dec. 1, 7 pm. The *North American and United States Gazette,* also published in Philadelphia, carried the same story on Dec. 3. George Kern to Jefferson Davis, Philadelphia, Dec. 19, 1853; George Kern to J. J. Abert, Philadelphia, March 30 and April 3, 1854; John Kern to Abert, Philadelphia, June 5, 1853; and John Kern to Abert, Philadelphia, Sept. 26, 1854, in LR, TB, NARS, M 506, r. 38, frs. 669, 680, 684, 699, 725. Among the replies to these letters are Abert to George Kern, March 31, 1854, and Abert to John Kern, June 7, 1854; on Sept. 28, 1854, Abert gave Lieutenant Beckwith's address to John Kern (LS, TB, NARS, M 66, r. 17, pp. 206, 381; r. 18, p. 121). R. to E. Kern, Philadelphia, Feb. 10, 1847, FS 117, mentions "George is in the custom house." He was still employed there in 1854.

60. J. H. Simpson to Brigham Young, Camp Floyd, Dec. 30, 1858; Young to Simpson, Feb. 7, 1859, containing a copy of a letter from Young to Beckwith and Morris, Salt Lake, Feb. 28, 1854. These items, respectively, are documents HM 20652, 20650, and 20653. In reply to a letter of Feb. 27, 1854, from George Kern, Brigham Young did not mention the

ring. George Kern had asked Young about his brother's body and personal effects. Young explained the circumstances of the burial and "presumed" that either Beckwith or Morris "took charge of the effects and papers of your brother in accordance with army regulations in such cases." Young to George Kern, Salt Lake, May 31, 1854, copy in Brigham Young Letterbook, Nov. 25, 1851–Feb. 21, 1855, p. 537, LDS Archives, copy courtesy of David H. Miller.

61. W. B. Wolfe to E. Kern, Philadelphia, Dec. 21, 1853, PC.

62. William H. Goetzmann, *Exploration and Empire* (New York: Alfred A. Knopf, 1967), p. 287.

63. Dec. 1, 1853, quoted in full in Mumey, *Gunnison,* p. 129, who quotes extensively from other newspapers on this question (pp. 123–38), and who devotes a chapter to some of the anti-Mormon literature (pp. 139–56). Miller, "Impact of the Gunnison Massacre," makes good use of Mormon sources to provide the best account of the aftermath in Utah.

64. Philadelphia *Public Ledger,* Dec. 3, 1853.

65. Schoolcraft, *Indian Tribes* 4:597.

65. See Beckwith to Abert, Camp near Fillmore, Oct. 29, 1853, in *Pacific Railroad Reports* 2:123–24, and the account of Anson Call in Mumey, *Gunnison,* p. 147.

67. Beckwith, "Report," p. 10.

68. Ibid., p. 88. Solomon Nunes Carvalho, *Incidents of Travel and Adventure in the Far West . . . ,* intro. by Bertram Korn (1st ed. 1857; Philadelphia: Jewish Publications Society, 1954), pp. 205–206. For a summary of Egloffstein's work, see Robert Taft, *Artists of the Old West, 1850–1900* (New York: Charles Scribner's Sons, 1953), pp. 263–64. David H. Miller has kindly given me Egloffstein's first name, citing the St. Louis census schedules of 1850.

69. Taft, *Artists,* pp. 12–13. A brief biographical sketch of Stanley appears in W. Vernon Kinietz, *John Mix Stanley and his Indian Paintings* (Ann Arbor: University of Michigan Press, 1942), pp. 3–10.

70. For the difference between a tinted lithograph and a chromolithograph, see Peter C.

Marzio, *The Democratic Art: Chromolithography, 1840–1900; Pictures for a 19th-Century America* (Boston: David R. Godine, 1979), p. 9. Taft, *Artists,* pp. 254, 261–62, notes that many variations occurred in the printing.

71. Taft, *Artists,* pp. 7–8, 256 n. 13.

72. A lithograph of one of Egloffstein's sketches from Frémont's fifth expedition also appeared in vol. 2 of the *Pacific Railroad Reports.* George Douglas Brewerton, who had crossed the Old Spanish Trail from California to Taos in 1848, might have given the public its first authentic view of this area, but he lost his sketches on the Grand (Gunnison) River. Drawings of the route, done by Brewerton, appeared as illustrations to his article, "A Ride with Kit Carson," published in *Harper's New Monthly Magazine,* in December 1853. Those drawings, as George Stewart has written, "are impressionistic, representing not what was actually to be seen along the trail in 1848, but a somewhat romanticized memory." George D. Brewerton, *A Ride with Kit Carson,* George Stewart, ed. (Palo Alto: Lewis Osborne, 1969), p. 107.

73. Trenton and Hassrick, *Rocky Mountains,* p. 90, assess Heap's work (the originals of which are lost), and conclude that "his sketches lack evidence of discipline and academic training" compared to the work of the Kern brothers.

74. One of the drawings that Egloffstein did while with Frémont appeared in vol. 2 of the *Pacific Railroad Reports.* After Egloffstein joined Beckwith, he did a number of sketches that were reproduced in vol. 11 of the *Reports.* See Taft, *Artists,* pp. 263–64. Carvalho published an account of the Frémont expedition in 1857, but apparently could not use his own illustrations because they belonged to Frémont. Only a few original paintings by Carvalho of Western scenes are known to have survived, and these were not done in the field (Carvalho, *Incidents of Travel,* pp. 39–40, 51, 204), but more, including remarkable portraits of Brigham Young and the Ute Chief "Warka," have been discovered in recent years and more may yet come to the surface. See Joan Sturhahn, *Carvalho: Art-*

ist, *Photographer, Adventurer, Patriot. Portrait of a Forgotten American* (New York: Richwood Pub. Co., 1976), pp. 102–03, 106, 114–23, 203. Trenton and Hassrick, *Rocky Mountains,* pp. 92–95, reproduce one of Carvalho's paintings in color, *Grand River,* and evaluate his work as revealing "the crudities associated with itinerant painters" (p. 95). Walt Wheelock, "Frémont's Lost Plates," *San Diego Corral of Westerners Brand Book II* (San Diego: San Diego Corral of Westerners, 1971), pp. 48–53, makes a convincing case that many of the plates in Frémont's *Memoirs* were drawn from Carvalho's sketches. Sturhahn, apparently unaware of Wheelock's work, draws the same conclusion, *Carvalho,* pp. 81–88.

CHAPTER 8
RICHARD KERN IN PERSPECTIVE

1. For Abert see chapter 1. For the other artists mentioned here, see Robert Taft, *Artists and Illustrators of the Old West: 1850–1900* (New York: Charles Scribner's Sons, 1953), pp. 1–35, 268–69, 276–78, and Robert V. Hine, *Bartlett's West: Drawing the Mexican Boundary* (New Haven: Yale University Press, 1968).

2. Rice's drawings have been reproduced in Richard H. Dillon, ed., *Cannoneer in Navajo Country: Journal of Private Josiah M. Rice, 1851* (Denver: Old West Publishing Co., 1970). Powell's drawings, which are mainly California scenes but which include views of Tumacácori and San Xavier del Bac, appear in Douglas S. Watson, ed. *The Santa Fe Trail to California, 1849–1852: The Journal and Drawings of H. M. T. Powell* (San Francisco: Book Club of California, 1931).

3. Brewerton's sketches were used to illustrate his own articles: "A Ride with Kit Carson," "Incidents of Travel in New Mexico," and "In the Buffalo Country," appearing in *Harper's* in the issues of December 1853, April 1854, and September 1862, respectively. A few of these woodcuts are attributed explicitly to

Brewerton; others, but not all, are presumed to be his. For Brewerton's training and later career as an artist, see Stallo Vinton, ed., *Overland with Kit Carson: A Narrative of the Old Spanish Trail in '48* (New York: Coward-McCann, 1938), pp. 23–26.

4. W. W. H. Davis, *El Gringo; or, New Mexico and Her People* (New York: Harper & Bros., 1857), frontispiece and pp. 50, 99, 140, 161, 235, 301, 344, 367, 377, 382, 398, 403. A new edition of this work (Santa Fe: Rydal Press, 1938), and a reprint edition (Chicago: Rio Grande Press, 1962), reproduce the illustrations following p. 255, but without the more detailed descriptions contained in the table of contents of the 1st edition. See, too, n. 48 below.

5. Robert Taft, *Photography and the American Scene: A Social History, 1839–1889* (1st ed., 1938; Macmillan Co., 1942), p. 263. Taft thought that the first use of a daguerreotype camera on a western expedition was in 1853 (pp. 261–62), but Frémont had taken a daguerreotype camera into the West in 1842. Donald Jackson and Mary Lee Spence, eds., *The Expeditions of John Charles Frémont,* vol. I, *Travels from 1838 to 1844* (Urbana: University of Illinois Press, 1970), p. xxxiii.

6. Quoted in Herman R. Friis, "The Documents and Reports of the United States Congress: A Primary Source of Information on Travel in the West, 1783–1861," in John Francis McDermott, ed., *Travelers on the Western Frontier* (Urbana: University of Illinois Press, 1970), p. 135.

7. Eugene Ostroff, *Western Views and Eastern Visions* (Washington, D.C.: Smithsonian Institution, 1981), pp. 13, 22. Weston Naef and James N. Wood, *Era of Exploration: The Rise of Landscape Photography in the American West, 1860–1885* ([Buffalo], New York: Albright-Knox Gallery and Metropolitan Museum of Art, 1975), p. 14.

8. Quoted in Martha A. Sandweiss, *Masterworks of American Photography* (Birmingham, Ala: Oxmoor House, 1982), p. 6. See, too, pp. 3–11, 14 for a discussion of the subjectivity of

photography. For a specific example, see Christopher M. Lyman, *The Vanishing Race and Other Illusions: Photographs of Edward S. Curtis* (Washington, D.C.: Smithsonian Institution Press, 1982).

9. John C. Ewers, *Artists of the Old West* (New York: Doubleday & Co., 1965), p. 117, makes this point about Catlin's and Bodmer's work.

10. Rex W. Strickland, *El Paso in 1854 with a 30-page Handwritten Newsletter by Frederick Augustus Percy entitled El Sabio Sembrador*, E. H. Antone and Carl Herzog, eds. and designers (El Paso: Texas Western Press, 1969), pp. 20, 23; compare these to James H. Simpson, *Journal of a Military Reconnaissance from Santa Fé, New Mexico, to the Navajo Country in 1849*, 31st Cong., 1st sess., Sen. Ex. Doc. 64 (Washington, D.C.: 1850), plates 12, 13.

11. G. Douglas Brewerton, "Incidents of Travel in New Mexico," *Harper's New Monthly Magazine* 7 (April 1854):591. Reprint editions of this article include: Vinton, ed., *Overland With Kit Carson*, p. 198, and *Incidents of Travel in New Mexico*, Ferol Egan, ed. (Ashland, Ore.: Lewis Osborn, 1969), p. 54. Egan, unaware that these sketches had appeared previously in Simpson's *Journal*, mistook the portrait of *Chapaton* for a Navajo girl (p. 74). For Theodore Rabuski, see George C. Groce and David H. Wallace, *The New York Historical Society's Dictionary of Artists in America, 1564-1860* (New Haven: Yale University Press, 1957), p. 522.

12. Abbé Em. Domenech, *Seven Years' Residence in the Great Deserts of North America*, 2 vols. (London: Longman, Green, 1860), 1, facing pp. 201, 208, 216, and 2, facing pp. 8, 52. Simpson, *Journal*, plates 4, 52. The Inscription Rock woodcut is adapted from Simpson, *Journal*, plate 60, with individual petroglyphs copied from various plates, such as 70 and 74. Lorenzo Sitgreaves, *Report of an Expedition down the Zuni and Colorado Rivers*, 32nd Cong., 2nd sess., Sen Exec. doc. no. 59 (Washington, D.C.: Robert Armstrong, 1853), plates 11, 15.

13. Samuel Woodworth Cozzens, *The Marvellous Country; or Three Years in Arizona and New Mexico, The Apaches' Home* (Boston: Shepard and Gill, 1873), pp. 268, 286, 307, 342, 343, 344, 437, 468, 504. Some of these drawings were taken from Schoolcraft, who also did not acknowledge Kern's authorship.

14. William Thayer, *Marvels of the New West . . .* (1st ed., 1887; Norwich, Conn.: Henry Bill Publ. Co., 1892), pp. 55, 145, 170, 174, 186. The *Pueblo of Laguna*, which appears on p. 174, derives from Seth Eastman's drawing of a Richard Kern sketch (figs 112 and 113).

15. "The First Americans," *Harper's*, 65 (Aug. 1882):342, 344.

16. (New York: Harper & Bros., 1886), pp. 51, 53, 215, 223.

17. For an example of a book that fails to credit its source, see Capt. J. G. Walker and Maj. O. L. Shepherd, *The Navajo Reconnaissance: A Military Exploration of the Navajo Country in 1859*, L. R. Bailey, ed. (Los Angeles: Westernlore Press, 1964), pp. 34, 76, 94.

18. (Albuquerque: University of New Mexico Press, 1968), pp. 7, 11, 13, 15, 19, 20, 23, 34, 40, 46, 54, 57, 59, 66, 67, 71, 160, 168. Gregg occasionally reproduces work that has been copied from Kern without attribution (such as the Pecos Indian from Domenech, p. 46), and he incorrectly attributes the view of Pecos on p. 24 to the Simpson report.

19. (Albuquerque: University of New Mexico Press, 1971), pp. 7, 18, 23, 33, 34, 56, 60, 64, 98—ten illustrations on these nine pages.

20. LeRoy R. Hafen and Ann W. Hafen, *Old Spanish Trail: Santa Fé to Los Angeles* (Glendale, Cal.: Arthur H. Clark Co., 1954), facing p. 310. Wallace, *The Great Reconnaissance: Soldiers, Artists and Scientists on the Frontier, 1848-1861* (Boston: Little, Brown & Co., 1955), contains three drawings by Richard Kern, all following p. 138. Goetzmann, *Army Exploration in the West, 1803-1863* (New Haven: Yale University Press, 1959), plates 3, 4; Goetzmann, *Exploration and Empire* (New York: Knopf,

1967), pp. 349, 50; Savage, *Discovering America, 1700–1875* (New York: Harper & Row, 1979), plate 34. Dodge, *The Road West: The Saga of the 35th Parallel* (Albuquerque: University of New Mexico Press, 1980), dust jacket and seven plates following p. 144; and Frank N. Schubert, *Vanguard of Expansion: Army Engineers in the Trans-Mississippi West, 1819–1879* (Washington, D.C.: Department of the Army, 1980), p. 79.

21. See, for example, *The Handbook of North American Indians,* William C. Sturtevant, ed., vol. 9, *Southwest,* Alfonso Ortiz, ed. (Washington, D.C.: Smithsonian Institution, 1979), pp. 213, 475, 619; J. Lee Correll, *Through White Men's Eyes: A Contribution to Navajo History. . . .* 6 vols. (Window Rock, Ariz.: Navajo Heritage Center, 1979), 1:239, 243, 245; David M. Brugge, *A History of the Chaco Navajos* (Albuquerque: National Park Service, 1980), pp. 28–29; *Wealth and Trust: A Lesson from the American Indian* (Sun Valley, Idaho: Institute of the American West, 1981), pp. 2, 14; and John L. Kessell, *Kiva, Cross, and Crown: The Pecos Indians and New Mexico, 1540–1840* (Washington, D.C.: National Park Service, 1979), pp. 461, 464, and three color plates between pp. 422 and 423.

22. *New Mexico: A Guide to the Colorful State. American Guide Series* (New York: Hastings House, 1940), p. 238, shows Kern's view of Santa Fe; *The Spanish West* (New York: Time-Life Books, 1976), p. 127, reproduces Kern's Zuni blacksmiths. For other works that copy the Zuni smiths, see chapter 5, n. 24. For examples of reproductions of Camp Yuma, see chapter 5, n. 69, and Anna Paschall Hannum, *A Quaker Forty-Niner: The Adventures of Charles Edward Pancost on the American Frontier* (Philadelphia: University of Pennsylvania Press, 1930), facing p. 254.

23. Alpheus H. Favour, *Old Bill Williams: Mountain Man* (Chapel Hill: University of North Carolina Press, 1936), frontispiece. The second edition of this biography (Norman: University of Oklahoma Press, 1962), contains a different set of illustrations.

24. Robert V. Hine, *In the Shadow of Frémont: Edward Kern and the Art of American Exploration, 1845–1860* (1st ed., 1962; Norman: University of Oklahoma Press, 1982), pp. 160–61. See also Hine, "The Kern Brothers and the Image of the West," *Utah Historical Quarterly,* 28 (Fall 1960): pp. 350–61; Frank McNitt, ed., *Navaho Expedition: Journal of a Military Reconnaissance from Santa Fe, New Mexico to the Navajo Country Made in 1849 by Lieutenant James H. Simpson* (Norman: University of Oklahoma Press, 1964), p. l; and Clinton Adams, "The Naked Land," in *That Awesome Space* (Sun Valley, Idaho: Institute of the American West, 1980), p. 10.

25. Trenton and Hassrick, *Rocky Mountains,* p. 20.

26. Compare, too, Kern's watercolor of Pueblo Pintado with the lithograph—both reproduced in Hine, *Edward Kern,* plates 23, 24. In suggesting that lithographers seldom added embellishments in preparing the plates for the Simpson *Journal,* I am in disagreement with Hine, p. 160, who argues that "one of the curious things about the Kerns' work is that few of the Romantic touches are present in the original sketches and drawings; they appear rather in the subsequent printings and engravings." To make his point, Hine cites "Dick's tall, balloon-like version of the cliffs above Casa Blanca in Canyon de Chelly," which he terms "fantastic." But the lithographer does not appear to have made the cliffs any more fantastic than Dick did. See Hine, *Edward Kern,* plates 26 and 27, where the original and the lithograph can be compared. Hine also cites as evidence of Romantic touches alterations of Kern's *Indian Blacksmith Shop.* See my discussion of this issue, below.

27. Nicholas B. Wainwright, *Philadelphia in the Romantic Age of Lithography* (Philadelphia: Historical Society of Pennsylvania, 1958), p. 77. For the accuracy with which some copyists did portraits, see Andrew J. Cosentine, *The Paintings of Charles Bird King* (Washington, D.C.: Smithsonian Institution Press, 1977), p. 60. The idea that lithographers may have used a

camera lucida, or some other device, is my own. The drawings from the Simpson expedition show no sign of having been traced upon.

28. The lithograph of this scene is attributed to Richard Kern, but the original drawing is signed by Edward Kern. For Schuessele, see Wainright, *Philadelphia,* pp. 62, 82.

29. The original drawing is unsigned; the lithograph attributes it to Richard.

30. McNitt, ed., *Navajo Expedition,* p. 1. Why Kern distorted this particular landmark is a mystery. He did a much better drawing, *Mesa Facada from the East,* Aug. 27, preserved in the Scrapbook, PC.

31. The pen-and-ink drawings are on blue paper (ca. ten by fourteen inches) and are in the Scrapbook, PC. Four of them correspond to plates 7, 10, 11, and 12 of Sitgreaves's *Report.* The fifth drawing is untitled and was not converted into a lithograph.

32. Some of Kern's field sketches are in Sketchbooks A and F, PC. Several of these sketches became the basis of drawings that Kern prepared for the lithographer, including *First View of the Big Colorado* and *Rough Bark Cedar, Camp 19.*

33. The quote is from Hine, *Kern,* p. 161. See above, chapter 5, n. 24. Hine did not have the sketch of the costumes of the smiths available to him, but only the sketch of the smiths in their shop that appeared in *Life* 46 (April 6, 1959):101. Sketchbook A, PC, in which Dick drew the Zuni smiths, contains other drawings (an Indian weaver and Indian dancers) that seem too crude to have been turned over to the lithographer, but that were clearly the basis of drawings that became lithographs.

34. The field sketch, reproduced in Trenton and Hassrick, *Rocky Mountains,* plate 26, is much rougher than any of the finished drawings that Kern did for the Simpson report. To use this, then, as evidence of the way in which lithographers take artistic license, as Trenton and Hassrick do (p. 74), makes little sense.

35. Taft, *Artists,* p. 272 n. 30.

36. The eight Stanley oils are in the Stark Museum of Art, Orange, Texas. The four scenes

that correspond to lithographs in Emory's *Notes* are: *San Felipe, New Mexico; Valencia, New Mexico; View of the Copper Mine;* and *The Hieroglypic Rock of the Gila.* I am grateful to the Stark Museum for making study slides available to me. It is possible that the oils were done from original field sketches, and that the lithographer also used the field sketches.

37. Ross Calvin, ed., *Lieutenant Emory Reports: A Reprint of Lieutenant W. H. Emory's Notes of a Military Reconnaissance* (Albuquerque: University of New Mexico Press, 1951), p. 4.

38. John Russell Bartlett, *Personal Narrative of Explorations and Incidents . . . ,* 2 vols. (New York: D. Appleton & Co., 1854), and Robert V. Hine, *Bartlett's West: Drawing the Mexican Boundary* (New Haven: Yale University Press for the Amon Carter Museum, 1968). Compare, for example, plates 1, 2, 5, and 18 in *Bartlett's West* with the corresponding Woodcuts in *Personal Narrative,* 1:118, 98, 189, 496; and plates 8, 17, and 19 in *Bartlett's West* with the corresponding lithographs in *Personal Narrative,* 1, following pp. 296, 486, 500.

39. John Galvin, ed., *Western America in 1846–47: The Original Travel Diary of Lieutenant J. W. Abert . . .* (San Francisco: John Howell Books, 1966), following pp. 46, 52. These correspond to the lithographs on pp. 87 and 111 of Abert's *New Mexico Report, 1846–'47* (1st ed. 1848; Albuquerque: Horn & Wallace, 1962). Other watercolors in Abert's sketchbook that have not yet been published may have been the subjects of other lithographs. Mr. Galvin has not been disposed to permit the study of the original sketchbook.

40. If the lithographer did work directly from these sketches, he made no effort to convey a greater sense of "drama or grandeur" than the artist had intended. The lithograph of Acoma is a straightforward copy, not especially attentive to detail, which makes one suspect that an intermediary drawing was actually copied. In the Acoma scene, the lithographer or another artist has changed the attire of a figure in the foreground, removing a sombrero and covering the person's head with a blanket, believing

perhaps that this dress was more suitable to a scene in an Indian pueblo. In the view of the ruins at Abó, we do find embellishments—either by the lithographer or by the artist who did a second sketch. In the foreground, a tall tree and two human figures appear in the lithograph that were not in the original watercolor drawing.

41. David H. Miller, "Balduin Möllhausen, A Prussian's Image of the American West" (Ph.D. diss., University of New Mexico, 1970), pp. 221–29. See also pp. 237, 250–52, 254–56 for other comparisons, in which it is less clear that the lithographer worked from the originals that Miller has reproduced. Since Möllhausen made more than one drawing of some scenes, confusion on this point seems inevitable. I am grateful to Professor Miller for graciously making a copy of his dissertation available to me and for advice that comes from long consideration of these questions.

42. Schott to John Torrey, Washington, Jan. 22, 1854, quoted in Gretchen Gause Fox, "Arthur Schott: German Immigrant Illustrator of the American West" (MA thesis, George Washington University, 1977), p. 45, called to my attention by Bernard L. Fontana, "Drawing the Line between Mexico and the United States: Nineteenth-Century Lithographs of People and Places along the Border," *American West* (July-Aug. 1982), p. 55. None of Schott's original drawings from the survey have been located (Fox, p. 52).

43. Miller, "Möllhausen," p. 271. Kern's original sketches of the dancers are in Sketchbook A, PC.

44. Miller, "Möllhausen," p. 224. For other examples of efforts to assure the accuracy of lithographs in government reports, see John Torrey to J. J. Abert, New York, April 29, 1853, in LR, TB, NARS, M 506, r. 71, frs. 223–24, and Samuel W. Woodhouse to Abert, Register of Letters Received, TB, M 505, r. 3, fr. 455.

45. William H. Goetzmann and Joseph C. Porter, *The West as Romantic Horizon* (Omaha: Center for Western Studies, Joslyn Art Museum, 1981), p. 26.

46. These two scenes, along with *San Luis Valley* and *Frémont's Christmas Camp,* appeared in a publisher's prospectus for Frémont's *Memoirs of My Life.* The first volume of this projected two-volume work was published in Chicago in 1887 by Belford, Clarke & Co., but the venture was a commercial failure and volume two, for which these engravings were intended, was not published. Allan Nevins, *Frémont: Pathmarker of the West* (1st ed., 1939; New York: Longmans, Green and Co., 1955), pp. 606–7. Trenton and Hassrick, *Rocky Mountains,* pp. 54 and 352 n. 91, provide a good analysis, but omit the *San Luis Valley,* perhaps because it is not a winter scene.

47. If I am correct that these scenes were substantially altered by the engraver, they are not as good an example of the Kerns' contribution to the "Romantic Reconnaissance," as William Goetzmann believed (*Exploration and Empire,* p. 213). Evidence linking these engravings to the Kerns remains circumstantial, but if they are based on drawings done by either of the brothers, Edward seems most likely, because he became involved in the Frémont project in 1858, five years after Richard's death (see chapter 2, n. 75) and because he was more skilled at representing people.

48. Two original watercolors by Joseph Horace Eaton, *Taos Pueblo* and *Santa Fe* are in the collection of Gerald Peters of Santa Fe and appear to be the originals from which illustrations were made for *El Gringo* (New York: Harper & Bros., 1857), pp. 99, 161. For biographical data on Eaton, see Groce and Wallace, *New York Historical Society's Dictionary,* p. 294.

49. Hine, *Edward Kern,* p. 70.

50. Peter C. Marzio, *The Democratic Art: Chromolithography, 1840–1900. Pictures for a 19th-Century America* (Boston: David R. Grodine, in association with the Amon Carter Museum, 1979), pp. 30–31.

51. Theodore E. Stebbins, Jr., *American Master Drawing: A History of Works on Paper . . .* (New York: Harper & Row, 1976), p. 138.

52. Hine, *Bartlett's West,* pp. ix, 86, came to this conclusion about Bartlett, whose work

had been known only through copies.

53. C. A. Hoppin to J. R. Bartlett, Doña Ana, New Mexico, Jan. 23, 1851, in the Mexican Boundary Commission Papers of John Russell Bartlett, 1850–1853, vol. 3, item no. 38, John Carter Brown Library, Providence, Rhode Island.

54. Kern to S. G. Morton, Santa Fe, July 3, 1850, Newberry Library. See, too, Dickinson's report to Kern that "Old Hoosta of Jamez [sic] has seen his portrait in Simpson's report and appears highly delighted" (as mentioned in chapter 5).

55. I am grateful to David H. Miller for bringing this episode to my attention. It is described in the November 24, 1851, entry of the manuscript journals of Lt. Amiel Weeks Whipple, which Miller is preparing for publication.

56. John C. Ewers, *Artists of the Old West* (New York: Doubleday & Co., 1965), p. 8.

57. "Please fix up the camera box so I can bring it on with me," Dick wrote to Ned from Washington, July 22, [1852], James W. Eldridge Collection, box 55, HEH. There is no firm evidence of Dick's use of either the camera or the camera lucida.

58. See above, n. 21, and my discussion of Kern's paintings of Indians and Indian artifacts in chapts. 2 and 4, in particular. The only criticism of Kern's accuracy in portraying Indians or an Indian-related subject is discussed in chapter 3, n. 22.

59. The watercolor drawings at the Amon Carter Museum reveal that Kern outlined his subject in pencil before applying washes.

60. R. Kern to J. R. Bartlett, Santa Fe, March 14, 1851, Mexican Boundary Commission Papers of John Russell Bartlett, 1850–1853, 3, 146, John Carter Brown Library, Providence, Rhode Island.

61. These include the portraits of *Ow-Te-Wa, Narbona, Mariano Martinez,* and *Chapaton.* *Yellow Wolf* carries Ned's signature alone, and the Pecos Indian *Wash-U-Hos-Te* is unsigned. Academy of Natural Sciences, Philadelphia.

62. See chapter 2, nn. 63, 76.

63. For a good introduction to the use of

pictoral evidence, see James West Davidson and Mark Hamilton Lytle, *After the Fact: The Art of Historical Detection* (New York: Alfred A. Knopf, 1982), pp. 113–38: "The 'Noble Savage' and the Artist's Canvas." For an example of analysis of lithographs as historical records, see Ronnie C. Tyler, *The Mexican War: A Lithographic Record* (Austin: Texas State Historical Association, 1973).

64. Trenton and Hassrick, *Rocky Mountains,* p. 54. See chapter 6, n. 31, above, for a discussion of why I believe Kern painted this in Washington.

65. Trenton and Hassrick, *Rocky Mountains,* p. 54. See chapter 2, n. 63, above.

66. See chapter 5, n. 69.

67. James Thomas Flexner, *That Wilder Image: The Painting of America's Native School from Thomas Cole to Winslow Homer* (1st ed., 1962; New York: Dover Publications, 1970), p. 16.

68. Quoted in Stebbins, *American Master Drawing,* p. 69. For the best discussion of this question see Peter C. Marzio, *The Art Crusade: An Analysis of American Drawing Manuals, 1820–1860* (Washington, D.C.: Smithsonian Institution Press, 1976), especially pp. 21, 24, 50, 53.

69. Quoted in Flexner, *That Wilder Image,* p. 36. See also Barbara Novak, *American Painting of the Nineteenth Century: Realism, Idealism, and the American Experience* (1st ed., 1969; New York: Harper and Row, 1979), pp. 170–72.

70. Novak, *American Painting,* p. 71.

71. Barbara Novak, *Nature and Culture: American Landscape and Painting, 1825–1875* (New York: Oxford University Press, 1980), p. 3.

72. Anonymous, *The Scenery of the United States Illustrated* (New York: 1855), quoted in Roderick Nash, *Wilderness and the American Mind* (1st ed. 1967; 3rd ed., New Haven: Yale University Press, 1982), p. 71. This discussion is based on Nash's splendid work, especially pp. 44–83; on Joseph Wood Krutch, "The Eye of the Beholder," *The American West* 4 (May 1967):18–20; and on Novak, *Nature and Culture,* pp. 3–17. See also Joshua C. Taylor, *America as Art* (Washington, D.C.: Smithson-

ian Institution Press, 1976), pp. 96–131.

73. Goetzmann, *The West as Romantic Horizon*, p. 12.

74. Nash, *Wilderness and the American Mind*, p. 47.

75. Larry Curry, *The American West: Painters from Catlin to Russell* (New York: Viking Press and the Los Angeles Museum of Art, 1972), p. 14.

76. David Carew Huntington, *Art and the Excited Spirit: America in the Romantic Period* (Ann Arbor: University of Michigan Museum of Art, 1972), p. 18. For trees, see for example, *On Proulx' Creek* (plate 3), and *Relief Camp* (plate 4). For the tradition of staffage in European landscape painting of the eighteenth century, see Novak, *Nature and Culture*, pp. 184–200.

77. See chapter 1, above, for more on *Proulx' Creek*, and chapter 3, above, for more on *Salto del Rito*. See Novak, *American Painting*, pp. 70–72, for idealization.

78. Novak, *Nature and Culture*, pp. 157–58.

79. Huntington, *Art and the Excited Spirit*, pp. 1–2.

80. Ibid., pp. 15–18 and plate 65.

81. Lee Clark Mitchell, *Witnesses to a Vanishing America: The Nineteenth-Century Response* (Princeton: Princeton University Press, 1981), pp. 113–17.

82. For Miller, see Carol Clark, "A Romantic Painter in the American West," in Ron Tyler, ed., *Alfred Jacob Miller: Artist on the Oregon Trail* (Fort Worth: Amon Carter Museum of Western Art, 1982), pp. 47–63. The quote is from p. 55.

83. Curtis M. Hinsley, Jr., *Savages and Scientists: The Smithsonian Institution and the Development of American Anthropology, 1846–1910* (Washington, D.C.: Smithsonian Institution Press, 1981), p. 22. Richard Kern's views of Indians do not fit easily into any of the "traditions" identified in John G. Cawelti, "The Frontier and the Native American," in Joshua Taylor, *America as Art* (Washington, D.C.:

Smithsonian Institution Press, 1976), pp. 133–83. John C. Ewers has pointed out that "a goodly number of the most significant pieces" of Indian art were collected by non-Indian artists: "Artists' Choices," *American Indian Art*, 7 (Spring 1982):40. I have not found any evidence that Kern's collections included Indian artifacts, although he was clearly fascinated with their drawing, architecture, costumes, and dances.

84. Trenton and Hassrick, *Rocky Mountains*, p. 51. This is a curious statement for these two perceptive writers to have made, and it is one that they themselves contradict in their fine analysis, pp. 20 and 55.

85. Goetzmann, *Romantic Horizon*, p. 15.

86. Stebbins, Jr., *American Master Drawings and Watercolors*, especially pp. 136, 141, 152; Carol Clark, *Thomas Moran: Watercolors of the American West* (Austin: University of Texas Press, 1980), p. 24; Trenton and Hassrick, *Rocky Mountains*, p. 57.

87. Quoted in Trenton and Hassrick, *Rocky Mountains*, p. 45, who provide a good discussion of this question. The watercolors of Joseph Horace Eaton and the oils of John Mix Stanley (see above, nn. 36, 48), also use a conventional palette.

88. James Ballinger shows how Stanley graduated from being a "factual" painter in 1846 into the Hudson River School by 1855: "John Mix Stanley, a 'Hudson River' Painter in Arizona," *Phoebus 3* (Tempe: Arizona State University, 1981), pp. 64–72.

89. Reference to Dick's work in oils in Washington appears in chapter 6, above. Evidence that he might have painted in oils in Santa Fe appears in a letter from H. Dickinson to E. Kern, Santa Fe, Sept. 10, 1851, FS 141, who refers to the "brushes paints canvass &c left in my possession by Dick."

90. Richard Kern to Eliza B. Weaver, on the death of her husband, Matthias, "my dearest friend." Philadelphia, Dec. 24, 1847, MS, Historical Society of Pennsylvania.

Bibliographical Essay

THIS BOOK IS built on a great variety of sources, many of them manuscripts, to which the notes will guide the specialist. A broader view may be useful for the general reader, who may want to know more about the art of exploration in the America of Kern's day.

For the exploration of the West, no finer introduction exists, or is likely to be written, than William H. Goetzmann's Pulitzer Prize winner, *Exploration and Empire: The Explorer and the Scientist in the Winning of the American West* (New York: Alfred A. Knopf, 1967), with its essays and portfolios on contemporary art. Firsthand accounts of the individual expeditions that Kern accompanied remain exciting reading. Frémont never published an account of his fourth expedition, but LeRoy Hafen and Ann Hafen have drawn together many of the letters and diaries, including Richard Kern's, and published them in *Fremont's Fourth Expedition: A Documentary Account of the Disaster . . .* (Glendale, Cal.: Arthur H. Clark, 1960). Utilizing such sources, William Brandon has written an account that captures the drama of the enterprise: *The Men and the Mountain: Frémont's Fourth Expedition* (New York: William Morrow and Co., 1955). James H. Simpson's report of his tour of the Navajo country has been reprinted with a fine introduction and annota-

tions by Frank McNitt (although he reproduced only eight of the Kerns' lithographs): *Navaho Expedition: Journal of a Military Reconnaissance from Santa Fe, New Mexico, to the Navaho Country Made in 1849 by Lieutenant James H. Simpson* (Norman: University of Oklahoma Press, 1964). The original government report of the Sitgreaves expedition across central Arizona has been printed in facsimile: *Report of an Expedition down the Zuni and the Colorado Rivers in 1851* (Chicago: Rio Grande Press, 1962). For the Gunnison expedition one must consult volume two of the original *Pacific Railroad Reports* (13 vols., Washington, D.C.: Beverley Tucker, 1854–60).

The best general overviews of images of the West in Kern's era are these: Robert Taft, *Artists and Illustrators of the Old West, 1850–1900* (New York: Charles Scribner's Sons, 1953); John C. Ewers, *Artists of the Old West* (New York: Doubleday & Co., 1965); and Peter Hassrick, *The Way West: Art of the American Frontier* (New York: Harry N. Abrams, 1977). Less comprehensive, but beautiful and analytical, is Patricia Trenton and Peter H. Hassrick, *The Rocky Mountains: A Vision for Artists in the Nineteenth Century* (Norman: University of Oklahoma Press, 1983).

For the broader currents in American art of

343

the mid-nineteenth century, see Thomas James Flexner's vividly written account, *That Wilder Image: The Painting of America's Native School from Thomas Cole to Winslow Homer* (1st ed., 1962; New York Dover Publications, 1970); Neil Harris, *The Artist in American Society: The Formative Years, 1790–1860* (New York: George Braziller, 1966); Barbara Novak, *American Painting of the Nineteenth Century: Realism, Idealism, and the American Experience* (1st ed., 1969; New York: Harper & Row, 1979); Barbara Novak, *Nature and Culture: American Landscape and Painting, 1825–1875* (New York: Oxford University Press, 1980); and Theodore E. Stebbins, Jr., *American Master Drawings and Watercolors: A History of Works on Paper from Colonial Times to the Present* (New York: Harper & Row, 1976).

Kern's contemporary artist-explorers in the Far Southwest have generally not been the subjects of full-length published studies. Two exceptions are by Robert Hine, who told Edward Kern's story in a masterful, engaging narrative, first published under the title *Edward Kern and American Expansion* (New Haven: Yale University Press, 1962), and reissued as *In the Shadow of Frémont: Edward Kern and the Art of American Expansion, 1845–1860* (Norman: University of Oklahoma Press, 1982). Hine has also examined the work of John Russell Bartlett in a finely wrought study: *Bartlett's West: Drawing the Mexican Boundary* (New Haven: Yale University Press for the Amon Carter Museum, 1968). Studies now underway of Balduin Möllhausen, by David H. Miller, and of John Mix Stanley, by Julie Schimmel, promise to bring these artists out of the shadow of the better known leaders of their respective expeditions.

Some artists and would-be artists, contemporary with Kern, did write accounts of their travels in the Far Southwest that have found their way into print. Lt. James W. Abert's original journals, with some of his original illustrations, have been published in two beautiful volumes edited by John Galvin: *Through the Country of the Comanche Indians in the Fall of the Year 1845 . . .* (San Francisco: John Howell Books, 1970) and *Western America in 1846–1847: The Original Travel Diary of Lieutenant J. W. Abert* (San Francisco: John Howell Books, 1966). The diaries of Charles Preuss, who was with the Kerns on Frémont's fourth expedition (and who also accompanied Frémont's first and second expeditions), have been translated and edited by Erwin G. Gudde and Elisabeth K. Gudde, *Exploring with Frémont: The Private Diaries of Charles Preuss . . .* (Norman: University of Oklahoma Press, 1958). John Francis McDermott has edited the letters of Alfred W. Waugh, who was in Santa Fe just before the Kern brothers: *Travels in Search of the Elephant: The Wanderings of Alfred S. Waugh, Artist, in Louisiana, Missouri, and Santa Fe, in 1845–1846* (St. Louis: Missouri Historical Society, 1951). John Russell Bartlett's *Personal Narrative of Explorations and Incidents . . . Connected with the United States and Mexican Boundary Commission . . .* (1st ed., 1854, 2 vols.; Chicago: Rio Grande Press, 1965), is a classic. Two artists left accounts of their journeys across the 38th parallel route in 1853, the same year Kern made that trip: Gwinn Harris Heap, *Central Route to the Pacific*, LeRoy R. and Ann W. Hafen, eds. (1st ed., 1854; Glendale: The Arthur H. Clark Co., 1957), and Solomon Nunes Carvalho, *Incidents of Travel and Adventures in the Far West . . . .* Bertram Korn, ed. (1st ed., 1857; Philadelphia: Jewish Publications Society, 1954). Never out of date, these and other firsthand accounts by Kern's contemporaries provide fascinating verbal descriptions of the same vanished world that Kern's drawings illuminate.

Index

Richard H. Kern
was designed by Emmy Ezzell.
Type was composed at the University of
New Mexico Printing Plant in Mergenthaler
Garamond #3 with handset Garamond display.
It was printed on Warren's Lustro Offset Enamel,
and bound in Whitman Imperial Bonded Leather
and Holliston Kingston Linen at Kingsport Press.
Color separations were made by Colorgraphics
of Fort Worth under the supervision of the
Amon Carter Museum.